# Toward an Entangling Alliance

# TOWARD AN ENTANGLING ALLIANCE

American Isolationism,
Internationalism,
and Europe, 1901–1950

## RONALD E. POWASKI

Contributions to the Study of
World History, Number 22

GREENWOOD PRESS
New York • Westport, Connecticut • London

# 22274865
DLC

10-21-91

**Library of Congress Cataloging-in-Publication Data**

Powaski, Ronald E.
  Toward an entangling alliance : American isolationism,
internationalism, and Europe, 1901 1950 / Ronald E. Powaski
    p.  cm. — (Contributions to the study of world history, ISSN
0885-9159 , no. 22)
  Includes bibliographical references and index.
  ISBN 0-313-27274-3 (alk. paper)
  1. United States — Foreign relations — 20th century.  2. United
States — Neutrality — History — 20th century.  I. Title.  II. Series.
E744.P68   1991
973.9 — dc20        90-45604

British Library Cataloguing in Publication Data is available.

Library of Congress Catalog Card Number: 90-45604
ISBN: 0-313-27274-3
ISSN: 0885-9159

First published in 1991

Greenwood Press, 88 Post Road West, Westport, CT 06881
An imprint of Greenwood Publishing Group, Inc.

Printed in the United States of America

The paper used in this book complies with the
Permanent Paper Standard issued by the National
Information Standards Organization (Z39.48-1984).

10 9 8 7 6 5 4 3 2 1

**Copyright Acknowledgment**

The author and publisher gratefully acknowledge permission to reprint material
from the following copyrighted source.

Henry L. Stimson Papers, Manuscripts and Archives, Yale University Library.

To the memory of my Father

# Contents

# Preface
# and Acknowledgments

For most of its history, the United States pursued what came to be called, in the twentieth century, an isolationist policy. (The words "isolationist" first appeared in 1862 and "isolationist" in 1899, while "isolationism" as a word apparently was not used until 1922.) Although this often emotionally charged term acquired a variety of meanings, depending on who was advocating or opposing it, and when they were doing so, isolationism can be defined generally as an attempt to avoid involvement in Europe's political and military (but not economic) affairs. To be more specific, isolationism came to mean the refusal of the United States to commit force beyond the limits of the Western Hemisphere and to avoid military alliances with overseas powers. On the other hand, the expansion of America's commercial ties with Europe was almost always considered vital to the economic prosperity of the United States, and thus exempted from the isolationist tradition.[1]

The principles of isolationism were gradually broadened in the nineteenth and twentieth centuries to include the avoidance of action with other nations in the pursuit of goals favored by the United States, such as upholding the Monroe Doctrine in Latin America; an emphasis on preserving unlimited American sovereignty, for example, by excluding U.S. immigration and tariff policies from international agreements; and a rejection of international political organizations and judicial bodies, such as the League of Nations and World Court.[2]

For nearly a century and a half after America's alliance with France ended in 1800, the United States successfully avoided what Thomas Jefferson called "entangling alliances" with European nations. In the nineteenth century, the United States fought the War of 1812, the Mexican War, and the Spanish-American War without allies and without engaging in military action in Europe. And when the United States entered World War I in 1917, it fought as an "associate" of Britain and France, rather than as their ally. After the war, the United States reverted to isolationism by rejecting membership in the League of Nations and the World Court.

But isolationism did not last. Soon America was drawn into another war with Germany, as well as Germany's Axis allies, Italy and Japan. Even before World War II, however, the United States led the effort to create, and then joined a world peace-keeping organization, the United Nations. Further, at war's end, all of America's military forces were not withdrawn from Europe, as they were after World War I. A small occupation force in Germany--roughly 30,000 men--would become the nucleus of a major American military presence on the Continent. Finally, in 1949 the United States abandoned isolationism as a policy once and (apparently) for all and joined an entangling alliance with European nations by signing the North Atlantic Treaty.

Why did the United States pursue an isolationist policy toward Europe for most of its history? Why did Americans abandon isolationism in the twentieth century? This book will attempt to analyze the factors, events, and personalities that were responsible for America's transition from isolationism to more extensive participation in the political and military affairs of Europe.

This study is the product not only of my own research, but also of the work of many authorities whose contribution to this book I have attempted to acknowledge in the end notes. I am also indebted to Yale University Library for permission to use the Henry L. Stimson Diary, and George Barnum of Case Western Reserve University's Freiberger Library, for his cheerful assistance in locating, and facilitating the use of, the library's government documents. I am very grateful to my research assistant, Kim Szendrey, and to Daniel Sirk, Peter Balunek, Adam Pawlowski, Richard Wherley, and Rosalie Fette for their generous help in the preparation of the manuscript. My appreciation also is extended to my editors, Cynthia Harris, William Neenan, and Susan Wells, for their caring and diligent editorial work. I cannot adequately express gratitude to my wife, Jo Ann, who, more than anyone else, inspired and supported this effort through her encouragement, wise counsel, and unlimited patience.

This book is dedicated to the memory of my father, who valued education and steadfastly encouraged mine.

Euclid, Ohio                                                              R.E.P

# Introduction:
# American Isolationism
# until 1901

## The Colonial Period

In a sense, American isolationism is as old as the nation itself. The first colonists who separated themselves from Europe--whether to escape religious or political oppression or economic hardship, or simply to make a profit or to satisfy a quest for adventure--in effect accepted the prospect of a life of virtual isolation from the Old World.

This separation from Europe, of course, was never complete. The early colonists were almost totally dependent on their mother countries for supplies and protection. And colonial Americans accepted and appreciated that their civilization in the New World was largely a product of the Old. In the late colonial period, American aristocrats traveled to Europe, modeled their fashions from those of Europe, and sent their sons to the best European universities. Until the very eve of the Revolution, Americans considered themselves Englishmen who had been transplanted to the New World.

It is also true that Americans who accepted independence from England did so only reluctantly, so strong were the bonds with the mother country. Even after independence, the former American colonies maintained important economic ties with the nations of Europe, and their cultural roots in the Old World continued to be fertilized by waves of new immigrants who helped account for the rapid growth and development of the new nation.

Nevertheless, the first settlers in America came to realize keenly that distance in space and time separated them from Europe, and that this separation had made them different from Europeans. To survive in their new environment, Americans began to develop new patterns of behavior and thought that ultimately helped to make them a new nation. It was a nation distinct in many ways from the Old World. Nowhere in Europe was there the degree of tolerance of expression, whether religious or political, that was found in America at the time of the Revolution. In no land was the gap between rich and poor so narrow, and class distinctions so unimportant. In no European country was there the absence of dynastic feuding and warfare that existed in colonial America.

Because of the relative peace, freedom, and opportunity that the New World offered, Americans quite naturally considered themselves morally superior to the inhabitants of the Old. The Puritans of New England, in particular, regarded themselves as the best of Englishmen, more God-fearing, more virtuous and harder working, and blessed in the isolation of the New World with the opportunity to create a "purified" religious society. As early as 1677, Increase Mather, a prominent Massachusetts clergyman, declared that "There never was a generation that did so perfectly shake off the dust of Babylon, both as to ecclesiastical and civil constitution, as the first generation of Christians that came into this land for the gospel's sake." To Massachusetts Governor John Winthrop, Puritan New England was "a city upon a hill" with "the eyes of all people" upon it, a noble experiment that would serve as a beacon to the world. The genesis of modern American idealism can be found in Puritan thought such as this.[1]

As a rule, the American colonists were not eager to become involved in European wars that did not directly concern themselves. In the first Anglo-Dutch war, the governor of New Netherlands, Peter Stuyvesant, proposed to the New England Confederation a policy of neutrality between the English and Dutch colonies in the New World. Stuyvesant was eager to prevent any disruption of the lucrative trade that flowed between the Dutch and English colonies. Nor was Stuyvesant's bid to preserve colonial neutrality an isolated case. Periodically, England's colonies refused to contribute men or money to that nation's wars. In 1651 the Massachusetts General Court reminded Oliver Cromwell, England's Lord Protector, that the colony's founders had left Europe to escape war. "We know not any country more peaceable and free from war," it stated, than America.[2]

Even the European countries themselves, at times, attempted to keep the affairs of the Old World and the New in separate spheres. The Franco-Spanish Treaty of 1604, the Anglo-French Treaty of Whitehall in 1686, and the Spanish-Portuguese Treaty of 1750 all tried to separate the colonies of America from the wars of Europe.

## The American Revolution

Nevertheless, the American colonists did participate in the wars of Europe, at least to the extent that these conflicts affected the North American continent. Between 1689 and 1763 Americans fought in four wars--King William's War, Queen Anne's War, King George's War, and the French and Indian War. Only the last had its origins in America, in the conflicting claims to the Ohio Valley of American settlers and French trappers.

The degree of American zeal that was displayed in these wars was influenced by the depth of American self-interest that was involved. In the case of the French and Indian War, American interests were considerable. Benjamin Franklin, in urging England to wage war upon France, argued that the removal of the French threat in America was necessary to the survival and expansion of the American colonies, on whose prosperity, he asserted, the real strength of the British Empire was based. Nevertheless, after the English defeated France, and removed the

French challenge from the North American continent, Franklin ungratiously told the English that the "enormous Load of Debt, which sinks us almost to Perdition," was not prompted by England's assistance to the colonies, but by her "romantick European Continental Connections."[3]

Thomas Paine, in his famous pamphlet, *Common Sense,* amplified Franklin's concern. The only way to avoid repeated American involvement in England's European wars, Paine insisted, was by establishing America's independence. He predicted that France and Spain would never be "our enemies as *Americans,* but as our being *subjects of Great Britain.*" Rather than by reliance upon British military power, Paine asserted, America's security could be maintained by her commerce. He argued, "it is in the interest of all Europe to have America a free port." And to ensure that Europe would be a market for American trade, Paine insisted, it was essential that America avoid political connections with any European state.[4]

Paine, and other American revolutionaries, found it necessary to accentuate and elaborate the myth of a virtuous New World in order to break the strong emotional ties of their countrymen with England. Paine's *Common Sense* heaped blistering scorn upon America's ties with the British monarchy, that "popery of government." "One of the strongest natural proofs of the folly of hereditary rights in Kings," Paine asserted, "is that nature disapproves it, otherwise she would not so frequently turn it into ridicule, by giving mankind an *Ass for a Lion.*"[5]

Although many, if not most, Americans agreed with Paine that European politics and society were rotten to the core, more than a few shared the belief of the Enlightenment that progress was inevitable, and that Europe must share in the values America was trying to establish. The Declaration of Independence, seen in this light, was not only a justification for America's separation from England, it was also a statement of her commitment to the inalienable rights of man. For American idealists, the Declaration of Independence provided the justification for a messianic tendency to remake Europe, and later the rest of the world, in the American image.

But the men who guided the American Revolution were, above all, pragmatic realists. While they may have deplored the amorality of the old diplomacy, with its emphasis on power politics, they also realized that the European balance of power offered opportunities as well as dangers, particularly the chance to advance American interests by playing off the European powers against each other. Without a foreign alliance, Richard Henry Lee stated in a resolution adopted by the Continental Congress on June 2, 1776, independence could not be won.

Yet the Congress accepted the need for an alliance only reluctantly. In seeking the assistance of France, Britain's chief European rival, America's negotiators, particularly John Adams, first sought only a commercial agreement, believing that the French would assist American independence simply to gain access to America's trade and to deny it to England.

The French, however, insisted that the price of their support was a "permanent" alliance that, had the French had their way, would have bound the fledgling United States indefinitely to the defense of French interests in Europe and elsewhere. While the Americans ultimately accepted the French demand for a permanent alliance, they obviously had no intention of allowing the interests of France to dictate the future foreign policy of the United States. In a manner that did justice to the duplicity that was characteristic of the old diplomacy, the American negotiators--Benjamin Franklin, John Adams, and John Jay--signed the preliminary peace with the English without first informing their French ally, an obvious violation of the treaty's prohibition against a separate peace.

# The Young Republic

The Americans clearly used the French for what they were worth--gaining independence--and then quickly, if tacitly, acted as though the alliance were no longer valid. Less tacitly, in 1778 Secretary of State John Jay asserted to the French minister that "It is our policy to be independent in the most independent sense, and to observe a proper distance toward all nations, minding our own business, and not interfering with, or being influenced by, the views of any, further than may respect us." The French rejected Jay's interpretation and stated that they regarded the alliance as still in force. The American government, during the period of the Confederation still too weak to stand up to the British alone, responded by maintaining the pretense that the treaty remained alive when it fact it had become a dead letter.[6]

To be sure, the French were not entirely blameless for the denouement of the alliance. They had helped the United States during the Revolution, not for altruistic reasons, but primarily because they had believed American independence would serve French interests, particularly the weakening of Britain. Without informing the Americans, the French also made an alliance with Spain, attempting thereby to tie America's struggle for independence to the unrelated war aims of Spain as well as France. In addition, the French were not eager to make the United States the dominant power on the North American continent or to lessen American dependence on French power. As a result, France did nothing to help the Americans gain satisfaction of their territorial claims against Britain or Spain.

Not surprisingly, considering the French subterfuge, the Continental Congress in 1783 passed a resolution that stated: "The true interest of these states requires that they should be as little as possible entangled in the politics and conflicts of European nations." Support for the resolution was motivated not only by fear that the alliance with France would drag America into a war in which she had no direct interest, but also by a general consensus that Americans should rely on themselves, rather than upon Europeans, for their own security.[7]

Four years later, the new American Constitution reflected the isolationist sentiment that once again prevailed after the Revolution. The provision requiring a two-thirds affirmative vote for the ratification of treaties was designed, at least in part, to make it difficult to conclude such agreements. The Constitution's explicit prohibition against the acceptance by any American official of "any present, Emolument, Office, or Title, of any kind whatever, from any King, Prince, or foreign State" also had a direct isolationist bearing. The strength of isolationist sentiment was also evident in the fact that the Congress in 1789 debated a motion to have only a temporary secretary of state. However, the motion was defeated, and the next year a Department of State with a secretary and five clerks was established.

## The Washington Administration

The new republic's first president, George Washington, did his best to preserve America's independence from foreign political entanglements. To avoid U.S. involvement in the European war that erupted after the French Revolution, Washington issued a proclamation in 1793 calling on all Americans to avoid any unneutral acts. He realized that the nation, divided between pro-British and pro-French factions, and with a new national government, a meager army, and no navy, was in no position to engage in war with either antagonist.

The Neutrality Proclamation, while supported by the Congress, widened the split between Thomas Jefferson and Alexander Hamilton, soon to be the leaders of America's first political parties. Jefferson insisted that the United States had a moral obligation to maintain the French alliance. Hamilton, ever the realist, argued against sentimental ties to France, asserting that America's first responsibility was to herself; that she had neither an interest nor the power to help the French win their European war. Yet Hamilton, while preferring an alliance with Britain, also realized that American public opinion, which was largely pro-French, made a British alliance an impossibility. He believed that American power, limited though it then was, should be harnessed to conquer the American continent, and should not be dissipated in wars with European powers that were sure to divide the American people, perhaps fatally.

Washington's Farewell Address, which set forth for over a century the bases of America's policy toward Europe, reflected Hamilton's thought. Indeed, it was partially drafted by Hamilton (as well as by James Madison). "Europe," Washington wrote, "has a set of primary interests which to us have no, or a very remote, relation. Hence she must be engaged in frequent controversies, the causes of which are essentially foreign to our concerns. Hence, therefore, it must be unwise in us to implicate ourselves by artificial ties in the ordinary vicissitudes of her politics or the ordinary combinations and collisions of her friendships and her enmities."[8]

America's geographical location, which Washington called her "detached and distant situation," enabled her to be separate from Europe's political squabbles. "Why forego the advantages of so peculiar a situation?" Washington asked his countrymen. "Why quit our own to stand upon foreign ground? Why, by interweaving our destiny with that of any part of Europe, entangle our peace and prosperity in the toils of European ambition, rivalship, interest, humor or caprice?"[9]

Washington asserted that it was the nation's "true policy to steer clear of permanent alliances with any portion of the foreign world." Permanent alliances concluded when America was weak were bound to work to her disadvantage when she became strong. Nevertheless, while Washington deplored alliances of a permanent nature, he did accept the possibility of America's participation in "temporary alliances for extraordinary emergencies." And yet he did not exclude, asserts historian Robert Ellis Jones, the possibility of American participation in military action to maintain the European balance of power. A statement in a first draft of the Farewell Address that was later erased read: "Belligerent European nations will not lightly hazard giving us provocation to throw our weight into the opposite scale."[10]

Nor, in the opinion of many historians of the Federalist period, did Washington think America's isolation from Europe's political affairs need be permanent. "If we remain one people, under an efficient government," he wrote, "the period is not far off when we may defy material injury from external annoyance; when we may take such an attitude as will cause the neutrality we may at any time resolve upon to be scrupulously respected; when belligerent nations, under the impossibility of making acquisitions upon us, will not lightly hazard giving us provocation; when we may choose peace or war, as our interest guided by justice, shall counsel." A year earlier, in 1795, he stated that "twenty years of peace with such an increase of population and resources as we have a right to expect, added to our remote situation from the jarring British power, will in all probability enable us, in a just cause, to bid defiance to any power on earth."[11]

Other historians, such as William Appleman Williams, have seen economic considerations as the primary motivating factors behind Washington's desire to avoid political entanglements with Europe. Isolation, according to Williams, would enable the United States to retain "complete freedom of action to secure and develop a continental empire in the Western Hemisphere." According to Williams, "Washington's proposition was classically simple: play from the strength provided by America's basic economic wealth and geographic location in order to survive immediate weakness and emerge as *the* world power."[12]

## The Jeffersonians in Power

Although Jefferson and his followers saw Washington's Farewell Address as a thinly disguised repudiation of the French alliance, they nevertheless took the first president's advice. Jefferson's 1801 inauguration statement--"Peace, commerce and honest friendship with all nations, entangling alliances with none"--was the essence of Washington's policy.[13]

Yet no American's view of Europe was more dichotomous than Jefferson's. From France, where he served as ambassador from 1784 to 1789, he wrote: "Were I to proceed to tell you how much I enjoy their architecture, sculpture, painting, music, I should want for words." Through Jefferson's travels in Europe, America was abundantly enriched. He returned to Virginia with some of the best things that the Old World had to offer the New: plants, architectural drawings, wines, furniture, and books (which would serve later as the nucleus of the Library of Congress). Nevertheless, Jefferson equated the social order of Europe with the Calvinists' hell. The Continent, he wrote, was "loaded with misery, by kings, nobles, and priests." He considered the "physical and moral oppression" of Europe's masses and the "intrigues of love" and "ambition" that preoccupied the aristocracy far inferior to "the tranquil, permanent felicity with which domestic society in America blesses most of its inhabitants."[14]

Jefferson did as much as anyone to perpetuate the myth of an America superior to Europe. "His rhetoric," wrote historian Cushing Strout, "transformed Americans into a group of idealized sculptured figures. On one side stand Liberty, Happiness, Innocence, and Simplicity, pointing toward the Future, while separated by a pool of water and facing them with menacing mien stand Despotism, Misery, Corruption, and Sophistication, wrapped in the shrouds of the Past." The Jeffersonian impression of the American-European dualism became a standard feature of America's image of Europe during the nineteenth century, an image that did much to underpin American isolationism.[15]

Like Washington, however, Jefferson's isolationism was based on hardheaded pragmatism. He realized that, as long as the United States stayed out of Europe's affairs, the European nations would be too preoccupied with their own quarrels to threaten America. Accordingly, he made no move to revive the French alliance, which had been formally abrogated in 1800 by his predecessor, John Adams, with the consent of France. However, like Washington, Jefferson was prepared to enter temporary alliances if they served the nation's interests. As president, he warned that he would marry America to a British alliance if France once again took possession of New Orleans.

To ensure insulation from Europe's troubles and to secure America's borders, Jefferson encouraged the westward expansion of his nation. The Louisiana Purchase in 1803, one of his greatest achievements, not only doubled the size of the United States, it also reduced the amount of territory on the North American continent still in the hands of European powers, thereby strengthening America's ability to stay aloof from Europe's affairs.

But while the nation's first presidents genuinely desired to avoid war with European nations, America's economic ties with the Old World made that impossible. Both Britain and France refused to recognize the neutral rights of the United States. Largely to protect American trade on the high seas, the United States, in the first quarter of the nineteenth century, engaged France in an undeclared naval war, defeated the pirates of Tripoli, and fought Great Britain in the War of 1812. Nevertheless, in each of these conflicts, America acted independently, without participating in even temporary alliances.

## The Monroe Doctrine

Having withstood successfully the might of Britain during the War of 1812, the United States was tempted to participate more actively in European affairs. In 1819 Czar Alexander I of Russia invited the United States to join a "Holy Alliance" ostensibly designed to promote worldwide peace. In rejecting the Czar's invitation, President James Monroe's secretary of state, John Quincy Adams, stated: "The political system of the United States is . . . essentially extra-European. To stand in firm and cautious independence of all entanglement in the European system has been a cardinal point of U.S. policy under every administration from the peace of 1783 to this day."[16]

American opinion toward the Holy Alliance soon became hostile when its members ruthlessly stamped out democratic movements in Spain, Portugal, Naples, and Greece. In fact, more than a few Americans were prepared to intervene on behalf of the oppressed people of Europe, arguing that the United States has a responsibility to extend to all peoples the blessings of justice, liberty, and peace. A collateral argument held that America's own liberties would be jeopardized if she did not combat the forces of reaction everywhere.

But Secretary of State Adams refused to be carried away by the emotional fervor of the interventionists. America, he said, "is the well-wisher to the freedom and independence of all, the champion and vindicator only of her own. . . . She well knows that by once enlisting under other banners than her own, were they even the banners of foreign independence, she would involve herself, beyond the power of extrication, in all the wars of interest and intrigue, of individual avarice, envy and ambition, which assume the colors and usurp the standards of freedom."[17]

Adams also took a negative view toward cooperation with European powers even when it would advance purely American interests. In 1823 George Canning, the British foreign secretary, called for joint Anglo-American action to prevent the Holy Alliance from assisting Spain to regain control of her New World colonies that had declared their independence. Jefferson advised Monroe that an exception should be made to the nonentanglement rule and Canning's proposal accepted. "By acceding to her [England's] proposition," Jefferson argued, "we detach her from the bands [of despots], bring her mighty weight into the scale of free government, and emancipate a continent at one stroke." But Adams refused to have the United States "come in as a cockboat in the wake of the British man-of-war." An American statement to the Holy Alliance, he insisted, should be made unilaterally. Monroe took his advice. In the doctrine of 1823 that bears his name, Monroe warned the European powers--including England--that the United States would consider any attempt to expand European rule in the Western Hemisphere as "dangerous to our peace and safety."[18]

In a further affirmation of the two-spheres theory, Monroe also stated that the United States had no intention of interfering in Europe's affairs. Justifying the two-spheres theory, Jefferson wrote: "America, North and South, has a set of interests distinct from those of Europe, and peculiarly her own. She should therefore have a system of her own, separate and apart from that of Europe. While the last is laboring to become a domicile of despotism, our endeavors should surely be to make our hemisphere that of freedom."[19]

Accordingly, the United States refrained from active involvement in the revolutions that erupted in Europe in 1848. When Louis Kossuth, the Hungarian patriot, visited America seeking help after the failure of the revolution in his native land, he was given much sympathy but little assistance. Henry Clay told him that the cause of liberty could best be served by Americans keeping their "lamp burning brightly on this Western shore, as a light to all nations, than to hazard its utter extinction, amid the ruins of fallen or falling republics in Europe." President Millard Fillmore told the Hungarian that he would pray for his cause.[20]

The Monroe Doctrine, in the opinion of historian Norman Graebner, "was a fitting climax to a quarter-century of Jeffersonian rule. Like Hamilton and Washington," Graebner wrote, "Adams and Monroe sought to limit the nation's political and military commitments to Europe while guaranteeing American predominance in the Western Hemisphere." It is also true, as Graebner pointed out, that what made the Monroe Doctrine a viable policy was the unacknowledged alliance with England that it created. It was the support of Britain, and particularly the British fleet, that enabled the United States to effectively oppose the expansion of French influence into the New World, and blocked the intervention of the Holy Alliance into the Americas during the first half of the nineteenth century, when U.S. naval power was virtually nonexistent.[21]

The Monroe Doctrine, according to historian Cushing Strout, also made unbridgeable the gulf between America and Europe. "No good American," Strout wrote, "could cross it without losing his political and moral integrity. The isolationist tradition thus acquired a sanctity which inspired a fierce belief, easily transformed into pharisaical righteousness and blind bigotry, that America was the favorite child of God, Nature, and History." Europeans, viewing the American exploitation of blacks and ruthless disregard for Indian rights, Strout added, might be forgiven if they could not take at face value American estimates of their own innocence.[22]

# Manifest Destiny and the Civil War

The development of American nationalism in the second quarter of the nineteenth century only encouraged isolationist sentiment. During this period, historian Foster Rhea Dulles wrote, "the belief was well-nigh universal that the United States was so strong, so vigorous, so dynamic--so morally superior--that it could ignore all other countries." Foreign visitors were astonished by the degree of self-confidence displayed by the American people and by their facile disregard for Europe. "Caught up in the excitement of the westward movement that was step by step bringing about the conquest of the continent," Dulles commented, "no bounds were placed upon the ultimate expansion of American power and influence."[23]

In the 1850s, after the Mexican Cession and the Gadsden Purchase rounded out the present continental boundaries of the contiguous United States, Americans for the first time gave meaningful attention to the prospect of overseas expansion. The opening of the markets of China and Japan to Western trade in the 1840s and 1850s prompted Americans to turn to the Pacific and Asia before they were fully exploited by America's European competitors. For the first time, Americans laid covetous eyes on islands of the Caribbean and the Pacific--Cuba, Hawaii, Samoa, and Guam--and thereby created the prospect of future conflict with nations of the Old World as well as the rising power of Japan.

But the outbreak of the Civil War delayed American overseas expansion. It also strengthened the American desire--at least on the part of Northerners--to maintain the two-sphere policy. In 1863 Lincoln's secretary of state, William Henry Seward, refused France's request for American cooperation to pressure Russia to deal more leniently with revolutionaries in Russian Poland. "Our policy of non-intervention, straight, absolute, and peculiar as it may seem to other nations,"

Seward asserted, "has become a traditional one, which could not be abandoned without the most urgent occasion, amounting to a manifest necessity." It also may be true that Seward's response was partly prompted by a desire to maintain Russian friendship in order to deter British recognition of the Confederacy. At any rate, Seward was not about to give Europeans any justification to intervene in the American Civil War by countenancing U.S. intervention in purely European matters.[24]

## The Post-Civil War Era

In the wake of the Civil War, Americans turned their attention and energy to Reconstruction, industrialization, the settlement of the West, and the development of the New South. To a degree even greater than before, Americans felt a sense of security, superiority, and power that made events in the rest of the world seem even less important than before. America's geographic location, the size of her territory, and her growing industry, according to President Andrew Johnson, made her "singularly independent of the varying policy of foreign powers" and served to protect Americans "against every temptation" to enter "entangling alliances."[25]

The great waves of immigration that America absorbed in the latter half of the nineteenth century, and the early years of the twentieth, also strengthened isolationist sentiment. To the immigrants, America symbolized freedom, opportunity, and peace; on the other hand, Europe represented suppression, poverty, militarism, and war. Most Americans probably would have agreed with Mark Twain's comment that Italy--and, by inference, all of Europe--was "one vast museum of magnificence and misery. For every beggar in America, Italy can show a hundred--and rags and vermin to match." Partly because countless immigrants were determined to keep their new country uncontaminated by the evils of the Old World, American isolationism in the latter half of the nineteenth century seemed virtually unshakable.[26]

Reflecting upon America's isolation, President Grover Cleveland stated that "The genius of our institutions, the needs of our people in their home life, and the attention which is demanded for the settlement and development of the resources of our vast territory dictate the scrupulous avoidance of any departure from that foreign policy commended by the history, the traditions, and the prosperity of our Republic. . . . It is the policy of neutrality, rejecting any share in foreign broils and ambitions upon other continents and repelling their intrusions here."[27]

## American Imperialism

Yet forces were at work that would make Cleveland's words the swan song of the old era. By the end of the nineteenth century, the United States had become an industrial giant with worldwide economic interests. Moreover, the oceans did not offer the degree of protection they once did. Technological developments--such as steel battleships and, later, submarines--exposed the nation's coasts, and particularly American shipping, to potential destruction.

Partly in response to industrialization and the increase of foreign trade, earlier American imperialist ambitions revived during the last quarter of the nineteenth century. The disappearance of the frontier, combined with widespread agrarian distress and worker unrest produced by the depression of 1893, caused some Americans to look favorably upon the possibility of overseas expansion as an outlet for apparent overpopulation and overproduction. Moreover, American imperialists argued that European nations were busy seizing new colonies in the Pacific and in Asia, and so, too, must America if she were going to protect her markets in these regions.

Carl Schurz, the liberal Republican senator from Missouri, was one of many who criticized the new imperialism. Overseas expansion, he argued, would violate the isolationist tradition, embroil the United States in foreign wars that did not directly affect its interests, and give cause for European intervention in the Western Hemisphere. By engaging in overseas expansion, Schurz asserted, America would be surrendering other, major advantages that nonintervention had brought her. "In our present condition," he explained, "we have over all the great nations of the world one advantage of incalculable value. We are the only one not under any necessity of keeping up a large armament either on land or water for the security of its possessions, the only one that can turn all the energies of its population to productive employment, and the only one that has an entirely free hand. This is a blessing for which the American people can never be too thankful. It should not lightly be jeopardized."[28]

In the end, however, the imperialists won the day. In the wake of the successful Spanish-American War in 1898, the United States annexed Puerto Rico, the Philippines, and Hawaii; established a protectorate over Cuba; helped Panama gain its independence from Colombia; and then began the construction of an isthmian canal. As a result of territorial acquisitions beyond its continental boundaries, the United States would find it increasingly difficult to remain isolated from the political affairs of other nations, particularly those of Europe.

# Toward an Entangling Alliance

# 1

# The Emergence of American Internationalism, 1901–1921

During the first two decades of the twentieth century, the United States rose to the pinnacle of world leadership, after intervening militarily on the European continent for the first time in history in World War I. Yet after a bout of internationalist fervor that was aroused by the war, the subsequent peace settlement and the battle between Woodrow Wilson and the Senate over American membership in a league of nations, the United States returned, even if somewhat incompletely, to the isolationism that characterized American foreign policy in the prewar period.

## Theodore Roosevelt: Internationalism and Power Politics

The assassination of William McKinley in 1901 brought to the White House one of the most colorful of America's presidents, Theodore Roosevelt. Brash, aggressive, flamboyant, but intelligent, Roosevelt was the son of a well-to-do New York businessman and banker. Throughout his life he had tried to compensate for a sickly youth by emphasizing "manly" activities--including horseback riding, boxing, weight lifting, then politics as state assemblyman, police commissioner of the city of New York, assistant secretary of the Navy, Rough Rider in the Spanish American War, governor of New York, and vice president in McKinley's administration. Concluded one historian, Richard Hofstadter, "A profound and ineluctable tendency to anxiety plagued him." Yet, as president, Roosevelt displayed an astute ability to rein in his aggressive tendencies and apply reason and often wisdom to the conduct of the nation's diplomacy.[1]

No individual more than Roosevelt inspired the emergence of internationalist sentiment in America at the turn of the century. Isolationism, he believed, may have been a wise course for an infant United States, but it was no longer possible in the twentieth century. "The increasing interdependence and complexity of international political and economic relations," he told the Congress in 1902, "render it incumbent on all civilized and orderly powers to insist on the proper policing of the world."[2]

Like his friend, the naval strategist Captain Alfred Thayer Mahan, Roosevelt emphasized that power, and particularly naval power, was the major determining factor in international relations. Mahan not only spoke of the necessity for a strong Navy with worldwide bases to protect America's growing trade, he also insisted that the United States must play a major role in upholding law and justice in the international community. Because Roosevelt believed that a United States economically rich but militarily weak would "invite destruction," he made the expansion of the Navy a major goal of his presidency. By the end of his second term, he had prodded the Congress into approving appropriations that enabled the Navy to double its size. By then, the U.S. Navy was second only to Britain in total capital ship tonnage. However, as historian Frederick W. Marks III has pointed out, while Roosevelt appreciated the importance of power in the conduct of diplomacy, unlike more ruthless practitioners of power politics, he also insisted that the employment of force must always be motivated and governed by moral values. As defined by Roosevelt, however, these moral values usually bore a striking resemblance to his conception of America's national interests.[3]

Roosevelt was also the first president to appreciate the threat of German economic and military power. Under the excitable and unpredictable Kaiser Wilhelm II, Germany posed a potential challenge to British control of the seas and to the stability of the European balance of power, both of which had helped to maintain American security for over a century. During the war with Spain, the German government had expressed its desire to obtain a share of the Philippine Islands if the United States did not annex them. The presence of a German naval squadron in Manila Bay during the U.S. attack on the Spanish fleet led many Americans to believe, incorrectly, that the Germans were preparing to intervene on Spain's behalf. Later, the Navy used rumors of alleged German attempts to acquire naval bases in the Galapagos Islands and in Haiti to support its case for a major expansion of the U.S. fleet.[4]

Roosevelt and other realistic internationalists favored closer relations with Britain to counter the German threat. By the beginning of his presidency, British and American interests, which once had seemed so diametrically opposed, had begun to merge. Both nations sought to maintain an open door for international trade in China. Both had interests in the Caribbean that they sought to protect against German intrusion. And, as one reporter wrote, "Wherever the American has gone in Europe, he has seen clearly that it is with Britain alone that his own country has much in common, whether in social or moral sentiments, political principles, or fundamental laws." In 1901 Roosevelt wrote his close friend, Senator Henry Cabot Lodge, that "we are closer to her [England] than to any other nation; and . . . probably her interest and ours will run on rather parallel lines in the future."[5]

Under Roosevelt, the slow, cautious, Anglo-American rapprochement that had begun under McKinley continued. After the Spanish-American War, during which time Britain had been openly sympathetic to the United States, the British surrendered their right to build an isthmian canal as well as most of their other ambitions in Central America. In 1902 Britain backed off from a potential confrontation with the United States by ending her participation in an Anglo-German blockade of Venezuela, brought about by that nation's refusal to pay its debts to European creditors. In 1903 the British helped cement its pro-American policy by siding with the United States in settling a Canadian-American boundary dispute over Alaska.

Like Britain, Roosevelt was also concerned about the expansionist tendencies of imperial Russia. As early as 1896, the British diplomat Sir Cecil Spring-Rice warned him: "Russia is self-sufficient. She is also practically invulnerable to attack. She is growing and has room to grow . . . it is not at all improbable that Europe may be in a given period at the mercy of a power really barbarous but with a highly military organization. No power will attack Russia--no one can afford to. Russia, therefore, has simply to bide her time."[6]

While the United States had a history of generally favorable relations with the Russians--Russia was benevolently neutral during the American Revolutionary War, openly sided with the North during the Civil War, and sold Alaska to the United States in 1867--Russian ambitions in Europe and in Asia bothered Roosevelt. As early as 1896 he wrote: "It has always seemed to me that the Germans showed shortsightedness in not making some alliance that would enable them to crush Russia. Even if in the dim future Russia should take India and become the preponderant power in Asia, England would merely be injured in one great dependency; but when Russia grows so as to crush Germany, the crushing will be once and for all."[7]

Roosevelt was also among the first to see that a major European conflict could not but affect the United States. In 1900 he stated that, if England were unable to preserve the European balance of power, the United States would have to do so: "In fact, we ourselves are becoming, owing to our strength and geographic situation, more and more the balance of power of the whole globe."[8]

Roosevelt, however, was frustrated by his inability to gain his nation's acceptance of its world responsibilities. "Here in the United States," he told a French statesman in 1908, "what is most lacking to us is to understand that we have interests in the whole world . . . the whole American people must become accustomed to this idea." But Americans were reluctant to abandon isolationism. They preferred to believe that geography alone--the two oceans that surround the North American continent--rather than the European balance of power, now threatened by Germany, was sufficient to preserve American security. Although they realized that America's overseas expansion and a shrinking world had made the aloofness of an earlier day impossible, they refused to surrender the freedom of action that isolationism provided.[9]

Without much enthusiasm from the American public or Congress, Roosevelt used his executive powers to do what he could to maintain the balance of power in Asia and in Europe.

To check the expansion of Russia in the Far East, he welcomed the conclusion of the Anglo-Japanese Alliance in 1902 and promised to act toward it as a silent partner. Secretary of War William Howard Taft told Japan's premier, Count Katsura Taro, that Tokyo could count on the American government "quite as confidently as if the United States were under treaty obligations." Two decades would pass before the American people learned about Roosevelt's secret circumvention of the Senate's treaty-making power. Yet after Japan dealt the Russian army and navy crushing defeats in the Russo-Japanese war of 1904-1905, Roosevelt intervened to prevent the Japanese from overthrowing the Far Eastern balance of power. He invited both belligerents to a conference at Portsmouth, New Hampshire. where he successfully mediated an end to the conflict.[10]

To preserve the balance of power in Europe, Roosevelt made a major and unprecedented departure from the traditional U.S. policy of nonintervention in purely European affairs. He agreed to permit American representatives to participate in the Algeciras Conference of 1906. Through Roosevelt's efforts, the conference settled a Franco-German dispute over Morocco, which threatened to ignite a major European war. But his intervention at Algeciras was the most criticized policy of his administration, for the Congress and the American people viewed it as an unnecessary abandonment of the isolationist tradition. The Senate, in ratifying the Algeciras agreement, stated that the United States was under no obligation to enforce its provisions.[11]

# International Cooperation

In spite of the reluctance of most Americans to participate in the maintenance of a global balance of power, by the turn of the twentieth century some had come to believe that the United States did have an obligation to play an active role in maintaining world peace, although most internationalists felt this should be accomplished by nonmilitary means. Advocates of international peace persuaded the McKinley administration to participate in a conference of twenty-six nations at The Hague in 1899, which was called by Czar Nicholas II of Russia to discuss disarmament and the prevention of war. While this first Hague Conference failed to bring about an agreement on disarmament, it did create a Permanent Court of Arbitration designed to settle international disputes. The Senate ratified the agreements signed at The Hague Conference, including one outlawing the use of so-called inhumane weapons. But once again it insisted that acceptance of the treaties represented no departure from the traditional policy of nonentanglement.[12]

A second Hague Conference in 1907 also failed to reduce armaments. Roosevelt offered to freeze the world's navies at their then current sizes in order to avoid additional congressional naval appropriations. But since the plan was opposed by most of the major powers--Japan, Germany, Russia, Austria-Hungary, and Italy-- and received only mild support from the British, it was not implemented. The second Hague Conference also rejected an initiative by Roosevelt's secretary of state, Elihu Root, to establish a more effective replacement for the Permanent Court of Arbitration. The conference also rejected treaties requiring the arbitration of international legal disputes. Nevertheless, within a year after the second Hague Conference, Root had negotiated twenty-four bilateral arbitration treaties with every major nation except Germany. However, because each treaty recognized the Senate's right to define the issues subject to arbitration, none was really meaningful.[13]

Roosevelt's successor, William Howard Taft, had no success expanding the areas subject to arbitration. Two treaties negotiated by his administration with Britain and France in 1911 required all international disputes that could not be settled diplomatically to be submitted to The Hague Court or some other suitable tribunal. However, Taft withdrew the treaties after the Senate added amendments reserving to itself the right to determine what disputes it would allow to be arbitrated.[14]

## Woodrow Wilson: Idealism and Internationalism

On March 4, 1913, Woodrow Wilson became the first Democrat since Grover Cleveland to enter the White House. A former history professor at Princeton, and later president of that university, Wilson had a background in politics as brief as it was meteoric. His only political office before the presidency was the governorship of New Jersey, a position he held for only one term, from 1911 to 1913. His presidential election was due not only to the progressive reputation he had built as governor of New Jersey but, more important, to the split in the Republican vote that occurred after Roosevelt decided to run as a third-party candidate.

While Wilson shared Roosevelt's belief that America must play a major role in world affairs, his philosophy for doing so was quite different. Where Roosevelt emphasized the use of military power to secure America's national interests, Wilson emphasized the force of American ideals--including peace, progress, brotherhood, liberty, democracy, self-determination, free enterprise, and free trade-- in the construction of a world based upon a community of interests rather than conflicting national interests. Because he believed it was America's duty to spread her liberal values, he was convinced that the United States must become an active participant in the new international community he envisioned, one that would be based on law and collective security rather than the balance of power. "My dream," he said in 1914, "is that as the world knows more and more of America, it will turn to America for those moral inspirations which lie at the basis of all freedom and [realize] that her flag is the flag of humanity."[15]

Unlike Roosevelt, who seemed to relish warfare, Wilson deplored violence. Reflecting the tenets of nineteenth century idealism, he believed that war was a product of irrationality. Properly educated, he believed, people would realize the futility of war. Yet Wilson was no pacifist. "There are times in the history of nations," he wrote, "when they must take up the instruments of bloodshed in order to vindicate spiritual conceptions," such as liberty. "When men take up arms to set other men free," he asserted, "there is something sacred and holy in warfare. I will not cry 'peace' so long as there is sin and wrong in the world."[16]

The disdain which Roosevelt displayed toward Wilson's brand of idealism prompted Robert E. Osgood to invoke Nietzsche's comparison of the "Warrior and the Priest." According to Osgood,

> The Warrior with all his natural strength and virility exults in the free and unabashed exercise of the will-to-power. . . . For the Priest he reserves a special loathing, since he sees that the Priest is also driven by the will-to-power, but in a perverted way that is forever confounding the Warrior, frustrating his manly passion, and denying him his rightful status in society. For the will of the Priest is not the frank, straightforward will of the Warrior but rather the devious influence of the crafty intellect, which compensates the Priest for his physical weakness by investing cowardice with the semblance of morality.

Osgood admitted that the comparison was imperfect because Roosevelt often cloaked his employment of power politics with "priestly" moralism and Wilson occasionally appeared as "a formidable Scotch Presbyterian Warrior." Nevertheless, it does serve to indicate why Roosevelt considered Wilson's attitude toward power utopian, hypocritical, and destined ultimately to undermine international confidence in the United States.[17]

Wilson's reluctance to use military power unless wedded to transcendent principles, some historians have argued, was a product of an unhappy childhood. His entrance into politics, Alexander and Juliette George concluded in a seminal psychobiography of the president, was motivated by a damaged sense of self-esteem caused by his tyrannical and demanding father. As a result, the Georges have argued, Wilson carried a burden of rage that he turned against anyone who dared to challenge him. For Wilson, the Georges asserted, "power was a compensatory value, a means of restoring the self-esteem damaged in childhood." However, they added, Wilson refused to admit the psychological need behind his quest for power and instead attempted to disguise it by insisting that power could only be used for virtuous ends. "This compelling personal need to purify the exercise of his power," the Georges argued, "partly explains Wilson's strong distaste for basing his foreign policy actions directly on power," and why "he, and by extension the nation, must act unselfishly and without hostile intent."[18]

On the other hand, a more recent study concludes that, while the Georges made a major contribution in pointing out that a political leader's personality can play a decisive role in his political conduct, their interpretation of Wilson suffered from three major deficiencies: inadequate research, misinterpretation of evidence to fit their theory, and a failure to consider how neurological disorders affected Wilson's behavior. The authors of this more recent study--Edwin Weinstein, James William Anderson, and Arthur S. Link--argue that, rather than hostility, Wilson's relationship with his father was characterized by great warmth. More important than his father in influencing Wilson's behavior, in their opinion, was the cerebral vascular disease that afflicted him intermittently from 1896 until his death in 1924. Wilson suffered a minor stroke in 1896, which caused a marked weakness in his right hand, and reoccurring, minor strokes in 1900, 1904, 1906, and 1907. These strokes, and especially the massive one he suffered in October 1919, the authors believe, made Wilson "less empathetic, more stubborn, and more prone to overgeneralize and personalize his problems."[19]

# World War I

In spite of Wilson's devotion to internationalism, the beginning of World War I in 1914 found him reasserting an essentially isolationist policy--America's traditional neutrality during European wars. World War I, he told the American people, was "a war with which we have nothing to do, whose cause cannot touch us." The president asked his fellow countrymen to remain neutral in thought as well as in deed. This proved impossible because most Americans resented German militarism and therefore favored an Allied victory. But the preponderant majority of the American people supported Wilson's neutrality policy; they did not want to sacrifice their sons to defeat the Germans.[20]

But neutrality for Wilson did not mean simply, as he put it, "the petty desire to keep out of trouble." He hoped that by staying neutral America could mediate a just peace. Such a peace, he insisted, could not be based on the paraphernalia of the old diplomacy--secret alliances, militarism, imperialism, and the like--for, in his opinion, the old diplomacy was responsible for the outbreak of the war in the first place. As a substitute for militarism and imperialism, Wilson emphasized the need for disarmament and a mandate system that would prepare the colonies of the world for eventual self-government. In place of a balance of power, he envisioned a "community of power," which would find expression, not in a system of entangling alliances, but in an association of nations designed to uphold the security of all--the League of Nations. Such an association, Wilson believed, would become a force "so much greater than the force of any nation now engaged, or any alliance hitherto formed or projected, that no nation, no probable combination of nations could face or withstand it."[21]

Contrary to the opinion of Wilson's critics, his defenders insist that he was not a visionary incapable of facing reality, nor was he obtuse to America's own interests. Rather, as historian Norman Gordon Levin, Jr. has argued, Wilson identified the national interest with America's duty to the rest of mankind in the creation of a new international order that shunned both traditional power politics as well as revolutionary socialism, and instead was based on collective security, democracy, free trade, and capitalism.[22]

Nor, Wilson's defenders assert, was he oblivious to the German threat. His closest advisers, "Colonel" Edward M. House and Secretary of State Robert Lansing, repeatedly impressed upon the president that a victorious Germany would expose American interests in the Western Hemisphere and in the Far East to the threat of a hostile naval power. Yet, while Wilson shared their concern, he did not emphasize it. Rather, he feared more that a German victory would produce a permanently militarized America in which democracy's survival would be endangered.[23]

But Wilson did not favor an Allied victory either--at least not until after the United States had entered the war. He worried that a German surrender, particularly if it were based on the harsh terms the Allies had in mind, would lead to Russian domination of Europe. What he wanted was a war that ended in stalemate, for only a deadlock would prompt both sides to accept a nonvindictive peace. A just peace in Europe, in Wilson's opinion, would not only preclude the necessity of a large American defense establishment, it would also lay the foundation for the new international order he envisioned. Yet, in the end, the belligerents would reject Wilson's repeated offer to mediate an end to the struggle.[24]

# The Preparedness Battle

As a result of the German threat in February 1915 to sink Allied merchantmen entering the Atlantic war zone and the sinking of the British passenger ship *Lusitania* the following May, Wilson felt compelled to bow to pressure from Theodore Roosevelt and other advocates of American "preparedness," and agreed to ask the Congress to approve a major expansion of the nation's military establishment. On October 15, 1915 he approved a plan drawn up by the General Board of the Navy that aimed at achieving naval equality with Britain by 1925. During the first five years of the plan, ten battleships, six battle cruisers, ten cruisers, fifty destroyers, and one hundred submarines and lesser craft would be built at a cost of $500 million. Wilson also approved a plan drafted by the Army calling for substantial increases in the Regular Army and the creation of a huge national reserve force of 400,000 men, called the Continental Army. The drafters of the plan hoped that the Continental Army would replace the National Guard as the nation's first line of defense.[25]

In a tour of the East and Midwest, Wilson defended his plans for a military buildup on the ground that the nation could not defend its honor without adequate military power. The United States, he said in a speech in St. Louis, must have "incomparably the greatest navy in the world." It was needed, he said, to defend the Western Hemisphere and to deal with the threatening situation in Europe. Privately, Wilson also expressed his concern about the growing power of Japan in the Far East. But the main reason for the military buildup, in the opinion of Robert E. Osgood, was not due to Wilson's concern about Germany's or Japan's threat to the balance of power. Rather, wrote Osgood, "He wanted to free the whole issue of preparedness from passion, prejudice, and partisanship so that the nation might remain true to its mission of service to the rest of the world."[26]

Nevertheless, Wilson's preparedness plans encountered considerable opposition, particularly from progressives in the South and Middle West, who insisted that America must serve as a model of social and economic justice for a decadent Europe. Strengthening the military, progressives feared, would revive American imperialism, lead to the nation's involvement in the war, and bring to an end the domestic reforms they had championed. Only bankers, munitions makers, and industrialists with overseas markets would profit from American intervention in the conflict, progressives insisted, while America's sons and their families alone would suffer. The only way to avoid these results, they argued, was to repudiate war and military preparedness and to champion disarmament and the compulsory arbitration of international disputes.[27]

The Democratic Party in Congress also deserted the president on the preparedness issue. Fearing the growth of the federal military establishment, congressional Democrats favored scrapping the Continental Army plan and replacing it with a strengthened but "federalized" National Guard. Without

Democratic support for his plan, Wilson had no choice but to capitulate. He accepted a compromise bill that increased the Regular Army from an authorized peacetime strength of 5,029 officers and 100,000 men to 11,327 officers and 208,338 men. The plan for the Contintental reserve was replaced by one designed to integrate more thoroughly the National Guard into the national defense structure and to increase its size to 17,000 officers and 440,000 men in five years.[28]

Wilson encountered less congressional opposition toward his plan to expand the Navy. He was able to persuade the House to accept the essentials of a Senate bill designed to complete the administration's naval program in three years, rather than five, and to provide funds for the construction of four battleships, four battle cruisers, four cruisers, twenty destroyers, thirty submarines, and a number of lesser craft during the first year of the plan. In addition, Congress also passed the Shipping Act, which established the modern American merchant marine. Asserted one heartsick opponent of preparedness, House Majority Leader Claude Kitchen, "The United States today becomes the most militaristic naval nation on earth."[29]

## American Intervention in World War I

Despite Wilson's sincere desire to keep America out of the war, like James Madison, he was confronted with a threat to the nation's shipping on the high seas that made neutrality difficult and ultimately undesirable. As in the Napoleonic Wars, World War I brought expanded American exports to Europe, particularly to Britain, whose control of the Atlantic hindered neutral trade to the Central Powers. While both sides violated neutral rights--the British opened American mail bound for the Continent, expanded the contraband list, blacklisted American companies that traded with the Germans, and mined the North Sea-- German violations proved to be deadlier: the Germans sank Allied ships carrying American passengers. The German submarine attack on the *Lusitania* killed almost 1,200 people, including 128 Americans. Yet rather than attempting to curtail trade and loans with the Allies or to prohibit Americans from sailing on the passenger ships of belligerent nations--which Wilson considered dishonorable alternatives, not to mention that their implementation would have contributed to the defeat of the Allies, an outcome he did not want either--he warned the Germans that they would be held to "a strict accountability" for the loss of American life. By doing so, the president committed American honor and prestige so deeply that the continuation of unrestricted submarine warfare would leave little room for diplomacy to avoid American involvement in the war.[30]

The Germans, at first, called off their attacks on Allied passenger ships and promised that all unresisting belligerent merchantmen would not be destroyed without warning and provisions for the safety of their crews. But by 1917 the German high command had come to believe that the resumption of unrestricted submarine attacks was the only way to end the war before the British blockade strangled the German economy. While the Germans appreciated that this strategy would probably bring the United States into the war, they felt certain they could defeat the Allies before substantial American military power was brought to bear on the Continent.[31]

The Germans also believed they had nothing further to lose and everything to gain by resuming unrestricted submarine attacks. Most American trade and loans were going to the Allies. Between 1914 and 1917 American exports to Europe rose from an excess over imports of $500 million to $3.5 billion. During the same interval, trade with the Allies increased 184 percent. And by 1917 the United States had exported over $1 billion worth of weapons and munitions to the Allies, in the process virtually creating a new munitions industry.[32]

However, to the very last, Wilson tried to avoid war with Germany, even after the Germans resumed unrestricted submarine warfare on February 1, 1917. Although he reluctantly broke off diplomatic relations with Berlin on February 3, he apparently believed the nation could defend its ships on the high seas without a declaration of war. On March 9 he approved the arming of American merchantmen by executive order after isolationists filibustered to death a Senate bill that would have accomplished the same purpose.[33]

Nevertheless, events beyond Wilson's control pushed the nation into war. The interception and publication by the British of a telegram from Germany's foreign secretary, Arthur Zimmermann, to the Mexican government enraged American opinion. The Zimmermann telegram offered Mexico an alliance with Germany, and possibly Japan, and, after the war, the return of territory lost in the Mexican Cession--Texas, Arizona, and New Mexico. More important, German submarines sank three American vessels in mid-March, causing a heavy loss of life. These attacks finally convinced Wilson that he had no choice but to ask for a declaration of war. Armed neutrality, he told the Congress in his war message on April 2, would not suffice to protect American ships against the brutal, German submarine onslaught.[34]

But the most compelling reason for Wilson's decision to accept belligerency was his conviction that only America's participation in the war could enable him to win the goals for which he had been working since August 1914--a reasonable peace settlement and the reconstruction of world order. America's entrance into the war, as her neutrality, Wilson insisted, was motivated by no selfish interests. Ignoring the economic and military stake the United States had in preventing an Allied defeat, Wilson portrayed America's intervention as a just crusade to end all wars. "We shall fight," he told the nation in his war message, "for things which we have always carried nearest our hearts--for democracy, for the right of those who submit to authority to have a voice in their own Government, for the rights and liberties of small nations, for a universal dominion of right by such a concert of free peoples as shall bring peace and safety to all nations and make the world itself at last free." "The world," he emphasized, "must be made safe for democracy."[35]

While Theodore Roosevelt was ecstatic that Wilson had finally asked Congress for a declaration of war, he was repulsed by the president's reasons for doing so. The nation should go to war, he argued, not to make the world safe for democracy but rather "to make the world safe for ourselves." "If Germany now conquered France and England," he wrote, we would be the next victim." The German submarine, he pointed out, ended the security for America that the oceans once offered. If the United States did not save the Allies from a German victory, "we shall some day have to reckon with Germany single-handed. Therefore, for our own sakes let us strike down Germany."[36]

American isolationists, on the other hand, denounced the decision to enter the war. Senator Robert La Follette declared that American intervention was a violation of everything for which the Founding Fathers had stood in warning the nation to avoid Europe's squabbles. Other isolationists believed Wilson was too eager to bail out the British Empire. "When did it come to pass," queried Senator William Stone, chairman of the Foreign Relations Committee, "that Uncle Sam must lay his head on the palpitating breast of Uncle Johnny Bull?" Senator George Norris stated a belief that would gain wide currency later, that the United States entered the war because bankers and munition makers undermined American neutrality. "The object in having war and in preparing for war is to make money," Norris asserted. "We are going to run the risk of sacrificing millions of our countrymen's lives in order that other countrymen may coin their lifeblood into money."[37]

But the faction against intervention was a distinct minority. The Congress, motivated primarily by the blatant German attacks on American ships, declared war four days later. The vote in the Senate was 82 to 6, while the House approved the war resolution 373-50. The Congress and the American people apparently believed that Wilson was justified in asking for a declaration of war. Yet, while they agreed with the president that Germany had dangerously violated American neutral rights, it is debatable how many were prepared to fight the war for the noble vision Wilson had in mind.

## War and Peace

American economic and military power was soon and decisively brought to bear against the Central Powers. American industry quickly converted to war production. Congress passed a draft law and loan authorization acts to finance the war. In the end, the total direct cost of the war amounted to $35.5 billion--$11.2 billion of which was loaned to other nations, primarily the Allies. (By contrast, the entire cost of running the federal government from 1789 to 1917 had amounted to only $24 billion.) The U.S. Navy sent hundreds of warships into the Atlantic to protect convoys of merchantmen and troop transports and to reinforce the Allied blockade of Germany. And, for the first time, American combat troops went into action on the European continent. General John "Black Jack" Pershing's American Expeditionary Force, some two million-men strong, helped check the great German offensive that began in March 1918 and then threw the German army into retreat in August. After the American and Allied armies broke through the German defensive line in early October, the German government, hoping to gain time to withdraw its forces behind the Rhine, asked Wilson to arrange an armistice as a prelude to a just peace.[38]

Well before the German request for an armistice, Wilson had crystallized his ideas regarding the peace terms. The end of the war, he told the Senate in January 1917, must produce a "peace without victory." A victorious peace, he insisted, "would leave a sting, a resentment, a bitter memory upon which terms of peace would rest, not permanently, but only as upon quicksand. Only a peace between equals can last." In early 1918, in his famous Fourteen Point plan, Wilson outlined the specific principles on which he believed a just peace must be based. They included self-determination for all nations, the end of secret diplomacy, freedom of the seas, removal of economic barriers, limitation of armaments, and an association of nations to guarantee the independence of great and small nations alike, the League of Nations.[39]

Not surprisingly, Wilson saw the American-inspired League of Nations as the logical extension to the entire world of the anti-reactionary principles of the Monroe Doctrine. "No nation," the president said," should seek to extend its polity over any other nation or people, but every people should be left free to determine its own polity, its own way of development, unhindered, unthreatened, unafraid, the little along with the powerful." He also proposed that the nations of the world replace "entangling alliances," which would draw them into power struggles, with a "concert of power," which would enable all people "to live their own lives under common protection." In the opinion of historian Lloyd E. Ambrosius, "By emphasizing the future League, Wilson hoped to establish extensive American control over world affairs while avoiding entanglement in European politics."[40]

To ensure a common purpose for the League, Wilson insisted that all members of the League must be democracies. "Nobody is admitted except the self-governing nations," Wilson explained, "because . . . only a nation whose government was its servant and not its master could be trusted to preserve the peace of the world." Henceforth, autocratic governments would be excluded from the "respectable society" upon which they depended for their existence.[41]

As a result, Wilson responded to the German request for an armistice by insisting that it must not only be based on the Fourteen Points but also preceded by the replacement of Germany's autocratic government with a republic. Two reservations were attached to the Fourteen Points. At the insistence of England, which did not want to surrender her ability to impose a naval blockade during wartime, Point 2, freedom of the seas, was left open for further discussion. The other reservation redefined Point 8, which concerned the evacuation of territory, to specify German payment for damage done to all civilian property. With the German army on the verge of defeat, and the German people in the throes of a revolution that anticipated the monarchy's downfall, the German government had no choice but to accept Wilson's terms. On November 9 Kaiser Wilhelm II was forced to abdicate and a republic was proclaimed. At five o'clock in the morning of November 11, 1918, the armistice was signed, and the fighting came to a close on the western front.[42]

## The Treaty of Versailles

In spite of Wilson's ardent efforts at the Versailles Peace Conference, which began in January 1919 and ended the following June, neither a just peace nor a peace without victory resulted. Germany and her allies were forced to accept the sole responsibility for starting the war and, on that basis, Germany was forced to pay reparations for the destruction her armies had wrought. She also was compelled to surrender her colonies and some of her European territory, and to accept the demilitarization of the Rhineland. In addition, she was virtually denuded of military power: her standing army was reduced to 100,000 men, her navy limited to thirty-six warships, and she was prohibited from possessing submarines, tanks, and combat aircraft.[43]

Wilson had proposed that the Allies also accept disarmament after the war. He wanted the peace treaty to abolish conscription, prohibit manufacture of weapons, and require the signatories to maintain armies adequate only for preserving domestic order and fulfilling their international obligations. But the French, and particularly their premier, Georges Clemenceau, feared the eventual resuscitation of German military power; they flatly refused to reduce their army and made only a vague promise to undertake general disarmament in the future. Nor was Wilson entirely blameless for the conference's failure to disarm the victors as well as the vanquished at war's end. He had refrained from proposing naval reductions because he believed he needed the threat of American naval expansion to win British support for the League of Nations. Wilson also believed a strong navy might be necessary to deter Japanese expansion in the Far East.[44]

To gain support for the League of Nations, Wilson also felt compelled to recognize secret territorial agreements concluded by the Allies during the war, agreements that often contradicted the principles of self-determination contained in the League Covenant. Germany's colonial possessions, for example, were awarded to Britain and Japan without the consent of their inhabitants. Even Germany's leasehold on the Shandong (Shantung) Peninsula in China was transferred to Japan over the vehement opposition of the Chinese. Wilson yielded on the Shandong issue after Japan threatened to walk out of the conference. In the end, the Versailles Treaty, by placing millions of Germans in the new Polish and Czechoslovak states, planted the seeds of another world conflagration twenty years later.[45]

Even Wilson himself admitted that the treaty was "undoubtedly very severe indeed," but he did not regard it as unjust, considering the "crimes" that Germany had committed. And while he hoped eventually to integrate a democratized Germany into the new international order he envisaged, she first would have to prove herself free from militarism and imperialism. Until then, Wilson agreed with the Allies that Germany would have to be disarmed and controlled.[46]

Wilson was also fully aware that the compromises he made on territorial issues violated the principles of the League Covenant. Yet there were important features of the treaty that reflected his Fourteen Points--Belgian independence was restored, Alsace-Lorraine was returned to France, and an independent Poland with access to the sea was created. Wilson believed that eventually the League would be able to redress the injustices of the treaty's territorial agreements, but first it must be created. The compromises he made, he believed, served this purpose.[47]

At the same time, Wilson was prevented from making a more successful defense of his Fourteen Points at the Versailles Conference by the sudden collapse of German power, which he had hoped would have remained sufficiently strong to check the extreme territorial ambitions of the Allies. With the threat of German military power gone, however, the Allies were no longer dependent on the United States for their survival, and they were much freer to resist Wilson's demands. According to Wilson scholar Arthur S. Link, the president's "only recourse-- withdrawal from the conference--would have resulted in a Carthaginian peace imposed by the French, as the British alone could have prevented the French from carrying out their plans to destroy Germany. In these circumstances, compromise was not merely desirable; it was a compelling necessity to avert, from Wilson's point of view, a far worse alternative."[48]

## The League of Nations

Wilson was not the first president to consider American participation in an association of nations. In 1910 Theodore Roosevelt called for the creation of a league of nations, but he insisted that, to be effective, American military power, backed by "righteousness" and allied with Britain, must be at its foundation. In 1915 the League to Enforce the Peace, with former President William Howard Taft at its head, called for a collective security system based on the mediation of international disputes and, if necessary, military action against aggressors. But Wilson was slow to accept the collective security idea, partly because of his reluctance to use military power to uphold it.[49]

Some of the credit for the eventual adoption of the league idea by Wilson belongs to Sir Edward Grey, Britain's foreign minister. By 1915 Grey had become convinced that direct and continuous American involvement in Europe's affairs was necessary if the postwar settlement were to prove stable and lasting. Grey saw the league idea as an indirect method to achieve this goal. He repeatedly prevailed on the president, through Colonel House, to accept a league of nations. At last, in November 1915, Wilson informed Grey that he favored a concert of nations organized to prevent war. Six months later, in May 1916, Wilson, for the first time in public, expressed his desire to create a League of Nations.[50]

In theory, the League of Nations Covenant, the drafting of which was presided over by Wilson, incorporated the concept of the equality of all nations. In the Assembly, or international parliament, every member would have one vote. But, in the end, the League would be dominated by the powers that had emerged victorious from the war--the United States, Britain, France, Italy, and Japan. The great powers would have the only permanent seats on the Council, the League's executive body. The "heart" of the Covenant, Wilson insisted, was Article 10. It pledged the Covenant's signatories to the collective defense of all the League's members against "external aggression," anywhere in the world. Other articles established machinery for the arbitration of international disputes, declared that the perpetrator of an aggressive war would be subjected to an automatic economic blockade, and empowered the League Council to consider military measures, if they proved necessary, to end the aggression.[51]

The French plan for the League of Nations differed essentially from Wilson's. Rather than a League Council recommending action by the member states, the French wanted the creation of an international army with a general staff, a scheme that did not see fruition until after the North Atlantic Treaty Organization (NATO) came into being in 1949. Wilson rejected the French concept primarily because he saw it as an attempt to maintain a Western alliance aimed at Germany. There must be, he insisted, "not a balance of power, not one powerful group of nations set off against another, but a single overwhelming, powerful group of nations who shall be the trustee of the peace of the world."[52]

To win French support for his league plan, Wilson went as far as to offer France a security treaty--a flat repudiation of the traditional American policy of no entangling alliances. It contained a firm and definite commitment by America to come to France's assistance at once if she became the victim of an "unprovoked movement of aggression" on the part of Germany. The treaty was also signed by the British, who saw it as another instrument of integrating American power into the maintenance of the postwar settlement. However, Wilson did not envision the French security treaty as a permanent obligation because, as he pointed out, it could be terminated by the League as soon as the world body was strong enough to guarantee France's borders. The French security treaty, however, never became a major point of contention in the United States, for it was soon eclipsed by the debate over the Treaty of Versailles and, as a result, died stillborn in the Senate Committee on Foreign Relations.[53]

## Intervention in Russia

Besides the fear of a resurgent, vengeful Germany, another matter created consternation at Versailles: the specter of Bolshevik Russia.

In March 1917 the Russian monarchy was overthrown and a provisional government, led by a moderate socialist, Alexander Kerensky, was proclaimed. Wilson, believing that democracy would take hold in Russia, responded by recognizing the provisional government on March 22 and by sending it $325 million worth of aid contingent on Russia remaining in the war. But the Russian army and people were exhausted by the conflict and susceptible to the demands of the Bolsheviks, led by Vladimir Lenin, for an immediate end to the war. On November 7, 1917, the Bolsheviks were able to overthrow the provisional government, and Lenin immediately initiated peace talks with the Germans.[54]

Wilson considered the Bolshevik regime a demonic conspiracy that had destroyed the democratic promise of the provisional government. He found particularly offensive its doctrine of class warfare, the dictatorship of the Communist Party, its hostility toward private property, and its proclaimed intention to overthrow existing governments. For Wilson, recognition of the Soviet regime was out of the question. Recognizing the Bolshevik government, Secretary of State Lansing stated, "would encourage them and their followers in other lands." Moreover, it would destroy any chance that a liberal Russian government could emerge from the civil war, which was the main goal of the president's policy toward Russia. As a result, Wilson joined the Allied effort to isolate Soviet Russia diplomatically, politically, and economically. The Bolsheviks were not invited to Versailles nor was the Soviet Union asked to join the League of Nations--at least, not until the 1930s.[55]

But Wilson refused, at least initially, to go beyond isolation of the Soviet regime. After the Bolsheviks made peace with the Germans in March 1918, the Allies implored him to permit U.S. troops to join an Anglo-French expedition to Murmansk in northern Russia and a Japanese expedition to Vladivostok on Russia's Pacific coast. The Allies not only wanted to keep the eastern front active, and thereby prevent the Germans from concentrating their forces in the west, they also wanted to assist the anti-Bolshevik forces that were trying to topple Lenin's government. But Wilson, at first, refused to intervene in Russia, asserting that the Russian people, as much as any nation, were entitled to self-determination. The internal affairs of Russia, he said, should be decided by the Russian people. More important, though, he feared that direct Allied intervention on the side of the so-called Whites would destroy the chance for reestablishing a liberal regime in Russia by enabling the Bolsheviks to portray Allied intervention as an attempt to restore the old regime.[56]

At the same time, Wilson did not believe that Bolshevism, as an ideology, could be crushed with military force. "The only way to act against Bolshevism," he insisted, "is to eliminate its causes"--including poverty, social disruption, and political degeneration. Wilson agreed with Lansing's statement that "Empty stomachs mean Bolsheviks. Full stomachs mean no Bolsheviks." Food, trade, and democracy, Wilson believed, were the only effective ways to prevent the communization of Europe.[57]

To save Europe from starvation and Bolshevism, Wilson appointed Herbert Hoover the coordinator of America's postwar European relief programs. In Hungary, Hoover used the pressure of American food, in conjunction with an invasion of that country by the Rumanian army, to help overthrow the communist government of Bela Kun. In the end, the yeoman work performed by Hoover, combined with Wilson's liberal peace program, did much to prevent the Bolshevization of Europe.[58]

Yet Wilson, after repeatedly rejecting Allied requests for U.S. military intervention in Russia, finally caved in. The necessity of maintaining Allied unity in order to defeat Germany, and to implement the League of Nations Covenant after the war, were primarily responsible for the change in the president's attitude. As a result, when a combined German-Finnish army threatened to seize Murmansk, Wilson in June 1918 agreed to send, as a part of an Allied military expedition to that city, three battalions of infantry, some 15,500 men. However, he also sent orders to the commander of the American force to refrain from any involvement in the Russian civil war. But the orders were not received before American troops, acting under the command of the British, were rerouted to another north Russian port, Archangel, where, soon after their arrival in September, they engaged Bolshevik soldiers in combat.[59]

In July Wilson also agreed to send some 9,000 American troops to Vladivostok, on Russia's Pacific coast. The first American troops disembarked in that city in August, shortly after British, French, and Japanese forces had done so. Some historians believe that Wilson's primary motive for approving the mission to Vladivostok was to counter a Japanese threat to intervene unilaterally and occupy eastern Siberia. They point out that Wilson not only feared for Russia's territorial integrity, he also believed that unilateral Japanese intervention would strengthen the resistance of the Bolsheviks, and might even force them to ally with the Germans.[60]

But rather than taking a public stance against the Japanese, Wilson defended his decision to intervene by saying that the American troops would enable a Czechoslovak army of 45,000 men, who were fighting the Germans in Russia, to withdraw safely to fight again on the western front. However, he neglected to emphasize that the Czechoslovaks were showing a marked reluctance to withdraw from Russia, primarily because they were assisting the White forces against the Bolsheviks.[61]

In spite of Wilson's reluctance to involve American troops directly in the fighting in Russia, he was not indifferent to events in that country. In January 1919 the president accepted a proposal of Britain's prime minister, David Lloyd George, to invite all the warring parties in Russia to attend a peace conference on Prinkipo Island, in the Sea of Mamora, near Istanbul, Turkey. Wilson hoped that by bringing the Bolsheviks to the negotiating table, he would be able to prevent Lenin from posing as the defender of a Russia endangered by foreign intervention. Lenin, for his part, believed that the Allies were prepared to recognize the Bolshevik regime and therefore accepted the invitation. But when his White opponents, who were backed by the bitterly anti-Bolshevik French, refused to attend the conference, the Prinkipo proposal collapsed.[62]

In February 1919, after the president had returned to Washington from Paris to attend to congressional matters, another attempt to communicate with the Bolsheviks was undertaken by William Bullitt, a young member of the State Department. Bullitt, a firm believer in a policy of recognizing and aiding the Bolshevik regime in order to moderate its behavior, apparently was sent to Russia, in Lansing's words, "to cure him of Bolshevism." However, Lansing did instruct Bullitt to report back on the "conditions, political and economic," in Russia. However, Bullitt was under the impression that he had been authorized to do considerably more than that, in fact, to find out if peace between the Bolsheviks and the Allies was possible. In this vein, he took with him proposals from Colonel House and Philip Kerr, Lloyd George's secretary, which indicated an Allied willingness to grant the Bolsheviks de facto recognition in exchange for a moderation of their behavior. Not surprisingly, Lenin, desperate for breathing space in order to save his embryonic Bolshevik regime, not only agreed to accept a cease-fire but also expressed his willingness to pay Russia's debts, to recognize the independence of the former Russian Empire's subject nationalities, and to declare a general amnesty in return for an end to Allied intervention.[63]

Much to his surprise, when Bullitt returned to Paris on March 25, with what he believed was a plan to end the fighting in Russia, he received a cold shoulder. Lansing flatly opposed Lenin's offer. And Wilson, who by this time had arrived back in Paris from the United States, shunned an appointment with Bullitt with the excuse that he had a headache--and he probably did, considering the severe case of flu, and possible minor stroke, he suffered soon thereafter. But more important, the president, as he said shortly before leaving Paris, did not favor "a rapprochement with the Bolsheviks." Confronted with opposition from Wilson, Lansing, and the French, who detested the idea of an understanding with the Bolsheviks, both House and Lloyd George abandoned Bullitt. Infuriated, Bullitt would later turn on Wilson during the Senate hearings on the Treaty of Versailles.[64]

After the failure of the Prinkipo proposal, Wilson agreed to cooperate with the Allies in providing food, supplies, and munitions to the White army of Admiral Alexander Kolchak. Moreover, he ordered American troops to secure from Bolshevik attack Kolchak's main supply line, the Trans-Siberian and Chinese Eastern railroads. However, Kolchak first had to agree--and he did--to create a freely elected constituent assembly after the Bolsheviks were defeated. In this way, Wilson could argue that American intervention in Russia was justified because it would help the Russians--albeit White Russians--to create a democratic regime.[65]

But before Kolchak could receive meaningful Allied and American assistance, his forces were decisively defeated by the Red Army in the summer of 1919. To avoid clashes with the advancing Soviet forces, American troops were withdrawn from Archangel in June 1919 and Vladivostok in April 1920. Needless to say, the American intervention in Russia left a long-lasting residue of distrust on the part of the Bolsheviks for the United States, a characteristic of the Soviet-American relationship that would endure, with alternating degrees of intensity, for over seventy years.[66]

Winston Churchill, who as British war minister wanted the Allies to "strangle the Bolshevik baby in its cradle," publicly lamented the Western failure to provide more meaningful assistance to the anti-Bolshevik forces. He wrote:

> When we observe the amazing exploits of the Czech Army Corps, it seems certain that a resolute effort by a comparatively small number of trustworthy American or Japanese troops would have enabled Moscow to be occupied by national Russian and Allied forces even before the German collapse took place. Divided counsels and cross-purposes among the Allies, American mistrust of Japan, and the personal opposition of President Wilson, reduced Allied intervention in Russia during the war to exactly the point where it did the utmost harm and gained the least advantage.[67]

However, others questioned the ability of either the White forces or the Allies to overthrow the Bolsheviks. After all, the German army, with a million men, had been unable to take Moscow. Nor did the Whites have the degree of unity and popular support they needed to overcome the Bolsheviks. And it is also quite clear that neither the American people nor the Congress supported the small-scale military intervention Wilson had conducted in Russia. On February 4, 1919, Hiram Johnson introduced a resolution in the Senate calling for the withdrawal of U.S. troops from northern Russia. It was defeated only by the vice president's tie-breaking vote. Moreover, after the armistice, the morale of the American troops in northern Russia sank rapidly. In March 1919 a company of U.S. soldiers near Murmansk refused to go to the front. There is no way American opinion could have been persuaded to countenance a lengthier or more massive U.S. involvement. And public opinion in war-weary Britain and France was, if anything, even more hostile to the idea of continued military intervention in Russia.[68]

# The Battle for the Treaty

While events in the spring and summer of 1919 were leading to the ultimate Bolshevik victory in Russia, Wilson embarked on his campaign to win the support of the American people for the Treaty of Versailles. He insisted repeatedly that U.S. ratification of the treaty would be a major turning point in the nation's history. "The isolation of the United States," he said, "is at an end" because "the sheer genius" of the American people and the growth of American power had made the United States "a determining factor in the history of mankind."[69]

Because the League of Nations was the one hope for maintaining world peace, he insisted, the United States had a moral obligation to ratify the treaty of which it was a part. Moreover, he argued that without American participation in the League, that organization would fail, and another war would become inevitable. Further, without a collective security system, he believed, the United States would have to maintain a large military establishment to ensure its national security. Without the League, he predicted, a president's civil responsibilities would be eclipsed by his role as "commander-in-chief, ready to fight the world."[70]

There is ample evidence to indicate that, in the early spring of 1919, most Americans supported ratification of the Treaty of Versailles and U.S. membership in the League of Nations. Newspaper polls, thirty-two state legislatures, labor unions, farm groups, women's organizations, and professional associations had all declared their support. Even the two leading opponents of the treaty, Senators Henry Cabot Lodge and William Borah, admitted that, had a plebiscite been held in early 1919, the treaty would have won by an overwhelming majority.[71]

Yet the Treaty of Versailles was not ratified by the Senate, and the United States did not join the League of Nations. Historians have debated the reasons for decades, but a number of factors stand out.

One was the opposition of isolationist senators, like Borah, the leader of the "irreconcilables"--those who under no circumstances would support the League. Tall, bushy-haired, and with a massive face and head, Borah was an idealist who feared that American democracy would be contaminated if the United States, through membership in the League, were to tie itself to the militaristic and imperialistic competition of European nations. Borah believed that the United States would serve its own interests, as well as promote world peace and democracy, by maintaining its complete independence in all foreign relations. Although he supported America's entry into war, he did so only to defend the nation's neutral rights, not to entangle it in Europe's postwar political affairs.[72]

All of the treaty's opponents, however, were not isolationists. In fact, more were internationalists who believed that the United States must play a role in preserving world peace. But, for a variety of reasons, most internationalists opposed committing the United States unreservedly to the collective security system contained in the League Covenant.

For one, they believed that a worldwide collective security system would not work. The great powers would not accept the Covenant's limitations on their sovereignty, nor would any nation go to war to uphold Article 10 unless its vital interests were involved. The American people, in particular, would not countenance the transfer to an international body of Congress' power to commit the United States to war. Nor would they accept a large standing military establishment to enforce the dictates of the League. Many were also concerned that the League would attempt to intervene in the affairs of the Western Hemisphere and thereby challenge the Monroe Doctrine. Nor would Congress or the American people tolerate the interference of an international body in the internal affairs of the United States, particularly on such issues as the tariff and immigration. Most internationalists favored American participation in the League but only if some method of preserving American sovereignty and special interests could be found.[73]

While the debate on the Treaty of Versailles crossed party lines, it nevertheless became highly partisan. More than a few Republicans, particularly conservatives who had opposed Wilson's progressive reforms, feared that ratification of the treaty would enable the Democrats to retain control of the White House and lead the country down the road to socialism. Republicans in general had been particularly angered by Wilson's attempt to turn the congressional election of 1918 into a referendum on the League, and by his failure to include a single senator or a prominent Republican in the American delegation to Versailles. Wilson had considered asking Republicans to serve on the delegation, but he feared that they would cause trouble. He clearly did not want any Republican interference with *his* peace plan. The ability of the Republican Party to gain control of both houses of Congress, for the first time in Wilson's presidency, convinced Republican conservatives that the treaty could become the instrument for undoing the Democratic Party's hold on the White House.[74]

The task of holding together a Republican Party divided between isolationists and internationalists fell to Henry Cabot Lodge, the Senate majority leader and chairman of the Foreign Relations Committee. Slender, narrow-shouldered, and aristocratically bewhiskered, Lodge had been educated at Harvard University, where he received a Ph.D. in history. Until Wilson entered the political scene, Lodge had been known as "the scholar in politics" because of the number of books and articles he had published on a wide variety of historical subjects. Although Lodge was an internationalist, like his friend, Theodore Roosevelt, he was also a realist who believed in the balance of power, harsh peace terms (which included the dismemberment of Germany), and an Anglo-French-American alliance to keep Germany weak.[75]

Lodge had little use either for Wilson personally or for the president's League of Nations. "As an English production," Lodge said of Wilson's Covenant, "it does not rank high. It might get by at Princeton but certainly not at Harvard." The kind of internationalist role Lodge favored for the United States was characterized by limited and specific objectives. "We want," he wrote Britain's Lord Charnwood, "the world made safe against Germany, and as long as that is done, we are content." He added: "So far as European matters are concerned, you are the people to settle them. . . . When it comes to Asia and Africa, of course we expect to have a voice; and we ask to be let alone in our hemisphere." Wilson, Lodge argued, had "undertaken to be the final umpire in every question. . . . meddling with things in which the United States has no interest whatsoever."[76]

The kind of league Lodge favored would not only protect American sovereignty and special interests, it would be backed by sufficient military power to ensure that its decisions could be implemented. It is "easy to talk about a league of nations and the beauty and necessity of peace," he said, "but the hard practical demand is, are you ready to put your soldiers at the disposition of other nations?" Lodge never believed for a minute that the American people would support such a league, or that a plan for U.S. participation in an international army could ever get through the Senate.[77]

On the other hand, historian Lloyd Ambrosius argues that Lodge and most other Republican senators would have supported ratification of the security treaty Wilson had offered the French, but the president refused to support ratification of that treaty until the Senate had first accepted the League of Nations. The failure to ratify the French security treaty, Ambrosius asserts, was far more important than the Senate's rejection of the League in undermining the European balance of power. Had France received an American security guarantee after the First World War, the second may never have occurred.[78]

To maintain the unity of isolationist and internationalist Republicans in the Senate, Lodge subdued his own strong skepticism about U.S. participation in an association of nations. In a shrewd, and ultimately successful, strategy, he moved to attach amendments to the treaty and, later, "reservations" (drafted by former Secretary of State Elihu Root) sufficient to "Republicanize" it, or at least to assure that Wilson would reject the treaty and thereby assume the onus for its defeat. On March 3 Lodge circulated a "Round Robin" that stated that the League Covenant was imprecisely phrased and unacceptable in its then present form. As drafted by Root, the Lodge reservations proposed that the Covenant be amended to prevent League intrusion into such domestic questions as immigration restriction. It called for the revision of Article 10 in order to uphold the Monroe Doctrine and to include safeguards that would prevent the involvement of the United States in any war without the consent of Congress. The Round Robin was signed by thirty-nine senators or senators-elect--six more than needed to defeat the treaty.[79]

Wilson accepted the Republican challenge with apparent relish. He imperiously stated that when the treaty came before the Senate, the League of Nations would be so intwined within it, that it would be impossible to "dissect the League Covenant from the treaty without destroying the whole vital structure." Further reflection, however, prompted the president to accept the need to win over some of the treaty's senatorial critics. As a result, he reluctantly induced the peace conference to revise the Covenant. Domestic issues, such as immigration and tariffs, were excluded from the League's jurisdiction, the right of withdrawal from the League was granted, and--most important--regional understandings like the Monroe Doctrine were specifically safeguarded. In return for supporting these concessions, Wilson promised Lloyd George that the United States would suspend naval construction after the 1916 program was completed in order to preserve British naval superiority, and he also accepted Clemenceau's demand for the temporary--fifteen years--military occupation of the German Rhineland.[80]

Nevertheless, Lodge and his fellow reservationists were unsatisfied with the changes Wilson had obtained in the Covenant. The clause affecting the Monroe Doctrine, in their opinion, was not strong enough. It did not state that the doctrine was a unilateral policy of the United States and that it was not, therefore, subject to the interpretation of foreign powers. Nor were the reservationists pleased that the League Council retained the right to decide whether a dispute fell within the domestic jurisdiction of one of its parties. They insisted that the United States must alone have that responsibility. Nor were they at all satisfied with the clause that stated that the right of withdrawal from the League would be contingent on the League's judgment that all of the withdrawing nation's international agreements had been fulfilled at the time of its withdrawal. The reservationists demanded that the United States alone must decide whether and when it would withdraw. And, most important, the reservations pointed out that Wilson had left Article 10 virtually intact and therefore totally unacceptable to them. The Lodge reservation to Article 10 declared that the United States "assumes no moral obligation" to preserve the independence or territorial integrity of any other country, or to employ the armed forces of the United States for such purposes, unless approved by Congress. Attached to the reservations was a preamble that stated that the treaty would not become binding on the United States until three of the four principal Allied powers had accepted it in writing.[81]

Wilson bluntly refused to make further changes in the Covenant, particularly the one required by Lodge's reservation to Article 10. This reservation, he argued, was unnecessary, for the Covenant's obligation to use force was binding on no nation. To prevent American involvement in military action by the League, Wilson suggested, the United States simply could employ its veto power in the League Council. Moreover, he pointed out, Congress would still retain the right to reject a declaration of war and the ability to refuse appropriations for any American military action. Furthermore, Wilson believed that it would be dishonorable for the United States to enter the League with reservations because they would mean that America would be demanding special treatment that other countries were not claiming. Accepting Lodge's reservations, Wilson feared, would open the floodgates to further demands for changes from other nations--including Germany --thereby requiring renegotiation of the entire treaty.[82]

In an attempt to meet Wilson's objections, seven "mild reservationists" offered four simplified reservations on August 1 that they believed would make explicit what the president insisted was implicit in the Covenant. But they stipulated that, although their reservations did not have to be a part of the treaty, they must be contained in the resolution of ratification, and they must be formally accepted by the other parties to the treaty. Again Wilson refused to compromise with any reservationists, whether "mild" or "strong." "Practically every so-called reservation," he said later, was "a rather sweeping nullification" of the terms of the treaty. In Wilson's opinion, there was no difference between "a nullifier" and "a mild nullifier."[83]

Blocked by the Senate, Wilson decided to tour the country and appeal directly to the people for their support of the treaty without reservations. However, shortly before leaving Washington, he made one last concession to his opponents. He gave Senator Gilbert Hitchcock, the Democratic minority leader, a draft of four "interpretations"--dealing with Article 10, the Monroe Doctrine, withdrawal, and domestic questions--which he said he would be willing to communicate to the Allies at the time of depositing the formal instruments of ratification. The interpretations were almost identical with the mild reservations. Wilson authorized Hitchcock to use the interpretations any way he saw fit, as long as he did not identify the president as their author. But Hitchcock was not permitted to make the one concession that was necessary to win over the mild reservationists--incorporating the interpretations in the resolution of ratification. More than a few have argued that, had Wilson compromised in this way, he could have won the votes needed for ratification.[84]

Unfortunately for the president, by the time he began his tour on September 4, public opinion had begun to turn against the treaty. Liberals who had thought he would bring home a peace based on the Fourteen Points were disillusioned by the Treaty of Versailles. It was not, they insisted, a peace without victory. The English economist John Maynard Keynes argued, in his best seller *The Economic Consequences of the Peace*, that the reparation provisions alone would reduce Germany to economic ruin and make a future war inevitable. Keynes could only conclude that the president had been "bamboozled" by the craftier Lloyd George and Clemenceau. Keynes' book, which appeared in the United States early in 1920, was used extensively by the opponents of the treaty to support their case. In addition, the return of America's soldiers, with their tales of the war's horrors, convinced many that American participation in future European wars should be assiduously avoided. Some of this antiwar sentiment found expression in the literature of the "lost generation" of postwar writers--including John Dos Passos, Ernest Hemingway, and F. Scott Fitzgerald.[85]

The treaty also was opposed by many ethnic Americans with strong ties to the Old World--including Germans, Italians, and Irish--who felt that it had betrayed the lands of their origin. Irish-Americans were angered by the exclusion of a provision in the treaty for Ireland's independence from Britain. Italian-Americans were upset that the treaty did not award Italy more territory, particularly the port of Fiume, which was awarded to the new Yugoslavian state. German-Americans were embittered by the treaty's punitive features against Germany.

Domestic developments in 1919 also worked against the treaty. Runaway inflation, violent strikes, bloody race riots in half a dozen cities, and a pervasive fear of Bolshevism helped to revive the traditional American desire to concentrate on domestic problems rather than foreign affairs. Many Americans blamed Wilson for the domestic turmoil that followed the war and they, no doubt, transferred some of that frustration to the Treaty of Versailles. The Republican refrain for a "return to normalcy"--relative domestic tranquility and noninvolvement in Europe's political affairs--struck a responsive cord in many Americans.

## The Defeat of the Treaty

In the end, Wilson was unable to overcome the forces against the peace treaty. In November 1919 the treaty, with Lodge's reservations attached, was defeated in the Senate by a vote of 39 in favor to 55 against. Another vote on the treaty, without the reservations, resulted in another defeat, 38 to 53. The treaty, with reservations, did much better in a third and final vote, on March 19, 1920, falling only seven votes short of the necessary two-thirds majority, with 49 votes in favor and 35 against.

Ironically, Wilson was primarily responsible for the treaty's defeat. On October 2, a week after collapsing from the physical exhaustion of his campaign in behalf of the treaty, the president suffered a stroke that left him partially paralyzed and, in the belief of some historians, less willing to compromise than he otherwise would have been. In fact, Edwin Weinstein, M.D., flatly asserts that the cerebral dysfunction that Wilson's stroke produced prevented ratification of the treaty. "It is almost certain," Weinstein wrote, "that had Wilson not been so affected, his political skills and his facility with language would have bridged the gap between the Hitchock and Lodge resolutions."[86]

Lodge apparently knew his intended victim well. He realized that Wilson's animosity toward him was as great as his hatred for the president. Wilson, Lodge predicted, would never accept reservations to which the senator's name was attached. When Senator James Watson urged the president to accept Lodge's reservations as the only way to save the treaty, Wilson vehemently refused. "Never! Never!" the president exclaimed. "I'll never consent to accept any policy with which that impossible name is so prominently identified!"[87]

Instead of compromising with Lodge, Wilson stubbornly urged Democratic senators to vote against any reservations. As a result, on the last vote, twenty-three Democrats, at Wilson's behest, stood with the irreconcilables and voted against the treaty, while twenty-one Democrats joined the Republican reservationists and voted for it. Had seven more Democrats abandoned the president and backed the treaty with reservations, the Treaty of Versailles would have been approved by the Senate. But even then, Wilson had warned, he would have vetoed it. The president thought that the defeat of the Lodge reservations would inevitably cause the Republicans to accept a more suitable compromise. But it did not. Republican "bitter-enders," like Senator Borah, threatened to bolt the party in an election year if Lodge tried to compromise further with Wilson. Lodge, who considered a Republican presidential victory more important than the ratification of the treaty, backed off and allowed it to die.[88]

Wilson wanted to run for a third term, with the treaty as his main issue, but his health prevented him from winning his party's nomination. Instead, the Democrats selected James M. Cox of Ohio and, as his running mate, Franklin D. Roosevelt. Both supported the League but agreed to accept reservations that did not cripple the Covenant. Their Republican opponent, Warren G. Harding, took an ambiguous stand on the League. While it cannot be said that Harding's overwhelming victory was a mandate against the League of Nations, it was, in effect, a repudiation of Wilson's brand of internationalism.[89]

# The Wilsonian Legacy

Wilson's critics, and historians to this day, have debated his impact on world history. Realists, not surprisingly, have been particularly harsh in their estimation of him. While they acknowledge his contribution to American internationalism and his effort to accentuate America's ideals as the basis of her foreign policy, they also assert that he failed to define an effective method for achieving them. In historian Norman Graebner's opinion, Wilson could have maintained the nation's ideals more effectively than he did by following the established rules of European diplomacy, as the nation's early diplomatists had done. Instead, by rejecting the importance of the European balance of power as a factor in America's security, Wilson made possible the return to American isolationism after the war. The subsequent inability of the United States to play a role in maintaining the European balance during the interwar era would inevitably lead to another world war, and another American military intervention.[90]

Wilson's defenders, on the other hand, have argued that it was not his system that failed, but rather those who refused to implement it. According to Arthur S. Link:

> The postwar version of the collective security failed in the crucial tests of the 1930s, not because the Treaty of Versailles was responsible or the peacekeeping machinery of the League of Nations was defective, but because the people of Great Britain, France, and the United States were unwilling to confront the aggressors with the threat of war. Consequently a second and more terrible world conflict came in 1939, as Wilson had prophesized it would.

In effect, Link has argued, Wilson demonstrated a "higher realism" than the so-called realists by aligning the national interests and power of the United States with a new world order based upon international law, the arbitration of international disputes, self-determination, and collective security rather than with the old diplomacy, based on the balance of power.[91]

However, Lloyd Ambrosius finds the traditional definitions of idealism and realism unsuitable for either Wilson or his chief antagonist, Henry Cabot Lodge. "Both Wilson and Lodge, despite their differences," Ambrosius writes, "believed in ideals and engaged in practical politics. On occasion, they both adhered to principle, or resorted to compromise, and both favored American military intervention in the European war." Moreover, Ambrosius asserts, Wilson was both an internationalist and an isolationist, because he wanted the United States to assume global obligations but insisted that the United States must alone define them--and this proved impossible to achieve. In Ambrosius' opinion, the collective security system was ultimately a failure because the rest of the world did not accept the American definition of "universal values" on which it was ostensibly based.[92]

Yet Gordon Levin argues that while Wilson's conception of a world order based on American values was not implemented in the short run, it did become the dominant goal of U.S. foreign policy later. "Wilson," wrote Levin, "established the main drift toward an American liberal globalism, hostile both to traditional imperialism and to revolutionary socialism." These characteristics were common to the foreign policies of such diverse personalities as Herbert Hoover, Cordell

Hull, Franklin Roosevelt, and John Foster Dulles--all of whom had been associated with Wilson or had been influenced by him. Whether Democrat or Republican, Levin has asserted, they all continued "to identify America's expansive national interest with the maintenance of a rational and peaceful international liberal order. Ultimately, in the post-World War II period, Wilsonian values would have their complete triumph in the bi-partisan Cold War consensus."[93]

# 2

# Republican Isolationism, 1921-1933

## The New Isolationism

Senator William E. Borah, the leader of the irreconcilables, hailed the results of the 1920 election as "the judgement of the American people against any political alliance or combination with European powers." "The United States," he observed, "had rededicated itself to the foreign policy of George Washington and James Monroe, undiluted and unemasculated." In his inaugural address, on March 4, 1921, the new president, former newspaperman and U.S. senator from Ohio, Warren G. Harding, appeared to agree with Borah. "Confident of our ability to work out our own destiny and jealously guarding our right to do so," the president said, "we seek no part in directing the destinies of the Old World. We do not mean to be entangled. We will accept no responsibility except as our own conscience and judgement may determine." One happy irreconcilable, Republican Senator Hiram Johnson of California, commented, "This is the end of the League of Nations."[1]

Even Harding's secretary of state, the former mild reservationist Charles Evans Hughes, acknowledged the strength of isolationist sentiment. Upon entering office, both Hughes and Harding believed that it would be possible to ratify the Treaty of Versailles and enter the League with reservations. But the irreconcilables in the Senate threatened to wreck the new administration if it attempted to revive the treaty and the League. Faced with this threat, both Hughes and Harding backed off. In July 1921 the president signed a congressional resolution that declared the war terminated. Attached to the resolution was an amendment drafted by Senator Henry Cabot Lodge ruling out American representation or participation "in any body, agency, or commission" except by act of Congress. The American people, Hughes was compelled to admit, were not prepared "to commit this government in advance to the use of its power in unknown contingencies."[2]

Yet because a congressional resolution is not binding on a foreign country, in October 1920 Harding and Hughes were able to persuade the Senate to approve, by a vote of 66 to 20, a separate peace treaty with Germany. Known as the Treaty of Berlin, the agreement reserved to the United States all the rights and privileges negotiated in the armistice and the Versailles Treaty. A procedure similar to the one used in concluding the Treaty of Berlin was followed in formally ending the state of war with Austria and Hungary. After the Lodge reservation was attached to the Berlin treaty, a pleased Senator Johnson could say: "We have accomplished all that we fought for."[3]

Publicly, Hughes justified the apparent return to isolation on the grounds that the Continent's interests and problems were not those of the United States. "The difficulties which beset Europe," he wrote, "have their causes within Europe and not in any act or policy of ours." Furthermore, he asserted, quite incorrectly, that the Europeans did not want American help. "The influence that is due to our attachment and impartiality could not be long maintained if we should substitute the role of a partisan in European quarrels." As historian Betty Glad has pointed out, "Like most Americans, Hughes remained unaware of the extent to which the policy of isolation had depended on British power and the political structure of Europe." He failed to consider not only the impact that the war had had on the European balance of power, and Britain's continued ability to maintain it, but also the possible consequences these changes may have had on the wisdom of maintaining the traditional policy of isolationism.[4]

However, unlike the extreme isolationists, Hughes never really thought that the traditional nonentanglement policy of the United States toward Europe implied complete separation from that continent. In the past, the United States had been forced to deal repeatedly with European nations in order to protect its interests. And now, at war's end, American interests in Europe were greater than ever. Neither Hughes, nor many other Americans, particularly those in the Congress, could forget that the Allies owed the United States more than $10 billion in war debts. Moreover, the United States and Europe had developed an extensive trade and investment relationship before and during the war. American businesspeople, as well as the Republican administrations of the interwar era, realized that Europe's economic recovery was vital to the economic well-being of the United States. As a consequence, they pursued a vigorous policy directed toward expanding American private loans, trade, and investment to, with, and in European countries. Indeed, historian William Appleman Williams has gone as far as to argue that the primary goal of the Republican administrations of the twenties was to create a worldwide "Open Door" for American economic activity-- as Harding put it, to "go on to the peaceful commercial conquest of the world"-- and that this in itself necessitated extensive U.S. involvement in the political affairs of Europe. At the same time, the enormous cost of the war in human life and property gave impetus to a burgeoning peace movement, both in the United States and Europe, which demanded positive steps to prevent another such holocaust. In an attempt to satisfy these economic and political demands, without making military commitments to do so, the Republican administrations of the interwar years would be compelled to deal with European nations repeatedly and extensively.[5]

However, for as much as the United States expanded its role in European and world affairs during the 1920s, the Republican administrations of that decade were determined to avoid political entanglements with European nations. Popular disgust with World War I, disillusionment with the fruits of the Versailles peace settlement, and fear that another war in Europe was inevitable, one in which the United States would again participate, all worked to prevent binding American military commitments to European security in the interwar period.

For these and other reasons, the United States in the 1920s adopted a policy historian Selig Adler has labled "the new isolationism," an approach that was midway between the isolationism of the prewar era, with its relative lack of interest in Europe's political affairs, and the global, messianic role called for by Wilsonian internationalists. The new isolationism was characterized by greater American participation in both the economic and political affairs of Europe as well as the wider relations of the world, but it was also marked by a persistent refusal to make commitments that would impair America's traditional freedom of action.[6]

## The League and the World Court

In January 1920, two months before the final rejection of the Treaty of Versailles by the Senate, the League of Nations began its ill-fated existence. Under pressure from Republican irreconcilables, Harding tried to ignore the League. "In the existing League of Nations, world-governing with its super power," he told Congress in his first message, "this Republic will have no part." For the next year, in fact, the State Department refused to answer League messages.[7]

By 1922, however, after the administration had demonstrated that it would not permit the United States to enter the League, it began a cautious approach to that body. Hughes began to respond to League messages. And, even earlier in the administration, in 1921, unofficial observers were sent to League-sponsored conferences dealing with humanitarian problems, such as the opium trade. Hughes' solution to the problem, he realized, was awkward, since the observers were unable to speak for the United States, let alone commit their country to League activities. But considering the restraints imposed upon the administration by Congress and the American public, Hughes believed it was the best that could be done. Subsequent administrations followed his pattern. The United States, in effect, recognized the League without playing a full part in it.[8]

While internationalists, like Hughes, were disappointed by the Senate's rejection of American membership in the League of Nations, they looked to U.S. participation in the World Court as the path to greater participation by the nation in world affairs. Authorized by Article 14 of the League of Nations Covenant, the Permanent Court of International Justice, the World Court's formal title, opened its first session in 1922. While its jurisdiction was ostensibly global in nature, in actuality the Court's power was quite limited: it could only deal with a dispute when all the involved parties asked it to do so, which in effect limited the Court to minor international incidents. Even in these cases, the Court's decisions were largely unenforceable.

In spite of the Court's limited power, American internationalists were attracted to it because it embodied the ideal of the rule of law rather than force in international relations. Indeed, the Court's inability to enforce its decisions was considered by many as an argument in its favor, because U.S. membership would require no American military commitment. Instead of military force, supporters of the Court argued, world public opinion would be its strongest weapon. "Fortunately for the Court's reputation," historian Robert Ferrell has pointed out, "the problem of obtaining obedience to the Court never came up in the interwar period."[9]

Despite the World Court's shortcomings, Hughes was able to persuade a reluctant Harding, who feared the inevitably hostile reaction of the isolationists, to support American membership. To head off the isolationists, Hughes drafted a letter, which Harding sent to the Senate in February 1923, listing four resevations that were designed to protect the United States against the slightest League involvement. The first declared that U.S. membership on the Court would not constitute a formal relationship with the League. The second stated that the United States intended to participate in the election of judges to the Court. The third announced that the United States would contribute to the expenses of the Court. And the last stated that the statutes of the Court could be amended only with American approval.[10]

In spite of Hughes' reservations, and the fact that U.S. membership on the Court was supported by a majority of the American people--and by both political parties in their 1924 election platforms as well as by the House of Representatives, which gave it a 301 to 28 favorable vote on March 3, 1925--the Court encountered formidable opposition in the Senate. Both Borah and Lodge considered American membership on the Court the first step toward U.S. participation in the League. In their opinion, the problem was that the Court was more a *League* court than a *World* Court. As a result, the isolationist-dominated Foreign Relations Committee, the chairmanship of which passed to Borah after Lodge's death in 1924, was able to delay a vote on the Court for two years.[11]

Eventually, on January 27, 1926, the full Senate voted 76 to 17 in favor of American membership on the Court. However, the irreconcilables managed to attach another reservation to the Senate resolution. It stated that the Court could not "without the consent of the United States entertain any request for an advisory opinion touching any dispute or question in which the United States has or claims an interest."[12]

Surprisingly, the League Council did not reject the American reservations out of hand. Instead, on March 18, 1926, it invited the United States to send a delegation to Geneva to discuss the matter. But President Calvin Coolidge, who had succeeded Harding upon the latter's death in 1923 (Harding suffered a fatal stroke), turned down the League's invitation. Coolidge insisted that "unless the requirements of the Senate resolution are met by the other interested nations, I can see no prospect of this country adhering to the Court."[13]

Coolidge's successor, Herbert Hoover, tried to break the impasse. He approved a compromise worked out by the eighty-four-year-old former secretary of state, Elihu Root, which would have allowed the United States to withdraw from the World Court if American objections to an advisory opinion were overruled by other members. However, the isolationists were able to delay a vote on the treaty until 1935, after Franklin D. Roosevelt had become president, when it was again defeated, by a vote of 52 in favor to 36 against--only seven votes short of the required two-thirds majority.[14]

The battle over the World Court, like that over the League, historian Norman Graebner has observed, revealed much about the nature of American internationalism in the 1920s. Wrote Graebner: "The United States would support world peace, not through specific commitments to the defense of the Versailles settlement but through the encouragement of any organization or procedure that promised to limit change in international life to peaceful processes."[15]

## The Peace Movement

In spite of America's refusal to make military commitments to European nations, the horror of the Great War helped to make the preservation of peace a central theme of American foreign policy in the interwar period. Indeed, the Senate's rejection of the League of Nations, and later the World Court, only added to the ferment for peace. But internationalists were not the only peace advocates. Isolationists like Senator Borah also spoke out strongly against war. Nor was the antiwar movement confined to a particular party or social class. Liberals, and conservatives, as well as radicals, favored steps to avoid war.

Among the more conservative peace groups were the Carnegie Endowment for International Peace, the World Peace Foundation, the Woodrow Wilson Foundation, and the League of Nations Association. Primarily eastern in origin and membership, these organizations also possessed considerable financial strength. The Carnegie Endowment, for example, was started with a $10 million gift from industrialist Andrew Carnegie. Believing that peace could only result from a gradual process of educating people, the conservative organizations built libraries, endowed university chairs, published educational materials, and lobbied politicians.[16]

In general, conservative peace advocates favored a legalist approach to the problem of war. Peace, according to the most prominent conservative legalist, former secretary of state and president of the Carnegie Endowment, Elihu Root, consisted in "the creation of right standards of conduct on the part of the people of the world." With American participation in the League of Nations a dead issue, Root, like many conservative legalists, believed the solution to war lay in "putting teeth" into The Hague conventions for the peaceable settlement of disputes. This included compulsory arbitration of international disputes and the further codification of international law.[17]

But not all legalists were conservatives; many were progressives who viewed law primarily as an instrument of reform rather than as a method for maintaining social order. Before America's entry into the war, progressives, through legislation and constitutional amendments, had remedied some of the worst abuses of industrialization and urbanization. Many believed that they could apply international law to the eradication of Europe's war system. However, while most progressive leaders wanted the United States to help the Old World prevent another war, like conservative internationalists, they wanted no part of Europe's internal politics. As the National Committee for the Prevention of War put it, peacemakers must keep "America First--In the Crusade for a Warless World."[18]

Perhaps the most interesting, if not the most influential, part of the peace movement was the more radical organizations--groups like the American Committee for the Outlawry of War, the American Committee for the Cause and Cure of War, the Women's International League for Peace and Freedom, the National Committee for the Prevention of War, the Committee on Militarism in Education, and the Fellowship of Reconciliation. Although by no means mass organizations, these radical peace groups were extremely influential. Robert Ferrell estimated that they influenced as many as sixty million Americans. "If they did not create opinion," he added, "they certainly crystallized existing attitudes, mobilized them, made them vocal."[19]

What the radical peace groups shared in common was an acute impatience with the war machine and a disdain for the gradual approach of eliminating conflict that was favored by their more conservative counterparts. Arbitration and conciliation treaties, free trade, the World Court, and the League of Nations--ideas that attracted either liberal or conservative support--had little appeal for the radicals. "Treat it [war] as a sin," declared Carrie Chapman Catt, sponsor of the American Committee for the Cause and Cure of War, "a crime, an iniquity, an unethical institution, an unpractical policy, or what you will. It is, in truth, a barbarism with no rightful place in an enlightened age." Catt exhorted her followers to subject war to the same grinding force of the American reform tradition that had freed the slaves, closed the saloons, and gained for women the right to vote. What radical peace advocates demanded was the *immediate* abolition of war. This meant the elimination as soon as possible of all traces of militarism--its uniforms, its banners, and, above all, its weapons.[20]

Of all the radical peace organizations, however, the most effective was the American Committee for the Outlawry of War. Fusing legalism and nationalism with the enthusiasm of Protestant evangelism, the outlawry movement sought to abolish war by declaring it illegal and by compelling nations to settle their disputes in an international court system modeled after the judicial system of the United States. The outlawry movement was the idea of an ebullient Chicago attorney, Salmon O. Levinson, who believed that once war was declared illegal, international disputes could be "fought out by experienced statesmen in the council chamber rather than by boys on the field of battle." To be sure, outlawry leaders were careful to distinguish between aggressive warfare and wars of self-defense. "Self defense," argued one outlawrist, "is a right, a principle, which no law or treaty can touch. A treaty renouncing war neither involves nor affects it." Critics pointed out, however, that war--no matter why it is fought, whether for reasons of legitimate self-defense or not--is still war.[21]

## Naval Disarmament

In spite of the commotion caused by the more radical peace groups, for the Republican administrations of the interwar period, disarmament was the preferred method of eliminating war. Many people had come to believe that the Great War would not have occurred had the prewar arms race been prevented. Because armies in both Britain and the United States had been reduced to a fraction of their wartime strength--the U.S. Army fell to 109,000 men in 1926--while navies remained relatively large, and threatened to grow even larger, warships became the primary targets of the postwar disarmers. "Big warships meant big wars," a popular epigram held. "Smaller warships meant smaller wars. No warships might eventually mean no wars."[22]

Moreover, with the defeat and disarmament of Germany, many Americans had come to believe that, not only was a larger navy unnecessary, continuation of the naval construction program of 1916 would only produce another wasteful and potentially dangerous arms race. Warships were also the most expensive weapons of war. With the cost of a battleship rising from $5 million in 1900 to $40 million by 1920, those in the know realized that financing the Navy's building program would be expensive. Politicians, faced with a short but intense postwar depression, were extremely reluctant to supplement the relatively heavy tax burden of the American people by building additional warships many people believed were unnecessary.[23]

Capitalizing on the crescendo against naval expenditures, in December 1920 Senator Borah introduced a resolution asking Harding to confer with Britain and Japan to reduce naval construction by fifty percent over the next five years. Borah saw naval reduction not only as a way to prevent another war but also as a method of deflecting attention from the criticism that, by rejecting membership in the League of Nations, the United States had shirked its responsibility to preserve world peace. He also believed that, by imposing naval limitations on Japan, the United States could preserve with less cost its interests in the Pacific. Borah's resolution passed in the Senate by a vote of 74 to 0 and in the House by a majority of 332 to 4. With Borah in the lead, a formidable coalition of church, women's, and peace groups joined the disarmament crusade.[24]

Although Harding declared that he favored "approximate disarmament," he still wanted to complete the capital ship program authorized by the 1916 program. Accordingly, he denounced as a "folly" a February 1921 House bill that reduced naval spending by $284 million from the previous year. The bill also omitted funds for any new ships and cut in half the money required to continue the 1916 naval construction program. Instead, Harding supported a Senate bill that added $100 million to the House measure. The Senate bill included funds for two aircraft carriers and for the construction of a naval base on Guam. But Borah was able to block passage of the Senate bill before the congressional session ended in March. Borah and the Congress, in effect, virtually ordered the administration to call a naval arms conference.[25]

Borah's push for naval reductions was supplemented by a similar effort by the British. Although David Lloyd George's government was prepared to engage the United States in a naval race if that proved necessary, it preferred, if possible, to avoid the expense and consequent increase in Anglo-American tensions that would result. Relations between the two countries were already strained by the question of renewing Britain's alliance with Japan, which would continue in force for at least another year unless terminated by July 13, 1921. As that date approached,

American opposition to renewal increased. Secretary of State Hughes went as far as to inform Lloyd George that Britain had to decide between the Japanese alliance and friendship with the United States; she could not have both. Hughes' ultimatum was reinforced by British ambassador Sir Auckland Geddes, who warned London that a naval race with the United States was inevitable unless the alliance were terminated. At the same time, the Canadian government, which viewed with horror the prospect of a Japanese-American war with the alliance still intact, bluntly informed the British that Canada could not promise how she would participate in such a conflict.[26]

While most Britons were willing to terminate the alliance with Japan, if only to ensure continued good relations with the United States--not to mention a favorable war-debt settlement--they nevertheless felt compelled to consider the sensibilities of the Japanese. While most Japanese considered the alliance something of a "lemon," in that they realized it would be of no value in a war with the United States, the Japanese government considered its renewal not only a matter of prestige but also a pillar of Japan's foreign policy. Nor could the British disregard the military threat a hostile Japan would pose to their vast interests in the Far East and the Pacific. Many Britons--as well as Australians and New Zealanders, who would be directly threatened by a hostile Japanese military machine--urged renewal of the alliance if only to preclude Japanese aggression, possibly in combination with a revived Germany or Russia.[27]

To escape the dilemma of choosing between the Japanese and the Americans, Lloyd George ingeniously approached the United States on the possibility of reaching a joint understanding with Japan. Only days before the Anglo-Japanese alliance was due to expire, he telegrammed Washington proposing that the United States convene a conference to discuss Pacific questions. Coincidentally, the British telegram crossed a message from Hughes inquiring how Britain would react to an invitation to a conference on naval armament limitations. Upon receipt of Lloyd George's inquiry, Hughes decided to merge the arms and Pacific conferences and to invite the French and Italians as well as the Japanese. Later, the agenda was expanded to discuss Chinese issues as well by including China, Holland, Belgium, and Portugal in a parallel Nine Power conference.[28]

Pointedly, one nation with major Far Eastern interests, Russia, was excluded from the conference. The Soviets were still a pariah in the eyes of the international community, and the Harding administration, which refused to recognize the Soviet government, would do nothing to enhance its prestige. Denying that Russia's form of government had anything to do with American nonrecognition, Hughes stated that it was due to the Soviet repudiation of the Czarist debt to the United States, the seizure of American property by the Soviet government, and efforts of the Soviets to overthrow the U.S. government. While nonrecognition did not prevent the American Relief Administration from sending $50 million worth of food to Russia during the famine of 1921, nor American companies from doing business with the Soviets, it did prevent normal diplomatic relations between the two countries.[29]

## The Washington Conference

The Washington Conference opened on November 12, 1921 with Hughes delivering a keynote address that shocked the assembled delegates. The secretary of state proposed that the three major naval powers--Britain, Japan, and the United States--together scrap no less than sixty-six capital ships built, building, or planned, with an aggregate displacement of over 1,878,000 tons. For the United States, this amounted to scrapping thirty vessels totaling 845,740 tons, of which fifteen were under construction. For Britain, it would require the scrapping of twenty-three ships, totaling 583,375 tons. The Japanese were asked to give up seventeen ships, aggregating 448,928 tons, and to postpone construction of eight other capital ships. In thirty-five minutes, one observer noted, Hughes sank more "ships than all the admirals of the world had sunk in a cycle of centuries."[30]

· The agreement that resulted from Hughes' proposal, the Five Power Treaty, required the United States, Britain, Japan, France, and Italy to halt construction of capital ships for ten years and to bring their tonnages of such ships to a fixed ratio of 5:5:3:1.75:1.75. Actually, the ratios broke down to 500,650 tons (eighteen capital ships) for the United States, 604,450 tons for Britain (twenty-two capital ships), and 299,700 tons (ten capital ships) for Japan. Britain was allotted a larger tonnage because more of her ships were older than those of the United States and Japan. France and Italy were required to scrap no ships because their allotments of 175,000 tons each matched the existing tonnages of their fleets. After the ten-year "holiday" on naval construction, replacements for ships twenty years old could be made as long as the new ships were no larger than 35,000 tons each.[31]

Hughes also suggested a similar 5:5:3 ratio for aircraft carriers and other classes of warships. The first aircraft carriers appeared, in experimental form, during the First World War. But they did not come into their own until General William "Billy" Mitchell of the U.S. Army Air Service demonstrated that aircraft could sink capital ships. In 1921 the captured German battleship, the *Ostfriesland*, was sent to the bottom by two one-ton bombs dropped from aircraft. The aircraft carrier limitations set at Washington were 135,000 tons for Britain and the United States, 81,000 tons for Japan, and 60,000 tons each for France and Italy.[32]

However, because France refused to accept a limitation on submarine construction smaller than the other major powers, it was impossible to include auxiliary craft--cruisers, destroyers, and submarines--in the agreement. The French wanted a large allotment of submarines--90,000 tons--to counter British superiority in surface vessels. But the British refused to restrict destroyers without strict limitations on the submarines they were designed to counter. Although Hughes was upset about the inability of the Washington Conference to limit auxiliary craft, he was confident that they could be restricted at a future conference.[33]

In return for accepting a smaller ratio of capital ships, the Japanese demanded--and received--a promise from Britain and the United States that they would refrain from fortifying their Pacific insular possessions. Hughes and the British agreed to apply the nonfortification provision to Hong Kong, the Philippines, Guam, and the Aleutians. For her part, Japan agreed to keep unfortified the islands adjacent to the Japanese homeland, including Formosa, southern Sakhalin, and the Ryukyus. The treaty was to remain in force until December 31, 1936, but any party could withdraw after two years' notice.[34]

A Four Power Pact accompanied the naval limitation agreement. It ended the Anglo-Japanese alliance and substituted an agreement under which Britain, Japan, France, and the United States pledged to respect each other's Pacific possessions and to consult with each other in case they were threatened. The agreement was to extend for ten years and to continue thereafter, subject to termination on twelve months' notice.[35]

A third agreement concluded at Washington, the Nine Power Treaty, dealt specifically with Chinese affairs. It bound the nine signatories to accept the principle of equal commercial and industrial opportunity in China as well as to uphold the independence and territorial integrity of that nation. In a major concession, Japan agreed to withdraw her forces from Shantung and China's Shandong Peninsula.[36]

The Harding administration was very pleased with the results of the Washington Conference. It appeared as though a new era of peaceful relations and economic cooperation would ensue in the Far East. The Five Power Naval Treaty checked a potential naval arms race far more effectively than even Senator Borah had thought possible. And the prospective reductions in naval expenditures would make possible lower taxes and balanced budgets. The security of America's Pacific possessions appeared to have been enhanced by the termination of the Anglo-Japanese alliance and its replacement by the Four Power Pact. Moreover, the Open Door policy, for the first time, was formally guaranteed by the major powers, including Japan. The return of the Shandong Peninsula to China by Japan can only be counted as a major achievement.[37]

Yet, while most Americans reacted favorably to the Washington Conference, it did not escape criticism. Isolationists, like Senators Borah and James Reed, concentrated their criticism on the Four Power Pact, which, they argued, was an entanglement as dangerous as the Versailles Treaty. Instead of terminating the Anglo-Japanese alliance, Reed argued, the United States had joined it. "We got rid of it just like the woman got rid of the old man, by marrying him," Reed said. In defense of the treaty, Senator Henry Cabot Lodge, who had the responsibility for guiding the Washington agreements through the Senate, told his colleagues that the Four Power Treaty carried not even a moral commitment to use force. It would help ensure peace, Lodge promised, "without alliances or penalties or the sanction of force lurking in the background." Nevertheless, the Senate refused to approve the Four Power Treaty before it had attached an amendment declaring that the pact was understood to contain "no commitment to armed force, no alliance, no obligation to join in any defense." With this amendment attached, twelve Democrats joined fifty-five Republicans in passing the treaty 67 to 27--only four votes more than the required two-thirds majority. The Five Power Treaty, on the other hand, passed with only one dissenting vote, 74 to 1, while the Nine Power Treaty was adopted unanimously.[38]

It was the unwillingness to use force to uphold the Washington agreements that made realists believe that the agreements not only had little value but were dangerous to the Far Eastern interests of the United States. Realists also had little liking for the broad and vague commitment, contained in the Nine Power Treaty, to defend China's territorial integrity and independence because it could not be enforced with military power. And the Five Power Treaty ensured that there would be little in the way of military force to restrain the Japanese in the Far East when they decided, as they would in the 1930s, to abandon their cooperative attitude toward the West. But realists centered their attack on the Five Power Treaty. They argued that its nonfortification provisions guaranteed Japan military supremacy in the Far East by precluding the possibility of effective naval operations against her in the northwestern Pacific; the nearest bases from which an attack could be mounted were Singapore and Hawaii.[39]

Hughes responded to the critics of the Five Power Treaty by arguing that the United States had surrendered nothing on the fortification issue because Congress would not provide the funds necessary to fortify the Philippines and Guam anyway. "We were thus," he argued, "able to agree not to do . . . what in any event we would not do, thus allaying a distrust which was even more threatening than armaments and creating an atmosphere favorable to peace and our best interests."[40]

In fairness to Hughes, he did attempt to maintain U.S. naval power as a bulwark of the Washington agreements. But once ratification of the treaties had been achieved, both political parties seemed so content with the agreements that they ignored Hughes' warning to "maintain the relative naval strength of the United States." Naval construction, as a result, was all but discontinued. Between 1922 and 1929, the United States built, or provided for the building of, only 11 ships, compared to 74 ships for Britain, 125 for Japan, 119 for France, and 82 for Italy.[41]

Nor did the Washington Conference do much to promote the security of Europe. The French complained, with justification, that the conference, by avoiding the issue of land armaments, had done nothing to safeguard France's frontiers, while, by holding the French navy to parity with Italy's, it had left France vulnerable in the Mediterranean Sea. Moreover, the French were excluded from the negotiations on capital ship limitations and were threatened with economic retaliation if they did not accept the Five Power Treaty. Not surprisingly, the French were extremely difficult to deal with at Washington, causing Hughes to believe "that France really had militaristic plans."[42]

## Reparations and French Security

Prompted by what was then perceived as a successful Washington Conference, Prime Minister Lloyd George in early 1922 thought he could draw the United States into a conference on European security and economic problems in Genoa, Italy. To this Genoa Conference were also invited the two outcast nations of Europe, the Soviet Union and Germany. But the Harding administration refused to participate. The administration not only did not want to have anything to do with a conference involving the Soviets, it also feared that American "entanglement" with European problems at Genoa might jeopardize the Washington accords, which still had to be ratified by the Senate.[43]

While America's nonparticipation was a factor in the inability of the Genoa Conference to resolve Europe's economic problems, French inflexibility was at least equally responsible. The fact is, France was too vulnerable, both economically and militarily, to accept the adaptation of Washington-style diplomacy, with its self-policing security schemes, to purely European issues. Excluding Russia, no country lost more in World War I. With a population of 40 million, France suffered more than a million-and-a-half deaths and counted another 700,000 of her citizens as disabled. Moreover, most of her northern departments were devastated by the conflict. Before the war, the north of France had produced 94 percent of French woolen products, 90 percent of the nation's linen yarn, 90 percent of its iron ore, and 80 percent of its steel. Nor could the French forget that much of the destruction was part of a deliberate German effort to eliminate French competition after the war. Needless to say, France expected the Germans to pay fully in reparations for restoring this region as well as the more than 22 billion gold francs she had borrowed to fight the war.[44]

But overshadowing all other French considerations was the realization that Germany was potentially far stronger than France. Germany's population of 70 million was not only much larger, it was also much younger than France's. In 1919 the ratio of German to French men of military age was 2 to 1 in favor of the Germans. And even though defeated, Germany was still the economic giant of Europe. Her heavy industrial potential alone was four times greater than that of France. Considering these factors, it is understandable why the French were obsessed with the German threat.[45]

At Versailles, French Premier Clemenceau had insisted that France's security required, at a bare minimum, the permanent Allied occupation of the left bank of the Rhine River as well as the bridges that crossed it. But Woodrow Wilson and Lloyd George refused to accept this. Instead, they persuaded Clemenceau to accept the permanent demilitarization of the Rhineland and its temporary occupation-- until 1935--by Allied troops. The French premier agreed only after Wilson and Lloyd George offered France a security treaty, which in the wake of the U.S. Senate's rejection of the Treaty of Versailles was never ratified, either by Washington or by London. Without a guarantee of American and British support, and without the Russian alliance, which expired with the Bolshevik Revolution, France feared that she would have to stand alone against the menace of a revived Germany bent on revenge.[46]

In what would prove a vain attempt to replace these former allies, France concluded alliances with Belgium (1920), Poland (1921), Czechoslovakia (1924), Rumania (1926), and Yugoslavia (1927). These nations were not only relatively weak but, in the case of Poland and Czechoslovakia, also objects of German revanchist ambitions. As long as French troops occupied the Rhineland and Germany remained disarmed, Poland and Czechoslovakia were useful allies. Later, when Germany rearmed and reoccupied the Rhineland, they became major liabilities.

France also tied her security to a rigid defense of the Treaty of Versailles, particularly the treaty's reparations provisions. The French demanded high reparation payments not only to finance the reconstruction of the French north but also to preclude full German recovery in the foreseeable future. At the London Reparations Conference in May 1921, German reparations were set at approximately $33 billion. This amount was much smaller than the astronomical figures that had been discussed at Versailles, but they were still lower than France considered sufficient to restore her northern departments or to defray her war debts. Not surprisingly, France rejected German demands for further reparations reductions and for a four-year moratorium on reparation payments. Indeed, the French agreed to attend the ill-fated Genoa Conference only after Lloyd George agreed to drop reparations from the agenda.[47]

The French reparation policy, and their almost paranoid quest for safety against a resurgent and vengeful Germany, strained nearly to the breaking point France's relationship with Britain. Where the French considered the London reparations schedule a political and economic necessity, the British came to regard it as excessively high and therefore the major obstacle to European recovery. And Britain's enormous wartime debt and postwar depression made the rapid economic revitalization of Europe--and particularly Germany, a traditionally major trading partner of the British--a vital necessity. The British insisted that the vindictive French policy toward Germany not only delayed German economic recovery, it exacerbated German hostility and thereby increased the risk of a future conflict. For this very reason, among others, Britain wanted no part of the French alliance system, which the British feared would drag them into another war with Germany over territories, in Eastern Europe, where British interests were not great. The British believed that the only way to ensure the security of France and the peace of Europe was through a policy of conciliating and cooperating with Germany, in other words, the "appeasement" policy that, after World War II began, would be almost universally derided. Needless to say, a conciliatory policy not only created the prospect of revitalizing European markets for British goods, it obviated the need for British military commitments on the Continent.[48]

## War Debts

As a way of removing in one stroke the problem of reparations, the British in August 1922 proposed one "great transaction" to cancel all inter-Allied debts and thereby enable reparations to be liquidated. Not surprisingly, not only the French but the Americans rejected this idea. The American people and the Congress clearly expected war debts to be paid. As Calvin Coolidge expressed the prevailing American sentiment, "They hired the money, didn't they?" To Senator Borah, debt cancellation would "simply fit into European schemes for armaments, huge land forces, more wars and therefore more debts."[49]

The European debtors, on the other hand, considered the American demand for debt payments selfish and unjustified. Nine-tenths of the money that was borrowed by the Europeans was spent in the United States, a fact that did much to stimulate American prosperity during the war. Moreover, in the European view, the war was fought for a common objective--defeat of the Central Powers--from which America as well as the Allies benefited. Furthermore, the United States had entered the struggle almost three years after it had started, and had lost much less in lives and property than the Allies. America's contribution was paid primarily in dollars, not in death and destruction, yet now the United States wanted its dollars back. Not surprisingly, Europeans called Uncle Sam "Uncle Shylock."[50]

The heart of the debt problem, however, was the European inability to pay. During the war, a large portion of the Allies' gold reserves had gone to the United States to pay for goods they desperately needed. After the war, they could not afford to pay war debts without destabilizing their currencies. The problem was compounded by high American tariffs (the Fordney-McCumber Tariff of 1922 and the even higher Smoot-Hawley Tariff of 1930) that made it very difficult for Europeans to sell enough goods to the United States to earn the currency needed to liquidate their debts. While Republican policymakers believed the economic recovery of Europe was vital to the United States, they also believed the health of the American economy was even more important. They somehow believed that they could protect the American home-market with higher tariffs while insisting that the Europeans could pay their war debts as well as moderate their reparation demands on Germany.[51]

The Congress, for its part, believed that the Harding administration was too sensitive to Europe's economic woes. Prompted by fears of default and excessive generosity by the executive branch, the Congress in 1921 passed legislation that placed debt settlement negotiations under a special agency, the World War Foreign Debt Commission. The same act also fixed interest rates at a minimum of 4.25 percent and set the maximum time limit for repayment of all principal and interest at twenty-five years.[52]

In practice, however, the debt commission virtually ignored the congressional guidelines. Instead, it applied a capacity-to-pay approach to negotiations with the debtors and then obtained congressional approval of each settlement. The settlement reached with Britain, which was more than eager to settle in order to restore its status as a major banking center, called for a low interest rate averaging 3.3 percent and a maturity date of sixty-two years. In this way, 19.3 percent of the British debt was canceled. The other settlements were even more generous. The settlement concluded with France in 1926 was set at an interest rate of 1.6 percent, in effect, canceling over half the French debt. The Italian settlement forgave 80 percent of that nation's debt.[53]

But further than this--either canceling war debts or assuaging French security concerns--the United States would not go. Constrained by Congress, and by its own inhibitions, the Harding administration refused to admit the link between war debts and reparations, or the cause and effect relationship between the lapsed Anglo-American security guarantee and the French alliance system. Instead, historian Carole Fink has written, "Washington preached against Europe's 'economic chaos' and called for 'disarmament,' as if its own decisive wartime intervention, its formidable role in the peace treaties, and its sudden withdrawal could be ignored."[54]

# The Ruhr Crisis and the Dawes Plan

The Germans, of course, were aware of the split in the Western camp, and throughout the twenties they attempted to exploit it fully as the primary way to bring down the Versailles system. At first they concentrated on the treaty's reparations provisions. Once they succeeded in nullifying reparations, the Germans believed, they could then demonstrate that other elements of the Versailles edifice were "only paper." Indeed, the government of Chancellor Joseph Wirth went to the extreme of virtually ruining the German economy to demonstrate to the Allies that reparations were impossibly excessive. Instead of raising taxes to cover reparations, the Wirth government paid the first reparation installments in foreign currency bought by printing paper marks. The result was immediate, runaway inflation that not only ruined the German middle class but did much to discredit, in the eyes of its citizens, the infant Weimar Republic.[55]

The French, however, were not fooled by the German effort to create a fraudulent bankruptcy. In January 1923, after the Germans defaulted on a reparations payment, the French, with the Belgians, sent a commission of engineers and several infantry and cavalry divisions into the Ruhr, the industrial heart of Germany. French Premier Raymond Poincaré believed that allowing the Germans to violate the reparations provisions of the Versailles Treaty would lead to its gradual, but nevertheless complete, abrogation. When the Germans responded with a government-directed program of passive resistance, France and Belgium broadened the area of occupation and established customs barriers between the Ruhr and the rest of Germany.[56]

The Ruhr invasion, however, failed. While France met no military opposition to her occupation of the Ruhr, she was condemned by Britain and the United States. Moreover, the program of German passive resistance that the invasion triggered deprived France of most of the material advantages she had expected. Indeed, by depriving France of German reparations, the Ruhr occupation helped to bring about the collapse of the French franc and the necessity for France to secure foreign credits to save it.

But the Ruhr occupation also hurt Germany. In fact, the Germans lost more in revenue from the Ruhr in the nine months of passive resistance than they had paid in reparations in all the years since the war. Further, the complete collapse of the German currency increased agitation from both the extreme left and right (in 1923 Adolf Hitler staged his unsuccessful Beer Hall Putsch) and called into question the continued existence of the Weimar Republic. In September 1924 a new government, headed by Gustav Stresemann, came to power, promised a policy of cooperation with the victorious Allies rather than economic confrontation, and called off the program of passive resistance. Stresemann then asked the United States for an initiative to end the Ruhr stalemate.

However much Americans might wish to stay out of Europe's problems, there was no way the United States could escape the consequences of a German economic collapse. Germany's inability, or refusal, to pay reparations would make it impossible for the United States to collect war debts from the Allies. And Europe's economic recovery, upon which the vitality of America's European trade and investments depended, would also prove impossible if Germany's economy were ruined. Further, an economically and militarily prostrate Germany, it was feared, could not serve as an effective barrier against Bolshevism, let alone remain a stable democracy.

As a result, for the first time since Versailles, the United States offered to play a direct role in European affairs. Hughes insisted that it was "imperative" to design a financial plan that would "prevent economic disaster in Europe, the consequences of which would be worldwide." To circumvent certain congressional objections to entanglement with Europe, Hughes proposed a committee of private financial experts, headed by an American banker, Charles G. Dawes, to determine Germany's capacity to pay as well as the conditions under which the Germans could be given a large foreign loan. The Dawes Plan, which the committee produced, provided that Germany would receive a loan of $200 million, $110 million of which would come from American banks. In return Germany promised to make reparation payments on a rising scale commensurate with her economic recovery. The payment for 1924 was reduced to $250 million; it would rise to $265 million in 1928. However, the total amount Germany would pay was left open. With the Dawes Plan, historian Betty Glad has written, "Hughes helped to start the dollars on their travels--from American investors to Germany as loans, to the Allied capitals as reparations payments, and back to the United States as payments on the war debts."[57]

Although Hughes insisted that the American role in the Dawes Plan was purely economic, it nevertheless had definite political repercussions. Not only did it compromise the nonentanglement policy of the United States, it also affected the structure of European political relations and especially the foreign policy of France. At the London Conference in 1924, an end to the Ruhr crisis was negotiated. The London agreement called for France to evacuate the Ruhr within one year, while imposing restrictions that would prevent independent French action if Germany defaulted again. The French approved the Dawes Plan only reluctantly, after Poincaré's hardline cabinet was replaced by the more conciliatory government of Edouard Herriot, and after the American banking firm of J. P. Morgan and Company was persuaded by Hughes to provide the French government with a six-month credit of $100 million in order to stabilize the franc.[58]

Despite this short-term gain, however, the French realized only too well that the Germans had gotten their way in demanding a reduction in reparations and that, in three or four years, they would be back for more. Worse, from the French perspective, the Dawes Plan had undermined France's ability to enforce unilaterally the Treaty of Versailles. By accepting a diminution in the powers of the Reparation Commission, agreeing to evacuate the Ruhr, and relinquishing control over a critical sector of the German economy, the French abandoned their ability to safeguard their vital interests through independent military action. French security now depended upon the goodwill of Germany and the aid of her former allies. The French, therefore, were reluctant to make additional readjustments until they had obtained further assurances of Germany's pacific intentions and had secured additional Anglo-American support. As a result, during the latter part of 1924 and early 1925 France rejected overtures to attend another disarmament conference and refused to withdraw troops from the Cologne occupation zone (one of three such zones; the other two were centered on Coblenz and Mainz) until Germany had abided fully by the disarmament provisions of the Treaty of Versailles. If European stabilization were to progress further, it was evident that French security apprehensions would have to be dealt with first.[59]

# The Geneva Protocol

Probably the most important of the early efforts to satisfy French security demands, while promoting disarmament, was the Geneva Protocol of 1924. The Protocol, which was offered to League members as well as nonmembers, including the United States, attempted to broaden the League's power to prevent war. It called for compulsory arbitration of disputes not settled by the League's Council, the compulsory submission of all domestic disputes to the World Court, military action against an aggressor, and an explicit definition of an aggressor as a nation unwilling to accept arbitration.[60]

In Britain, the Protocol was championed by the Labour Party, which, by accepting its principles, became the leading British advocate of the collective security approach to international peace. Labourite Arthur Henderson argued that the Protocol "will restrain aggressors by making greater the deterrent power of the obligations already enshrined in the Covenant." Philip Noel-Baker, one of the Protocol's most fervent supporters, called it "the outlawry of war with a vengeance." However, the British Left adopted the Protocol not because they desired to use sanctions or military force, but rather because they thought the mere threat to use sanctions or force would be sufficient to deter aggression. If coercion became necessary, economic sanctions alone would be adequate, Henderson explained, because of the "supreme value of supplies of raw materials and foodstuffs, and conversely, the enormous effect of a blockade." Indeed, the British Left believed the Protocol would advance the cause of disarmament, since it would only come into force after a plan for the reduction of armaments was adopted.[61]

While the French refused to disarm until their security was guaranteed, they accepted the Protocol because it seemed to commit Britain to the defense of the status quo that France was so determined to preserve. By making the arbitration of international disputes compulsory, the Protocol precluded the forceful revision of treaties. As historian Arnold Wolfers has pointed out, "Arbitration means the application, not the change, of treaties. Instead of facilitating revision, the effect of the Protocol was unquestionably to consecrate the international status quo with a definite position of legality, not to be disturbed by force." What the advocates of collective security failed to realize, or refused to admit, was that by accepting the possibility of a coercive response to aggression, they had committed themselves to fighting any nation that preferred to risk war rather than accept the status quo.[62]

The Geneva Protocol, however, ran into the rock solid opposition of the United States. Both Hughes and Coolidge's second secretary of state, Frank B. Kellogg, opposed it on the grounds that it would create an unfriendly European concert--"a new Holy Alliance," in Hughes' words--that could threaten the Monroe Doctrine.

Under the terms of the Protocol, the United States would not be able to act unilaterally against a Latin American country. Instead, it would have to submit inter-American disputes to League arbitration or face economic sanctions. "America," Hughes warned, "could hardly help regarding the League of Nations as a potential enemy" if the Protocol were adopted without change.[63]

Some commentators believed that the negative American attitude toward the Geneva Protocol was the major factor behind its rejection by the Conservative British government of Stanley Baldwin. In defending that decision, British Foreign Minister Sir Austen Chamberlain argued that American cooperation was essential for the Protocol's success. But it is also true that British conservatives had no use for the Protocol's sweeping commitments. American opposition, in other words, reinforced rather than determined Britain's negative, and ultimately fatal, attitude toward the Protocol. Chamberlain, historian David D. Burks has commented, "could only feel gratified at American disapproval of the Protocol; British distrust of the League and American isolationism were walking hand in hand."[64]

## The Locarno Agreements

In place of the Geneva Protocol, the European powers signed a number of treaties at the Swiss town of Locarno in October and November 1925. The most important was signed by Britain, France, Belgium, Italy, and Germany. It guaranteed the western boundaries of Germany and the demilitarization of the Rhineland. The three powers most directly concerned, France, Belgium, and Germany, promised never "to attack or to invade each other or to resort to war against each other," except for a flagrant violation of the agreement or on League authorization. In addition, Germany signed a series of arbitration treaties with Poland, Czechoslovakia, Belgium, and France.[65]

Locarno represented a complex bargain between Germany and the Western powers. In effect, Germany promised to maintain the status quo in the West, to arbitrate disputes in the East, and to join the League of Nations. In return, the British and French released Germany from any obligation to participate in League sanctions against Russia (with whom the Germans had no ability or desire to wage war), and promised to evacuate the Cologne occupation zone as soon as possible. The Locarno agreements also preserved American loans, which were contingent on German approval of Locarno, protected western Germany from military sanctions by the Allies, and guaranteed continued German sovereignty over the Rhineland. Moreover, Locarno helped to rule out the prospect of another Geneva Protocol, or worse, from the German perspective, an Anglo-French-Belgian alliance. In subsequent months, the Allies withdrew their troops from the Cologne occupation zone and Germany entered the League of Nations. In 1927, after the Allies declared that Germany was effectively disarmed, the Inter-Allied Military Control Commission was withdrawn.[66]

The Conservative government in Britain supported the Locarno agreements as a way of guaranteeing the security of France and Belgium without offending

Germany and without tying Britain to French alliance commitments in Eastern Europe. In fact, the British saw no prospect of military obligations in the West either, as long as Germany remained disarmed.[67]

Both Coolidge and Kellogg also were pleased with the Locarno accords. They were certainly, from the American perspective, a far better alternative to the defunct Geneva Protocol. "These recent Locarno agreements," Coolidge said, "represent the success of [our] policy . . . of having the European countries settle their own political problems without involving this country."[68]

The French, on the other hand, accepted the Locarno agreements with reluctance. They realized all too readily that while Locarno may have enhanced the security of the French frontier, it did nothing to augment the safety of France's eastern allies. In fact, the Locarno agreements actually weakened the French alliance system. Before Locarno, France was free to assist Poland and Czechoslovakia by invading Germany. After Locarno, the French could only invade Germany if France were attacked first, or after the League of Nations had condemned Germany as an aggressor and economic sanctions had failed. Furthermore, if France attacked Germany first, she risked the prospect--highly unlikely though it may have been-- of British military assistance to Germany, since Locarno made Britain a guarantor of Germany's western boundary as well as the borders of Belgium and France. Austen Chamberlain, recognizing the restrictions Locarno placed upon France, happily concluded: "It is all in the German interest and in ours."[69]

One result of the Locarno agreements was to make France less willing to leave the Rhineland. Although the Cologne occupation zone was evacuated in January 1926, the last French troops did not leave the Rhineland until 1930. In February 1927 the French Superior Council of War, believing that the Great War had demonstrated the supremacy of the defense, approved a project to build a fortified barrier along the frontier with Germany--the Maginot Line. The French delayed their withdrawal from the Rhineland to permit completion of the Maginot project. Nor were the French prepared to consider total withdrawal until a final, acceptable reparations settlement was reached.[70]

## The Geneva Disarmament Conference

Inspired by the temporary easing of international tensions that resulted from the signing of the Locarno agreements, President Coolidge in early 1926 accepted an invitation to participate in the work of the League-sponsored Preparatory Commission for the Disarmament Conference, which was established in Locarno's wake. Coolidge wanted to head off an arms race with the British and thereby save American taxpayers hundreds of millions of dollars a year. At the same time, however, he was intent on securing American interests while avoiding entangling commitments. As a result, the Coolidge administration insisted upon separate discussions for naval, air, and land armaments. The administration also rejected proposals to establish machinery to enforce disarmament agreements as well as any commitment to apply sanctions or respect naval blockades.[71]

Not surprisingly, the American approach to disarmament was in marked contrast to the policy of France. The French were determined to ensure that Germany's industrial revival after the Dawes Plan became effective was not channeled into resuscitating German military power. For this reason, the French insisted that a nation's industrial capacity and war-making potential must be factors in any disarmament scheme. Moreover, German violations of the disarmament provisions of the Treaty of Versailles convinced the French that any new disarmament accord must be rigorously enforced. Nor were the French going to reduce their armaments until international guarantees were provided for the security of their East European allies. Fortunately for American-French relations, the two powers did not clash at Geneva over their conflicting disarmament philosophies. Kellogg stated that the United States, with a small army and weak neighbors, had only an "academic interest" in land disarmament. Yet, while the Americans also acknowledged the validity of France's claim that her security was an essential prerequisite to disarmament, they also insisted it was a regional matter and not the business of the United States.[72]

The French, of course, had no choice but to accept the fact that the United States would not guarantee their security. Consequently, they tried to draw the British into an expanded security role by proposing to strengthen the coercive features of the League Covenant, particularly Article 16. Specifically, the French wanted the British to commit their navy to the enforcement of League-authorized sanctions or an economic embargo against an aggressor. When the British rejected these measures, the French took a noncommittal attitude toward Britain's disarmament proposals. As a result, the Preparatory Commission on Disarmament soon found itself in an impasse that would extend into the next decade.[73]

With land disarmament obviously going nowhere, the Coolidge administration turned its attention to naval armaments. In early 1927 the the president invited Britain, Japan, France, and Italy to attend a conference that would attempt to reach an agreement limiting naval vessels that were not affected by the Washington Treaty, that is, cruisers, destroyers, and submarines. Because the other powers were building these ships in larger quantities than the United States, Coolidge realized that the only alternative to their inclusion in the Washington limits was a major and expensive American naval construction program.[74]

Britain and Japan accepted Coolidge's invitation, but France and Italy did not. The French refused to consider naval disarmament until the interrelated problems of security and land armaments had been resolved to their satisfaction. And they were not about to endure a repetition of the humiliation they had suffered at the Washington Conference when they had felt compelled to accept parity in capital ships with Italy. The Italians, for their part, were mesmerized by Benito Mussolini's plan to build another Roman Empire and consequently lost interest in naval disarmament.[75]

In the end, the Geneva Naval Conference proved to be, in the words of one historian, "one of the most dramatically unsuccessful international gatherings of the twentieth century." Perhaps the main reason was the fact that, unlike the Washington Conference, the Geneva Conference was conducted by naval officers rather than diplomats. But the major obstacle proved to be an Anglo-American controversy over cruiser limitations. The Americans wanted to extend the

Washington capital ship ratio of 5:5:3 to cruisers, destroyers, and submarines and to reduce the total tonnage of each of these classes. Because the United States lacked the worldwide network of naval bases possessed by Britain, the Americans wanted to build cruisers with large cruising radii, displacements of 10,000 tons, and eight-inch guns. The British were willing to extend the capital ship ratio to cruisers over 7,500 tons, but they wanted to leave unrestricted smaller cruisers, which had six-inch guns and small cruising radii, because, based at Britain's many naval bases, these ships were ideally suited for protecting the long trade routes of their empire and for enforcing a naval blockade. The inability of the British and American naval officers to resolve these incompatible positions caused the conference to end on August 4 without an agreement.[76]

Stymied by the United States, the British turned to France. In a "Compromise on the Limitation of Armaments," concluded in July 1928, Britain and France agreed that, in any future naval disarmament agreement, heavy cruisers and large submarines would be restricted, but smaller varieties of these classes would not. In exchange for France's support on naval reductions, Britain accepted the French position on the restriction of land forces, which excluded limitations on France's large numbers of trained reserves, thereby preserving a key element in the French military superiority over the Germans, who were denied large reserves by the Treaty of Versailles.[77]

The Americans angrily rejected the Anglo-French understanding, which they regarded as a circuitous attempt by the British to maintain their naval superiority over the United States. Coolidge recommended that Congress fund a five-year, billion-dollar naval construction program, which included twenty-six cruisers of 10,000 tons each, three aircraft carriers, eighteen destroyers, and five submarines. As enacted by Congress in February 1929, the program called for the construction of fifteen light cruisers and one aircraft carrier. However, the act permitted the president to suspend the construction program, in whole or part, if a naval limitation agreement were concluded. The breakdown of the Geneva Conference, and the prospect of another naval race, frayed Anglo-American relations further.[78]

# The Kellogg-Briand Pact

Before the Geneva Naval Conference failed, the American peace movement had accelerated its effort to outlaw war. In 1923 the "father" of the outlawry movement, Salmon O. Levinson, managed to win the support of Senator Borah, who in February of that year introduced a resolution in the Senate calling for a universal treaty that would make war "a public crime under the law of nations." The senator saw the outlawry idea not only as a way to prevent an entangling American military commitment to Europe, but also as a device to unite the peace movement behind a Borah presidential campaign. The outlawry idea was supported by other peace leaders, including Dr. Nicholas Murray Butler, president of Columbia University and of the Carnegie Endowment for International Peace, and James T. Shotwell, a professor of history at Columbia and a director of the Carnegie organization. But because Butler and Shotwell tied their plan to closer

American cooperation with the League of Nations, an organization that was anathema to both Levinson and Borah, the two groups became rivals.[79]

It was not until 1927, however, that the outlawry idea finally caught hold. In March of that year, Shotwell convinced France's foreign minister, Aristide Briand, that a bilateral Franco-American treaty declaring war illegal could be the way to reduce the strained relations between the two countries as well as the risks of war. Briand bought the idea, not because he thought it could prevent war, but primarily because he hoped to reduce the risk of a clash with the United States over American neutrality policy in the event the League of Nations applied sanctions against an aggressor. On April 6, 1927, the tenth anniversary of America's entry into the Great War, Briand called for a bilateral treaty in which the two countries would forever renounce war as a means of resolving their differences.[80]

The Coolidge administration at first ignored Briand's offer. It was angered by the manipulations of the outlawrists and convinced that Briand's proposal was simply a ploy to entangle the United States in the French alliance system and draw the attention of the American people away from France's uncompromising stands on disarmament and debts. Yet, much to the surprise of the administration, the Briand proposal caught the imagination of the American people. Mrs. Catt's American Committee on the Cause and Cure of War collected tens of thousands of signatures on petitions supporting a treaty to outlaw war. In December 1927 the White House received as many as 200 letters a day, and the State Department as many as 600 a day, supporting the outlawry treaty.[81]

The Coolidge administration began to give serious consideration to Briand's proposal, not only to mollify public opinion, but also because it feared that the proposal would complicate America's strict neutrality policy in the event the treaty failed and France became involved in another war. In the Senate, Kansas Republican Arthur Capper introduced a resolution, inspired by Shotwell's ideas, that called for an alteration in America's traditional neutrality policy by requiring the United States to cooperate with League-imposed sanctions or blockades. The Capper Resolution also defined aggression strictly (essentially as any hostilities initiated without first attempting to settle a dispute peaceably) and required the U.S. government to withhold national protection from any citizen dealing with an aggressor state. Adoption of the Capper Resolution, historian Francis P. Walters observed, "might well have changed the face of history."[82]

Fortunately for the Coolidge administration, Senator Borah, who feared the entangling ramifications of the Capper Resolution as much as anyone, came to the administration's rescue. Instead of the Capper Resolution or the bilateral treaty proposed by France, Borah proposed a multilateral pact that would include Britain, Japan, Italy, and Germany and that would prohibit all forms of international war, not just aggression. In December Borah was able to persuade Kellogg that his proposal was a far safer route than the one outlined by either Briand or Capper. On December 28 Kellogg wrote to Briand suggesting that the outlawry pact should include all the major powers as well as all types of war.[83]

Briand, however, reacted only with tepid enthusiasm, primarily because Kellogg's proposal said nothing about America's neutrality policy in case of aggression. Moreover, Briand feared a multilateral pact would undermine the French alliance system by making it difficult for France to wage defensive war on behalf of her European allies. Nevertheless, on January 5, 1928, Briand accepted Kellogg's proposal to extend the pact to all nations, but he rejected the suggestion that it should outlaw all wars. France, he said, was unable to adhere to a universal antiwar compact that denied the crucial distinction between aggressive and defensive war.[84]

Kellogg, for his part, reacted to Briand's emphasis on the issue of aggressive war with the same coolness that he had displayed toward the Capper Resolution. A definition of the term aggression would implicitly require the United States to cease relations with the designated aggressor, compromise American neutrality, and end America's effort to avoid political entanglement in Europe. Not surprisingly, Kellogg informed Briand that the United States would renounce all wars or none at all.[85]

Once more, Borah came to the rescue. He circumvented the whole aggression issue by proposing that nations pledge themselves to renounce all war while agreeing that, in the event of a breach of the pact, all signatories were immediately released from their obligation under it not to go to war. By this maneuver, the United States was able to promote a treaty that promised to condemn all war, even as the French were assured that their obligations to fight in defense of their treaty commitments remained unimpaired. In the end, Briand accepted the principles of a multilateral treaty but with the understanding that it would not impair France's right of self-defense.[86]

The Kellogg-Briand Treaty was signed by fifteen nations in Paris on August 27, 1928. It contained only two articles. They pledged the signatories to renounce war "as an instrument of national policy" and to seek to solve their disputes "by pacific means." However, the interpretive notes that were attached to the treaty made it almost meaningless. Kellogg had insisted that the pact contain no sanctions, no commitment for the United States to go to war, and nothing that would draw it into European affairs. "Every nation is free at all times and regardless of treaty provisions," he said officially, "to defend its territory from attack and it alone is competent to decide whether circumstances require war in self-defense." And although the Senate added no formal reservations to the treaty, it did adopt a number of interpretations drafted by the Foreign Relations Committee. They stated that the treaty did not impair the right of self-defense, interfere with the Monroe Doctrine, commit the nation to the use of force, or alter its position under its other treaties.[87]

Not surprisingly, the full Senate offered no important opposition to the treaty, though some senators said it was worthless because it made no provision for its own enforcement and would lull the United States into a state of unpreparedness. One of them scoffed that it would be "as effective to keep down war as a carpet would be to smother an earthquake." But it was precisely the absence of enforcement machinery that made the treaty palatable to isolationists and internationalists alike. On January 15, 1929, the Senate approved the treaty 85 to 1. And, after all fifteen signatories and thirty-one adhering nations had ratified the pact, President Hoover declared it in force on July 24, 1929. "I dare predict," he said, "that the influence of the Treaty for the Renunciation of War will be felt in a large proportion of all future international acts."[88]

Others were not so sure. Former Secretary of State Robert Lansing considered the pact an exercise in futility. "War cannot be outlawed," he said, "because . . . it is often the only means of protecting the rights to which a nation and a people are entitled by every principle of justice and morality. The law, which far transcends any man-made law, is the supreme law of self-preservation."[89]

In response to Lansing, Borah placed his trust in the "invincible force of public opinion." War, he believed, could be prevented by depriving it of its legality and glory, and by educating people that no war was worth the death and destruction that accompanies it. He insisted, however, that a "code of international law declaring war a crime and making criminally liable those who foment war could be carried out as successfully as any provision of domestic law in the United States."[90]

More perceptive, however, was the observation of a British statesman, Lord Lothian. America, he said, "wants on the one hand to prevent war, and on the other to retain the right to be neutral in the event of war, and to assume no obligation for maintaining world peace."[91]

# Herbert Hoover

Herbert Hoover, historian Robert Ferrell has pointed out, "was one of the most learned and capable men ever to rise to the presidency. In sheer mental power, in administrative ability, the thirty-first president of the United States has had few equals." Today, few scholars would argue with Ferrell that Hoover "had the makings of a superb president," and likely would have been one had it not been for the Great Depression, an event which, given the economic knowledge of his day, was largely beyond his control.[92]

Hoover brought to the White House considerable experience in both foreign and domestic affairs. As a mining engineer before the world war, he had traveled and lived abroad, both in Europe and in the Far East. After the war he had organized relief work in Belgium and in Russia, undoubtedly saving millions from starvation in the process. Unlike his predecessor, Calvin Coolidge, who slept as many as eleven hours a day, Hoover was a hard working president. He lived his motto, "Work is life," arriving at his desk before 8:30 in the morning, and working with but short breaks until the early hours of the next morning. His secretary of state, Henry L. Stimson, by contrast, rarely spent more than three hours a day in his office and liked frequent vacations, which Hoover took much less often. The contrasting work habits of the president and his secretary of state were a source of friction that did much to strain their relationship.[93]

Like Woodrow Wilson, under whom he had served, Hoover believed that moral power was more effective than military force. He was certain that the unprecedented horror of the Great War had made people everywhere determined to prevent another such holocaust. Again like Wilson, Hoover believed that the United States, with its democratic ideals and traditional policy of nonentanglement, was ideally suited to the task of helping the world create a new international system based upon peace and justice.[94]

# The Great Depression

Try though he did, Hoover was no more successful in avoiding Europe's problems than was Harding or Coolidge. Bouyed by economic recovery in the late twenties, France once again reverted to a vindictive German policy. She refused to complete the evacuation of the Rhineland or to settle her debts with the United States until the Germans agreed to a final reparations settlement. With German pressure for French withdrawal from the Rhineland mounting, and with reparation authorities increasingly concerned about Germany's public finances and borrowing practices, Hoover reluctantly accepted an old solution--a commission of private experts headed by an American banker, in this case, Owen D. Young--to arrange a "definitive settlement" of the reparations problem. Not surprisingly, the Germans jumped at the opportunity to tie reparations once again to American money and Allied evacuation of the Rhineland. The French reluctantly agreed to participate, but only after they were assured that the settlement would be sufficient to cover restoration of France's northern departments as well as French debts owed to Britain and the United States.[95]

The Young Plan proved to be a far-reaching revision of Germany's reparations. It reduced total reparations from the initial amount of $33 billion set at the London Conference in 1921 to a little over $8 billion, payable in fifty-nine annual payments, the same term as the inter-Allied debts-funding agreements. French resistance to the plan was quickly overcome by the combined pressure of Britain, Belgium, and the United States. At The Hague Conference on August 21, 1929, France and the other principals accepted the Young Plan and agreed to evacuate the two remaining occupied zones in the Rhineland, Coblenz and Mainz. By January 30, 1930, when the last Allied occupation troops left the Rhineland, Germany was finally free of foreign controls.[96]

Unfortunately, the Young Plan was crippled before it could be fully implemented. In October of 1929 the New York Stock Exchange crashed, wiping out, in a few short weeks, $30 billion worth of stock--an amount almost as great as the entire cost of American participation in the First World War. Implementation of the Young Plan, like the Dawes Plan before it, required private financial assistance to Germany, much of which was to come from American investors. But that became impossible after the full effects of the stock market crash were felt. By 1932 American investments abroad had dwindled to a trickle of their former flow, and many foreign holdings were called home, with dire consequences for the economies of Europe and the world as a whole. Many nations reacted to the the cessation of American credit by abandoning the gold standard, devaluating their currencies, increasing their tariff rates, and ultimately by defaulting on their debts. In Austria, the near collapse of the Kreditanstalt, that nation's largest bank, in May 1931 had a chain-reaction effect throughout Europe, but especially in Germany, where a precipitate flight from the mark threatened the Reichsbank's reserves of gold and foreign currency.[97]

With Germany and much of Europe on the verge of economic collapse, Hoover was forced to act, if only to save the American gold standard and banking system, which had extensive holdings in German banks. Moreover, German debtors owed American citizens a total of $2,369,750,000. If the German economy collapsed, there would be little chance of regaining this money. On June 20 Hoover responded to the crisis by announcing a one-year moratorium on the collection of war debts, contingent on the deferral by other governments of their war debt and reparation collections.[98]

The French reacted with shock to the announcement of the moratorium. They deplored the fact that they were being asked to give up more in lost reparation payments than they would receive from postponed war debt obligations. More important, the French feared the political implications of postponing German reparation payments so recently declared final by the Young Plan. If reparation payments were allowed to go by the boards, the French wondered, what would happen to the remaining provisions of the Versailles Treaty? The moratorium, in short, affected more than intergovernmental finances; it threatened the entire Versailles system. Not surprisingly, Hoover considered the French attitude toward the moratorium "intolerable." With no concern whatever for the Treaty of Versailles, the president insisted that the moratorium was not only essential to restore the world economy, it was vital to the continuation of democracy in Germany, in his opinion, France's best security insurance. In the end, the French accepted the moratorium after Hoover agreed that the suspended payments would be repaid over a ten-year period.[99]

But the problem of reparations would remain after the one-year moratorium expired. To deal with it, Britain, France, and Germany met in Lausanne, Switzerland, in June 1932. The Lausanne Conference agreed to a three-year moratorium on reparation payments and a reduced reparation total of only $2 billion, but they did so contingent upon similar reductions of American war debts. However, the Hoover administration, fully aware of the Congress' opposition to debt reduction, rejected the Lausanne conditions. Yet, with the world economy reeling from the effects of the deepening depression, the president did agree to participate in a World Economic Conference in 1932--a major departure from the avowed Republican policy of avoiding European economic conferences. However, Hoover agreed to do so only after insisting that tariff rates and war debts must be excluded from the conference's agenda.[100]

In the end, neither the Hoover moratorium nor the approaching World Economic Conference, which was postponed to 1933 because of Hoover's defeat in the presidential election in November, averted the complete collapse of the postwar debt-reparations structure. Most nations failed to resume debt payments when the moratorium ended on December 15, 1932. In France the Herriot government was overthrown on a parliamentary vote after it insisted that French war debts must be paid, if only to ensure the continued payment of German reparations. Britain and five other nations did make the December payment, but, with the exception of Finland, it was the last payment they made. American isolationist sentiment, already strengthened by the depression, was only reinforced by the default of the Europeans.[101]

# Hoover and Disarmament

The horrible economic situation served as a backdrop to Hoover's efforts to reduce armaments. Despite his Quaker background, Hoover was not a pacifist, but he did believe that a large U.S. military establishment was not only expensive but unnecessary. The Washington treaties and the Kellogg-Briand Pact, backed by an aroused public opinion, in Hoover's view, had made war less likely than ever before. Moreover, both the Army and the Navy had assured the president that there was no imminent threat to America's vital interests anywhere in the world. This comforting assessment convinced Hoover that military budgets could be trimmed safely and the surplus returned to the taxpayer or transferred to useful civilian projects. It also meant that the president could initiate a new round of disarmament talks.[102]

In the summer of 1929 Hoover met with J. Ramsay MacDonald, the first British prime minister ever to visit the United States, at the president's fishing lodge in Virginia. There, both men agreed to convene another five-power conference on naval reductions in London. Unlike the Conservative government of Stanley Baldwin, which MacDonald replaced in May 1929, MacDonald's Labour government was eager to avert an arms race with the United States and anxious to improve Anglo-American relations. As a step in that direction, MacDonald accepted approximate naval parity with America in all categories of ships.[103]

While the Japanese, for their part, accepted an invitation to the London Conference, they did so after they had made it very clear that they wanted a higher ratio in cruisers, destroyers, and submarines than the capital ship ratio they had accepted at the Washington Conference.[104]

But the key to a successful naval conference lay in the hands of the French. They bluntly stated that they would not agree to naval reductions unless they were given additional security guarantees against Germany. As a starter, the French wanted the United States to assure Britain that American neutral rights would be suspended when members of the League of Nations were acting collectively to deter aggression. They also proposed a Mediterranean security pact, a new and stronger interpretation of Article 16 of the League Covenant, and a general consultative agreement to supplement the Kellogg-Briand Pact. Moreover, the French bluntly stated that they were unwilling to accept parity with Italy, something Mussolini insisted upon.[105]

Under the weight of these obstacles, the London Naval Conference, which opened on January 30, 1930, quickly became stalemated. In an attempt to break the logjam, on March 24 Secretary of State Stimson, who led the American delegation to London, informed the British that the United States would consider signing a consultative pact with France if Britain offered her a stronger security guarantee. While the consultative pact would concern only American neutrality policy in the event France were attacked, Stimson's offer was much more than either Hoover or, in all probability, the Senate was prepared to accept. Stimson, realizing that his proposal had caused the president some embarrassment, assured Hoover that he would not offer any American military commitments, and that he would not even discuss the specific phrasing of a consultative pact until Britain and France had agreed to additional security guarantees and an arms reduction agreement. At the very least, Stimson informed Hoover, his proposal produced some flexibility in the French.[106]

In the end, the London Naval Treaty was signed on April 22, 1930. Among other things, the treaty extended until 1936 the capital ship "holiday" that was formulated at the Washington Conference. It also established for the same period tonnage ratios acceptable to the Japanese: 10:10:6.5 for cruisers, 10:10:7 for destroyers, and parity in submarines. (The ratios broke down to the following tonnage limitations. Heavy cruisers: United States 180,000 tons, Britain 146,800 tons, Japan 108,400 tons. Light cruisers: United States 143,500 tons, Britain 192,200 tons, Japan 100,450 tons. Destroyers: United States and Britain 150,000 tons each, and Japan 105,500 tons. Submarines: 52,700 tons for each nation.) However, because the French and Italians could not agree on their respective ratios, they did not accept limitations on these categories of ships. To safeguard the other naval powers in the event of a Franco-Italian naval race, an "escalator clause" was inserted in the treaty permitting the signatories to exceed the established tonnage levels if their security were adversely affected by construction programs by the nonlimited powers. Yet, although the French and Italians were excluded from the construction limits of the treaty, they were allowed to sign the treaty's other articles, which included a series of regulatory agreements under which the five powers established rules for replacement, scrapping, and conversion of war vessels, and established rules prohibiting unrestricted submarine warfare.[107]

Although weakened by the exclusion of France and Italy from the construction limitations on cruisers, destroyers, and submarines, the London Naval Treaty was a significant step in disarmament history. It was the first time that all categories of warships were restricted by an international agreement. The Hoover administration signed the treaty because, although it did not produce the reductions the president desired, it did promise to stop competitive building in all categories of ships, recognized American parity with Britain, and enabled both the United States and Britain to make substantial cuts in military appropriations. Hoover estimated that the agreement would save the naval powers $2.5 billion and be "a great stimulus to world prosperity."[108]

The treaty encountered only minor opposition in the Senate, where it was approved on July 21 by a vote of 58 to 9. But neither France nor Italy ratified the agreement, so great was the opposition to it in both countries. And while the treaty was ratified by Japan, over the strong opposition of the Japanese navy, which denounced the agreement for keeping the country in a "position of inferiority," ratification triggered considerable domestic violence that contributed to the assassination of the Japanese premier, the fall of his government, and the subsequent militarization of Japan's foreign policy. In the end, the London Naval Treaty did not produce the results it had promised. Because Japan's fleet of cruisers, destroyers, and submarines was below the London limitations, the Japanese kept building these categories of ships. Moreover, France and Italy, excluded from the limitations on these craft, embarked on a naval race. In short, the London Naval Treaty did not end the construction of naval warships, as Hoover had hoped it would.[109]

Nor did it give the French the security they demanded. Before leaving London, Briand reminded Stimson that France did not expect a security guarantee from the United States but only an amendment to the Kellogg-Briand Pact providing for joint consultation in the event of a crisis. The French request was ignored by the Hoover administration. Bills in both houses of Congress, which would have provided for consultation and made American neutrality policy more compatible with European security arrangements, did not receive administration support. While Hoover criticized the French for rejecting arms limitation, he refused to give them even the minimal guarantees that they demanded before they would assume the risks of reducing their armed forces.[110]

Not surprisingly, the French proved difficult to deal with at the World Disarmament Conference that finally convened, after seven years of preparation, in Geneva in February 1932. French Premier André Tardieu proposed the creation of a League-sponsored international military force, to which all states would surrender their offensive weapons. However, the Tardieu plan received little support, not only because it was opposed by states, like the United States and the Soviet Union, that were not members of the League, but because few nations were prepared to turn over their military forces to an international body, League-sponsored or not. Moreover, as in the ill-fated Geneva Protocol, the employment of an international police force required a precise definition of aggression, which few nations, particularly Britain, were prepared to make.[111]

In May 1932, fearing a breakdown in the talks, and abhorring the economic consequences of an arms race during the severe depression, Hoover made what he called some "practicable and far-reaching proposals." They included the reduction of all armies to one-third more than the strength that would be required to maintain internal order. In addition, Hoover called for the abolition of weapons designed essentially for offensive operations--including tanks, chemical weapons, large mobile guns, and bombers. The president also proposed a one-third reduction in battleships and submarines and a 25 percent decrease in aircraft carriers, cruisers, and destroyers. And, in an important departure from the traditional nonentanglement policy of the United States, he approved an August 8 speech by Stimson in which the secretary of state declared that in times of crisis the United States would consult with other nations about the application of American neutral rights in the event that Britain used her navy to enforce League sanctions.[112]

The Hoover proposals, however, went nowhere. France, with the largest army in Europe, again insisted that she would not reduce her forces without additional security guarantees, which neither Britain nor the United States were prepared to make. In the end, the Hoover administration simply could not see how America's strategic interests were related to France's security. The Germans added to the French anxiety by demanding military parity with France. The conference adjourned in stalemate after agreeing to meet again in January 1933, a date that was postponed until June, following the election victory of Franklin D. Roosevelt.[113]

## The Manchurian Crisis

The failure of the World Disarmament Conference and the collapse of the debt-reparations regime were not the only portents of a worsening international situation during the last months of Hoover's presidency. In September 1931 Japanese troops stationed near Mukden in southern Manchuria attacked local Chinese forces. The Mukden affair was the first step in the Japanese conquest of Manchuria, a prelude to their later invasion of China proper. The action of the Japanese army in Manchuria, in violation of the Nine Power Pact, the League of Nations Covenant, and the Kellogg-Briand Pact, was taken without the consent or even foreknowlege of the Japanese government. But as Japan's government was soon to realize, its army increasingly would determine that nation's foreign policies in the decade ahead. The Japanese militarists were convinced that the only way to relieve the chronic economic crisis that gripped their nation as tightly as it did Europe was to make Japan economically self-sufficient by conquering the markets and raw materials of the Far East.[114]

Confronted with problems related to the Great Depression, the West was reluctant to act against the Japanese aggressor. In the first major test of the world collective security system, the League of Nations called for Japanese evacuation of the conquered territory and, when that failed to have any effect, sent an investigating committee to Manchuria that subsequently issued a report (the Lytton Report) that determined that the Japanese action in Manchuria was not in self-defense. But the League refused to take any coercive measures against Japan, not even the implementation of economic sanctions, primarily because both Britain and France did not want to jeopardize their extensive interests in China and elsewhere in the Far East by antagonizing the Japanese militarists.[115]

Nor was the United States prepared to take coercive measures against Japan. While Stimson favored a policy of economic coercion, Hoover rejected economic sanctions because he believed that they would lead to war with Japan in an area he did not believe was vital to American security. Instead of coercion, Hoover and Stimson settled for a policy of not recognizing Japanese territorial conquests. Japan responded by ignoring American nonrecognition, walking out of the League of Nations in 1933, and scrapping the Five Power Naval Treaty in 1936. With good reason, many have regarded the Manchurian Crisis as the opening shot of the Second World War.[116]

## The Legacy of Interwar Republican Foreign Policy

The inauguration of Franklin D. Roosevelt in March 1933 brought to an end twelve years of Republican foreign policy. In that interval the fabric of America's relations with her allies in Europe was badly frayed by her refusal to join the League of Nations and the World Court and to meet European demands for a cancellation of their war debts to the United States. More important, the United States refused to give the Europeans, and particularly the French, security guarantees that, had they been provided, may have averted the catastrophe of the

Second World War. At the very least, an American guarantee may have made unnecessary the vindictive and inflexible policy that France pursued toward Germany during the twenties, a policy that facilitated Hitler's successful assumption of power in 1933. But this is hindsight. As historian Melvyn Leffler points out, "while European stability was important to the United States, it was [considered] neither vital to the security of the nation nor to the survival of the capitalistic system." Americans felt secure behind the two oceans during the twenties and well into the thirties, and until then perceived no threat to the United States from Europe.[117]

As a result, the Republican administrations of this era, which were strongly influenced by the prevailing isolationist and pacifist sentiment, as well as by the dominant probusiness attitude of the predepression twenties, thought they could promote Europe's political stability through expanded American loans, trade, and investments rather than by making military commitments to the Europeans. Accordingly, American bankers and investors were encouraged by the Republican presidents to tackle Europe's economic problems, particularly the German reparations issue. However, while American private loans made possible the continued payment of German reparations payments, and thus Allied debt payments to the United States, the program of American loans to the Germans-- and with it the ability of Germany to make reparations payments--collapsed with the Great Depression, an event that caused American opinion in the thirties to be even less concerned with the problem of maintaining the European balance of power. "Only after the cumulative impact of world depression, totalitarian aggression, and universal conflict," Melvyn Leffler points out, "did American policy makers come to believe that European stability was vital to American well-being."[118]

# 3

# Franklin D. Roosevelt, the Isolationists, and the Aggressors, 1933–1939

## Franklin D. Roosevelt: The Pragmatic Internationalist

As a young man, Franklin D. Roosevelt was an ardent admirer of his distant cousin, Theodore Roosevelt. Like Theodore, Franklin believed that the United States must play a major role in international affairs and that, to do so, America must have a great navy. He had no sympathy, he wrote in 1917, for those who tried to hide behind the Allegheny and Rocky mountains and the "impregnable" Atlantic and Pacific oceans. The oceans were impregnable, he insisted, only if the U.S. Navy controlled them.[1]

But the younger Roosevelt was a Democrat and a supporter of his cousin's archrival, Woodrow Wilson. Named the assistant secretary of the navy by Wilson, Roosevelt became a vigorous advocate of preparedness before America's entrance into World War I. Displaying little sympathy for pacifism, he complained to his wife, Eleanor, that what the country needed was a stronger army and navy "instead of a lot of soft mush about everlasting peace which so many statesmen are handing out to a gullible public."[2]

Franklin Roosevelt, like Theodore, also believed that the United States must also play a major role in maintaining a European balance of power that was increasingly threatened by the growth of German power. He was disgusted when William Jennings Bryan resigned as secretary of state because he feared that Wilson's warnings to Germany about her submarine attacks on passenger ships would lead to American involvement in the war. Roosevelt welcomed Congress' declaration of war because he believed that Germany was a menace not only to Europe but also to the United States.[3]

At first, Roosevelt had little use for Wilson's idealistic world view. But, if he was anything, Roosevelt was flexible, and he was an astute judge of public opinion. Although he continued to berate utopianism, he came to appreciate the importance of dreams and ideals in mobilizing the American people. This helps to explain why, after accompanying Wilson to the Versailles peace conference and, more important, after experiencing the president's tumultuous return to the United States, Roosevelt became a convert to the League of Nations. Instead of seeing it as "a beautiful dream, a Utopia," he now called the League a realistic alternative to the imperialism, militarism, and aggression of the old diplomacy, and a vehicle for bringing about a greater international role for the United States.[4]

It is not surprising, considering Roosevelt's sensitivity to public opinion, that he downplayed the idea of U.S. participation in Wilson's League after the Senate rejected the Treaty of Versailles. Without U.S. membership, he argued, the League had become primarily a forum for dealing with European problems. Yet he really never gave up on the idea of collective security or an effective association of nations to preserve the peace. As late as July 1932 he told a friend that he believed it might be necessary for the United States to join the League in order to preserve world order. And early in his first term he considered sending an American ambassador to the League. But he backed off from both ideas after considering the consequences such a move would have on American opinion, which was still strongly opposed to U.S. entanglement in Europe's affairs. Indeed, during his successful campaign for the presidency in 1932, Roosevelt felt compelled to repudiate the League in order to win the support of American isolationists.[5]

Yet while Roosevelt shared many of Wilson's ideals, he was far more pragmatic and realistic in attempting to achieve them. Unlike Wilson, he was willing to compromise and accept a half a loaf rather than lose everything. Nor could he forget Wilson's humiliation at the hands of the Senate. As a result, he was reluctant--indeed, fearful--of getting too far in front of American opinion. Roosevelt also had a feel for diplomacy, and especially power politics, which Wilson never attained or even pursued. While Roosevelt's employment of power politics was not sophisticated, as historian Robert E. Osgood pointed out, he did "perceive one fact of immense importance, and that was that the domination of either Europe or Asia by a hostile or aggressive power would be a disaster for America's hemispheric security."[6]

Nevertheless, throughout the thirties, Roosevelt experienced considerable difficulty in coping with the threat posed to the global balance of power by aggressive regimes in Germany, Italy, and Japan. As he prepared to take office during the interregnum that followed his election victory in November 1932, Japanese troops, having overrun Manchuria, were advancing toward the Great Wall of China. On January 30, 1933, only five weeks before Roosevelt's inauguration, Adolf Hitler became chancellor of Germany. Within a few weeks after taking power, Hitler took the first steps toward creating a totalitarian regime bent on tearing up the Treaty of Versailles, restoring German military power, and embarking on a program of territorial expansion designed to give Germany *lebensraum* (living space).[7]

## The World Economic Conference

One reason why Roosevelt was unable to deal effectively with the aggressor states during his first term was his preoccupation with the Great Depression. Near starvation, massive unemployment, and business and financial collapse forced foreign relations into a position of secondary importance both to the president and to the American people. The view of Senator Henrik Ship of Minnesota was typical in 1933: "The best way to discourage the dictators is to make our democracy secure by solving our own problems" and "by putting our own house in order." Echoing this sentiment, Roosevelt in his inaugural address said: "I shall spare no effort to restore world trade by international economic readjustment, but the emergency at home cannot wait on that accomplishment."[8]

The first victim of Roosevelt's emphasis on the depression was the World Economic Conference, whose original objectives had been debt reduction, restoration of the international gold standard, and currency stabilization. After agreeing to send a delegation to the conference, Roosevelt took a decidedly nationalist course. He refused to accept the Lausanne formulation for linking diminished reparations to reductions in war debts. And in May 1933 he persuaded Congress to end the convertibility of gold and the dollar, in effect, removing the United States from the gold standard. But the real American "bombshell" for the Europeans was the president's statement of July 3 rejecting the idea of stabilized currencies. His primary motive for torpedoing the World Economic Conference was directly related to his desire to raise domestic prices through monetary inflation, a goal quite opposed to the stabilization of international currencies favored by the Europeans. However, Roosevelt did not see economic nationalism as a viable long-term policy. He hoped that the success of his New Deal monetary and economic policies would enable him to support currency stabilization and lower tariffs at a later date.[9]

The Europeans, however, reacted to the Roosevelt bombshell with shock and anger. The British viewed an inflated American dollar as a major threat to their export trade, while the French saw it as a menace to the gold-backed franc. Faced with American intransigence on the war debt issue and American unilateralism on monetary policy, the World Economic Conference came to an end on July 27 without any notable accomplishments. Perhaps worse, the British and French saw in American economic nationalism the specter of resurgent American political isolationism, for if Europe and and the United States could not cooperate in dealing with economic problems, what prospect was there of coordinating their security policies?[10]

Insult was added to injury the following year, on April 13, 1934, when an isolationist Congress passed the Johnson Debt Default bill. Sponsored by the old irreconcilable, Senator Hiram Johnson of California, the act prohibited American citizens from making loans to governments of nations in default to the United States. Although Roosevelt did not publicly urge Congress to adopt the bill, neither did he publicly oppose it. The fact is, he needed the support of progressive isolationists, like Hiram Johnson, for his New Deal programs, and he did not want to lose it over the debt question, on which the isolationists enjoyed overwhelming public support. But, as historian Frederick W. Marks III has pointed out, while Roosevelt struck one pose with the Congress, he privately took another one with the British and the French. To both, he suggested that he would not object if they repaid nothing or made only a token repayment. In this way, Marks argues, "FDR eased the path of their default." In the long run, Roosevelt paid for his short-term pragmatism and duplicity. His economic nationalism alienated the Europeans, strengthened isolationist sentiment in America, and made it impossible for him to do anything effective to check the aggressor states before they led the world, and ultimately the United States, into a second global conflict.[11]

## The Failure of the Geneva Disarmament Conference

To be sure, Roosevelt did not neglect the problem of international security while trying to deal with the domestic effects of the depression. He came out strongly for disarmament, not only because he believed it could reduce international tensions but because the disarmament movement was popular in America. Nevertheless, Roosevelt was not naive; he had legitimate doubts about Hitler's willingness to accept German disarmament. However, should the disarmament movement fail, he wanted the odium for its failure to fall squarely on the Nazi dictator, not on the United States.[12]

As a result, soon after Roosevelt entered the White House, he initiated a vigorous effort to instill life into the floundering Geneva Disarmament Conference. He heartily endorsed the proposal of British Prime Minister J. Ramsay MacDonald to abolish gradually offensive weapons, including gas, heavy mobile artillery, airplanes, and tanks. Said Roosevelt: "If all nations will agree wholly to eliminate from possession and use the weapons which make possible a successful attack, defenses automatically will become impregnable, and the frontiers and independence of every nation will become secure." The MacDonald plan also called for equality of armaments within five years for France, Germany, Poland, and Italy, with each allowed 200,000 men in their continental armies. France would have the right to an additional 200,000 men for her overseas possessions, while Italy could have an additional 50,000 men for that purpose. In addition, a disarmament commission would be established to supervise implementation of the plan with full power of investigation. In an attempt to satisfy French security concerns, the MacDonald plan called for consultation between the signatories of the Kellogg-Briand Pact if the disarmament pact were violated.[13]

To reinforce the MacDonald plan, the Roosevelt administration also announced that it would not impede European collective security efforts. In May, Norman Davis, the U.S. delegate to the Disarmament Conference, stated that America was prepared "to consult with other states in case of a threat to the peace," and "to refrain from any action tending to defeat the collective effort . . . to restore peace." The administration, however, took much of the value out of Davis' pledge by also stating that it would not join in implementing any program of economic sanctions. In spite of this qualification, many regarded the administration's announcement as the most significant American contribution to preserving world peace since World War I.[14]

Unfortunately for the administration, Roosevelt's plan for American cooperation with European collective security became entangled with an arms embargo resolution that he had sent to Congress in March. The resolution, which would have empowered the president to decide when and against whom American arms shipments would be embargoed, was a major departure from the traditional policy of impartiality toward belligerents and freedom of the seas for American traders and travelers during wartime. Roosevelt favored the measure because he wanted control over trade to belligerents, not only to deter aggression, but also to prevent the United States from being dragged into a war by special interests. The House passed the resolution by a two-thirds majority. But the isolationist-dominated Senate Foreign Relations Committee, fearing the consequences of the Davis pledge on continued American neutrality, attached to the administration's arms embargo bill an emasculating amendment drafted by Hiram Johnson. The Johnson amendment required that, in the event of war, an arms embargo must be applied to all belligerents, thereby denying the president the discretionary power to embargo only the aggressors and not their victims. Johnson's amendment, in effect, changed a collective security measure into an isolationist one. However, because Roosevelt wanted the continued support of progressive isolationists like Johnson, he at first accepted the amendment. But after Secretary of State Cordell Hull argued that acceptance of the Johnson amendment would nullify the Davis pledge, Roosevelt agreed to kill the arms embargo resolution. The president's retreat was an early indication of the influence congressional isolationists would have on the conduct of the administration's foreign policy in the years ahead.[15]

Growing isolationist sentiment in the United States, however, was not the primary reason for the failure of disarmament in the thirties. The fact is, Hitler had no intention of keeping Germany disarmed. Without rearmament, there was no way he could achieve the conquests he envisioned. Yet with Germany still too militarily weak to preclude a preventive war by France, the Nazi leader went through the motions of favoring disarmament while Germany secretly rearmed. Rather than rejecting disarmament outright, he instead demanded immediate equality of armaments with France--in other words, German rearmament and French arms reduction--and rejected the idea of inspection, which would have revealed the extent of the massive German rearmament effort. Not unexpectedly, the French as well as the British rejected the German demand. Fearing that further German participation in the conference might expose the extent of Germany's rearmament program, in October 1933 Hitler called home his delegation and, for good measure, withdrew Germany from the League of Nations.[16]

But the United States does not escape responsibility for the failure of the Geneva Conference. Before Hitler's withdrawal, Britain's foreign secretary, Sir John Simon, wanted to force the disarmament issue by exposing Germany's rearmament program. But he was dissuaded from doing so by Norman Davis, the U.S. delegate, who feared "a new Treaty of Versailles." Moreover, after Hitler withdrew from the conference, Roosevelt instructed Davis to declare publicly that the United States was at Geneva only to discuss disarmament and was not interested "in the political element or any purely European aspect of the picture." As a result, there would be no effort to coerce the Germans to return to the conference or to abandon their rearmament effort. Concluded Neville Chamberlain, the British chancellor of the exchequer, "The Americans are chiefly anxious to convince their people that they are not going to be drawn into doing anything helpful for the rest of the world."[17]

# The Destruction of the Versailles System

While the Geneva Disarmament Conference dragged on, with Davis and the British hoping that Hitler could be persuaded to return to the negotiating table, any prospect that he would do so was obliterated in March 1935. In that month, in violation of the disarmament clauses of the Treaty of Versailles, Hitler announced the formation of a German air force and his intention to increase the size of the German army to 550,000 men. The following year, on March 7, 1936, Hitler violated not only the Versailles Treaty but also the Locarno agreements by sending German troops into the demilitarized Rhineland.[18]

Ironically, Britain and France permitted Hitler to knock down the the last foundations of the interwar treaty structure. However, although France was still stronger militarily than Germany, she was also politically unstable, economically weak, deeply divided on social and economic issues, and intensely fearful of another war. Consequently, the French refused to force a German withdrawal from the Rhineland. The British, for their part, were neither prepared for war nor willing to fight one over territory in Germany's "own back garden." In fact, the British pressured the French to take no retaliatory actions against the Germans. Meanwhile, the United States remained entirely aloof during the crisis. In the end, the French lost more than the protection offered by a demilitarized Rhineland; they also lost an ally. With the demise of the Locarno Treaty, to which Belgium was a party, the Belgians announced that they would follow a policy of "independence." The loss of Belgium as an ally, combined with Hitler's occupation of the Rhineland, made France even more dependent on Britain in dealing with the German threat.[19]

Not surprisingly, then, the French were shocked when the British on June 18, 1935, signed a treaty with Hitler permitting Germany to build a surface fleet 35 percent of the size of the British Commonwealth's navy. The agreement also recognized the right of Germany to possess 45 percent of the submarines possessed by Britain. The French, who were not consulted in advance about the Anglo-German naval agreement and its abolition of the naval clauses of the Versailles Treaty, felt betrayed by their former ally. In Berlin, U.S. Ambassador William Dodd wrote Roosevelt: "This is the first time . . . in modern history that England has sided with a threatening imperialist power, rather than guide a combination of weaker powers against the threatening one."[20]

Roosevelt, while discouraged by the absence of any meaningful Anglo-French efforts to check Hitler's actions, was himself at a loss as to what to do. In March 1935 he had privately considered proposing the formation of an anti-German bloc that would include England, France, Italy, Belgium, Holland, Poland, and possibly Russia. To Secretary of the Treasury Henry Morgenthau he suggested that these countries should conclude a ten-year disarmament agreement and then ask the Germans for their adherence. If Hitler refused to comply, Roosevelt believed the nations of Europe should blockade Germany into submission. He insisted that he could authorize U.S. participation in such a blockade without congressional approval because recognition of a blockade was a traditional power of the executive branch. If the blockade did not succeed, Roosevelt believed that war would result. In the opinion of historian William E. Kinsella, the president abandoned the blockade idea because both Britain and France were unwilling to take a stand against Hitler. But another historian, Robert Dallek, believes that Roosevelt was less interested in the idea as a workable proposal than he was in making it known that he wanted to act against the aggressors.[21]

## Another World Court Rejection

Yet most Americans, and especially the Senate, were opposed to a stronger U.S. role against the aggressors. This was demonstrated once again in 1935, after Roosevelt revived the question of American membership on the World Court. The president had resurrected the Court issue because he believed that, with isolationist influence as strong as it was, supporting Court membership was just about the only thing he could do to promote the cause of world peace. Moreover, it appeared that popular support for the Court was overwhelming and, with the Democrats holding sixty-nine out of the Senate's ninety-six seats, the two-thirds majority that was needed for ratification would not be impossible to achieve.[22]

But Roosevelt's request for U.S. membership on the Court produced a storm of opposition from isolationists. The Detroit "radio priest," Father Charles Coughlin, called the Court, like the League, the tool of international bankers and "plutocrats" who would use it to drag the United States into wars to preserve their investments. "I am a believer in democracy and will have nothing to do with the poisonous European mess," declared Senator Homer T. Bone of Washington. "To hell with Europe and the rest of those nations!" Minnesota's Senator Thomas D. Schall announced. Prompted by sentiment like this, as well as by a deluge of telegram opposition generated by Coughlin and the Hearst newspapers, only fifty-two senators voted in favor of Court membership--seven short of the required two-thirds majority. The defeat strengthened Roosevelt's belief that there was very little that he could do in cooperation with Britain and France to check the aggressor nations. Shortly after the Senate's action, he predicted, "We shall go through a period of noncooperation [with Europe] in everything for the next year or two."[23]

Still, in the opinion of some historians, the president himself must bear a large share of the responsibility for the Senate's rejection of the World Court. At the height of his popularity, Roosevelt nevertheless was easily intimidated by the isolationists and, as a consequence, refused to take the lead in pushing the Court through the Senate. The rejection of the World Court had a direct impact on America's foreign policy. It dispirited internationalists while it encouraged isolationists to take even bolder actions to ensure American neutrality in another European conflict, all of which would tie the president's hands even more than he had believed possible.[24]

# The Disintegration of the Washington System

While the attempt to cut land armaments in Europe was failing at Geneva, the effort begun in 1922 to reduce navies also faltered. Because the U.S. Navy had declined far below the ceilings established by the Washington and London naval treaties, while the Japanese navy remained at the treaties' limits, Japan's total naval tonnage had reached 80 percent of America's. To redress the imbalance, in June 1933 Roosevelt allocated $238 million in public works funds for the construction of thirty-two ships totaling 120,000 tons. When added to five ships of 17,000 tons already provided for by the Congress, the total amounted to a threefold increase in allocated construction costs, the largest building program since 1916. The following year, Roosevelt augmented this initial effort by fully supporting the Vinson-Trammel bill, which when passed in March 1934 authorized funds to bring the Navy to the limits of the Washington and London naval treaties by 1942.[25]

The president's naval construction program was also motivated by a desire to check Japanese aggression in the Far East. In May 1933 Japan withdrew from the League of Nations to protest that body's condemnation of the Japanese conquest of Manchuria. More ominously, in the following year, during preparatory discussions for another naval reduction conference that would take place in London during 1935, the Japanese insisted that they must have naval equality with Britain and the United States. The practical effect of the Japanese proposal would have been to reduce relative British and American power in the Pacific, leaving Japan a virtual free hand to expand in the Far East. While Roosevelt was prepared to reduce the existing naval ceiling as much as 20 percent, if the other parties agreed to do so also, he firmly insisted that he would not accept Japanese naval equality.[26]

But the British at first wavered in their support for Roosevelt's stand. Preoccupied with growing German military power in Europe, and with a Far Eastern empire increasingly vulnerable to rising Japanese militarism, the British were most anxious to avoid offending Japan. When Roosevelt suspected that they would attempt to mediate a revision of the Washington naval ratio in favor of Japan, he told his chief delegate, Norman Davis: "If Great Britain is even suspected of preferring to play with Japan to playing with us, I shall be compelled, in the interest of American security, to approach public sentiment in Canada, Australia, New Zealand, and South Africa in a definite effort to make these Dominions understand clearly that their future security is linked with us in the United States." But the president did not have to carry out his threat. Prime Minister MacDonald disavowed any intention of making a separate deal with the Japanese. Instead, Britain joined the United States in pressing Japan for a continuation of the existing treaties.[27]

Confronted with Anglo-American opposition to Japanese naval equality, in December 1934 Japan gave formal notice that, effective two years later, she would no longer be a party to the Five Power Naval Treaty. And although Britain, the United States, France, and Italy signed a new naval treaty on March 25, 1936, without Japanese adherence, it proved stillborn. Taking advantage of escalator clauses in the treaty, in 1936 Roosevelt requested the largest peacetime naval appropriations in American history. But it was another two years before Congress passed the second Vinson bill, which authorized a twenty percent increase in the size of the Navy. The delay was largely due to an American reluctance to provoke the Japanese into a naval race, Japan's success in keeping secret the size of the naval construction program she had begun in 1936, and Congress' desire to balance the budget during the recession of 1937. As a result, until 1940, when the American naval buildup reached high gear, the Japanese were ahead in the naval construction race.[28]

# The First Neutrality Act, 1935

The failure of the disarmament movement prompted some Americans to look for villains. In 1934 two books, *Merchants of Death* by H. C. Englebrecht and F. C. Hanighen, and *Iron, Blood, and Profits* by George Seldes, placed the blame for the failure to end the arms race on the munitions industry, which they accused of lobbying against disarmament efforts and promoting wars to guarantee profits. Prompted by the public outrage created by the two books, and by pressure from pacifist groups, a Senate committee was set up to investigate the impact of the arms industry on America's foreign policy. Chaired by isolationist Republican Senator Gerald P. Nye of North Dakota, the committee found that the munitions companies had lobbied extensively and at times "resorted to a form of bribery of government officials or of their close friends in order to secure business." Moreover, the Nye Committee reported, the munitions makers had made enormous profits during the war. While the committee conceded that the evidence did "not show that wars have been started solely because of the activities of munitions makers and their agents," it insisted that it was "against the peace of the world for selfishly interested organizations to be left free to goad and frighten nations into military activity."[29]

The growing suspicion that sinister forces were behind America's entrance into the First World War was reinforced by a number of revisionist histories that appeared in the thirties. Among the most influential was Walter Millis' *Road to War: America, 1914-1917,* which argued that the primary reason why the United States entered the war was to preserve economic interests in Britain and France-- primarily trade and loans. Shocked by the revelations of the Nye Committee and the work of revisionist historians, many Americans were more convinced than ever that the United States should not become involved with foreign problems.[30]

Roosevelt apparently was sympathetic to the view that bankers and munitions makers needed regulation, and he even admitted that William Jennings Bryan had been right in favoring legislation to prevent U.S. citizens from sailing on belligerent ships. Consequently, he cooperated with the Nye Committee, giving it access to the documents it requested, including even income tax returns. And, much to his later regret, and against Hull's advice, Roosevelt even encouraged the Nye Committee to consider neutrality revision, a subject that was not within its original jurisdiction. Roosevelt hoped that, by cooperating with the committee, he would gain its support for an arms embargo bill that would give him discretionary power to prohibit the sale of arms to aggressor nations, while allowing arms sales to continue to their victims.[31]

But the isolationists refused to give Roosevelt the discretionary power he wanted. They feared that America partiality in applying an arms embargo would lead inevitably to retribution against U.S. interests by the slighted party, with the result that the American people would be dragged into a war they did want. Consequently, the isolationists introduced a resolution that required the president, whenever he proclaimed a state of war to exist, to declare an arms embargo against all belligerents, without distinction. It also gave him the authority to warn Americans that they could take passage on belligerent ships only at their own risk. While the embargo covered arms, ammunition, and implements of war as defined by the president, it did not prohibit the shipment of food, raw materials, or other categories of manufactured goods--all of which would be important to a belligerent in a long conflict. The neutrality bill passed both houses of Congress in August, even though Roosevelt argued that their "inflexible provisions might drag us into war instead of keeping us out." Nevertheless, the president signed the bill on August 31, after the Congress agreed to his request to limit the bill's duration to six months.[32]

## Ethiopia

The first Neutrality Act met its initial test only five weeks after passage by Congress. On October 3, 1935, Italian troops invaded Ethiopia as a first step in Benito Mussolini's bid to create an African empire. Four days later the League of Nations Council formally declared that the Italian attack constituted an act of aggression requiring the implementation of sanctions against Italy. Soon thereafter, the League voted to prohibit arms shipments, loans, and credits to Italy, and then placed a ban on Italian imports. While some exports to Italy were also prohibited, coal, steel, and oil exports were not.[33]

The Roosevelt administration refused outright to cooperate with the League sanctions. The president feared not only isolationist sentiment but also the influence of the powerful Italian-American lobby, which opposed any action against Mussolini's Ethiopian adventure. In fact, to preclude the possibility that the League would ask the United States to participate in the sanctions, on October 5 the administration invoked the new Neutrality Act. Arms exports to both countries were prohibited and Americans were warned to refrain from travel on ships of either belligerent. In addition, Hull released a statement by the president warning Americans who engaged in trade with either belligerent that they did so at their own risk.[34]

At the same time, however, both Roosevelt and Hull realized that the embargo would hurt Ethiopia, the victim of aggression, more than the aggressor, Italy. As a result, the administration called on American exporters to participate in a voluntary "moral embargo" on the export to Italy of oil, steel, and other vital warmaking materials, all of which were not affected by the Neutrality Act. Yet, in spite of the administration's pleas, the moral embargo proved to be a resounding failure because U.S. exports to Italy, particularly oil, increased dramatically in October 1935, seemingly substantiating the thesis of the Nye Committee that businessmen were more interested in profits than peace.[35]

But American businessmen were not the only collaborators of Mussolini. Neither Britain nor France, and especially the latter, was prepared to risk alienating the Italian dictator, whom they hoped to keep unaligned with Hitler, by crippling the Italian war effort. France had just concluded an agreement with Italy that provided joint military action in the event either was attacked by Germany. While the British were now more eager than the French to preserve the League, they nevertheless refused to close the Suez Canal to Italian shipping, a move that most certainly would have terminated Mussolini's Ethiopian venture. In early December 1935 French Foreign Minister Pierre Laval worked out a proposal with Britain's foreign secretary, Sir Samuel Hoare, which would have ceded to Italy large parts of Ethiopia and designated the remainder of that country an Italian sphere of influence. However, when the Hoare-Laval plan was leaked to the press, the public outcry it produced in Britain and France compelled both Hoare and Laval to resign and the governments of both nations to repudiate their scheme.[36]

Faced with no effective opposition from either the West or Ethiopia, the Italians completed their conquest of that nation in May 1936. Ethiopian Emperor Haile Selassie fled to Geneva, where he pleaded in vain before the League of Nations for assistance for his country. However, on July 4 the League voted to end its sanctions against Italy. As in Manchuria, the League in Ethiopia proved to be ineffective in preventing or punishing aggression. Its failure convinced Roosevelt that a general war was probable.[37]

But while it was easy to blame others--particularly Britain and France--for the collapse of the collective security system, the United States also played a role in its failure. Three weeks before the League terminated its sanctions against Italy, the administration ended its embargo. While Roosevelt had preferred to see the Italian venture in Ethiopia fail, he had not been prepared to align the United States with Britain and France in an effort to help it do so. Roosevelt, historian David Schmitz argues, was anxious to prevent the Ethiopian conflict from triggering a world war; as a result, he was determined to maintain a friendly relationship with Mussolini, whom the president believed was a moderating influence on Hitler.[38]

To be sure, even if Roosevelt had been inclined to take vigorous action against Italy, his hands would have been tied by isolationist sentiment in the Congress and in the country. Rather than attempting to cooperate with the Western powers to prevent further acts of aggression, the Congress passed a new neutrality act in February 1936 that was designed to close the loopholes in the first act. The new act, which would expire on May 1, 1937, added a ban on loans to belligerent governments and made mandatory, rather than discretionary, the application of an arms embargo on states entering a war already in progress. Roosevelt, who again was denied the powers he believed he needed to discriminate between aggressors and their victims, signed the bill on February 29 without comment. With his New Deal program still incomplete, and with a presidential election approaching in the fall, he believed there was nothing more that he could do to challenge the isolationist hold on the Congress and American public opinion.[39]

# The Spanish Civil War

No sooner did the war in Ethiopia end than another erupted, this time in Spain. The Spanish turmoil was directly related to the overthrow of the monarchy and the establishment of a republic in 1931. As the result of a parliamentary election in February 1936, control of the republican government was won by a popular-front coalition of socialists, liberals, and communists. The new government was anathema to the Spanish Right, which included conservatives, monarchists, fascists, the armed forces, and the Catholic Church. A rebellion of army units in Spanish Morocco in July 1936 triggered a bloody civil war that would last three years before the forces of the Right under General Francisco Franco gained control of the country.[40]

The Spanish Civil War served as a prelude to the approaching global conflict. Both Italy and Germany intervened quickly, and probably decisively, on the side of Franco. Some 50,000 Italian troops and 10,000 German soldiers and airmen saw action in Spain. The republican or "Loyalist" side, on the other hand, received considerable--but, as it turned out, insufficient--support from the Soviet Union in the form of supplies and weapons. While the French popular-front government of Léon Blum wanted to aid the republicans, it was blocked in its effort to do so by the French Right, which opposed the anticlericalism and communist leanings of the Loyalists, and by the British government, which warned France that if war with Germany resulted because of French intervention in Spain, Britain would not come to France's assistance. As a result, both Britain and France signed a nonintervention agreement that significantly reduced Western aid to the Loyalists.[41]

The Spanish Civil War also divided many Americans. Conservatives and Catholics opposed the republican side for its anticlericalism and close ties to Moscow. The American Left, on the other hand, saw the civil war as an epic struggle between democracy, embodied in the republican forces, and fascism, represented by the rebels. But most Americans were not concerned about the conflict in Spain. What they wanted most of all was to ensure that the United States would not become involved in the struggle.[42]

Roosevelt's attitude was fully in line with this sentiment. With a presidential election approaching in the fall, he was determined to do nothing to challenge prevailing isolationist sentiment nor alienate the pro-Franco, American Catholic vote. However, in the opinion of historian Douglas Little, even more important in the president's consideration was the assumed threat to American economic interests in Spain from the leftist republican government. Accordingly, on August 7, 1936, Hull notified American diplomats and consular agents in Spain that, while the administration had no authority to embargo arms to belligerents in a civil war, it hoped that U.S. citizens would "scrupulously refrain from any interference whatsoever in the unfortunate Spanish situation." One week later, in a memorable speech at Chautauqua, New York, Roosevelt reaffirmed his opposition to American involvement in European conflicts, including civil wars. "I have seen war," he told his audience. "I hate war." He concluded: "We can keep out of a war if those who watch and decide possess the courage to say 'no' to those who selfishly or unwisely would let us go to war."[43]

However, in January 1937, after Roosevelt was overwhelmingly reelected to a second term, he asked the Congress for discretionary power to apply arms embargoes during a civil war. But after the Congress refused to give him a free hand in the matter, he asked for a mandatory arms embargo applied exclusively to Spain. Roosevelt realized that the arms embargo would hurt the Loyalists more than the rebels, but he did not want to undermine the Anglo-French policy of nonintervention, which was designed to prevent the Spanish conflict from escalating into a world war. The Congress granted this request with only one dissenting vote on January 6. However, by June 1937 Roosevelt was willing to extend the embargo to include Germany and Italy because, through their assistance to Franco, they had become cobelligerents in the conflict. But he decided not to do so after he was advised by his ambassador in London, Robert W. Bingham, that an embargo on Germany and Italy would probably require one on Russia and France as well, both of which were sending supplies to the Loyalists. Moreover, Acting Secretary of State William Phillips warned that U.S. recognition of a state of war between Italy and Spain might "spread the conflict beyond the Spanish frontier" and even escalate into a wider European conflict. Prompted by this advice, Roosevelt decided to leave American policy unchanged. In effect, like the British, Roosevelt was willing to accept Franco's victory to prevent a world war. Without Western help to counter the German and Italian aid received by Franco, the Loyalist cause collapsed with the fall of Madrid on March 28, 1939. Four days later, Roosevelt recognized the Franco government and terminated the U.S. embargo.[44]

Franco's victory emboldened the aggressors. Drawn together by their common goal of helping the Spanish fascists, in October 1936 Hitler and Mussolini signed a treaty that came to be known as the Axis Pact. Although not yet an alliance, the pact pledged both states to collaboration in various political matters, including the Spanish Civil War, and particularly the suppression of international communism. On November 25, 1936, Japan aligned herself loosely to Germany by concluding the Anti-Comintern Pact. Publicly this agreement committed Japan to the Axis struggle against world communism. But a secret provision of the pact also obliged each party to refrain from concluding any agreement with the Soviet Union that would impair the other's interests. While not a formal alliance, the Anti-Comintern Pact did help to reduce the possibility that the Soviet Union would play a major role in checking the aggressive designs of Germany, a development that did not go unnoticed in Paris and London. When Mussolini joined this treaty a year later, the Rome-Berlin-Tokyo Axis was completed.[45]

Some historians have faulted Roosevelt's timidity during the Spanish crisis. Howard Jablon has argued that Roosevelt "was too much the politician intent on preserving good will, and not enough the leader willing to sacrifice his popularity for the national interest." Refusing to consider the consequences of allowing the Axis powers to win in Spain, Jablon adds, "Roosevelt joined the master chefs of appeasement and served another morsel to the voracious Axis appetite." In Jablon's opinion, Roosevelt should have placed the Axis threat ahead of his domestic priorities and challenged the isolationists in Congress by going over their heads and appealing directly to public opinion. His refusal to do, Jablon argues, left him vulnerable to the isolationists on the neutrality issue.[46]

# The 1937 Neutrality Act

The passage of the Spanish embargo in January 1937 was the prelude to a more extensive, and ostensibly permanent, neutrality revision later that year. The original Neutrality Act, which had been extended in 1936, was due to expire on May 1. Its basic features--an impartial arms embargo, a ban on travel, and the prohibition of loans to belligerent governments--were not in question. What was debatable was the extent to which the nation's export trade in goods other than arms should be sacrificed if war broke out in Europe. As Senator Borah sarcastically put it: "We seek to avoid all risks, all dangers, but we [must] make certain to get all the profits." The so-called cash-and-carry provision, fashioned by financier Bernard M. Baruch, appeared to meet these requirements. Baruch graphically described cash-and-carry this way: "We will sell to any belligerent anything except lethal weapons, but the terms are 'cash on the barrel-head and come and get it.'"[47]

Roosevelt supported Baruch's idea for a number of reasons. First, he thought it was the best proposal that he could get enacted by a Congress dominated by isolationists and infuriated with him for his effort that year to "pack"--or increase the membership of--the Supreme Court. At the same time, public opinion polls, which were just coming into widespread use in 1937, indicated that the American people believed that the Congress rather than the president should determine the nation's neutrality policy. But most important, Roosevelt realized that cash-and-carry would enable the United States to help Britain and France, whose navies would control the seas if war broke out with Germany.[48]

Congressional sentiment also supported the cash-and-carry plan. Senator Nye endorsed the idea as a reasonable alternative to a total embargo on trade with belligerents, which he preferred, but which he also realized could not be enacted. On the other hand, extreme nationalists, like Senators Borah and Johnson, protested that cash-and-carry amounted to a cowardly abandonment of America's traditional neutral rights. They insisted that the United States should stand firmly for freedom of the seas in time of war, and should not, as Johnson said, "sell goods and then hide." Borah also contended that cash-and-carry would favor the Japanese, whose navy dominated the western Pacific, thereby undermining the Open Door policy in China.[49]

But Congress was not swayed by these arguments. By April 30 both houses had passed the revised neutrality bill, and the next day, Roosevelt signed it into law. The new act required that, if the president proclaimed the existence of a state of war between other nations, or a civil war that endangered the peace of the United States, the shipment of arms, ammunition, and implements of war, excluding raw materials, would be embargoed. In addition, loans to belligerents were banned, but not short-term commercial credits, travel on belligerent ships was prohibited, as was the arming of American merchant ships trading with belligerents. And, finally, the law contained the cash-and-carry provision, but it was limited to a two-year period.[50]

In the end, the Neutrality Act of 1937 proved to be, in the words of historian Robert A. Divine, "a haphazard compromise which failed to establish a clear-cut neutrality policy for the nation." On the one hand, Divine explained, "the United

States would abstain from the arms trade and refuse to finance foreign wars, but at the same time it would supply the basic sinews of modern warfare to any nation able to buy and ship the goods itself." As events would prove, the act did little to discourage the aggressors. Nor did it guarantee that the United States would remain uninvolved in foreign wars. Many predicted that, if war erupted in Europe, the same type of economic links that had existed between the United States and the Allies during World War I was likely to be forged again.[51]

## The Sino-Japanese War

The first test of the new Neutrality Act occurred in the Far East. On July 7, 1937 Japanese troops stationed in North China, under the terms of the Boxer Protocol of 1900, clashed with elements of the Chinese army near the Marco Polo Bridge, ten miles west of Beijing. Apparently unpremeditated, the incident quickly became the initial engagement of an all-out Japanese invasion of China. By the end of the month, Beijing was occupied and in the following month Shanghai was attacked. Though neither side declared war--or even suspended diplomatic relations--the prelude to the coming Pacific conflict had begun.[52]

The new Neutrality Act required the president to implement its provisions when a state of war existed. But since war was not declared by either Japan or China, Roosevelt chose not to invoke the act. He realized that the imposition of the embargo would hurt China more than Japan, since the Chinese were almost entirely dependent on arms imports while the Japanese were largely self-sufficient in weapons. When it became clear that the Neutrality Act would not be implemented, isolationists and pacifists reacted angrily. Senators Nye and Bennett Clark issued a public statement on August 18 that reminded the president that the purpose of the Neutrality Act was not to favor one side or the other but to keep America out of war. Twenty-five members of the House signed a statement demanding the immediate application of the arms embargo in order to "stop feeding the war which means destruction of thousands of lives in the Orient and the danger of war to all the world." Roosevelt reacted to the criticism that he was nullifying the Neutrality Act by declaring that the administration would not permit any American ship to carry arms to either China or Japan. Yet he permitted American munitions to reach China via British ships destined for Hong Kong. While this was technically legal, as well as popular, it did violate the spirit of the Neutrality Act.[53]

Emboldened by his successful circumvention of the Neutrality Act, in the fall of 1937 Roosevelt made his first major attempt to mobilize American opinion against the Axis. On October 5, in a speech delivered in Chicago, the president dramatically ended his public silence on the Far Eastern crisis. With forceful words Roosevelt described the breakdown of peace as an "epidemic of world lawlessness" caused by 10 percent of the planet's population. "When an epidemic of physical disease starts to spread," he continued, "the community joins in a quarantine of patients in order to protect the health of the community against the spread of the disease." Although Roosevelt did not spell out explicit measures for quarantining the aggressors, he did call for "a concerted effort" to restrain countries "creating a state of international anarchy and instability." He added, "there is no escape through mere isolation or neutrality."[54]

However, as historian Frederick Marks points out, there was no other action to back up the president's words. Indeed, the next day Roosevelt told reporters that the word "quarantine" implied no coercive intent. As a result, French Premier Camille Chautemps was prompted to complain to William Bullitt, U.S. ambassador to Paris: "You Americans from time to time talk as if you really intended to act in the international sphere when you have no intention of acting in any way that can be effective. . . . Such a policy on the part of the United States merely leads the dictatorships to believe that the democracies are full of words but are unwilling to back their words by force, and force is the only thing that counts today in the world."[55]

Still, the quarantine speech, as it was so labeled by the press, was addressed primarily to the American people, not the Europeans. As such, it did represent a change in Roosevelt's attitude, if not yet his policy, toward the aggressors. The previous year, at Chautauqua, he had spoken as an isolationist, even as a pacifist. However, at Chicago he was able to reemphasize the internationalist sentiments he had submerged since 1935. His decision to do so was not only a result of his growing concern for the Axis threat. It was also due to the fact that, despite the recession of 1937, the economic emergency seemed to be easing and, with the New Deal running out of steam, Roosevelt was no longer as dependent on progressive-isolationist support as he was in his first term. While the speech produced a loud outcry from isolationists, the president did not seem disturbed. Public opinion, at least editorial opinion, appeared supportive. In a letter to Colonel House, Roosevelt wrote that the speech was part of a gradual process of educating the American people to the dangers of isolation, which, he added, "seems to be working slowly but surely."[56]

However, Under Secretary of State Sumner Welles believed the president had to do more than wait for public opinion to change. On October 6, the day after the quarantine speech, Welles suggested to Roosevelt that he call a world conference in Washington to deal with problems of international conduct, disarmament, and trade. Welles' proposal was designed to prevent war by persuading the Germans to abandon economic autarchy, a policy Hitler was pursuing in order to make Germany self-sufficient during war. Roosevelt, who had been considering an international conference for months, approved the Welles plan. It would enable him to do something dramatic that would draw public attention to the problem of preserving peace, yet would not directly challenge the prevailing isolationist sentiment.[57]

But before Roosevelt could implement the Welles plan, events in the Far East took a decided turn for the worse. On December 12 Japanese aircraft bombed an American gunboat, the *Panay,* on the Yangtze River in China. The administration, which believed the attack was no accident, demanded and received an explanation and apology from Japan. While Roosevelt accepted the Japanese response, encouraged by the angry reaction of the American public to the *Panay* incident, he proposed to British Ambassador Sir Ronald Lindsay, in the event of another Japanese "outrage," the implementation of a joint, long-distance, Anglo-American "peaceful blockade" of the Japanese home islands, one that would deny

Japan the raw materials she needed to continue her war with China. The president believed the blockade could be conducted covertly and denied as official policy if it became public knowledge. A blockade of Japan was clearly what Roosevelt had in mind in the quarantine speech but dared not say so publicly. But while the British were prepared to conduct a joint naval maneuver to impress the Japanese, they were not about to consider a blockade of Japan. Nevertheless, in December both sides did agree to conduct secret naval staff talks the following month, the result of which was the first plan for joint cooperation in the event either country became embroiled in a war with Japan. The following March three American cruisers were sent to Britain's new naval base at Singapore. More important, in April 1939 the bulk of the U.S. fleet--including twelve battleships and four carriers--was transferred to the Pacific.[58]

## The Ludlow Amendment

Although the isolationists were unaware of Roosevelt's proposals for joint Anglo-American naval cooperation, the president's forceful response to the *Panay* incident reinforced their fears of U.S. involvement in an extrahemispheric war. Their fear prompted renewed support for a constitutional amendment, first proposed in 1935 by Representative Louis Ludlow, an Indiana Democrat, which would have required a nationwide referendum before Congress could declare war-- except if the United States were attacked first. By placing the decision for war in the hands of the people, Ludlow intended to ensure that no president could ever lead the nation into war against their will. However, until the *Panay* incident, the Ludlow amendment had been tied up in the House Judiciary Committee. But as a result of the *Panay* attack, Ludlow was able to obtain the required number of signatures for a House vote on a discharge petition designed to permit debate on the proposed amendment.[59]

The Roosevelt administration was horrified by the implications of the Ludlow amendment. Shortly before the vote on the discharge resolution on January 10, 1938, Speaker of the House William Bankhead read a letter from the president in which Roosevelt called the Ludlow amendment "impracticable in its application and incompatible with our representative form of government." He also stated that the proposed amendment "would cripple any president in his conduct of our foreign relations, and it would encourage other nations to believe that they could violate American rights with impunity." Under extreme pressure from the administration, the House voted to defeat the discharge resolution, but only by the narrow margin of 209 to 188. The "size of the minority," British Ambassador Lindsay reported to the Foreign Office, "shows that isolationist elements are impressively strong."[60]

Yet the close vote on the Ludlow amendment did not dissuade Roosevelt from launching a campaign to prepare the nation's defenses and the American people for a war he thought was more and more probable. On January 28, 1938, in a special message to Congress, he called defense expenditures "inadequate for national security." He added that, in the absence of international disarmament, the nation needed armed forces strong enough to "keep any potential enemy many hundred miles away from our continental limits." Accordingly, he recommended increasing by 20 percent the existing naval building program and called for appropriations to lay down two additional battleships and two additional cruisers during 1938.[61]

Although there was some debate about the president's defense program, Congress went along with his requests. While isolationists opposed U.S. involvement in foreign wars, most believed that America must be militarily strong to deter foreign attacks. As a result, by May 1938 a $1.1 billion naval expansion bill was passed by both houses. Rearmament also won overwhelming support of the American people. A *Fortune* poll in July 1938 revealed that 63.6 percent approved the president's rearmament policy, while only 13.2 percent opposed it. But while Roosevelt was winning congressional and public support for American rearmament, he still remained reluctant to challenge the existing Neutrality Act.[62]

## British Appeasement

On the other side of the Atlantic, Neville Chamberlain, who had become prime minister of Britain in May 1937, had little use for Roosevelt's blockade idea or for Welles' conference scheme when the latter was proposed to him in January 1938. "In the present state of European affairs, with the two dictators in a thoroughly nasty temper," Chamberlain confided to his colleagues, "we simply cannot afford to quarrel with Japan." Chamberlain realized that Britain lacked the necessary military or financial resources to deal with the possibility of aggression in both Europe and the Far East. Prompted by the same consideration, the British chiefs of staff had warned him the preceding month that they could not "exaggerate the importance of any political or international action which could be taken to reduce the number of our potential enemies and to gain the support of potential allies." Moreover, the close vote on the Ludlow amendment appeared to indicate to the British prime minister that American isolationist sentiment was so strong that Roosevelt would be unable to do anything effective against the aggressors. Indeed, Chamberlain feared that, as he put it, "after a lot of ballyhoo, the Americans will somehow fade out and leave us to carry all the blame and the odium."[63]

Chamberlain's lack of enthusiasm for the Welles plan was reinforced by the failure of the Brussels Conference in November 1937. The conference, to which the signatories of the Nine Power Treaty of 1922 and other interested nations were invited, was called to discuss ways to terminate the Sino-Japanese conflict. But both Japan and Germany refused to attend. And while Italy was represented, her accession to the Anti-Comintern Pact on November 6 guaranteed that she would not do anything to oppose Japanese aggression in the Far East. Nor, as it turned out, would the Americans. "The United States cannot afford to be made, in popular opinion at home, a tail to the British kite," Roosevelt informed Norman Davis, who headed the American delegation. Any action, he added, would have to have the support of the overwhelming majority of the conference, including the United States. However, Roosevelt ruled out the possibility of economic sanctions--or any other coercive action--against Japan because he did not believe they would win the support of the American people. The collapse of the Brussels Conference on November 24, and with it the Nine Power Treaty, convinced Chamberlain that nothing would come of any other international conference.[64]

Chamberlain also feared that the Welles plan would interfere with his own effort to appease Germany and Italy. In this regard, he was prepared to offer the Italians *de jure* recognition of their Ethiopian conquest and the Germans the prospect of colonial acquisitions outside of Europe. In his response to Roosevelt rejecting the Welles plan, Chamberlain asked the president "to consider holding his hand for a short while to see what progress we can make in beginning to tackle some of the problems."[65]

But conflicting diplomatic strategies were not the only reason for Chamberlain's unwillingness to cooperate with Roosevelt against the Axis. Part of the explanation was also economic in nature. The Americans were pressuring the British to accept a reciprocal tariff reduction agreement in order to promote world economic recovery. The main target was the British imperial preference system, which was established in 1932 as a response to the depression and the tariff increases of other nations, including the United States. Americans considered imperial preference an act of economic aggression against the United States. In its first year of operation, American exports to the British Empire fell by $10.5 million. Moreover, after Britain and Germany had concluded a trade agreement in 1934, Washington began to fear that the British were attempting to conclude a "selfish deal" with Germany that would close the major markets of the world to the United States. An Anglo-American trade agreement, the Roosevelt administration believed, would not only put these fears to rest, it might also serve to spread economic liberalism throughout the world, thereby undermining the system of economic autarchy Hitler had established in Germany as well as checking his aggressive inclinations.[66]

Chamberlain, however, feared that the reciprocal tariff reductions envisioned by the Roosevelt administration would expose older British industries to more vigorous American industrial competition, with the results that American economic dominance of the world would be ensured, the empire would be wrecked, and Britain would be reduced to the status of an economic and political client of the United States. While the prime minister agreed to negotiate a new trade treaty with the United States, the British concessions in the resulting agreement, which was concluded in November 1938, were far more modest than the Roosevelt administration had anticipated. In the end, only the pressure of another catastrophic world war would compel the British to bow to the wishes of the United States and completely dismantle the imperial preference system.[67]

Roosevelt and his advisors were shocked by Chamberlain's outright rejection of the Welles plan and by the prime minister's stated intention to recognize the Italian conquest of Ethiopia. In a note to Chamberlain on January 17, Roosevelt stated that he would defer for "a short while" his conference proposal, but he also argued that British recognition of the Italian conquest of Ethiopia would not only receive a hostile reaction from the American people, it would also encourage the Japanese to conquer China.[68]

British Foreign Secretary Anthony Eden, who was not consulted by Chamberlain in advance of the prime minister's response to Roosevelt, was appalled by the rejection of the Welles plan. In striking contrast to Chamberlain, Eden attached great importance to any involvement of the United States in world affairs, and he welcomed any tangible evidence of Anglo-American solidarity in order to deter Hitler's aggressive inclinations. Under pressure from Eden, Chamberlain reversed himself and agreed to cooperate with the Welles plan and to delay approaching Italy "for at least a week."[69]

Although Roosevelt expressed pleasure with Chamberlain's reversal, he was privately upset and discouraged by the obvious reluctance of the British to support the international conference proposal. Sumner Welles likened it to a "douche of cold water." As a result, Roosevelt delayed and eventually abandoned the implementation of the Welles plan. Years later, Winston Churchill, whose refusal to accept appeasement made him a political outcast in the late thirties, condemned Chamberlain for turning away "the proferred hand stretched out across the Atlantic," thereby losing "the last frail chance to save the world from tyranny otherwise than by war." On the other hand, L. S. Amery, a member of Chamberlain's cabinet, argued that the prime minister was justified in believing that the Welles plan would only irritate the dictators without doing anything meaningful to restrain them. Historian William Rock argues that Roosevelt was put off by Chamberlain's effort to appease the dictators, and as a result disassociated himself from the British effort to do so. According to Rock, this was exactly what Chamberlain wanted.[70]

There were other reasons for Roosevelt's reluctance to proceed with the Welles plan. One was an internal crisis in Germany. In February 1938 Hitler cashiered the leadership of the German army, Generals Werner von Blomberg and Werner von Fritsch, and made himself supreme commander of the German armed forces. He also replaced Konstantin von Neurath as foreign minister with the more aggressive Joachim von Ribbentrop. By these moves it appeared that Hitler had decided that a program of territorial conquest was better than abandoning Germany's goal of economic autarchy. However, Roosevelt did not want to launch the Welles plan until the motives behind the German purge became more definite. The delay was also due to the resignation from the British cabinet of Anthony Eden on February 20. Eden disliked Chamberlain's effort to appease Italy, which he believed would alienate American opinion while doing nothing to lure Mussolini away from his tie with Hitler. But an even more important reason for his resignation was Chamberlain's refusal to cooperate with the United States. Roosevelt feared that Eden's demise meant that Chamberlain was preparing to sell out to the Axis.[71]

But it was the German occupation of Austria--the *anschluss*--on March 12 that ended once and for all Roosevelt's support for the Welles plan. That same day he informed the British that his plan was indefinitely postponed and opportunity for its use "would not recur." However, while American opinion was outraged by Hitler's brutal occupation of Austria, few Americans were prepared to do anything about it. Said Senator Borah, the loss of Austria's independence, while lamentable, was "not of the slightest moment" to the United States. The administration apparently agreed. While Roosevelt's first inclination was to condemn the *anschluss,* Welles persuaded him to do nothing that might preclude the chance for an international conference at a later date. As a result, on April 6 the State Department tacitly recognized the *anschluss* by downgrading the American embassy in Vienna to a consulate.[72]

The *anschluss* also made Chamberlain even more determined to reach an understanding with Italy. As a result, an agreement was concluded with Mussolini on April 16, 1938. By its terms the British promised to bring before the League of Nations the issue of *de jure* recognition of Italy's conquest of Ethiopia, but only after Italian volunteers were withdrawn from Spain.[73]

A British request for American support for the Anglo-Italian agreeement divided the Roosevelt administration. Hull and Assistant Secretary of State Jay Pierrepont Moffat opposed American association with British appeasement, while Welles saw the Anglo-Italian agreement as a way to divide the Axis. To the disgust of Hull and Moffat, Welles persuaded Roosevelt to issue a sympathetic statement calling the Anglo-Italian agreement a step in the right direction of settling international disputes through negotiations rather than war. While Roosevelt did not want to be associated with Britain's appeasement policy, he also did not want to block it either. Yet the president also made clear that Washington would not recognize Italy's Ethiopian conquest. Moffat privately criticized Roosevelt's inconsistency: "In one breath we praise the British for getting together with the Italians; in the next breath we imply that the Italians are treaty breakers and unworthy to be dealt with on a footing of equality."[74]

## The Turn of Czechoslovakia

After Austria, Czechoslovakia was Hitler's next target. Urged on by the führer, in the spring of 1938 the leader of the Sudeten Germans demanded complete autonomy for his 3.5 million people. The Czechs, whose army was one of the best in Europe, refused the Sudeten demands and prepared to defend their homeland. The Czechs also turned to France and England for support against Hitler. But the French, who were committed by treaty to defend Czechoslovakia, would not act without the cooperation of Britain. As result of a Czecho-Soviet alliance in 1935, the Soviets were also obliged to defend Czechoslovakia. But their commitment was dependent on prior action by France. Thus, ultimately, the fate of the Czechs was in the hands of the British, who were not obliged by any treaty to come to Czechoslovakia's assistance.[75]

Winston Churchill argued that "the Nazification of the Danube states" would be a "danger of the first capital magnitude to the British Empire." He called for Britain and France to join with the Soviet Union in a "grand alliance" to check further German expansion. Chamberlain, however, believed that Hitler's aims were limited to the acquisition of lands inhabited by Germans. And he feared that Churchill's call for a grand alliance with Russia would only enhance that country's status while jeopardizing his plan to appease Hitler. The alternative to appeasement--a war with Germany over Czechoslovakia--was unthinkable to the prime minister, and many other Britons as well. Rather than allying with France and Russia to uphold Czechoslovakia, on September 15 Chamberlain traveled to Berchtesgaden, Hitler's mountain retreat, where he accepted the führer's demand that the Sudetenland must be turned over to Germany. In return, Hitler promised to respect the independence of what remained of the Czechoslovak state. Chamberlain then journeyed to Paris where he persuaded French Premier Edouard Daladier to pressure the Czechs to accept the settlement. The Czechs were told that, if they turned it down, Britain and France would "wash their hands" of the consequences.[76]

In desperation, on September 25 Czech President Eduard Benes pleaded with Roosevelt to prevent the Anglo-French sellout to Hitler. While Roosevelt realized that a sellout would probably be the outcome of the negotiations, he refused to intercede on behalf of the Czechs. In fact, on September 19 he had told British Ambassador Lindsay in the utmost secrecy that, although the Anglo-French plan demanded "the most terrible remorseless sacrifice" ever demanded of a country, and that it most certainly would provoke an unfavorable response in America, if it succeeded in averting war, he would be "the first to cheer." Moreover, he told Lindsay that he would not publicly condemn Germany's aggressive intentions "lest it might encourage the Czechs to vain resistance."[77]

At the same time, however, Roosevelt expressed his fear that Hitler would not be satisfied with the rape of Czechoslovakia, but that Poland, Denmark, and Rumania would be next. As one alternative, he again suggested an international conference to reorganize "all unsatisfactory frontiers on rational lines." If this proved unworkable and Britain and France decided to resist Hitler, he recommended that both Germany and Italy should be blockaded. He warned, however, that America's contribution to this effort would be limited. All he, as president, could do without violating the Constitution or the Neutrality Act was to prohibit American ships from entering the war zones, except at their own risk. Lindsay reported his conversation with Roosevelt to British Foreign Secretary Lord Halifax. While Halifax thanked the president for his concern, he did not think a blockade alone would be effective against the Axis.[78]

Roosevelt's timidity during the Czech crisis was undoubtedly influenced by the political situation he faced at home. Both the Congress and the American people were unwilling to risk war to help the Czechs. It was also due, in the opinion of some historians, to Roosevelt's belief that, if war came, Britain and France were too weak to win. It was for this reason primarily, in this view, that Roosevelt encouraged Chamberlain's effort to appease Hitler at Munich. But despite his suspicions about Hitler's intentions, on September 26 he cabled the Nazi leader, as well as Chamberlain, Daladier, and Benes, urging further negotiations to achieve "a peaceful, fair and constructive settlement of the question at issue." The following day Roosevelt wrote a personal message to Hitler in which he called for a conference of European leaders to negotiate a settlement of the issues that threatened to produce a war. But he also informed the führer that "the Government of the United States has no political involvement in Europe, and will assume no obligations in the conduct of the present negotiations." Some historians believe that in this way Roosevelt unintentionally gave Hitler a green light to deal with the Czechs and the Western powers without fear of American retaliation.[79]

At Munich on September 29-30 Chamberlain and Daladier met with Hitler and Mussolini to complete the sellout of Czechoslovakia. They agreed to hand over the Sudetenland to Germany in return for Hitler's pledge that he would not seek an additional foot of European territory. The Czechs, who were not present at the Munich Conference, bowed to the inevitable and accepted the settlement on the morning of September 30. Roosevelt was relieved that a peaceful solution to the crisis had been found. In a private message to Chamberlain on October 5, he stated: "I fully share your hope and belief that there exists today the greatest opportunity in years for the establishment of a new order based on justice and on law." In this way, historian Robert Divine has written, "American isolationism had become the handmaiden of European appeasement."[80]

## The Aftermath of Munich

It was not long before Roosevelt admitted that his hopes for the Munich Conference were illusory. On October 9 Hitler announced his intention to reinforce Germany's western fortifications. Three days later, the American ambassador in Tokyo, Joseph Grew, learned that the Germans were putting intense pressure on Japan to strengthen the Anti-Comintern Pact. This news was accompanied by reports of increased German subversive activities in South America, including a plot to establish a pro-Nazi government in Brazil. By the end of October, Hitler was saying that the Munich settlement did not represent a final solution to Germany's grievances in Europe. After the Nazis launched a general attack on the Jews in Germany in early November, Roosevelt publicly condemned the Nazi excesses, and then called home the American ambassador to Berlin.[81]

In the wake of Munich, Roosevelt also initiated a campaign to prepare the United States for what he believed more and more was an inevitable European war. On October 12 he announced his intention to ask Congress for an additional $300 million in defense appropriations. On November 14 he told the cabinet that he wanted Congress to fund an air force of 12,000 planes and a production capacity of 24,000 per year. "The recrudescence of German power at Munich," he said, "had completely reorientated our own international relations; for the first time since the Holy Alliance, the United States now faced the possibility of an attack on the Atlantic side in both the Northern and Southern Hemispheres." A large air force, he said, would preclude the need to have a large army.[82]

But Roosevelt's plan for a large air force ran into the opposition of both the armed forces and the Congress. The Army, which favored defense in breadth rather than depth, feared that large-scale aircraft production would result in a large amount of quickly obsolescent planes with too few pilots to fly them. The Army favored a more balanced program, with less funds for aircraft and more money for ground forces. The Congress, on the other hand, did not believe the international situation was sufficiently menacing to warrant the construction of a large air force. Faced with this opposition, Roosevelt reduced his request to 3,000 planes.[83]

At the same time, however, Roosevelt took the first steps toward making America the arsenal of democracy. In December he overruled the Army's opposition to aircraft sales to France, which he believed would not only deter Hitler but also make possible the rapid expansion of the American air force at a later date. In addition to selling France aircraft, Roosevelt also assured Chamberlain that he had "the industrial resources of the American nation behind him in the event of war with the dictatorships." The president insisted that the defense of Britain and France was vital to the security of the United States. If they fell to Hitler, he was certain the Western Hemisphere would be the next Nazi target.[84]

## Neutrality Revision

To make rearmament effective as a deterrent to Axis aggression, Roosevelt realized that the Neutrality Act would have to be revised. Retention of the act in its then current form made it impossible for the president to impress upon Hitler that America would intervene to prevent German domination of Europe. Although he preferred total repeal of the Neutrality Act, he also realized that the strength of the isolationists made repeal an impossibility. As a result, he accepted the advice of Senator Key Pittman, chairman of the Foreign Relations Committee, to ask Congress to remove the ban on munitions sales and to put all trade, including armaments, on a cash-and-carry basis. In his State of the Union message on January 4, 1939, Roosevelt announced his intention to ask for a revision of the Neutrality Act to enable the United States to aid the victims of aggression by all means short of direct American military participation.[85]

However, while wanting neutrality revision was one thing, getting Congress to agree to it was quite another. As 1939 began, Congress was in a distinctly anti-Roosevelt mood, the consequence of the president's unsuccessful bids to pack the Supreme Court in 1937 and purge conservative Democrats in the congressional election of 1938. With his political prestige at low ebb, Roosevelt was reluctant to lead the assault on the Neutrality Act. Consequently, he quickly approved Senator Pittman's offer to direct the battle for neutrality revision.[86]

But before Pittman could launch his campaign, the cause of neutrality revision was dealt a severe setback on January 23 when an experimental American bomber crashed in California, killing its pilot and badly injuring a passenger, who happened to be a representative of the French air ministry. As a result of the crash, the American people learned for the first time that the administration was selling aircraft to France. Roosevelt tried to quell the uproar that resulted by meeting with the Senate Military Affairs Committee on January 31. He told the senators that he had "pretty definite information that there was in the making a policy of world domination between Germany, Italy, and Japan." To prevent the success of the Axis plan, Roosevelt said, it was vital to sell aircraft to France. "Practically speaking," he explained, "if the Rhine frontiers are threatened the rest of the world is, too. Once they have fallen before Hitler, the German sphere of action will be unlimited."[87]

The isolationists who were in attendance at the meeting with Roosevelt were stunned by his presentation. Senator Nye found it "shocking" that "even before the war comes, the president considers our first line of defense to be in France." He was convinced that Roosevelt was "determined to utterly ignore the neutrality law" and "to aid the so-called democracies." Senator Hiram Johnson added that Roosevelt "cares no more for what may happen to us in a war than the man in the moon. He has developed a dictator complex." Despite a pledge of secrecy, one or more senators leaked word to the press that Roosevelt had stated that America's defensive frontier lay on the Rhine. The president responded by calling that statement a "deliberate lie," and by reasserting that his foreign policy had "not changed and is not going to change." Nevertheless, he did not discontinue the aircraft sales to France. But production problems delayed deliveries, with the result that France possessed less than 200 American planes at the outbreak of war in September 1939. Yet, while the isolationists were unable to block the aircraft union to France, they were successful in convincing Pittman that neutrality revision had little chance of success. With Hull's grudging consent, Pittman decided to postpone the effort.[88]

While Pittman procrastinated, a group of internationalists led by Clark Eichelberger of the League of Nations Association devised a revised neutrality bill, which Senator Elbert D. Thomas of Utah introduced on February 13. The bill authorized the president, with the consent of Congress, to exclude the victims of aggression from the restrictions of an arms embargo. The Thomas amendment, which was designed to help Britain, France, and China, was enthusiastically supported by American internationalists. But Roosevelt ignored it, choosing instead to support Pittman's decision to delay the battle for neutrality revision.[89]

Adolf Hitler finally forced the Congress and the Roosevelt administration to act on neutrality revision. On March 15, 1939, in violation of the promise the führer had made at Munich, German troops occupied Czechoslovakia. Two days later, Roosevelt publicly spoke in favor of neutrality revision. He was probably encouraged by a poll published on March 12 showing that 72 percent of the American people favored aiding the democracies with food supplies while 52 percent favored sending war materials. *The New York Times* commented that the poll had demonstrated that public opinion had "gone beyond some of the provisions of the present Neutrality Act." Privately, Roosevelt told Senator Tom Connally of Texas: "If Germany invades a country and declares war, we'll be on the side of Hitler by invoking the act. If we could get rid of the embargo, it wouldn't be so bad." The next day Senator Pittman introduced another neutrality measure that the State Department had been advocating since November, that is, repeal of the arms embargo section and adoption of cash-and-carry for all trade with belligerents. The other provisions of the 1937 measure were retained in the Pittman bill, including the prohibition of loans to belligerents, travel on belligerent ships, and the arming of American merchantmen. But two additions were made. One required the president to put the law into effect within thirty days after the outbreak of either a declared or an undeclared war. The other addition gave him discretionary authority to proclaim combat zones from which he could ban all American ships and travelers.[90]

In a radio address, Pittman argued that his bill would enable America to help Britain and France, because they controlled the seas, while ensuring U.S. neutrality. But isolationists argued that, by permitting American aid to reach Britain and France, the United States again would be drawn into a war with Germany. As a result, Senators Nye, Clark, and Bone introduced a measure designed to strengthen the 1937 act by retaining the arms embargo and adding a mandatory cash-and-carry provision for all other exports.[91]

Roosevelt was also upset with the Pittman bill but for a different reason. The cash-and-carry plan, he complained to Hull, "works all wrong in the Pacific." It would penalize China and favor Japan because the Japanese navy controlled the western Pacific. To the president, the only solution was to repeal the Neutrality Act altogether. In an attempt to mollify Roosevelt and prevent his bill from helping the Japanese, Pittman introduced a separate resolution that would permit the president to embargo exports to any country violating the Nine Power Treaty. But the isolationists were not fooled. They realized the real intent of the Pittman bill was not the preservation of neutrality but rather the facilitation of aid to the victims of aggression. In the opinion of historian Robert Divine, "It would have been far more honest, and perhaps even more expedient, for the administration to have come out early for the Thomas amendment, and fight for a policy of all-out opposition to aggression."[92]

Much to Roosevelt's chagrin, Pittman caved into isolationist pressure and agreed to conduct lengthy hearings before the Senate Foreign Relations Committee. The hearings dragged on past May 1, the date the cash-and-carry provisions of the 1937 act expired. Worse still, from the administration's perspective, was Pittman's decision in mid-May to postpone neutrality revision for several weeks, because he no longer believed the situation in Europe required urgent action.[93]

Checked in the Senate, Roosevelt for the first time openly supported repeal of the arms embargo in the House. However, instead of leading the battle personally, the president gave the assignment to Cordell Hull. Under intense pressure from the White House, in early June the House Foreign Affairs Committee approved a bill repealing the arms embargo and erasing the distinction between munitions and raw materials. But on June 30, by a two-vote margin, 159 to 157, the House passed a revised neutrality bill that retained an embargo on arms and ammunition, though not on the implements of war. The next day William C. Bullitt, then U.S. ambassador in Paris, cabled Hull to tell him that the French were asking "if the House of Representatives desires to precipitate war at this moment" and permit "the triumph of Hitler and Mussolini."[94]

Defeated in the House, Roosevelt on July 4 again turned to the Senate and asked that body once again to repeal the arms embargo. But the Senate Foreign Relations Committee, by a 12 to 11 vote, decided to postpone action on the neutrality bill until the next session of Congress. An infuriated Roosevelt complained in a press conference three days later that the Republicans had deprived him of the means to avert the outbreak of a European war.[95]

But Roosevelt also must share the blame for the failure to revise the Neutrality Act. Motivated by fear of further damaging his political prestige, he had stayed in the background too long and allowed Pittman and Hull to lead the administration's battle for neutrality revision. "If Roosevelt had risked his prestige by entering into the thick of the debate," Robert Divine has written, "he might have overcome this stubborn resistance. He at least could have the satisfaction of knowing that he had made a supreme effort to use American influence to prevent war in Europe." Still, it was highly unlikely that even revision of the Neutrality Act to permit American arms shipments to Britain and France would have checked Hitler's determination to conquer Europe. The Nazi dictator was not at all frightened by what he termed Roosevelt's "Bluffpolitik." The United States, in Hitler's opinion, "was incapable of conducting war." As a result, he did not allow American actions or opinion to sway him from his aggressive plans.[96]

## The Eve of War

Following the German conquest of Czechoslovakia in March 1939, Hitler made clear that Poland would be his next victim. He increased pressure on the Poles to accept German annexation of the free city of Danzig as well as to grant Germany exclusive road and railroad rights across the so-called Polish corridor, which separated East Prussia from the rest of Germany. The Poles rejected the German demands and turned to France and Britain for support. Badly burned by Hitler's violation of the Munich agreement, on March 31 Chamberlain promised to come to Poland's assistance if her independence or vital interests were endangered by another power. On April 13, following Italy's occupation of Albania, Britain also promised to defend the independence of Greece and Rumania. In May an Anglo-Turkish agreement committed both countries to joint action to defend the eastern Mediterranean. In response to the sudden change in British policy, Hitler denounced the German-Polish nonaggression treaty of 1934 and the Anglo-German Naval Treaty of 1935. In May Germany and Italy concluded a formal alliance, the "Pact of Steel." The Nazi dictator clearly intended to test the newly found assertiveness of the British.[97]

Although hampered by his inability to revise the Neutrality Act, Roosevelt nevertheless supported the new British policy of confronting Hitler. On March 25-26 the president had told an old English journalist friend, Sir Arthur Willert, that he was doing his best to educate American opinion about the necessity of the United States playing an active role in maintaining world peace and that, if war came, he was prepared to assist Britain economically as well as patrol the seas with the U.S. Atlantic fleet. But Roosevelt also told Willert that Britain must take the lead in confronting Hitler. Willert got the impression that the president "would welcome circumstances, or perhaps even help to bring them about, which would enable him to persuade his countrymen that the best way to save themselves from Hitler would be to fight him."[98]

As a way of educating American opinion, on April 14 Roosevelt sent a message to Hitler and Mussolini asking them to pledge not to attack any other additional countries for at least ten years. Both dictators responded with scathing personal attacks on the president, but they made no promises to curb their territorial appetites. On April 16 Roosevelt also announced that major elements of the U.S. fleet, which were stationed in the Atlantic, would be transferred to the Pacific. The move came in response to a British request the previous month asking the

United States to send a fleet to Honolulu in the event Britain became involved in a war with Germany and Italy. The American action was designed to deter aggressive moves by the Japanese while the British navy defended the Atlantic and the Mediterranean.[99]

Despite these measures, in the spring of 1939 it was obvious that, because of American isolationism, the most effective way of checking Axis aggression in Europe would be an alliance of Britain, France, and the Soviet Union. Joseph Stalin, the Soviet leader, was apparently more than anxious to conclude such an agreement. Since 1934 he had pressed the Western powers for a stronger collective security system to check Hitler. With this end in mind, the Soviet Union had joined the League of Nations in 1934 and, the following year, had concluded alliances with France and Czechoslovakia. However, because of British opposition to a Soviet alliance and French doubts about the military effectiveness of the Red Army, the French were never willing to conduct the military staff talks with the Soviets that were necessary to make the alliance viable. In addition to seeking assistance from the powers of Western Europe, the Soviets had sought from the United States some token of military collaboration that would act to check Japanese aggression in the Far East.[100]

Roosevelt, for his part, was eager to use the Soviet Union as a counter to Axis expansion in the Far East and in Europe. His decision to extend diplomatic recognition to the Soviet regime in 1933 had this end in mind. And, for the same reason, in 1936 he had responded favorably to Stalin's request to allow the United States to build a battleship for the Soviet fleet. However, the request was blocked by anti-Soviet hardliners in the State Department and in the War Department, who opposed any American effort that might enhance the international prestige or the military power of the Soviet Union. Fearing hostile congressional and public reaction if the Soviet request became public knowledge, Roosevelt for the time being abandoned his attempts to help the Soviets economically and militarily. The president's inability to deliver what he promised earned him the disdain of Stalin, who could not believe that a U.S. president could not get anything he really wanted.[101]

Blocked in his own efforts to strengthen Soviet-American ties, Roosevelt encouraged the British to conclude an alliance with the Soviet Union. But for several reasons the British were unwilling to do so. For one, Britain's new protectorates, Poland and Rumania, feared the Soviets as much as the Germans and, as a result, flatly refused to permit Soviet troops to enter their territory, even after a German attack. Second, the British, like the French, did not have much regard for Soviet military power following the brutal purge of the Red Army that Stalin had conducted in the late thirties. Some 80 percent of the Soviet military leadership above the rank of captain was removed from command--and many were executed. At the same time, Chamberlain feared that Hitler would use an Anglo-French-Soviet alliance as the excuse for launching the war the British prime minister was still very much determined to prevent. However, at the heart of Chamberlain's reluctance to conclude an alliance with Russia was his "most profound distrust" of Soviet motives. In addition to the military alliance, the Kremlin demanded the right to occupy the Baltic states, without their consent, in the event that they were threatened by German occupation. Chamberlain feared that what Stalin really wanted was a war between Germany and the Western powers, the result of which would leave Europe prostrate before the Red Army. Before relying on a hungry Russian bear, Chamberlain still hoped to appease the Nazi dictator.[102]

Despite Chamberlain's reluctance to conclude an alliance with the Soviets, at the insistence of the French and members of his own cabinet, who argued that Soviet assistance would be vital to the defense of Poland, he agreed to joint Anglo-French talks with the Russians. They began on May 27. However, instead of an alliance, Chamberlain offered the Soviets a consultative pact that would come into operation if Britain, France, or the Soviet Union became involved in war directly, or as the result of aggression against another European state that offered resistance. This arrangement would remove the appearance of a Soviet threat to Poland and Rumania while avoiding any British guarantee to the Soviet Union. However, the two Western powers refused to accept the Kremlin's demands for boundary adjustments or the right to occupy the Baltic states.[103]

The inability of the Soviets and the Western Allies to reach an agreement gave Hitler an opportunity that he skillfully exploited. Putting aside for the time being the hostility he felt for communism, in early August he responded to earlier Soviet suggestions for an understanding by instructing his ambassador in Moscow to suggest a political agreement between the two governments. Stalin, who by this time had given up on the prospect of a meaningful alliance with the Western Allies, or aid from the United States, jumped at the German offer. On August 20 a Soviet-German commercial agreement was concluded. Three days later both countries startled the world by signing a nonaggression treaty that required both to refrain from attacking each other and to remain neutral if either became involved in a war with other countries. In a secret protocol to the treaty, Germany recognized Finland, Latvia, Estonia, and the eastern half of Poland to be within the Soviet sphere of influence.[104]

In the short term, the German-Soviet Nonaggression Pact was extremely advantageous to both parties. The agreement enabled Hitler to attack Poland without fear of Soviet opposition. Stalin, on the other hand, gained territory the Western Allies would not allow him to take, as well as the benefits of neutrality that would result from a war between the Germans and the Western powers. Roosevelt had tried in vain to wreck the German effort to strike a bargain with Stalin. According to Joseph Davies, U.S. ambassador in Moscow, the president warned the Soviet dictator that, in Davies' words, "if his government joined up with Hitler, it was as certain as that the night followed the day that as soon as Hitler had conquered France, he would turn on Russia, and it would be the Soviet turn next."[105]

Unable to alter Stalin's course, Roosevelt tried to avert war by urging Britain to stand by her commitment to Poland. On August 24 Chamberlain responded by informing U.S. Ambassador Joseph P. Kennedy that, while Britain had every intention of honoring her guarantee to Poland, if war were to be averted, Poland would have to negotiate with the Germans. Reported Kennedy: "The British wanted one thing of us and one thing only, namely that we put pressure on the Poles." Roosevelt was not prepared to comply. "As we saw it here," Moffat noted, "it merely meant that they wanted us to assume the responsibility of a new

Munich and to do their dirty work for them." Instead of meeting the British wish, on August 24 Roosevelt appealed to both sides to seek a negotiated settlement of their differences. After concluding a formal alliance with Britain the following day, the Poles indicated that they were willing to discuss their differences with the Germans. But Hitler, who was determined on war, demanded the appearance in Berlin of a Polish plenipotentiary prepared to accept his demands. After the Poles refused to be so humiliated, German troops invaded their country on September 1. Three days later, Britain and France declared war on Germany, and the European phase of World War II began.[106]

# Afterthougths

The question of assessing responsibility for the outbreak of the European war has divided and fascinated historians and other interested persons until this day. It is now generally accepted that Hitler was determined to bring about a war that would lead to German domination of the European continent and much else besides, and that both the Western Allies and the Soviet Union were foolhardy to believe that they could satisfy him with proposals that offered less.[107]

But the United States also bears a large share of the responsibility for the conflict. American disgust with Europe's failure to reduce armaments and pay war debts owed to the United States, the refusal of Britain and France to cooperate with one another in checking Axis expansion, and the popular revulsion from what increasingly appeared to be the inevitability of another European conflict did much to reinforce isolationist opinion in the United States. Reinforced by the American public's hostility toward Europe, isolationists made it impossible for Roosevelt to exercise U.S. military and economic power in a way that may have deterred Hitler, or at least strengthened the resolve and ability of the Western powers and the Soviet Union to resist his aggressive moves.

Yet even after acknowledging the obstacles that Roosevelt faced at home and abroad, some historians have criticized him for not challenging the isolationists sooner and more directly. They argue that Roosevelt was too concerned with the impact of American congressional and public opinion, particularly after they began to become concerned about the Axis menace. As J. Garry Clifford has pointed out, "the thrust of public opinion research since World War II indicates that a president's power to persuade is greatest during international crises, when a frightened public tends to rally behind strong leadership." As early as 1940, pollster George Gallup observed that "the best way to influence public opinion" on an issue "is to get Mr. Roosevelt to talk about it and favor it."[108]

In addition, critics argue, Roosevelt was unnecessarily nebulous, and even duplicitous, in his offers of assistance to the Western Allies and the Soviets. Considering the probable consequences--the Axis conquest of Europe--they regard Roosevelt's actions not only as inadequate but also as excessively cautious. In this vein, Edward C. Bennett has argued: "England and France might not have responded to a more direct policy of leadership from the United States, but the results of the attempt could scarcely have been more injurious than the policy of inaction which evolved."[109]

Frederick Marks believes Roosevelt's policy was duplicitous because the president was "a public crusader for collective security against totalitarian aggression and a closet appeaser whose erratic efforts to avert war in Asia and Europe actually accelerated global conflict." Not once, Marks asserts, "did FDR demonstrate a capacity to coordinate military and political factors in the interest of shaping a coherent and consistent foreign policy." As a result, Roosevelt "accumulated the largest overseas credibility gap of any president on record. Scores of promises made to leaders of other nations were retracted or broken."[110]

Still, when one considers the difficulty Roosevelt encountered in getting the Neutrality Act revised, one can only conclude that the president was doing as much as he could without bringing about a public backlash against him. Always remembering the lesson of Woodrow Wilson, who got too far in front of public opinion and lost his battle for American membership in the League of Nations, Roosevelt engaged in a program of public education the slow pace of which eventually enabled it to bear fruit. If Roosevelt appeared to favor appeasement it was only because, under the leadership of Neville Chamberlain, the British refused to consider, until it was nearly too late, any other course. Until war had erupted, and Winston Churchill became prime minister in May 1940, the British refused to initiate a policy of forceful resistance to Axis aggression that Roosevelt could, and wanted to, support. Given the state of American opinion in the late thirties, to have asked Roosevelt to initiate such a policy before British resistance began is simply asking too much of a politician as astute as Franklin Roosevelt was.

Needless to say, the question of how much more Roosevelt could have done-- considering the obstacles under which he labored, including Hitler's determination to dominate Europe, his disregard of the United States, the unwillingness of Britain and France to resist until it was almost too late, and the refusal of the American Congress and people to play a role in maintaining the global balance of power--is one that will remain unanswerable.

# 4

# The Road To War, 1939-1941

## The Outbreak of War in Europe

The outbreak of war in Europe moved Franklin Roosevelt to assure the nation that he would do all in his power to keep the United States out of the conflict. "I give you assurance and reassurance," he told the American people in a fireside chat on Sunday evening, September 3, "that your government will make every effort to prevent a black-out of peace in the United States." Two days later, as required by the Neutrality Act, he placed an embargo on arms shipments to the belligerents. Yet, while Roosevelt sincerely desired and expected to keep the country out of war, he rejected strict neutrality. "I cannot ask that every American remain neutral in thought," as Woodrow Wilson did in 1914. "Even a neutral has a right to take account of facts. Even a neutral cannot be asked to close his mind or conscience."[1]

Personally and privately, the president believed that the preservation of America's values and security obliged him to do all he could to help Britain and France beat Hitler. The defeat of the Allies would give the führer control of the European continent, and with it, Hitler would be able to strike at the Middle East, Africa, and even the Western Hemisphere. As a result, Roosevelt specifically delayed implementation of the arms embargo until September 5 in order to give the Allies additional time to procure weapons and munitions from the United States. He also virtually ignored violations of international law caused by the Allied blockade of Germany. Further help came by way of the Declaration of Panama on September 25. In it the administration declared the Western Hemisphere south of Canada and from 300 to 1,000 miles off the Atlantic coast a neutral zone. While he publicly justified the action as a way of keeping war away from the Western Hemisphere, he privately hoped that it would reinforce the British blockade.[2]

## Neutrality Revision Again

While Roosevelt did what he could to help the Allies, he was slow to strengthen the nation's armed forces. In the fall of 1939 the U.S. Army consisted of only 14,000 officers and 227,000 men, of whom but 80,000 (five divisions) could be used as a field force. There was not enough equipment to put even an army of 500,000 men into combat, let alone the 1,200,000 envisaged by the War Department's Protective Mobilization Plan. The small air corps had only 1,800 planes of all types, but most were obsolescent. The armored forces had only 329 tanks, most of which were light tanks. On September 7, by executive order, Roosevelt authorized an increase of the Regular Army by 17,000 men, the National Guard by 35,000, and the Navy by 60,000. But he turned down the request of General George C. Marshall, the Army chief of staff, for a more rapid buildup of the nation's armed forces. The president was determined to avoid any action that might arouse "undue excitement" or in any way suggest an American intention to participate in the hostilities. Instead, he preferred to take the indirect path of aiding the Allies, and this, he believed, could be best achieved by concentrating on repeal of the arms embargo.[3]

As a result of the brutal German conquest of Poland, American opinion was increasingly sympathetic to the idea of helping the Allies--short of direct U.S. military involvement. Prompted by this change in the public attitude, as well as by the events in Europe, the president called Congress into special session on September 21 to revise the Neutrality Act. However, he did not try to get too far in front of public opinion with the revised neutrality bill. While the bill called for repeal of the arms embargo, it kept the cash-and-carry trade policy, continued to ban loans to belligerents and American travel on belligerent merchant ships, and retained the prohibition on the arming of merchantmen as well as the president's power to declare combat zones closed to American ships. Although Roosevelt did not say so publicly, he realized that the cash-and-carry feature of the bill would help the Allies more than Germany because Britain and France controlled the high seas. In an attempt to head off anticipated isolation opposition, the administration portrayed the effort to repeal the arms embargo as motivated solely by the desire to keep the nation out of war.[4]

The isolationists were not fooled by the administration's subterfuge. They asked, quite logically, that if the purpose of revision was to ensure neutrality, why not simply retain the arms embargo and add cash-and-carry for all other trade with belligerents? Senator William Borah argued that the only purpose of repeal was to help Britain and France, and as such would constitute "an act of intervention." Repeal of the arms embargo, Senator Nye argued, would be "followed by other steps by this administration which will have us wrapped up in Europe's war overnight." The isolationists insisted that even if Hitler were victorious in Europe, he did not have the power to conquer the United States. The administration, the anti-interventionist America First Committee argued, should concentrate on strengthening the nation's defenses, rather than endangering American neutrality by aiding the Allies.[5]

In the end, Congress passed the revised neutrality bill. Quite clearly, the president had convinced the American people that they could aid the Allies without themselves becoming directly involved in the conflict. On October 27 the Senate approved the bill by a vote of 63 to 30, and six days later the House gave it a favorable vote of 243 to 182. On November 4 Roosevelt signed the bill into law. He then declared a combat zone to exist in the North Atlantic off the European coast from Spain to Norway as well as in the Baltic Sea. American ships were prohibited from entering these areas even if they were bound for a neutral port. While the restrictions on loans and travel contained in the 1937 act remained in force, for the first time since the outbreak of the war, Americans could sell arms, ammunition, and implements of war to the European belligerents, provided that title to them was transferred before they left the United States, and that they were paid for in cash and carried away in foreign ships.[6]

While isolationists could take consolation from the restraints on presidential action that were retained in the revised Neutrality Act, they also realized that their effort to keep the country out of foreign wars had been severely damaged by the repeal of the arms embargo. "The same emotions which demand the repeal of the embargo," Republican Senator Arthur Vandenberg of Michigan recorded in his diary, "will subsequently demand still more effective aid for Britain." The nation, Senator Borah accurately predicted, would become associated "with the European balance of power." That this was Roosevelt's intention is indisputable. Yet he still dared not say so publicly. A month after his legislative victory, the president wrote a letter to William Allen White, editor of the *Emporium* (Kansas) *Gazette* and, later, chairman of the Committee to Defend America by Aiding the Allies. Stated Roosevelt: "My problem is to get the American people to think of conceivable consequences without scaring [them] into thinking that they are going to be dragged into this war."[7]

## *Blitzkrieg* in the West

After the defeat of Poland, the European war entered into a period of relative inactivity during the winter of 1939-1940, the so-called Phony War. Taking advantage of this lull, in February 1940 Roosevelt sent Under Secretary of State Sumner Welles to Europe to see if there was any chance of restoring peace. While the president was not optimistic about the prospects of Welles' mission, he believed that it might at the very minimum buy time for the Allies to prepare for the expected German offensive. Not surprisingly, after Welles visited Britain, France, Germany, and Italy, Roosevelt could only conclude that there was no prospect of an early peace. On April 9, 1940, the Phony War came to an abrupt end when German troops invaded Denmark and Norway. Four days later, Roosevelt denounced this latest German aggression. "If civilization was to survive," he said, "the rights of smaller nations to their independence, to their territorial integrity, and to their unimpeded opportunity for self-government must be respected by their more powerful neighbors."[8]

But the president's words had absolutely no impact on Hitler's plans. On May 10 German forces invaded Belgium, Luxembourg, and the Netherlands in the opening move of Hitler's great western offensive. Although Britain and France immediately came to the assistance of the Dutch and Belgians, they were unable to halt the German blitzkrieg. Relying on massed concentrations of tanks and aircraft, the Germans broke through the Allied lines, overran the Dutch and Belgian armies, and forced the British army and some French forces to retreat to the coast near Dunkirk, from where most of them were ultimately withdrawn by boats and ships to England. The Germans then turned against the remaining French armies to the south, driving almost to the gates of Paris by June 10. On that day Italy entered the conflict by declaring war on France and Britain. In desperation, French Premier Paul Reynaud immediately appealed to Roosevelt for all possible American aid, short of an expeditionary force. A few hours before receiving Reynaud's plea, Roosevelt condemned the Italian attack on France in an address at Charlottesville, Virginia. "The hand that held the dagger," the president said, "has struck it into the back of its neighbor." He then announced that the United States was taking immediate steps "to extend to the opponents of force the material resources of this nation."[9]

In truth, however, there was little the United States could have done to help France avert disaster. There were too few available planes, guns, and ammunition to help the Allies substantially. Nevertheless, on June 7 Roosevelt approved the sale to France of fifty vintage Navy dive bombers and ninety-three obsolete Army attack bombers. But the American assistance proved to be too little and too late for the French. On June 14 German troops entered Paris. Fleeing the French capital, Reynaud cabled Roosevelt that in France's "most tragic hour," the only hope was to throw into the balance "this very day the weight of American power." Unless the president could promise that the United States would enter the war within a very short time, Reynaud added, "you will see France go under like a drowning man and disappear after having cast a last look towards the land of liberty from which she has awaited salvation."[10]

For Roosevelt, however, there was no possibility of U.S. military intervention. Neither the Congress nor American opinion would support it. According to an opinion poll published on May 29, only 7.7 percent of the people favored immediate American entry into the war. Only 19 percent believed that the country should intervene if the defeat of the Allies appeared certain. Forty percent opposed U.S. participation under any circumstances. The president, who by this time had decided to run for an unprecedented third term, could not ignore the public's attitude on the war and still expect to stay in the White House after January 1941. As a result, he responded by saying that he was doing all he could to help without a declaration of war from Congress, something that was not forthcoming.[11]

Soon thereafter, on June 17, Marshal Henri Pétain, who that day had replaced Reynaud as France's premier, asked the Germans for an armistice. Hull implored the French government to ensure that its fleet would not fall into German hands, and warned that if France failed to do so, she would "permanently lose the friendship and goodwill of the government of the United States." The following day, the French assured the United States that their fleet would "never be surrendered to the enemy." On June 22 the French signed an armistice agreement with the Germans that placed the northern half of France and her Atlantic coast under German occupation. A puppet regime under Pétain was established at Vichy, in the unoccupied southern part of France. While some French forces continued to fight outside of France, Britain was left virtually alone to face Hitler's wrath.[12]

It is no exaggeration to say that the American people were shocked by the impact of the German blitzkrieg. Taking advantage of the almost universal cry for American preparedness, on May 16 Roosevelt asked the Congress for a supplemental defense appropriation of $1.2 billion, which would include the initial funds for 50,000 military aircraft. By the end of the month, the Congress responded by giving the president more money than he had requested--$1.5 billion. The following month the Congress appropriated an additional $1 billion for the Army and $700 million for the Navy and authorized an increase of 95,000 men in the Army's authorized strength of 280,000 and a 25 percent increase in new carrier, cruiser, and submarine tonnage already authorized in May 1938. In July Congress authorized additional funds for the construction of a "two-ocean Navy"--1,325,000 tons of new battleships, battle cruisers, carriers, cruisers, destroyers, and submarines, and the purchase or conversion of 100,000 tons of auxiliary vessels. An additional request by Roosevelt for another $5 billion after the fall of France was approved by the Congress in September. All totaled, $10.5 billion were appropriated for defense in 1940, a fivefold increase over the previous year.[13]

## The Destroyer Deal

As the American people began to realize the gravity of the Nazi threat to the Western Hemisphere after the fall of France, they also started to appreciate the value of Britain as America's first line of defense. An opinion poll in July showed that 73 percent of the people thought the United States should do everything possible to help Britain, except go to war. Only 13 percent favored armed intervention. Surprisingly, 50 percent said the United States should intervene against Germany if Britain were defeated.[14]

But helping Britain became more difficult after the fall of France, as German submarines, operating in "wolf packs" from French ports, attacked British shipping in the Atlantic. In June Britain lost 290,000 tons of shipping, compared to 75,000 tons the previous month. If these losses continued at the same rate, Britain would be strangled into submission. To meet this threat, on May 15 Winston Churchill, who became prime minister five days earlier, cabled Roosevelt imploring him to declare American nonbelligerency immediately and to provide all aid short of direct military participation. The immediate needs of Britain, he told the president, were a loan of forty or fifty old destroyers (the British had only 68 destroyers on active duty in their home waters) and several hundred aircraft which were then being delivered to the U.S. Army.[15]

Although Roosevelt appreciated the dire straits in which Britain found herself, he was reluctant to provide the destroyers. He feared that a destroyer loan would leave the Atlantic approaches to the United States inadequately defended. The Navy had already commissioned 172 of the more than 200 destroyers that dated back to World War I. Moreover, Congress had decreed that U.S. military equipment could not be transferred to a foreign country without the approval of the chief of naval operations, who had to certify that the transfer was vital to American security. And Roosevelt also feared the hostile reaction from congressional isolationists that such an obvious violation of American neutrality was sure to produce. It could become, he believed, a major issue in the approaching presidential election.[16]

It was not until September 1940, at the height of the Battle of Britain, that Roosevelt removed the obstacles standing in the way of the destroyer deal. Wendell Willkie, the Republican presidential candidate, promised he would not make an issue of the destroyer transfer, and the chief of naval operations also authorized the deal. In addition, to help facilitate the transfer, the British agreed to hand over to the United States, as an outright gift, air and naval bases in Newfoundland and Bermuda, granted ninety nine year leases to additional bases in the Caribbean, and promised never to surrender the British fleet to the Germans. In return, the president gave the British fifty over age destroyers. Fearful that the Congress would not approve the destroyer deal, Roosevelt accomplished the transfer by executive order. While he was attacked by the isolationists for taking this step without the consent of Congress, a public opinion poll revealed that 70 percent of the American people supported the move. It obviously did not prevent Roosevelt's successful reelection bid in November.[17]

The destroyer deal clearly marked the end of American neutrality. But it was only one step toward America's involvement in the European war. In September 1940 Congress gave the president power to call the National Guard for service in the Americas and passed a selective service act for men between the ages of twenty-one and thirty-five. The measure was passed over the vehement opposition of isolationists and pacifists who said it would commit American boys to foreign wars and "slit the throat of the last great democracy still living." Looking for an issue that would defeat Roosevelt in the fall election, Wendell Wilkie, who also had called for conscription, attacked the president as a warmonger. The impact of Wilkie's attack prompted Roosevelt to reassure the nation repeatedly that he had no intention to lead it into war. On October 30 he told a Boston audience: "I have said this before, but I shall say it again and again and again: Your boys are not going to be sent into any foreign wars." Although Roosevelt defeated Wilkie in the November election by 5 million votes (out of 49 million cast), it was the smallest winning margin since Wilson's election in 1916. Nevertheless, Churchill was elated by Roosevelt's victory. He wrote the president: "I prayed for your success and I am truly thankful for it. We are entering upon a sombre phase of what must evidently be a protracted and broadening war."[18]

## Lend-Lease

But Churchill also had bad news for Roosevelt. "The moment approaches," he cabled the president on December 8, "when we shall no longer be able to pay cash for shipping and other supplies." He then expressed his confidence that the president would find "ways and means" to continue the flow of munitions and goods across the Atlantic. In a novel approach to the problem, Roosevelt decided that he would simply lend or lease Britain the supplies she needed. Hitler, he told the nation on December 29, wanted to dominate the world. If England fell, "all of us in the Americas would be living at the point of a gun." While he repeated that he had no intention of committing American boys to the war, he insisted that America must become "the great arsenal of democracy."[19]

The Lend-Lease bill was introduced in Congress in January 1941 under the symbolic title, House Resolution 1776. It authorized the president to sell, transfer, exchange, lease, or lend--under such terms as he thought suitable--supplies of munitions, food, weapons, and other defense articles to any nation whose defense he deemed vital to the security of the United States. The administration argued that the measure was imperative to maintain control of the high seas, which were "the key to the security of the Western Hemisphere." The president himself used an analogy everyone could understand to justify Lend-Lease: "Suppose my neighbor's home catches fire, and I have a length of garden hose. . . . If he can take my garden hose and connect it up with his hydrant, I may help him to put out his fire." Once the fire was out, the hose could be returned. There was no need, the president argued, to sell the hose to the neighbor. There was, however, one major string attached to the formal Lend-Lease agreement that was signed in February 1942. The British had to agree to work with the United States to eliminate "all forms of discriminatory treatment in international commerce" and to reduce "tariffs and other trade barriers," including imperial preference.[20]

The debate on the Lend-Lease bill consumed two months. Isolationists argued that the bill not only dissipated resources vital to the defense of the United States but represented another step toward war with Germany. "Make no mistake about it," Senator Nye told reporters, "this is a last ditch fight. If we lose it, war is almost inevitable." At the same time, many who favored aid to Britain were reluctant to grant the president the sweeping power to extend support to any nation--possibly including Soviet Russia--whose defense, on his sole authority, he deemed vital to the national interest. Only after several amendments seeking to limit presidential powers had been defeated, did Congress approve the bill. The margin in the House was 260 to 165, and in the Senate 60 to 31. On March 11, 1941, the Lend-Lease Act became law with the president's signature. Shortly thereafter, Congress approved an initial Lend-Lease appropriation of $7 billion. In the end, Lend-Lease proved to be the last great battle fought by the isolationists. A disconsolate Senator Vandenberg wrote in his diary: "We have torn up 150 years of traditional foreign policy. We have tossed Washington's Farewell Address into the discard. We have placed ourselves squarely into the power politics and power wars of Europe, Asia, and Africa. We have taken the first step upon a course from which we can never hereafter retreat."[21]

## Toward an Anglo-American Strategy

While the debate on the Lend-Lease bill raged in Congress, secret Anglo-American military staff talks got under way in Washington on January 29, 1941.

Their purpose was to outline a common strategy both powers could follow in the event the United States entered the war. It was decided, with Roosevelt's approval, that every effort would be made to keep Japan out of the war. If that proved impossible, the primary effort of the two countries would be made against Germany, which was considered the immediate threat to Britain. But the two sides could not agree on how Hitler was to be defeated. To save lives, the British preferred to wage a war of attrition against Germany. They ruled out an invasion of the Continent until Germany had been weakened first by blockade and aerial bombardment, and possibly after the Soviet Union had entered the conflict. In the meantime, Britain would attempt to maintain its peripheral positions in North Africa, the Mediterranean, and the Middle East, not only to drain German resources, but as eventual jumping-off points for an assault on Europe. The Americans, on the other hand, feared that the British strategy would drain more resources from the Allies than the Germans. Rather than supporting a diversionary strategy, the Americans wanted to invade Western Europe as soon as possible. Only there, they believed, could Hitler be defeated decisively.[22]

The joint staff talks concluded on March 27 with a report entitled "ABC-1," which was tacitly approved by the president two days later. Yet, while the implementation of the common strategy envisioned in the report was contingent on American involvement in the war, six months before the Japanese attack on Pearl Harbor, the United States in many ways was already at war with Germany. Not only was American Lend-Lease aid beginning to flow to Britain, British and American scientists were exchanging top-secret scientific information (including research on atomic energy), pooling their military intelligence, and exchanging military and technical specialists. In addition, damaged British warships were being repaired in American shipyards and Royal Air Force pilots and aircrews were being trained in the United States.[23]

In retaliation for the increasing assistance America was giving Britain, on March 25 Hitler extended the German war zone westward to the coast of Greenland. As a result, it became clear that only an American naval escort could protect the Atlantic shipping lanes from the expanded German threat. But Roosevelt did not believe the American people would support U.S. convoy protection all the way to Greenland. As Roosevelt's aide and confidant Harry Hopkins pointed out, the president "would rather follow public opinion than lead it." But Roosevelt also was not averse to creating situations that would cause public opinion to move in the direction he desired. As a result, on April 24 he extended the American neutrality zone to the mid-Atlantic--26 degrees west longitude--and ordered American warships to patrol it. Not announced was his decision to permit the Navy to alert the British to the presence of any German raiders or submarines that were discovered. Reporting the position of German warships to the British navy, admitted Henry Stimson, whom Roosevelt had made secretary of war in May 1940, was "a clearly hostile act." Stimson could only conclude that "the president shows evidence of waiting for the accidental shot of some irresponsible captain on either side to be the occasion of his going into war." On May 17 Roosevelt admitted as much when he confided to Secretary of the Treasury Henry Morgenthau, "I am waiting to be pushed into this situation." Morgenthau interpreted this to mean that "he wanted to be pushed into the war rather than lead us into it."[24]

While waiting for an incident to occur, Roosevelt increased the pressure on Germany. On March 29 he authorized the seizure of sixty-five ships of Axis and Axis-occupied nations in American ports. In April Greenland was occupied by U.S. marines for reasons of "hemispheric defense," that is, preventing its conquest by the Germans. In May the president ordered fifty oil tankers transferred to British use, and on May 27 he declared a state of "unlimited national emergency." By now, Roosevelt was no longer talking about defending solely the United States. "Our Bunker Hill," he said, "will be several thousand miles from Boston." Yet the president did nothing to implement the state of emergency, much to the chagrin of interventionists, who believed he should have ordered naval escorts into the Atlantic. (Between April 15 and June 9 public support for American convoy escorts rose from 41 percent to 55 percent.) But, with the nation almost evenly divided on the issue, Roosevelt did not yet want to risk war by initiating convoy escorts. Instead, on June 14 he took the less risky steps of freezing German and Italian assets in the United States and, two days later, closing their American consulates.[25]

## "Barbarossa"

While Roosevelt moved cautiously toward conflict with Germany, the Germans made war on the Soviet Union. On June 22, 1941, 190 German and German-satellite divisions attacked Russia. The invasion ended the brief, unnatural period of cooperation between Hitler and Stalin that had begun with their nonaggression pact of August 23, 1939. Although Stalin had observed the collateral Soviet-German trade agreement by providing Germany with strategic raw materials until the very day of the invasion, Hitler had become alarmed by Soviet ambitions in Eastern Europe. Taking advantage of Germany's preoccupation with the Western powers, Soviet troops invaded Finland in November 1939 and, after stubborn resistance on the part of the Finns, forced them to cede the entire Karelian Isthmus, several islands in the Gulf of Finland as well as territory in Finland's north. In June 1940, shortly before the collapse of France, the Soviets annexed the Baltic states of Latvia, Lithuania, and Estonia. On June 27 Stalin forced Rumania to cede to the Soviet Union northern Bessarabia and northern Bukovina.[26]

In a November 1940 conference with Soviet Foreign Minister Vyacheslav Molotov, Hitler tried unsuccessfully to divert Russia's expansionist impulses toward the Middle East and to the south of Asia, away from German interests in Europe. But Molotov was not about to be lured away from the prime areas of Soviet interest, which, he told Hitler, included Bulgaria, Turkey, Hungary, Rumania, Yugoslavia, Greece, and Finland. The infuriated führer responded to Molotov's arrogant demands by ordering his generals to prepare for the invasion of the Soviet Union, which was code named "Barbarossa." As a prelude to the invasion of Russia, German troops occupied Rumania and Bulgaria, and conquered Yugoslavia and Greece in the spring of 1941.[27]

On the day of the Nazi invasion of Russia, Winston Churchill extended to the Soviet Union Britain's unsolicited offer of help. While he admitted that "the Nazi regime is indistinguishable from the worst features of communism," he also stated that German success in Russia would only increase Britain's peril. "The Russian danger," he concluded, "is therefore, our danger, and the danger of the United States." Three weeks later, on July 12, the Soviet Union and Britain concluded a formal treaty of alliance.[28]

A week before the German invasion, Churchill had sounded out Roosevelt about the idea of publicly welcoming Stalin as an ally in the event Russia were attacked by Hitler. The State Department, which was staffed by people with bitter memories of Stalin's purges and recent Soviet expansion in Eastern Europe, was reluctant to help the Russians. "We should steadfastly adhere to the line that the fact that the Soviet Union is fighting Germany does not mean that it is defending, struggling for, or adhering to the principles in international relations which we are supporting." At most, the department recommended a relaxation of export restrictions to permit the Soviets to buy supplies not needed by either the United States or Britain. The War Department, on the other hand, believed that the shipment of any supplies to Russia would be pointless because it did not believe that the Russians could hold out against the German blitzkrieg for more than three months.[29]

Roosevelt ignored the War Department's predictions and the State Department's hostility to Russia. Instead he accepted the view of Joseph Davies, former U.S. ambassador to Moscow, that the resistance of the Soviet army would "amaze the world." Davies warned that, if the United States withheld assistance to Russia, Stalin might conclude a separate peace with Hitler after the latter seized the Ukraine and Byelorussia. Unlike the State Department's Soviet specialists, Davies did not believe it would be possible "for many years, for the Soviets to project Communism, even if they wished, in the United States or even Europe."[30]

Roosevelt himself was not ignorant about the nature of the Soviet regime. He told a group of left-wing students in 1940 that "everyone who has the courage to face the facts" realized that the Soviet Union "is run by a dictatorship as absolute as any other dictatorship in the world." But he also thought that, under Stalin, the Soviet Union had become less a vanguard of revolution than a conventional imperialist power, with ambitions quite similar to those of the former czarist regime. As a result, the president believed he could deal with Stalin as a realist rather than a radical. However, the paramount consideration that motivated Roosevelt's Soviet policy, both before and after the German invasion of Russia, was his belief that Russian participation in the war was vital to the defeat of Hitler. He realized that the German conquest of Russia, or a separate Soviet-German peace, would be disastrous. Germany would then be able to dominate the Eurasian land mass and nullify the impact of the British blockade. German success in Russia also would encourage further expansion by the Japanese, thereby creating the prospect of Axis domination of the entire Eastern Hemisphere.[31]

On the other hand, continued Russian participation in the war would not only preclude the worst effects of an Axis victory, Roosevelt believed, it would also be the key element in the ultimate defeat of Germany, a victory that he still hoped might be possible without the direct military participation of the United States. Slowly, the military came to share this view. A War Department report, "Major Military Policy," stated: "The maintenance of an active front in Russia offers by far the best opportunity for a successful land offensive against Germany, because only Russia possesses adequate manpower, situated in favorable proximity to the center of German military power. . . . The effective arming of Russian forces would be one of the most important moves that could be made by the Associated Powers."[32]

To keep open the possibility that Stalin would eventually join with the West against Hitler, Roosevelt did not take a hardline position against the Soviets after their nonaggression pact with the Germans. He refused to designate the Soviet Union a belligerent in the wake of its invasion of Poland. Nor did he take a strong stand against Soviet occupation of Estonia, Latvia, and Lithuania. The administration preferred to view Soviet aggression against these countries as a defensive response to German expansion. While he publicly condemned the brutal Soviet attack on Finland, he restrained America's reaction, not only because he believed the American people opposed U.S. intervention in behalf of the Finns, but also because he did not want to take action that would work to tighten the bonds between Russia and Germany. As a result, he did not invoke the Neutrality Act, using the excuse that neither Finland nor the Soviet Union had declared war. And while he invoked a "moral" embargo cutting off the shipment of aircraft and strategic metals to Russia, other Soviet purchases were allowed to more than double over the previous year. Moreover, although he helped to arrange a $20 million loan to the Finns, the amount proved to be much less than the $60 million credit and $20 million worth of war material the Finns had desired. In effect, the United States did little to aid Finland before she capitulated to the Russian demands in March 1940. Afterward, in December of that year, Roosevelt removed the "moral" embargo and once more permitted strategic materials to be sold to Russia.[33]

## Aid to Russia

In response to the German attack on Russia, Roosevelt approved a statement drafted by the State Department condemning the German aggression, and personally added a sentence that read, "Hitler's armies are today the chief dangers of the Americas." When reporters wondered if this meant the United States would aid the Soviets, Roosevelt responded, "Of course we are going to give all the aid we possibly can to Russia." Although he dodged the issue of providing Lend-Lease assistance to the Soviets, he unfroze Russian assets in the United States and refrained from invoking the Neutrality Act, thereby enabling American ships to deliver supplies to Vladivostok.[34]

By the end of July, Roosevelt's close aide, Harry Hopkins, was in Moscow laying the foundation for long-range American aid to Russia. Stalin, who had been pressing the British for a second front in France or the Balkans to divert German divisions from the Russian front, said he would welcome the presence of American troops in Russia. Roosevelt, who had no intention of complying, saw American economic aid not only as a way of keeping Russia in the war but also as the only alternative to a second front neither the United States nor Britain was prepared to establish. For the time being, Stalin accepted the aid alternative. He told Hopkins that the Russian front would not collapse as long as meaningful American aid arrived in time to stem the German advance. That fall, an agreement was concluded in which the United States promised to provide the Soviets, over a nine-month period, 1.5 million tons of supplies valued at $1 billion.[35]

Roosevelt never wavered in his decision to give all possible assistance to the Soviets. On July 9 he told Sumner Welles that he wanted substantial aid sent to Russia before October 1. The next day he personally assured Soviet Ambassador Constantine Oumansky that the United States would do everything possible to deliver supplies to Russia. If the Russians could just hold out until the onset of winter in October, Roosevelt told the Soviet ambassador, he was convinced that the "ultimate defeat of Hitler" would be assured.[36]

But getting aid to the Soviet Union was not accomplished without much difficulty. The effort to keep Britain in the war placed severe demands on American supplies and shipping. There was also bureaucratic reluctance to hasten aid to a country, the Soviet Union, that appeared to be on the verge of collapse. As a result, Roosevelt was compelled to intervene personally to unsnarl delays in getting supplies to Russia. On August 30 he ordered Stimson to prepare immediately a list of supplies that could be delivered to Russia by June 30, 1942. The increase in supplies to the Soviet Union came at the expense of America's armed forces and the British services, which, Churchill commented, considered the reductions analogous to "flaying off pieces of their skin."[37]

Although Roosevelt had the authority to extend Lend-Lease aid to Russia, for a number of reasons, he proceeded cautiously in doing so. For one, the Congress retained control of Lend-Lease appropriations, and could have blocked aid to Russia simply by not funding it. In addition, there was widespread antipathy for the Soviet Union both in Congress and in the nation. According to a Gallup poll on June 24, only 35 percent favored military aid to Russia on the same basis as that to Britain, while 54 percent opposed it. Many felt that a German victory or a Soviet triumph would be equally heinous. More than a few Americans shared the sentiments of Senator Harry S. Truman of Missouri, who suggested: "If we see that Germany is winning, we ought to help Russia and, if Russia is winning, we ought to help Germany, and that way let them kill as many as possible." However, he added: "I don't want to see Hitler victorious under any circumstances. Neither of them think anything of their pledged word."[38]

# The Atlantic Conference

Besides anti-Soviet opinion, another factor complicating Roosevelt's Soviet policy was the issue of postwar boundaries. Almost immediately after Churchill had offered help to the Russians, Stalin began pressing the British and the Americans for recognition of the gains the Soviet Union had made in Eastern Europe after the war began. No matter that these territories were now being overrun by the Germans! At the same time, however, the Polish government-in-exile (the so-called London government) was pressuring both Churchill and Roosevelt to recognize Poland's prewar boundaries, including territory seized by the Russians in September 1939. Prompted by rumors that the British had reached a postwar understanding with Yugoslavia, Assistant Secretary of State Adolf Berle warned, "If we want to have anything to say about the postwar settlement, we had better start now. Otherwise, we shall find, as President Wilson did, that there were all kinds of commitments which we shall be invited to respect; and we shall not be able to break the solid front any more than we were at Versailles."[39]

But Roosevelt was not yet about to deal with the thorny issue of postwar boundaries. In a letter to Churchill, the president expressed his firm belief that it was premature to deal with postwar frontiers at a time when it appeared that Hitler alone would determine them. Moreover, he did not want to do anything that would fracture the Anglo-Russian alliance, and nothing was sure to do that more, or at least so he thought, than taking a position on boundaries. At the same time, the president feared that any discussion of postwar frontiers was bound to upset ethnic Americans with ties to Eastern Europe, thereby upsetting his plans to support Russia against Germany. Churchill responded by saying that Britain had concluded no secret deal with Yugoslavia nor had any desire to do so with any other nation. The British also informed both the Soviets and the Poles that Britain did not recognize any territorial changes that had occurred since the outbreak of the war. As a result, the Polish-Soviet Pact of July 30 left unresolved the matter of Poland's postwar boundaries.[40]

Even though Roosevelt refused to consider postwar frontiers, even before America was committed to the conflict, he found it necessary to address postwar issues. His ability to obtain public and congressional support for the war effort would depend to a great extent on the ability of the American people to understand why the conflict was being fought. Consequently, Roosevelt secretly met Churchill in Placentia Bay, off the coast of Newfoundland near Argentia, between August 9-12, 1941, in the first of a series of wartime conferences between the two leaders. A primary purpose of the Atlantic Conference, at the president's suggestion, was to "draw up a joint declaration laying down certain broad principles which should guide our policies along the same road."[41]

The document that resulted, the so-called Atlantic Charter, paralleled Woodrow Wilson's Fourteen Points. In an effort to preclude secret postwar agreements, the charter stated that the two powers sought no territorial aggrandizement or territorial changes without the freely expressed wishes of the concerned peoples. Moreover, it declared America's and Britain's mutual respect for the right of all peoples to choose the form of government under which they will live. It also called for equal access for all nations to the trade and raw materials of the world, and for a peace in which all people would live in freedom from want and fear. Finally, the Atlantic Charter asserted that, pending the establishment of a permanent system of general security, the disarmament of aggressor states was essential.[42]

Although no one argued that the principles of the Atlantic Charter were so vague that they would be inadequate to address actual postwar conditions, they were soon accepted as the basis of America's policy toward Eastern Europe. In September the governments at war with Germany, including the Soviet Union, accepted the Atlantic Charter. However, the Soviets added a significant reservation to their endorsement of the charter. Its application, they insisted, would have to be adapted to "the circumstances, needs and historic peculiarities of particular countries," a formulation that cast doubt on their simultaneous profession of respect for "the sovereign rights of peoples" and for every nation's "independence and territorial integrity."[43]

While Roosevelt was eager to announciate the principles on which he thought peace should be reestablished, he rejected a British proposal for an international organization designed to uphold them. Fearing that the mere mention of such a body would stir memories of the League of Nations and rattle American isolationists, Roosevelt told Churchill that he preferred to see a joint Anglo-American police force operate for a period after the war before another international organization was created. American isolationists were offended by the Atlantic Charter anyway. They feared that Roosevelt's association with the charter amounted to a joint Anglo-American declaration of war on Germany. The public, for the most part, did not react to the charter as favorably as the president desired. While most Americans supported its principles, 74 percent still opposed U.S. involvement in the war.[44]

## Lend-Lease for Russia

At the Atlantic Conference, both Roosevelt and Churchill promised to create a common pool of resources that would be shared with the Soviet Union. But in the drafting of the Atlantic Charter, Roosevelt blundered by making no mention of religious freedom as a war aim. It was an omission opponents of aid to Russia were quick to condemn. In an attempt to correct his error, the president persuaded the Soviets to engage in what Stalin would later call a "little propaganda work." Roosevelt informed Soviet Ambassador Oumansky that "if Moscow could get some publicity back to this country regarding the freedom of religion in Russia, it might have a very fine educational effect before the next Lend-Lease bill comes up in Congress." Not surprisingly, the Russians complied with Roosevelt's request. On October 4, 1941 they publicly proclaimed that freedom of worship was guaranteed in the Soviet Union as long as it did not challenge the authority of the state. In spite of the incredulous reaction the Soviet statement caused among religious leaders in America, United States ambassador to the Vatican, Myron Taylor, reported in early October that the pope, who had opposed any aid to atheistic Russia, had given a "sympathetic" reception to the American case for supporting the Soviet Union in order to facilitate the defeat of Nazi Germany. A relieved Roosevelt believed he could go ahead with Lend-Lease to Russia without fear of major religious opposition in the United States.[45]

After preparing the ground of public opinion, in September the administration introduced a second Lend-Lease bill in the Congress. To divert public attention from the issue of aiding Russia, however, the administration tried to create the impression that the bill was a separate matter by not specifically including--but not excluding--the Soviet Union from its language. One angry isolationist, Congressman William P. Lamberston of Kansas, reacted by saying that "everyone has insisted this is not the Russian bill, when everyone knows it is." Nevertheless, the bill passed the House on October 10, 1941 by a vote of 328 to 67 and the Senate on October 23 by a vote of 59 to 13. Interventionists supported the bill because they preferred sending American dollars to Russia rather than American boys to fight the Germans. Even some isolationists supported the bill, believing that aid to Russia would preclude direct U.S. military involvement in the war. A week after passage of the bill, Roosevelt sent Stalin a cable announcing his decision to furnish $1 billion worth of supplies under Lend-Lease. In return, Russia had to agree to pay this sum, without interest, over a ten-year period after the war. On November 4 Stalin replied that the Soviet government "accepted with sincere gratitude" the American assistance.[46]

## Preparing for War

In order to extend aid to Russia as well as to Britain, and still prepare the American armed forces for war, on July 9 Roosevelt asked Secretary of War Stimson and Secretary of the Navy Frank Knox to explore at once "the overall production requirements required to defeat our potential enemies." The product of this order was the so-called Victory Program, which was outlined in a report completed on September 25. It called for an expansion of the nation's armed forces to 8,795,658 men and the creation of an army of 215 divisions, including 61 armored divisions. But Roosevelt had no intention of creating an army as large as that recommended by the Victory Program (in fact, the Army never exceeded 90 divisions during World War II). Above all else, he considered American mobilization primarily an industrial effort, with munitions the key to victory. Nevertheless, Secretary of War Stimson was pleased by the president's request for a war program, even one emphasizing industrial production. "It means," he recorded in his diary, "a strategic plan for the means necessary to produce a successful termination of the war against Hitler." But he warned Roosevelt that the industrial mobilization program would not move ahead at full speed as long as the American people believed they could stay out of the war. He wanted the president to ask Congress for a declaration of war "so as to get the benefit of the speed which could be obtained by a war psychosis." But Roosevelt was not ready for so drastic an action. He told Lord Halifax, now the British ambassador to Washington, that "if he asked for a declaration of war, he wouldn't get it, and opinion would swing against him."[47]

The validity of Roosevelt's assessment of the public mood was demonstrated in the fight to extend the Selective Service Act. The original act limited service for all "selectees" to one year and limited their service to the Western Hemisphere. In June, at the insistence of Army Chief of Staff General George Marshall, Roosevelt decided to ask Congress to extend the period of service for the duration of the national emergency. He also wanted Congress to remove the restriction limiting service to the Western Hemisphere and the 900,000-man ceiling on the size of the Army. Unless these steps were taken, Marshall warned, the new Army being created would melt away by the winter of 1942, and it would be impossible to defend either Hawaii or the Philippines, let alone the Atlantic approaches to the United States.[48]

The opposition to Roosevelt's requests was even greater than he had anticipated. Many congressmen argued that extending the period of service would amount to a breach of faith with draftees who had been promised a return to civilian life after twelve months of duty. More than a few congressmen feared giving the president power to send the new Army overseas. Public opinion was also hostile. Most Americans opposed removing the restriction limiting service to the Western Hemisphere, while only a small majority favored extending service for the duration of the national emergency. The strength of the opposition forced Roosevelt to go for half a loaf. He dropped the effort to remove the restriction on service outside the Western Hemisphere but told his supporters to go all-out for extended service. In the end, after Congress approved the new Selective Service bill on August 12, the president was also forced to accept an eighteen-month extension on service rather than the unlimited duration he wanted. The Congress did, however, agree to remove the limit on the number of men that might be trained at any one time. But the incredibly close vote in the House, with 203 votes for and 202 votes against the measure, revealed that many legislators deeply distrusted the president. It also demonstrated that Roosevelt was moving on the war issue as fast as Congress and the public would permit.[49]

## Undeclared Naval War with Germany

Shortly after the German invasion of Russia, Roosevelt took additional steps to protect the transatlantic convoys, now that they had to provide supplies for Russia as well as Britain. On July 1 an agreement was reached with Iceland that permitted U.S. Marines to be stationed in that nation. On July 11 the president approved Hemispheric Defense Plan Four, which provided for "escort convoys of U.S. and Icelandic flag shipping, including shipping of any nationality which may join such convoys between U.S. ports and bases, and Iceland." In this way, British ships traveling with Icelandic vessels could be protected more than halfway across the ocean by the U.S. Navy. But before the new policy was scheduled to go into effect on July 25, Roosevelt, fearing hostile public reaction, backed off from extended convoy protection to any nationality. He still did not believe the American people were ready to protect British convoys.[50]

When Churchill was first informed of Roosevelt's plan to protect American and Icelandic shipping, he was elated. "The president," he told his cabinet after the

Atlantic Conference, "had said that he would wage war but not declare it, and that he would become more and more provocative." Hitler would be compelled to choose between attacking the convoys and risking the involvement in the war of the United States, or lose the Battle of Britain by letting the convoys through. "Everything was to be done to force 'an incident,'" Churchill explained, "which would justify [Roosevelt] in opening hostilities." Stimson was distressed by the president's obvious effort to circumvent Congress' constitutional prerogative to declare war. The situation reminded Stimson of the period between Abraham Lincoln's inauguration and the Confederate attack on Fort Sumter, when there had been considerable "pulling back and forth, trying to make the Confederates fire the first shot."[51]

But Hitler was determined to deny Roosevelt any excuse for leading the American people into the conflict, especially after the invasion of Russia began in June. He ordered German submarine commanders to refrain from attacking American ships. Nevertheless, on September 4 a German submarine fired torpedoes at an American destroyer, the *Greer*. Although the *Greer* was not damaged, Roosevelt denounced the German attack as an unprovoked and deliberate assault on the United States. He did not, however, reveal that the *Greer* had been tracking the submarine and had radioed its position to the British, who unsuccessfully bombed the submarine.[52]

Still, the attack on the *Greer* was the incident Roosevelt wanted. On September 11 he announced that the Navy would henceforth protect all merchant ships regardless of their flag. Two days later, the Atlantic fleet was ordered to shoot on sight any Axis warship operating in the area of American patrol, which was now extended to longitude 10 degrees west, little more than 400 miles off the northern coast of Scotland. On October 9 Congress was asked to repeal the section of the Neutrality Act that prohibited the arming of American merchant ships. Said Senator Vandenburg, the Congress' response to the president's request would "settle the question whether America deliberately and consciously shall go all the way into a shooting war, probably upon two oceans. The ultimate acknowledgement by Congress of a state of war, I fear, will be a mere formality."[53]

While the House was debating the question of arming merchantmen, the Germans again inadvertently came to the administration's assistance. On October 16 a German submarine torpedoed the U.S. destroyer *Kearny*, on convoy patrol some 400 miles south of Iceland. It was not revealed that the *Kearny* had dropped several depth charges on the submarine before it was torpedoed. Yet Roosevelt, in a Navy Day address on October 27, declared: "We have wished to avoid a shooting war. But the shooting has started. And history has recorded who fired the first shot." Four days later, another American destroyer, the *Reuben James*, was attacked and sunk by a German submarine, with the loss of 115 American sailors. A week later Congress repealed both the ban on arming American merchant ships and the provision in the Neutrality Act that prohibited them from entering combat zones. But while the Senate vote was 50 to 37, the margin of victory in the House was only 18 votes, 212 to 194. Despite the closeness of the vote, the end result was still clear: the Neutrality Act was weakened further. Only the bans on loans to belligerents and American travel on belligerent ships remained in force from the original neutrality legislation.[54]

Roosevelt's undeclared naval war on Germany won the overwhelming support of the American people. Sixty-two percent of a national poll approved the "shoot-on-sight" policy. Even after a congressional inquiry into the *Greer* incident revealed that the president had been less than forthright with the American people, neither the Congress nor the public demanded a change in policy toward Germany. As a result, the British were able to concentrate on the German submarine threat in the waters surrounding the British Isles, while the Americans patrolled the rest of the North Atlantic. But the new U.S. policy also made all-out war with Germany virtually inevitable. Only Hitler's determination to knock out Russia first precluded a formal state of war between Germany and the United States.[55]

## War with Japan

But events in the Pacific, rather than in the Atlantic, were ultimately responsible for America's entrance into World War II. Japan's continued aggression in China, her alignment with the Axis powers, and her threat to Anglo-American interests in the Pacific increasingly alarmed Roosevelt while he tried to help Britain and Russia resist Hitler.

Roosevelt's initial inclination was to deal harshly with the Japanese. On January 1, 1938, he imposed a "moral" embargo on aircraft and parts to Japan, and the next month he cut off credit to the Japanese. On July 26, 1939, the administration announced its decision to abrogate the 1911 Japanese-American commercial treaty, which was due to expire in January 1940. During the summer of 1939 he talked privately of intercepting the Japanese fleet if it headed south against Indochina or the Dutch East Indies--although his top naval commanders wondered where he would get the ships to do so. In September he reacted favorably to a Chinese request for additional credits ($25 million had been extended in 1938) by lending China another $20 million. After the Japanese pressured France to close the Indo-Chinese border with China, and Britain the Burma Road in June 1940, Roosevelt the following July 26 ordered the emplacement of restrictions on the export to Japan of aviation gasoline, lubricants, and high-grade, melting scrap iron. (From the United States, Japan imported 80 percent of its oil products, 90 percent of its gasoline, 74 percent of its scrap iron, and 60 percent of its machine tools.) On September 26, after the Japanese successfully pressured the French for troop transit rights, airfields, and economic concessions in northern Indochina, Roosevelt responded with a complete embargo on all exports of scrap iron and steel to Japan. The next day Japan joined the Tripartite Pact with Germany and Italy. That agreement obliged each party "to assist one another with all political, economic and military means when one of the three contracting Parties is attacked by a power at present not involved in the European War or in the Sino-Japanese Conflict." There was no doubt that the pact was directed against the United States.[56]

In the eyes of Roosevelt, the Tripartite Pact transformed what was previously a regional conflict between China and Japan into a major segment of an Axis plot to dominate the world. As a result, the president came to see the continued struggle by the National Chinese forces of Chiang Kai-shek as a vital element of the effort to maintain a world balance of power. If China fell, Southeast Asia would be next. With Japan in control of the Far East and Hitler threatening to conquer Russia, how could Britain expect to hold out? Accordingly, on November 30, the same day Japan recognized a puppet Chinese government in Nanking, Roosevelt announced that the United States would lend $100 million to Chiang. The following month, the president dispatched additional ships and planes to the Philippines. In April 1941 he permitted American military personnel to join Colonel Claire Chennault's "Flying Tigers," a group of U.S. Air Corps volunteers fighting for China.[57]

Most Americans, according to polls taken at the time, supported tightening the economic noose on the Japanese, although they did not favor direct U.S. military involvement in the conflict. But not everyone supported Roosevelt's actions. The New York chapter of the America First Committee wrote:

> The battle in Asia is Britain's battle--and a battle not for democracy, but to continue her hold on 300,000,000 people in India, millions more in Malaya and other territories of Asia, to say nothing of a hundred million in Africa. She is parked there for the gold, the oil, the rubber, the silver, the diamonds, the rich supplies which her capitalists own there--which belong to the peoples of those countries, but which Britain has stolen.

Former Under Secretary of State William Castle, a chief organizer of the Washington Chapter of the America First Committee, argued that what Japan did in China was none of America's business. He felt that the United States should stay out of Japan's way in China until the Japanese experienced their inevitable inability to control the Chinese masses and, as a consequence, withdrew from China. American pressure on the Japanese to leave China before this experience occurred, he warned, could only lead to war with Japan, a conflict from which only the forces of communism in the Far East would prosper.[58]

On the other hand, some of Roosevelt's advisers--particularly Stimson, Treasury Secretary Morgenthau, Navy Secretary Frank Knox, Interior Secretary Harold Ickes, and Stanley Hornbeck of the State Department's Far Eastern Division-- believed that stronger measures were necessary to check Japanese aggression, especially an embargo on oil shipments to Japan. But Roosevelt at first refused to take that step. From Japan, Ambassador Joseph Grew warned that an oil embargo would only make Japan more aggressive, perhaps leading her to seize the oilfields of the Dutch East Indies. Roosevelt did not want a war with Japan that would make it more difficult to counter Hitler. On July 1, 1941, he told Harold Ickes: "It is terribly important for the control of the Atlantic for us to keep peace in the Pacific. I simply have not got enough Navy to go around--and every little episode in the Pacific means fewer ships in the Atlantic."[59]

However, on July 25, after Tokyo demanded the right to occupy eight air and two naval bases in southern Indochina, and Japanese troop transports were observed sailing for Saigon, Roosevelt responded by authorizing a limited freeze of Japanese assets in the United States and a restricted embargo on oil and gasoline exports to Japan. Yet, when the president's order was implemented by the State Department, acting under the instructions of Assistant Secretary Dean Acheson--instructions that were not counteracted by Roosevelt--the embargo on oil to Japan became virtually total. The British and Dutch followed suit by impounding Japanese assets and embargoing all further oil exports to Japan. With only a one-year supply of oil, Japan would be forced to give up her dreams of a new order in East Asia or seize the oilfields of the Dutch East Indies. Grew had no doubts about which alternative the Japanese would choose. "The obvious conclusion," he confided to his diary, "is eventual war."[60]

In August, at the Atlantic Conference, Churchill pressed Roosevelt to deliver an ultimatum to Japan stating that the president would ask Congress for a declaration of war if the Japanese attacked British or Dutch possessions. Churchill saw such an ultimatum not only as a way to ensure that Britain would not be compelled to fight the Japanese alone but also as a way to bring the United States into the war. But Roosevelt continued to delay a showdown with the Japanese. A war at this time, Sumner Welles explained to a British official, "would not only tie up the major portion of, if not the entire, American fleet, but would likewise create a very serious strain upon our military establishment and upon our productive activities at the very moment when these should be concentrated upon the Atlantic." Although Roosevelt warned Japan on August 17 that further Japanese encroachments in the southwest Pacific would compel him to take all measures "necessary . . . toward insuring the safety and security of the United States," he also expressed an interest in a Japanese offer to resume negotiations. The president told Churchill at the Atlantic Conference that his desire to negotiate with the Japanese was motivated primarily by a desire to put off what he believed was an inevitable conflict with Japan.[61]

But while Roosevelt was willing to negotiate with the Japanese, he was not prepared to sell out the Chinese. And that would have been the ultimate result of the Japanese peace plan that was offered to the United States on August 6. In it the Japanese promised not to advance into the southwest Pacific beyond Indochina and to withdraw their forces from Indochina after the China "incident" was ended. In return, the Japanese expected the United States to halt all military preparations in the southwest Pacific, restore normal trade relations with Japan, help the Japanese obtain raw materials from the Dutch East Indies, use its good offices to get Chiang Kai-shek to make peace with Japan, and recognize that the Japanese were entitled to a special position in Indochina even after the withdrawal of their forces.[62]

Events in Japan took an ominous turn on October 16, when Premier Konoye Fumimaro, who favored a negotiated settlement with the United States, resigned and was replaced by the more aggressive war minister, Tojo Hideki. Three weeks later, on November 5, an Imperial Conference decided that, if a diplomatic accommodation with the United States proved impossible to achieve by November 25 (a deadline that was later extended to November 29), the emperor would be asked to approve a decision for war. At the same time, the Japanese military was instructed to prepare for the commencement of hostilities in early December. The operational orders issued on November 5 included preparations for an attack on Pearl Harbor.[63]

Fortunately for the United States, American cryptographers had been able to break the Japanese secret code that was used to transmit messages from Tokyo to its embassy in Washington. The intelligence so derived was code named "Magic." As a result, by early November Roosevelt was aware that the Japanese were about to make their final offer. It came on November 20. Japan offered to transfer her troops from southern to northern Indochina, and to withdraw all of her forces from Indochina upon the conclusion of the conflict with China. In return, the Japanese expected the United States to restore full commercial relations with Japan, including the sale of oil to Japan, to assist Japan in obtaining goods from the Dutch East Indies, and "to refrain from such measures and actions as will be prejudicial to the endeavors for restoration of general peace between Japan and China."[64]

Although the Japanese proposal was unacceptable to Roosevelt and Hull, primarily because it would have required the United States to give Japan a free hand in China, both tried to string out the negotiations in order to give the U.S. military time to complete defensive preparations in the Philippines and western Pacific. On November 24 Roosevelt informed Churchill that the United States intended to offer Japan a State Department designed, three-month *modus vivendi,* which would include "a monthly quota of oil for civilian needs and a limited amount of a few other supplies, in return for a Japanese promise not to advance either northward or southward." But the president was compelled to add: "I am not very hopeful, and we must be prepared for real trouble, possibly soon." However, after Churchill and Chiang objected to any relaxation of the economic pressure on Japan, Hull persuaded Roosevelt to drop the idea of a *modus vivendi* with the Japanese. Instead, the secretary of state on November 26 restated the extreme American position, calling for an end to Japan's aggression in China as the prerequisite to reestablishing normal commercial relations.[65]

By then, thanks to "Magic," it was quite apparent to the president that negotiations with Japan had failed, and that military action was now inevitable. From Magic he had learned that the Japanese considered November 29 the last day for signing an agreement, after which time, one Japanese cable warned, "things are automatically going to happen." On November 25 Roosevelt warned his top advisers that Japan was likely to initiate a war with a surprise attack. "The question," Stimson recorded in his diary, "was how we should maneuver them into the position of firing the first shot without allowing too much danger to ourselves." After Japanese troop transports were sighted moving south toward Indochina on November 25-26, Roosevelt and his advisers were led to believe the Japanese were more likely to strike at Thailand, Malaya, or the Dutch East Indies than the Philippines or Hawaii. Nevertheless, on November 27 Admiral Harold Stark, the chief of naval operations, alerted both the American forces in the Philippines as well as the Pacific fleet based at Pearl Harbor to the possibility of a surprise attack. On December 1 and 3 Roosevelt told Lord Halifax that he was prepared to defend the threatened non-American territories with force, and he instructed Hull to prepare a statement explaining the rationale for doing so.[66]

Contrary to charges by some isolationists, and later by some revisionist historians, all available evidence indicates that Roosevelt and his advisers were surprised by the Japanese attack on Pearl Harbor on December 7. But they were also relieved by the Japanese action. "All of us believed," Harry Hopkins recalled, "that in the last analysis the enemy was Hitler, and that he could never be defeated without force of arms; that sooner or later we were bound to be in the war and that Japan had given us an opportunity." On December 8 the president asked Congress for a declaration of war against Japan. Both houses complied with only one dissenting vote. Three days later, Germany and Italy declared war on the United States, and on the same day the United States reciprocated. "So we had won after all!" an elated Churchill recalled telling the president. "No doubt it would take a long time. . . . But there was no more doubt about the end."[67]

Years later, Senator Vandenberg, who became the leader of the isolationists upon the death of William Borah in 1940, remembered the impact of Pearl Harbor: "That day ended isolationism for any realist." After months of struggle, Franklin D. Roosevelt finally had overcome the isolationist effort to keep America out of the war.[68]

## The Continuing Debate

But the methods Roosevelt employed in bringing the nation into the war have remained controversial to this day. Historian Jonathan G. Utley places at least partial blame for the outbreak of the Pacific war on Hull and Roosevelt. Hull, Utley argues, refused to make the kind of compromise with the Japanese--for example the *modus vivendi* suggested by Roosevelt in late November 1941--that could have purchased valuable time that the United States needed to aid England or at least to complete preparations for the defense of the Philippines. The president, for his part, refused to overrule the secretary of state with respect to Japan, not only because Hull had made Japanese diplomacy his "turf," but also because Roosevelt was heavily preoccupied with European affairs. In Utley's estimation, Roosevelt's handling of Japan was a major failure of his leadership.[69]

Some recent interpreters of Roosevelt's policy toward the Axis powers, including Utley and Frederick Marks, consider that policy as often muddled, unnecessarily devious, and too heavily dependent on the views of an excessively cautious Hull. On the other hand, Waldo Heinrichs believes that Roosevelt was very much in charge of the administration's policy, in spite of the unstructured procedures he followed. In Heinrichs' opinion, the president timed the increasing pressure he brought to bear upon the Japanese, as well as America's step-by-step intervention in the Atlantic war, with the public's improving perception of the Axis threat to American security, which did not allow Roosevelt to proceed faster than he did.[70]

In the same vein, historian Robert Dallek has argued that, considering the reluctance of the American people to fully confront the international dangers facing the country, Roosevelt cannot be criticized for being less than forthright with them. "Had he directly presented his views to the public of what it must do in response to the world crisis," Dallek has written, "it would have won him few converts and undermined his popularity and ability to lead by confronting ambivalent Americans with a choice they did not care to make." Had he not provoked an undeclared naval war with Hitler, and instead waited until the American people would support a resort to arms, he would have had to risk the defeat of both Britain and Russia. That course, Dallek has argued, "would have been a failure of his responsibility as commander-in-chief."[71]

Less sympathetic to Roosevelt, however, is historian Robert Divine. Roosevelt, Divine has written, became a "prisoner of his own policies." By telling the American people repeatedly that U.S. intervention in the war would not be necessary, and that Hitler could be defeated simply by providing all-out American aid to England, Roosevelt had deprived himself of the option of truthfully telling the American people that the nation must enter the war to ensure its security. As a result, Divine concluded, "all he could do was edge the country closer and closer, leaving the ultimate decision to Germany and Japan."[72]

But even if one accepts, as Dallek and others do, that Roosevelt's deviousness was necessary to protect the nation's security, it nevertheless set a precedent that, in the long run, would be harmful to constitutional government in the United States. "FDR's deviousness in a good cause," Senator William J. Fulbright commented at the height of the Vietnam War, "made it easier for LBJ [President Lyndon Baines Johnson] to practice the same kind of deviousness in a bad cause." And, as subsequent events would demonstrate, Lyndon Johnson would not be the last president who was less than candid with the American people and Congress when it came to employing the nation's military power.[73]

# 5

# The Grand Alliance, 1941–1943

## The ARCADIA Conference, December 1941-January 1942

Soon after the Japanese attack on Pearl Harbor, Winston Churchill invited himself to Washington to discuss strategy with the president and his advisors. This first Washington Conference, code named ARCADIA, extended from December 22, 1941, to January 14, 1942. Churchill's primary fear--that in the wake of the Pearl Harbor attack the United States would concentrate its energies on the defeat of Japan--was quickly relieved. The Americans reaffirmed the decision of the ABC-1 Report to defeat Germany first. The British were also assured that U.S. military production would not be diverted from Britain to equipping the American armed forces. Nevertheless, an acute shortage of shipping, combined with German submarine attacks on ships destined for Britain, would be a major problem in the first two years of the war.[1]

The major area of disagreement concerned the proper strategy for defeating Germany. As in the ABC-1 Report, the British wanted to ensure American military involvement in northern Africa in order to defeat German and Italian forces under the command of Field Marshal Erwin Rommel, which were threatening the Suez Canal, Britain's lifeline to the oil of the Mideast and her Asian empire. Driving the Axis from Africa, Churchill believed, would "close the ring" around Germany and would make possible an invasion of Europe in 1943. The Continent could be invaded, he argued, at several points, including the Balkans, Italy, and finally France--but only after Germany had been sufficiently weakened by Allied aerial bombardment and blockade. Following this strategy, he believed, the Germans could be defeated by late 1943 or early 1944.[2]

However, the American military, led by Army Chief of Staff General George C. Marshall, vehemently opposed U.S. participation in a North African campaign. They insisted that only an invasion of France, which they believed should take place as soon as possible, would give meaningful relief to the hard-pressed Soviets. "We would be guilty of one of the grossest blunders of history," argued General Dwight D. Eisenhower, the head of the War Plans Division of the War

Department, "if Germany should be permitted to eliminate an Allied [Soviet] army of 8,000,000 men." In addition to giving meaningful relief to the Russians, an invasion of France would strike the Germans in the most direct manner possible, permitting maximum utilization of shipping and air power without endangering the security of the British Isles by sending troops far from them. Churchill's "side show" in North Africa, America's military chiefs argued, would only delay the invasion of France and thereby the termination of the war. The Americans suspected that the primary objective of Churchill's Mediterranean strategy was the preservation of Britain's empire.[3]

For a number of reasons, however, Roosevelt was strongly attracted to the Mediterranean theater of operations. For one, he was concerned about the possibility of a German thrust into the western bulge of Africa, near Dakar, a move he believed would threaten Brazil. Occupation of French North Africa would remove that danger. In addition, the opening of the Mediterranean would greatly shorten Allied supply routes to the Middle East and India and relieve the acute shortage of shipping the Allies were experiencing. But more important was the fact that no other plan could provide the opportunity to employ American soldiers against the Germans in the near future. Sufficient forces for a successful invasion of France could not be amassed until 1943, perhaps too late to help the Soviets avoid disaster. Finally, an early invasion of North Africa would counter the apathetic attitude the American people were displaying toward fighting the Germans and diminish pressure from the public, the Congress, and the Navy to concentrate America's main military effort against the Japanese, a move Roosevelt believed would be disastrous to the overall conduct of the war. It was "very important to morale," he told Marshall, "to give this country a feeling that they are in the war, [and] to give the Germans the reverse effect, to have American troops somewhere in active fighting across the Atlantic."[4]

As a result, on January 14, 1942, Roosevelt supported Churchill's plan for an Anglo-American invasion of North Africa (first code named SUPERGYMNAST; later simply GYMNAST). Although the invasion was tentatively scheduled to begin in May, it soon became obvious that the operation would have to be postponed. On January 21 Rommel resumed his offensive in Libya and pushed the British Eighth Army back toward the Egyptian frontier, thereby raising doubts about its ability to apply effective pressure on the Axis from the east when Anglo-American forces landed in northwestern Africa. In addition, the Allies learned that it would not be possible to obtain the support, or at least acquiescence, of Vichy troops in French North Africa. Marshal Pétain warned that his government would "resist invasion by British, Gaullists, Germans, or Americans."[5]

In addition to the North African invasion, Roosevelt approved Churchill's overall strategy for Europe, which consisted of four major elements. First, the "ring" around Germany would be closed by holding and strengthening a line running from Archangel to the Black Sea and along the northern coast of the Mediterranean and the western coast of Europe. Second, all possible support would be given to the Soviets. Third, the air-offensive against, and blockade of, Germany would be intensified, and subversive movements in the occupied countries would be organized and assisted. And finally Europe would be invaded during 1943 from "across the Mediterranean, from Turkey into the Balkans, or by landings in Western Europe." To help implement this strategy, in addition to the steps already taken, it was agreed that American troops would be sent to Northern Ireland and American bombers would be based in the British Isles. Most of the remainder of the conference's time was occupied with plans for defensive deployments of ships and troops in the Pacific and the Far East.[6]

Still, there was time, on New Year's Day 1942, for twenty-six nations, including Britain, the Soviet Union, and the United States, to sign the Declaration of the United Nations, the name Roosevelt gave to the Allied nations. The signatories pledged to follow the principles of the Atlantic Charter, to launch efforts to defeat "Hitlerism" (a word made necessary by the Soviet Union's firm decision to avoid war with Japan), and to refrain from signing a separate peace with any of the common enemies.[7]

Another accomplishment of the ARCADIA Conference was the creation of the Combined Chiefs of Staff, with representatives from the military establishments of Britain and the United States (but not from the Soviet Union). The primary function of the Combined Chiefs was to translate the overall objectives of the president and the prime minister into operational orders for the military forces of the two nations. The establishment of the Combined Chiefs prompted the creation of the U.S. Joint Chiefs of Staff in February 1942. The Joint Chiefs were given the responsibility of coordinating the operations of the American armed services.[8]

## The Second Front

Part of the reason why Roosevelt approved GYMNAST at the ARCADIA Conference was the failure of the American General Staff to create an alternative plan that could compete with Churchill's Mediterranean strategy. By late March 1942, however, Marshall and his staff formulated an alternative to the British strategy. Code named Operation ROUNDUP, the American plan called for an invasion of France between Le Havre and Boulogne with forty-eight divisions, thirty of them American, in April 1943. However, if the Soviets appeared to be on the verge of collapse before then, the American military chiefs envisioned an emergency invasion that could take place as early as the fall of 1942, code named Operation SLEDGEHAMMER. This was to be a limited action designed to seize and hold a bridgehead in France until the major assault could be launched the following spring. SLEDGEHAMMER, it was hoped, would draw not only German troops from the Soviet front but also a large portion of the Luftwaffe. Roosevelt approved the plan on April 1 primarily because, with GYMNAST postponed as a result of Rommel's advance into Egypt, it offered the only prospect of giving prompt aid to the Soviets. "The Russians," Roosevelt emphasized to Churchill, "are today killing more Germans and destroying more equipment than you and I put together."[9]

Churchill, however, had serious misgivings about the American plan. For one, he believed that an early cross-Channel invasion had no chance of success. Too few forces would be available in 1942 to ensure the success of SLEDGEHAMMER, meaning it would be a sacrificial venture. Moreover, because American troops could not be trained and equipped soon enough to participate in large numbers in SLEDGEHAMMER, it would be the British who would do most of the sacrificing. Churchill could not accept this outcome either for political or military reasons. Not only would he be subjected to a parliamentary vote of confidence that he might lose, but there were not enough British troops as it was to defend the vast empire without engaging in the sacrificial venture in France the Americans contemplated. It was impossible, Churchill felt, to defend Egypt and India while simultaneously engaging in a military buildup (which was code named Operation BOLERO) for a cross-Channel invasion.[10]

The British, however, had to be careful in the way they reacted to the American plan. Open opposition could encourage the Americans to shift their attention to the Pacific. As a result, Churchill and the British Chiefs agreed with the parts of the American plan that they liked and ignored the parts they disliked. They supported the plan for a rapid buildup of American forces in Britain as a prelude to a Continental invasion in 1943. But they also stated that before such an invasion could occur, Germany would have to be weakened first. SLEDGEHAMMER, the sacrificial invasion in 1942, was ignored by the British. Yet the Americans received the impression that the British had accepted the U.S.-backed strategy in its entirety, SLEDGEHAMMER included. Pleased with the British response, Marshall promised that India would receive enough supplies to check a Japanese invasion.[11]

Later, Major General Hastings Ismay, Churchill's representative to the Chiefs of Staff Committee, admitted that it had been a mistake to delude the Americans. "When we had to tell them, after a most thorough study of SLEDGEHAMMER, that we were absolutely opposed to it, they felt that we had broken faith with them. . . . I think we should have come clean, much cleaner than we did, and said, 'We are frankly horrified because of what we have been through in our lifetime. We are not going into this until it is cast-iron certainty.'" The British faux pas did much to strain Anglo-American relations for the rest of the war.[12]

## Dealing with Stalin

The problems the British experienced with the Americans were only compounded by the difficulties they encountered with the Russians. In November 1941, when the German advance toward Moscow had not yet been checked, Britain's inability to start a second front or to send large forces to fight in Russia led to sharp exchanges between Stalin and Churchill. After the German drive was stopped short of Moscow in early December, the Soviet need for a second front lost some of its urgency, thereby allowing the Russians to raise once again the matter of the postwar settlement. Stalin told British Foreign Secretary Anthony Eden, when the latter visited Moscow that month, that after the war Germany should be partitioned and reparations in kind collected from German industry. Stalin also wanted the prewar boundaries of 1941 reestablished, meaning that the British would have to recognize the Soviet annexation of the Baltic states, as well as parts of Finland, Poland, and Rumania. Without such recognition, Stalin told Eden, he could not conclude a formal treaty of alliance with Britain. Churchill, however, wanted no part of any agreement recognizing the transfer of territory in advance of a future peace conference. Such an agreement would not only alienate the Americans, who had taken a strong line against secret agreements and territorial settlements made in advance of a general peace conference, it could also give the Russians more territory than they might be strong enough to take.[13]

Confronted by British opposition to his postwar territorial ambitions, Stalin turned to a technique he would employ more than once--the threat of a separate peace with Germany. In a speech on February 23, 1942, the Soviet dictator said: "It would be ridiculous to identify Hitler's clique with the German people and the German state. History shows that Hitlers come and go, but the German people and the German state remain." Stalin's threat may have persuaded Churchill to be more conciliatory on the territorial issue. By March 1942 the British were ready to accept Soviet annexation of the Baltic states, although they continued to resist Stalin's claim to eastern Poland.[14]

In a letter to Roosevelt on March 7, Churchill asked the president to give him "a free hand to sign the treaty which Stalin desires as soon as possible." Churchill felt that it was essential to make territorial concessions to the Soviets before the anticipated German spring offensive, in lieu of the material or military assistance neither Britain nor America could provide, in order to keep the Russians in the war. Roosevelt responded by stating that the proposed Anglo-Soviet treaty had to provide for those Baltic peoples who might not wish to live under Soviet rule. He wanted a clause added to the treaty permitting the Lithuanians, Latvians, Estonians, and Finns affected "to leave those territories with their properties and belongings." Though the Soviets rejected this proposal when Eden tried to add it to the treaty, the very fact that Roosevelt suggested it was a sign of his willingness to accept the Soviet territorial demands. Like Churchill, historian Robert Dallek has argued, Roosevelt was "unwilling to raise questions that might weaken the Soviet resolve to fight."[15]

But Secretary of State Cordell Hull refused to recognize the territorial transfer. "The Soviet Government," he wrote, "has tremendous ambitions with regard to Europe. It would seem that it is preferable to take a firm attitude now, rather than to retreat and to be compelled to take a firm attitude later when our position had been weakened by the abandonment of general principles." On May 22 Hull sent the British a message warning that, if the impending Anglo-Soviet treaty recognized the 1941 Soviet frontiers, "we might have to issue a separate statement clearly stating that we do not subscribe to its principles and clauses." Roosevelt, who did not want a major fight with Hull on postwar boundaries, a fight that might leak to the press, approved the secretary of state's message.[16]

Blocked in his attempt to use territorial concessions to ensure continued Soviet participation in the war, Roosevelt tried another tactic. In London, U.S. Ambassador John G. Winant informed Soviet Foreign Minister Molotov on May 24 that while the United States could not recognize territorial settlements before a peace conference, America was very much interested in creating a second front as soon as possible. With such a prospect dangled before their eyes, the Soviets dropped, for the time being, their territorial demands. The Anglo-Soviet treaty that was signed by Molotov on May 26 made no mention of postwar frontiers. In it both countries merely promised to provide assistance to each other and to make no separate peace.[17]

After his talks in London, Molotov arrived in Washington on May 29 expecting a payoff for his concession on the territorial issue in the form of an American commitment to an early second front. In a conference with Roosevelt and General Marshall the next day, he pointedly asked the president if it would be possible for the Western Allies to mount an operation in 1942 that would draw forty German divisions from the Russian front. Roosevelt turned to Marshall and asked him if it was possible to tell Stalin that a second front was being prepared. After Marshall responded affirmatively, Roosevelt authorized Molotov to inform the Soviet leader that "we expect the formation of a second front this year." Bothered by such a definite commitment, Marshall tried to qualify the president's statement by adding a description of the difficulties a cross-Channel operation would encounter that year. But when Marshall urged the president to remove all reference to a date for the invasion, Roosevelt refused.[18]

Yet Roosevelt exacted a price for his promise of a second front. He told Molotov that in order to free shipping for the invasion it would be necessary to reduce Lend-Lease shipments to Russia from 4.1 to 2.5 million tons in the coming year. Molotov sarcastically replied that "the second front would be stronger if the first front still stood." He then asked what would happen if the Soviets accepted these reductions "and then no second front eventuated?" To reassure him, Roosevelt agreed to Molotov's suggestion that the communiqué released at the end of the Russian's visit would read: "In the course of the conversations, full understanding was reached with regard to the urgent tasks of creating a Second Front in Europe in 1942."[19]

The British, however, were not about to permit Roosevelt to commit them to a premature cross-Channel operation. When Molotov stopped in London on his way back to Russia, Churchill personally handed him an *aide-mémoire* that stated, in part: "It is impossible to say in advance whether the situation will be such as to make this operation feasible when the time comes. *We can therefore give no promise in this matter.* But the Soviets ignored Churchill's qualifications and instead emphasized Roosevelt's promise that a second front would be created in Europe that year. On June 22 the American ambassador in Moscow, William H. Standley, warned "that if such a front does not materialize quickly and on a large scale, these people will be so deluded in their belief in our sincerity of purpose that inestimable harm will be done."[20]

# TORCH

In June 1942 the European Theater of Operations: U.S.A. was established with General Dwight D. Eisenhower in command. Eisenhower arrived in Britain determined to put SLEDGEHAMMER into operation. But it was soon apparent to the Americans that a cross-Channel operation could not take place in 1942. For one reason, SLEDGEHAMMER received no support from the British. During a second Roosevelt-Churchill conference, held in Washington from June 19 to 25, the prime minister and the British Chiefs argued that there was no way a cross-Channel operation could be mounted that year that would be large enough to succeed. Any doubts concerning this would be laid to rest, at least in the minds of the British, by a raid on the French port of Dieppe that would be conducted two months later by 7,000 Canadian and British troops. The Canadians suffered 3,000 casualties in only nine hours of fighting before they and the British forces were withdrawn from the encounter. In addition, while Churchill was in Washington in June, Rommel scored a stunning victory in Libya by capturing Tobruk with a force inferior in size to that of its British defenders. The position of the British Eighth Army was so desperate that Roosevelt approved the immediate transfer to Egypt of 300 new Sherman tanks. With Egypt in danger of being overrun, Roosevelt and Churchill agreed to postpone a strategic decision and instead study all the offensive possibilities, including landings in France, North Africa, Norway, and the Iberian peninsula. Although the American military buildup in Britain was permitted to continue, the inability of Roosevelt and Churchill to make a definite strategic decision at Washington in effect meant that there would be no cross-Channel operation in 1942.[21]

Disillusioned by the prospect of no major American operation in Europe during 1942, the U.S. Joint Chiefs of Staff tried to shift the main American military effort to the Pacific theater. But Roosevelt refused, as he put it, to "turn our faces away from Germany and toward Japan." In his estimation, Germany remained the major threat to Britain and Russia; their surrender, he insisted, would cause Axis power to be concentrated against the United States. Furthermore, after the Japanese navy suffered major defeats in the battles of the Coral Sea in May and Midway Island in June, the Japanese naval threat to Australia and Hawaii had diminished appreciably. As a result, Roosevelt insisted that Germany would remain the primary target of America's war effort and that an invasion of France must take place in 1943.[22]

But the president refused to delay a major American ground operation against Germany until then. He believed that it was important, for the sake of American morale, to get U.S. soldiers into action as soon as possible. And it was vital to give Stalin's demand for a second front some satisfaction, not only to lift Soviet morale but also to prevent a collapse of the Russian army.

Roosevelt had good reason for concern about his Soviet ally. When Stalin received word in July that there would be no invasion of Europe in 1942, he complained that the Soviet Union was being betrayed by its allies. He was further outraged when, in that same month, the British suspended for the rest of the summer the northern convoys to Russia. The British decision was prompted by the disaster that struck one convoy (PQ 17) that had sailed for Archangel that month: the Germans sank twenty-three of its thirty-four merchant ships, destroying 500 of the 600 tanks it carried. Nevertheless, at a time when the German forces were once again rolling across the plains of southern Russia, Stalin found the postponement of the cross-Channel invasion and the suspension of the northern convoys bitter pills to swallow.[23]

Roosevelt also believed that the defense of the Middle East was vital to both Britain and the Soviet Union. If the Germans overran Egypt and the Suez Canal, they would be in a position to cut off the West's access to Persian Gulf oil and to strike at Russia through Turkey and Iran. With these considerations in mind, on July 25 the president gave his approval to Churchill's proposal for an invasion of North Africa, which was code named TORCH.[24]

As planned by Eisenhower, TORCH called for two Anglo-American forces to attack the ports of Oran and Algiers on the Mediterranean coast, while a third force would cross the Atlantic from the United States and land on the Moroccan coast near Casablanca. Six hundred vessels would be required to transport six divisions--three British and three Americans, some 90,000 men and their supplies and equipment--in the initial assault, with some 200,000 to follow, 1,500 miles from Britain and over 3,000 miles from the United States. It was decided that the invasion would take place no later than October 30, 1942, and that General Eisenhower would be the Allied commander.[25]

## The French and TORCH

To ensure the success of TORCH, the Americans were eager to find a French leader with whom they could work to preclude any resistance to the invasion. Charles de Gaulle, the leader of the Free French, could not play this role because he was considered a traitor by the Vichy forces that controlled French North Africa. Another alternative, General Henri Giraud, who had escaped from a German prison camp and expressed his willingness to work with the Allies, also had little support in North Africa. As a result, the Americans were compelled to seek the assistance of a prominent Vichy leader, Admiral Jean Darlan, who happened to be in Algiers when the North African invasion began, on November 8, one week later than originally planned. Although Darlan had collaborated with the Germans, he alone had the authority to order a cease-fire in French North Africa. In return for Darlan's cooperation to that effect, Eisenhower agreed to recognize him as the head of the civil government in North Africa, subject to Eisenhower's supervision, while General Giraud was given command of French military forces in the region.[26]

As a result of Darlan's cease-fire order, French resistance in Oran and Casablanca was relatively brief, although fierce, and within three days the fighting ended in Algeria and Morocco. However, the French authorities in Tunisia permitted German forces to occupy that colony and, as a result, the battle for North Africa would last until May. In reaction to the Allied invasion, Pétain broke off diplomatic relations with the United States. The move did not, however, prevent the Germans from occupying that part of France under Vichy control. Fortunately for the Allies, the Germans did not gain control of the French fleet based at Toulon. Unfortunately, neither did the Allies. In one day, on November 25, the French scuttled their entire Toulon fleet--177 warships, including three battleships, seven cruisers, thirty destroyers, and sixteen submarines.[27]

The deal worked out between Eisenhower and Darlan provoked considerable criticism on both sides of the Atlantic. But Eisenhower, with Roosevelt's support, defended his action on the ground that it saved Allied lives and time. Churchill only reluctantly accepted the Darlan deal because he feared the repercussions it would have on Allied relations with the Free French. Needless to say, de Gaulle would have nothing to do with Darlan. Fortunately for the Allies, Darlan's timely assassination by a disgruntled French royalist on December 24, 1942, ended an embarrassing situation.[28]

Even with Darlan out of the way, relations between the Anglo-Americans and de Gaulle remained strained for the remainder of the war. De Gaulle considered himself the embodiment of French honor and prestige, both of which had been dragged through the mud by the Vichyite collaboration with Hitler. De Gaulle tried to impress upon Roosevelt that the restoration of a stable Western Europe depended on the reestablishment of France as a great power. "Of all the great nations of Europe," de Gaulle told the president, France "is the only one which was, is, and always will be, your ally."[29]

While Churchill considered de Gaulle arrogant, egotistical, and inflexible, he nevertheless supported the Free French movement because he saw it as the best hope of restoring a strong France allied to Britain after the war. But Roosevelt, who believed that de Gaulle was more concerned with securing his postwar position in France than in doing what he could to help the Allies win the war, wanted nothing to do with him. De Gaulle, he told Churchill, was trying to be another Napoleon, with a personal dictatorship as his ultimate goal. To prevent this, Roosevelt refused to recognize any French provisional government until the people of France had the opportunity to approve it, which, of course, would not be possible until France was liberated.[30]

Roosevelt's policy only infuriated de Gaulle. "From the moment America entered the war," he complained in his *Memoirs*, "Roosevelt meant the peace to be an American peace, that the states which had been overrun should be subject to his judgement, and that France in particular should recognize him as its savior and arbiter." What aggravated de Gaulle even more about Roosevelt was the latter's willingness to work with Vichy France before the Allied invasion of North Africa. Not until July 1942 did the president decide to hedge his Vichy bet by accrediting representatives to de Gaulle's National Committee and making the Free French directly eligible for Lend-Lease. After the North African invasion, Roosevelt preferred to work with Giraud, who was given the title "Military and Civil Commander in Chief of French North Africa." But as de Gaulle's prestige in the French community increased, Giraud's declined, and Roosevelt ultimately was forced to give de Gaulle the recognition he had long desired. Yet it was not until after the invasion of France in June 1944 that the United States finally recognized de Gaulle's Committee of National Liberation as the de facto government of France. The animosity that divided Roosevelt and de Gaulle would have a long-lasting impact on Franco-American relations.[31]

Soviet recognition of de Gaulle and the Free French movement was far less grudgingly granted. On September 27, 1941 the Soviets recognized de Gaulle "as the leader of all Free Frenchmen" and promised "to afford the Free French every possible help and assistance in the common struggle against Hitlerite Germany."

Stalin even ordered the French communists to cooperate with de Gaulle, since the Soviet leader was much more interested in defeating Germany than in inciting a communist revolution in France. To Stalin, it was deplorable that Roosevelt was trying to undermine de Gaulle at a time when he considered it imperative to reinforce him.[32]

# Aftermath of TORCH

In retrospect, even General Marshall came to regard TORCH as a strategically wise move. The operation provided the Allies with valuable experience in using large masses of troops in an amphibious operation in an area where the risks of doing so were far less than would have to be faced later in Italy and France. Moreover, while providing the Americans with needed combat experience, TORCH also deprived Hitler of a quarter of a million troops, and thus provided some immediate relief to the Russians. Not surprisingly, however, Stalin was not effusive over the TORCH landings. He simmered over the cancellation of the northern convoys caused by the diversion of Allied shipping to North Africa. And while he sent his congratulations after the successful Allied landings, he did not buy Roosevelt's argument that the North African invasion fulfilled his promise of a second front in 1942. To Stalin, TORCH was no substitute for a cross-Channel invasion. How livid he would have been had he only realized at that time that TORCH would delay the invasion of France for another year, another year in which the brunt of the Nazi war effort would fall on Russia. The duplicity practiced by Roosevelt in defending TORCH would not be forgotten by the Russians.[33]

# Turning Points of the War

TORCH was only one of a series of decisive campaigns that began during 1942 that would become turning points in the war. While Anglo-American forces advanced from the west toward Tunisia, the British Eighth Army, which had thrown Rommel into retreat after the battle of El Alamein on October 23-24, advanced from the east. Now under the command of General Bernard Montgomery, the Eighth Army captured Tobruk on November 12 and Tripoli on January 23, 1943. But the Germans quickly rushed reinforcements into Tunisia, and it was not until after much hard fighting that the Germans and Italians were finally driven from North Africa in May.

The Germans suffered an even more decisive defeat on the Russian front. On November 19, 1942, only eleven days after the Allied landings in North Africa, Soviet forces attacked both north and south of Stalingrad, encircling the German Sixth Army within the city. When it fell to the Soviets on January 31, 1943, the Red Army had dealt the Wehrmacht a blow from which it would never recover. Stalingrad marked the beginning of the end of Hitler's great Russian campaign.

No less important to the Allied cause was victory over Germany's submarines in the Atlantic. By the end of August 1942, Allied shipping construction finally exceeded losses from submarine attacks. The turnaround was due partly to increased shipbuilding, the use of more effective antisubmarine weapons, particularly radar-equipped search planes, and in December the ability of the British, using a deciphering apparatus called ENIGMA, to break the German code used in U-boat communications. As the German submarine menace declined, it would be possible to transport increasingly larger numbers of Allied troops and supplies to the coastal reaches of the Axis empire.[34]

The war in the Pacific also experienced a turning point during 1942. In May the American naval victory in the battle of the Coral Sea effectively halted the Japanese threat to Australia. A month later, the Japanese navy was decisively defeated in the battle of Midway, thereby precluding any possibility of a Japanese invasion of Hawaii. After Midway, American and Australian troops assumed the offensive against the Japanese on New Guinea. And on August 7 U.S. marines landed on Guadalcanal and other islands in the Solomons chain. By February 1943 Guadalcanal was secure, and the long process of pushing the Japanese back in the central Pacific could begin. With the Japanese on the defensive, the war in the Pacific had turned the corner.

# The Casablanca Conference, January 1943

In the European-Mediterranean theater, the successful Anglo-American invasion of North Africa raised the immediate military question of what to do next. With the American buildup in Britain slowed by the invasion of North Africa, and with the Americans taking the offensive against the Japanese in the Pacific, Churchill again feared that the United States would reduce its military effort in the European-Mediterranean theater.

The prime minister was horrified by the likely consequences on relations with the Soviet Union of taking no action on the European continent in 1943. To preclude both outcomes, Churchill outlined a three-part strategy in late November and early December 1942. One part called for an attack upon Sicily and Italy using the forces assembled in North Africa. The second part called for an invasion of the Balkans from Turkey, whose government he would try to persuade to enter the war. It is quite probable, even at this early date, that Churchill saw a Balkan operation as a way to stop the Russians from dominating Eastern Europe at war's end. The third part of Churchill's strategy called for a limited invasion of France in August or September 1943, but only after German power had been dispersed and weakened by peripheral attacks along the Mediterranean coast, on the Soviet front, and as a result of intensified Allied bombing of Germany.[35]

Churchill's strategic proposals divided the Americans. General Marshall argued that an expansion of the Mediterranean operations would be indecisive and would only delay a cross-Channel invasion indefinitely. Some members of his staff insisted that all Allied resources should be concentrated on the cross-Channel attack in 1943, and if the British refused to cooperate, the United States should turn to the Pacific. But other Army planners found compelling reasons for accepting Churchill's strategy. For one, the close of the North African operations would free a large number of veteran Allied troops to attack Sicily without creating major demands on scarce Allied shipping. The fact that an attack on Sicily might force Italy out of the war and Germany into assuming her commitments also made this an attractive operation. In addition, there were telling arguments against an early cross-Channel invasion. One related to the Allied inability to drive the Germans out of Tunisia quickly, thus making it improbable that sufficient good weather would remain in 1943 to make a major invasion of France possible that year. Moreover, the North Africa invasion suggested that more than twice the men and far more landing craft would be needed for a major cross-Channel operation than originally had been anticipated. Both Marshall and Eisenhower reluctantly admitted that it was unlikely that this force could be assembled before 1944.[36]

With a major cross-Channel attack looking improbable in 1943, and with the Soviet army continuing to tie down almost three-quarters of the German army, the thought of standing pat until 1944 was simply unacceptable to Roosevelt. As a result, the president essentially accepted Churchill's strategy at a conference both leaders attended in Casablanca, Morocco, from January 14 to 25, 1943. There they decided that Sicily would be invaded as soon as possible after the Tunisian campaign ended. (The Sicilian operation was code named HUSKY.) In addition, American air power in Britain would be increased substantially to permit the heaviest possible bombing of Germany. It also was agreed that the anti-submarine campaign in the Atlantic would be intensified and everything short of "prohibitive cost" would be sent to the Russians. At the same time, the buildup of ground forces in Britain would be accelerated to make possible an invasion of the Cotentin Peninsula in France by August or September 1943 (Operation ROUNDUP). This would not be the all-out invasion Marshall wanted, but a smaller operation designed to secure a bridgehead for the major invasion that would take place in 1944. Marshall, however, was not fooled; he realized that, due to the requirements of HUSKY, a Cotentin invasion in 1943 was more a pious hope than a firm commitment.[37]

The terms of Axis surrender were also stated at Casablanca. Roosevelt insisted upon "unconditional surrender" as the only terms the Allies would offer to their enemies. There were a number of reasons for Roosevelt's uncompromising stance. For one, he wanted to avoid the type of detailed and generous promises Wilson had made to Germany in the Fourteen Points. This time, the Germans must realize that they were soundly defeated and not, as Hitler had asserted after World War I, betrayed by the Allies. There would be no compromising with anyone tainted by Nazism, fascism, or Japanese imperialism. Finally, Roosevelt saw the unconditional surrender formula as a way to assure Stalin that the West would not seek a separate peace with the Axis powers, assurance he felt was necessary at a time when fears of a Soviet-German deal were very much alive and a major, second front in Western Europe looking less and less probable in 1943.[38]

More than a few have considered Roosevelt's unconditional surrender policy a mistake, arguing that it only strengthened the enemy's will to resist. They argue that Hitler could have been overthrown by an army coup at any time after the Normandy landing (and, indeed, he nearly was assassinated by a bomb planted by army conspirators on July 20, 1944), and that Germany may have sued for peace much earlier than she eventually did, had it not been for Roosevelt's unconditional surrender demand. But the point is, Roosevelt did not want to deal with the German army, as Wilson did during World War I. He wanted Germany to be reconstituted after the war, and he insisted that the German General Staff must play no role in that endeavor. In vain did Stalin, Churchill, and others attempt to persuade him to modify his demand. As a result, unconditional surrender became the ultimate war aim of the Grand Alliance, eclipsing even the Atlantic Charter in the importance it was given. Yet, in the end, none of the Axis powers surrendered unconditionally. Italy, Germany, and Japan were able to negotiate contingencies of great significance when they finally agreed to lay down their arms.[39]

## Troubles with Stalin

In reporting the results of the Casablanca talks to Stalin, who was invited to the conference but piquedly chose not to attend, Churchill and Roosevelt were deliberately evasive on the matter of a second front. They stated that the invasion of Western Europe would occur "as soon as practicable." Stalin chose to interpret this as a promise of a cross-Channel attack in 1943 and asked to be informed "of the concrete operations planned and of their timing." Churchill, with Roosevelt's approval, responded by informing Stalin: "We are pushing preparations to the limit of our resources for a cross-Channel operation in August [1943]." Stalin was not pleased with the news. On February 16 he insisted to Churchill that "the blow from the West, instead of being put off till the second half of the year, should be delivered in the spring or early summer." He further stated that he would not consider an invasion of Sicily a substitute for a second front in France. Stalin also was angered by the news from Churchill on March 30 that convoys to Murmansk would again be suspended, this time until the fall of 1943, because of HUSKY's demands on Allied shipping.[40]

Relations between the Soviets and the West were also strained by the growing animosity between Moscow and the London Poles. On April 13 the Germans announced that they had discovered a mass grave in the Katyn Forest near Smolensk in the Soviet Union, where, they alleged, ten thousand Polish soldiers had been slaughtered by the Russians after they had occupied eastern Poland in 1939. After the Polish government in London demanded an investigation of the event by the International Red Cross, the Soviets responded by breaking diplomatic relations with the London Poles on April 26. (A later investigation by the British supported the German accusation but lowered the number of bodies to 4,510.) The British, fearing that the Katyn massacre would disrupt the Grand Alliance, tried to dismiss the massacre as merely German propaganda. Roosevelt also downplayed the incident. "The winning of the war is the paramount objective for all of us," he stated in a letter to Churchill (dated April 30 but not sent). "For this, unity is necessary. . . . The Russians and the Poles . . . must subordinate factional differences to the common struggle for victory." As a result, the Katyn massacre was not permitted to impair the operation of the Grand Alliance.[41]

Nevertheless, the massacre at Katyn reinforced the arguments of those who believed that the West must make a strong stand during the war to block Soviet expansion after the conflict was over. In a long memorandum to Roosevelt on January 29, 1943, former ambassador William C. Bullitt warned the president that postwar'Soviet expansion could extend "as far west as the Rhine, perhaps even beyond." Stalin's tactics, Bullitt said, were intelligent and realistic: "He moves where opposition is weak. He stops where opposition is strong. He puts out pseudopodia like an amoeba rather than leaping like a tiger. If the pseudopodia meet no obstacle, the Soviet Union flows on." Bullitt asserted that America's ability to check Soviet expansion would only decline as the Soviets advanced into Eastern Europe. He wanted Roosevelt to act immediately to prevent the Russians "from replacing the Nazis as the masters of Europe." He suggested reorganizing the State Department to enable it to deal effectively with the problems of the postwar world, setting up American administrations in territories occupied by U.S. troops in order to promote the formation of strong democratic governments, forming a united front with Britain to resist Soviet demands, and pressing Stalin to dissolve the Comintern and renounce his claims in Eastern Europe. In addition, Bullitt wrote, an "adequate force should stand behind the eastern frontier of Europe ready to resist the Red Army." Without it, Europe would become "a military vacuum for the Soviet Union to flow into." That force, Bullitt suggested, should enter Europe through the Balkans in order to check Soviet expansion as far to the east as possible. "War is an attempt to achieve political objectives by fighting," he reminded Roosevelt, "and political objectives must be kept in mind in planning operations."[42]

"I don't dispute your facts," Roosevelt responded to Bullitt. "They are accurate. I don't dispute the logic of your reasoning." But the president rejected Bullitt's advice. "I just have a hunch," he said, "that Stalin is not that kind of man. Harry [Hopkins] says he's not, and that he doesn't want anything but security for his country, and I think that if I give him everything I possibly can and ask nothing from him in return, *noblesse oblige*, he won't try to annex anything and will work with me for a world of democracy and peace."[43]

At first glance, especially from hindsight, Roosevelt's statement appears the height of naiveté. But in the opinion of historian John Lewis Gaddis, Roosevelt's "hunch" was based on sound reasoning. A precipitous move against Russia could have jeopardized the ultimate outcome of the war. A Soviet-German separate peace was still not out of the question. And Soviet assistance was still deemed necessary to defeat Japan. "Furthermore," Gaddis argues, "Roosevelt was extremely conscious of the limits of American power. U.S. troops could not counteract Russian moves in Europe without imposing unacceptable demands on the nation's manpower pool and productive facilities--already stretched to the limit by simultaneous operations against Germany and Japan." Both the State Department and the Pentagon believed an Anglo-American invasion of the Balkans would do nothing to forestall a Soviet invasion of Western Europe, if that were the ultimate Soviet goal, but would only extend the length of the war by delaying the cross-Channel operation, which alone, in their opinion, would put substantial Anglo-American forces into a position to check Soviet expansion westward. Nor could the president bring himself to believe that the American people would tolerate a substantial and indefinite military presence in Europe after the war, which, it was believed, would be necessary if Soviet expansion were to be checked by military means. Moreover, a Balkan campaign would increase Russian suspicion and hostility at a time when Moscow's future plans were still unclear and subject to numerous interpretations. More important, it would come at a time when the Russian army was fighting three-quarters of the German army virtually alone.[44]

For these reasons, Roosevelt rejected Bullitt's recommendations for a forceful response to the Soviet postwar threat, and particularly a campaign in the Balkans. While he later, in August 1943, approved a plan (Operation RANKIN) to put American troops into Europe as quickly as possible in the event of a precipitous German collapse, and even stated that it was vital "to get to Berlin" as quickly as the Russians, Roosevelt did not anticipate, nor did he implement, a policy of military confrontation toward the Soviet Union. Instead, for the remainder of his life, he would follow a policy designed to accommodate Soviet security demands, particularly in Eastern Europe, where, he realized, Soviet military power was certain to predominate after the war.[45]

Accordingly, in the spring of 1943 Roosevelt went out of his way to assure the Soviets that Britain and the United States were doing all in their power to create a second front in Europe. In early May he sent former ambassador Joseph Davies to Moscow with a personal message for Stalin suggesting that they meet that summer to plan the defeat of Germany. On May 9 the president met with the Joint Chiefs of Staff and reaffirmed his support for a cross-Channel assault "at the earliest practicable date." Stalin received Davies warmly, dissolved the Comintern that month, and responded that he would be pleased to attend a summit meeting that summer.[46]

## The TRIDENT Conference, May 12-25, 1943

With the conquest of Tunisia about to be completed, Roosevelt again met with Churchill in Washington from May 12 to May 25 to reconsider Anglo-American strategy. In this so-called TRIDENT Conference, the prime minister argued that, after conquering Sicily, the main effort for the remainder of 1943 should be the defeat of Italy. An Italian surrender would add to Germany's defensive burden not only in the Mediterranean theater but also in the Balkans, where major Italian forces were stationed. Italy's surrender might also persuade Turkey to join the Allies, something Churchill badly wanted in order to justify an Anglo-American invasion of the Balkans. But most important, Churchill emphasized, "In no other way could relief be given to the Russian front on so large a scale this year." ROUNDUP, the invasion of France, Churchill argued, could not be launched before the spring of 1944, and the Allies could not sit idle in the Mediterranean for ten months while preparations for the cross-Channel operation ensued.[47]

While Marshall and his advisers feared that expansion of the war into Italy would jeopardize the logistical buildup for the cross-Channel invasion, the Joint Chiefs of Staff admitted that only further action in the Mediterranean would offer the Soviets immediate assistance. This argument had the greatest impact on Roosevelt. As a result, he agreed to permit Eisenhower to study and submit proposals for action in the Mediterranean after the conquest of Sicily. However, he refused to commit the United States to an Italian invasion after HUSKY, for fear that it would jeopardize ROUNDUP. To preclude that possibility, Churchill accepted Roosevelt's condition that on November 1 Eisenhower would be required to transfer seven divisions from the Mediterranean to Britain for use in the cross-Channel invasion, which was now set for May 1, 1944. Due to logistical difficulties, however, the new cross-Channel operation was cut from the forty-eight divisions originally called for in ROUNDUP to thirty-six divisions, and was further reduced to twenty-nine divisions before the conference ended. This placed the new operation about midway in size between ROUNDUP and SLEDGEHAMMER, and was therefore called ROUNDHAMMER, a name that was soon dropped in favor of the less confusing OVERLORD.[48]

Neither Roosevelt nor Churchill, however, could bring himself to draft a statement informing Stalin that the invasion of France would not be launched until 1944. In the end, it was Marshall who drafted the message giving the Soviet leader the bad news. Stalin angrily replied on June 11 that the decision ran counter to the Casablanca promise, created "exceptional difficulties" for the Red Army which, as a result, was left "to do the job alone" against the Germans. The Soviet Union, he insisted, would not accept the TRIDENT decision. And he subsequently announced that he would not attend a summer summit meeting. After further livid exchanges with Stalin that month, Churchill could only conclude that their correspondence had come to an end. The following month, after another German offensive began on July 5, Stalin recalled his ambassadors from Washington and London, launched a virulent campaign for a second front, demanded Western recognition of the Soviet annexation of the Baltic states, and announced the establishment of a puppet "Free Germany Committee" on July 13. With Allied-Soviet relations at a new low, rumors of a separate Soviet-German peace again circulated.[49]

And there was substance to the rumors. Scattered but convincing evidence indicates that Soviet agents conducted conversations with subordinate German officials in Stockholm during the summer of 1943, apparently to determine if the basis of a peace settlement could be found. Hitler, however, was not interested in a negotiated end to the war. As a result, nothing came of the Soviet initiative. Furthermore, after the Red Army broke the back of Germany's Army Group Center in the great battle of Kursk at the end of July, the Soviets lost interest--if they ever seriously had any--in a separate peace with the Germans. Instead, they embarked on the longest sustained offensive in military history, advancing 650 miles on a 1,500-mile front by the end of the year.[50]

With relations between the West and Russia deteriorating, another decision made at the TRIDENT conference would gain importance for the long-term future. It concerned the atomic bomb. Some of Roosevelt's advisers, particularly Vannevar Bush, the director of the Office of Scientific Research and Development, opposed pooling atomic-bomb research with Britain, which began in June 1942, for fear that the British would become rivals of the United States in the development and sale of commercial atomic energy after the war. Roosevelt responded by sharply curtailing the amount of research data that was offered the British. But after Churchill had protested vigorously that the new restrictions were a violation of the president's earlier pledge to share the benefits of atomic research, Roosevelt reversed himself at the TRIDENT Conference and agreed to restore the collaborative atomic relationship between the two countries.[51]

# The Invasion of Italy

A month and a half after the TRIDENT Conference ended, the invasion of Sicily began. On the night of July 9-10, 1943, the British Eighth Army under Montgomery and the American Seventh Army under General George S. Patton landed on the eastern and southeastern coasts of the island. The Italians did not put up much resistance, but German troops on Sicily fought vigorous, rearguard actions until August 17, when the last of them escaped across the Straits of Messina to the mainland of Italy.

Despite the reluctance of American planners to invade the Italian mainland, as Churchill had foreseen, events ultimately overcame their objections. The rapid Allied advance in Sicily, the low state of Italian morale, a defeatist Italian military establishment, and Hitler's refusal to allow Italian troops in the Balkans to return to Italy to defend their homeland, all contributed to a coup d'état on July 25 that drove Mussolini from power and led to his replacement by Marshal Pietro Badoglio.

While Roosevelt welcomed the overthrow of Mussolini, the establishment of a Badoglio government created a problem for the president quite analogous to the one that he had experienced with the Darlan deal the previous November. Badoglio had been one of Mussolini's top commanders in the Ethiopian campaign. Churchill, motivated by his fondness for monarchism and fear that communism would triumph in Italy if the Badoglio government collapsed, found it easy to inform Roosevelt that he was "not in the least afraid to recognize the House of Savoy or Badoglio, provided they are the ones who can make the Italians do what we need for our war purposes." Badoglio's cooperation, Churchill believed, would facilitate a rapid Allied advance through Italy, perhaps as far as to the Alps, thereby weakening Hitler's empire in its "weak underbelly." Consequently, Churchill urged Roosevelt to accept Badoglio's government and attempt to get it to switch sides. But Roosevelt, who was much more sensitive to public opinion than Churchill, could not forget the criticism he had received in the wake of the Darlan deal. Therefore, he assumed a hardline attitude toward the new Italian government and refused to modify the unconditional surrender formula. The Italian government, he insisted, must eventually be reconstituted along democratic lines.[52]

Yet, like Churchill, neither Roosevelt nor his military advisers were insensitive to the military advantages Badoglio's defection to the Allied camp would bring. As a result, at the second Quebec conference (code named QUADRANT) between August 14 and 24, Roosevelt approved an invasion of the Italian mainland that would begin in early September. As planned, the Allied invasion called for one amphibious assault force to cross the narrow Straits of Messina, and another to disembark along the coast at Salerno, thirty miles south of Naples. In return for supporting the Italian invasion, Churchill accepted an American condition that the invasion force would not advance beyond a line from Ancona to Pisa. He also reaffirmed the TRIDENT decision stating that OVERLORD would remain the primary operation for 1944.[53]

But before the invasion of the Italian mainland could begin and Badoglio could surrender, both on September 3, the Germans rushed reinforcements into Italy. As a result, Italian resistance, which was spotty at best, proved to be futile, the Italian army disintegrated, Badoglio and the king fled the capital, and Italy was effectively knocked out of the war. In addition, the Germans were able to put up stiff resistance to the Allied landings, particularly at Salerno, where the American Fifth Army was nearly hurled back into the sea. However, after difficult fighting, Allied air superiority, naval supporting fire, and the approach of General Montgomery's Eighth Army from Calabria (where it had landed on September 3) turned the tide against the Germans. By the beginning of October, Naples was captured. But much to the chagrin of the Allies, the Germans were able to build a strong defensive line to the north of the city, where they stopped the Allied advance well to the south of Rome.

In the meantime, on September 29 Badoglio's government signed a formal armistice agreement. In what amounted to a major alteration of the unconditional surrender formula, the armistice permitted the monarchy and the Badoglio government to continue in power, but they were made subject to the overall supervision of the Allied commander-in-chief, whose orders would be executed through an Allied Control Commission. In addition, the armistice agreement required the arrest of all war criminals and the removal of all fascists from office as well as the dissolution of fascist organizations. On October 13, the king and his government declared war on Germany. However, although the Italian fleet joined the Allied side, the Italian army refused to fight. In effect, Italy ceased to play an active role in the war, and was soon under Allied military occupation.[54]

Although both Churchill and Roosevelt attempted to keep Stalin informed of their dealings with the Italians, the Soviets were denied an equal share in directing Allied policy in Italy. While the Russians were given a seat on the Advisory Council for Italy, whose power was negligible, they were assigned only an observer status on the Allied Control Commission, where the major decisions concerning Italy were made. In October Roosevelt reminded Churchill that the occupation of Italy would "set the precedent for all such future activities in the war." It was likely to provide the Soviets with the excuse to minimize the postwar role of the West in Eastern Europe. But that did not persuade Churchill to give the Soviets a greater role in Italy. The prime minister did not want to increase the chances that Italy would fall under communist domination by giving Russia a greater voice in her affairs, and Roosevelt did not push the matter. By excluding the Soviets from all but a nominal role in the affairs of Italy, the Western powers ensured that they would be excluded by the Soviets from obtaining any meaningful role in the postwar affairs of Eastern Europe.[55]

# The Washington Conference, September 1943

While these momentous events were taking place in Italy, in early September, after the Quebec Conference, Churchill traveled to Washington. On September 11 he tried to persuade the American military chiefs that the invasion of Italy would cause the Germans to withdraw divisions from the Balkans, thereby making an Allied invasion of that region feasible. If the twenty-four Italian divisions stationed in the Balkans joined the Greek and Yugoslav guerrilla forces, Churchill argued, and if Turkey could be persuaded either to declare war on Germany or to allow British air forces to use bases on Turkish soil, the German position in the region would crumble. Churchill suggested that some of the Allied troops in Italy be diverted to the Dalmatian coast or to the Dodecanese Islands, located in the Aegean Sea off the coast of Turkey. The success of this strategy, he certainly realized, would require postponement of OVERLORD, yet he vehemently asserted that he was against "whittling down" the latter operation.[56]

America's military leaders remained unmoved by Churchill's argumentation. They remembered all too well how the prime minister had substituted TORCH for SLEDGEHAMMER, and they would not agree to any change in the scheduled buildup for OVERLORD. Marshall insisted that nothing needed for OVERLORD should be retained in the Mediterranean, no matter how enticing the opportunities offered by the Italian invasion might seem. The only new enterprise that was approved by the Combined Chiefs was Churchill's plan for a campaign in the Dodecanese Islands. But the Americans would not permit it in any way to delay OVERLORD. Consequently, after the Germans occupied the largest Dodecanese Island, Rhodes, and drove the British from the three smaller islands they had managed to capture, the Americans repeatedly rejected Churchill's pleas for the transfer of reinforcements to the islands. The Americans even opposed Churchill's scheme of enticing Turkey into the war for fear that the Turks would drain resources from OVERLORD. Roosevelt backed his military advisers to the hilt on these decisions.[57]

# The Moscow Conference, October 1943

The Soviets did not allow their exclusion from Italy to end their relations with the Western Allies. In fact, as a consequence of the reaffirmation of the cross-Channel assault at the QUADRANT Conference, relations between the Soviets and the Anglo-American Allies actually improved after the Italian invasion. Stalin accepted the Italian surrender terms and even empowered Eisenhower to sign for the Soviet Union. He also agreed to attend a tripartite summit meeting in the fall. To prepare an agenda for the summit, the Soviets agreed to hold a preliminary foreign ministers' conference in Moscow in October.[58]

The Moscow Conference of foreign ministers opened on October 18 with Eden, Hull, and Molotov in attendance. At Soviet insistence, not surprisingly, the first order of business was the second front. Only after Eden and Hull assured Molotov that OVERLORD would take place in May, 1944, were the Soviets willing to discuss political issues, the main item on the agenda of the conference.[59]

For Hull, the most important political issue was the Four Power Declaration on General Security. Prepared by the State Department, it stated that the representatives of Britain, China, Russia, and the United States promised to fight to war's end and to cooperate afterward to create a new international peace organization, the United Nations. When the four powers signed the document, an overjoyed Hull believed that the basis for a new Wilsonian world order had been established. Upon his return to Washington, he told Congress: "There will no longer be need for spheres of influence, for alliances, for balance of power, or any other of the special arrangements through which, in the unhappy past, the nations strove to safeguard their security or promote their interests." The signature of the U.S. government, at the same time, seemed to ensure that United States would not revert to isolationism at war's end. The passage of the Connally Resolution by the Senate on November 5, by an overwhelming 85-5 vote, reinforced this view. It declared that the Senate "recognized the necessity" of establishing an international organization for the maintenance of peace, one the United States would join.[60]

The Moscow Conference adopted another document drafted by the State Department. This one declared that after Germany had surrendered unconditionally, she would be occupied by the Big Three, totally disarmed, and required to make reparation payments in the form of goods and services. In addition, the foreign ministers agreed that Germany should be compelled to surrender all territory acquired since 1938, and that East Prussia should be separated from the rest of the country. The question of additional partitions was referred for further study to an inter-Allied commission for Germany, which was established to enforce the terms of the German surrender.[61]

At Eden's suggestion, the foreign ministers agreed to set up a European Advisory Commission with headquarters in London. It would consider all questions relating to the terms and execution of the German and Italian surrenders. The commission could make recommendations for common action, but it had no mandatory authority of its own.[62]

The Americans were pleased by the outcome of the Moscow Conference. The Soviets not only had signed the two American-sponsored documents, they also promised to join the war against Japan as soon as Germany was defeated. In the euphoria of the moment, Stalin's refusal to discuss independence for the Baltic states or to restore diplomatic relations with the London Poles was glossed over.[63]

Churchill was also pleased by the results of the Moscow Conference, but for a different reason. When Eden informed Stalin on October 29 that the operations in the Aegean might delay OVERLORD for a few months, Stalin did not raise any objections, leading Churchill to believe that he might be able to pull off a major Aegean campaign after all. With OVERLORD not coming until the spring or summer, Stalin may have concluded that additional pressure in the Mediterranean might be the only immediate way to divert German divisions from the eastern front. He admitted to Eden that the Italian campaign had had that effect. Whatever Stalin's motives, the American military chiefs were forced to conclude that he might indeed support Churchill's Mediterranean strategy at OVERLORD's expense. Fearful that Roosevelt might approve another Mediterranean campaign, Stimson tried to head it off in a meeting with the president on October 29. Roosevelt assured the secretary of war that he "would not think of touching the Balkans"--unless the Russians requested it. Anxious to please the Soviets, Roosevelt, in effect, was going to permit Stalin to determine whether OVERLORD should take place as scheduled! [64]

## The Cairo and Tehran Conferences, November-December 1943

Roosevelt had been trying to arrange a summit with Stalin for months. However, the Soviet leader did not want to be out of telephone contact with his frontline commanders, while Roosevelt, for reasons of convenience and prestige, was not willing to go to Russia. It was not until November that the president finally accepted Stalin's suggestion that the conference convene in Tehran, Iran. Roosevelt also accepted another of Stalin's conditions for attending the tripartite summit (which was code named EUREKA): that the representatives of all other powers would be excluded, meaning specifically Chiang Kai-shek, whose participation the president had badly wanted, but which Stalin opposed for fear that it would provoke the Japanese.[65]

To salve any hurt feelings on Chiang's part, Roosevelt invited him to attend a conference (code named SEXTANT) with himself and Churchill in Cairo between November 22 and 26, shortly before the president and the prime minister traveled to Tehran. Roosevelt wanted to guarantee that the Cairo Conference would concentrate on Far Eastern, rather than European affairs, in order to avoid creating the impression that he and Churchill, as the president put it, had "ganged up" on Stalin. The president believed that if he distanced himself from Churchill, he would be able to convince the Soviet leader that the United States posed no threat to the Soviet Union and thereby establish a sound foundation for Soviet-American cooperation after the war.[66]

At Cairo, Admiral Lord Louis Mountbatten, the British commander in the Far East, presented a plan for an invasion of Japanese-occupied Burma. Chiang agreed to cooperate with invasion, but only after Churchill and Roosevelt promised to launch an amphibious assault on the Andaman Islands in the Bay of Bengal and to equip ninety Chinese divisions. Churchill, however, approved the Burma operation only reluctantly because he feared it would interfere with his plan to expand Allied operations in the Mediterranean, particularly in the Balkans. However, as Churchill had feared, nothing concerning strategy in the European-Mediterranean theater was decided at Cairo. Apparently, the president was still prepared to allow Stalin to determine whether OVERLORD or further action in the Mediterranean would be the main Anglo-American effort in 1944.[67]

Roosevelt and Churchill arrived in Tehran on November 27, where they met with Stalin until December 2. Much to Churchill's chagrin, the Soviet leader decisively threw his weight behind OVERLORD rather than a Balkan operation or a more intensified Italian campaign. Stalin even suggested that some Allied troops in Italy might be used for a supplementary invasion of southern France. He also promised to coincide a major Soviet offensive with OVERLORD. Roosevelt backed Stalin's recommendations fully, not only to win the gratitude of the Soviet leader but also to satisfy the U.S. Joint Chiefs of Staff, who vehemently opposed any expansion of Mediterranean operations. Isolated by Roosevelt and Stalin, Churchill had no choice but again to go along with OVERLORD, which was scheduled to begin no later than June 1, 1944. The invasion of southern France, code named ANVIL, was also approved at Tehran. Stimson, who had feared that Churchill would talk the president into another Mediterranean campaign, was relieved. "I thank the Lord, Stalin was there," he recorded in his diary; "he saved the day." Having disposed of military matters, the Big Three turned their attention to postwar political issues.[68]

Roosevelt took the lead in advocating the postwar partition of Germany into five independent states: (1) a small and weakened Prussia; (2) Hanover and northwestern Germany; (3) Saxony and the Leipzig area; (4) Hesse-Darmstadt, Hesse-Kassel, and the area south of the Rhine; and (5) Bavaria, Baden, and Württemburg. Churchill, however, proposed that only two German states should be created, Prussia and the rest of Germany, which might be organized into a Danubian confederation. But Stalin strenuously opposed any Germanic confederation, as he did Churchill's desire to establish a confederation in Eastern Europe. The Germans, he said, would simply use a confederation to create a new state. But he probably also feared that any European confederation would be hostile to the Soviet Union. For Stalin, the key to the German problem was the liquidation of the Prussian military class. Unable to reach agreement on the partition of Germany, the three leaders decided to refer the problem to the European Advisory Commission.[69]

Poland was another problem the Big Three discussed at Tehran. The Soviets wanted to move Poland's boundaries westward at Germany's expense and for Russia's benefit. German territory east of the Oder River would become a part of Poland, while a part of East Prussia and much of eastern Poland would become Soviet territory. While Roosevelt sympathized with the Soviet plan for Poland's postwar boundaries, he refused to publicly commit the United States to the arrangement because the London Poles refused to recognize any Polish territorial settlement in which they did not participate. Roosevelt feared that opposition from the London Poles would cause him to lose Polish-American votes in the next presidential election. When he so informed Stalin, in a private session between the two leaders, the Soviet leader said he understood the president's reluctance to publicize the Polish arrangement.[70]

But Roosevelt was not about to let the Poles disrupt his effort to create a harmonious postwar Soviet-American relationship. Later, he told the Polish ambassador:

> Do you expect us and Great Britain to declare war on Joe Stalin
> if they cross your previous frontier? Even if we wanted to,
> Russia can still field an army twice our combined strength, and
> we would just have no say in the matter at all. What is more,

> I'm not sure that a fair plebiscite, if there ever was such a thing, would not show that those eastern provinces of Poland would not prefer to go back to Russia. Yes, I really think those 1941 frontiers are as just as any.[71]

Roosevelt, however, had less success trying to persuade Stalin to preserve an illusion of freedom for the Baltic states. He asked the Soviet leader to permit an internationally supervised referendum in the Baltic states before incorporating them into the Soviet Union. The president expressed his confidence that the Baltic peoples would choose to remain a part of the Soviet Union. Stalin, however, firmly rejected Roosevelt's plebiscite proposal, no doubt because he realized that the Baltic states would vote to be independent. Instead, he argued that the Soviet constitution provided sufficient opportunities for the Baltic people to express their views. Faced with Stalin's opposition, Roosevelt did not press the matter further.[72]

At Tehran Roosevelt also informed Stalin that he was opposed to any long-term American occupation of European territory. Neither the Congress nor the American people, he said, would condone it. Because of this, he wanted to limit America's postwar occupation duties to northwestern Germany, Norway, and Denmark, where political stability was likely to be restored quickly, thus permitting U.S. troops to be withdrawn in a year or two. Under no circumstances, he told the Joint Chiefs of Staff on November 19, did he want the United States to acquire a sphere of influence in Europe, which he believed would be the result of American occupation duty in France, Italy, or the Balkans.[73]

Roosevelt also informed Stalin that it would take "a terrible crisis such as the present," before Congress would agree to send U.S. troops back to Europe. Had the Japanese not attacked Pearl Harbor, he added, it would have been virtually impossible to have sent any American troops to Europe. If peace were to be threatened again in Europe, he told Stalin, the United States might send planes and ships, but Britain and Russia would have to provide the ground forces. To what extent Roosevelt was being candid with the Soviet leader, or merely attempting to reassure him that the United States would pose no threat to Soviet security, is impossible to determine, for Roosevelt did not always mean what he said. But one can safely conclude that Stalin was not disappointed by the president's views.[74]

Roosevelt, however, had a more permanent structure of international relations in mind, one that he believed would satisfy American idealists as well as provide a realistic framework for peace. In a private conversation with Stalin on the second day of the conference, the president proposed the creation of a postwar peacekeeping body based on the United Nations. It should have, he suggested to Stalin, three parts: a thirty-five to forty-member body that would meet periodically in different places to make recommendations; an executive committee of ten nations, including the great powers, which would deal with all nonmilitary problems; and a third group, "the Four Policemen"--America, Britain, the Soviet Union, and China--that would have the power to deal immediately with any threat to the peace or any sudden emergency requiring action.[75]

Stalin's initial reaction to Roosevelt's world-body idea, like that of Churchill, was not favorable. He told the president that the smaller nations would prefer to deal with their own problems rather than be dictated to by the Four Policemen. Stalin said he preferred regional police forces to a global one. But Roosevelt replied that the American people and Congress would regard regional security arrangements as spheres of influence and would oppose them. Although Roosevelt did not push the issue, by the end of the conference Stalin informed the president that he was ready to accept a worldwide, rather than a regional, peacekeeping body. However, Stalin did not believe that such a body would be strong enough to check future German or Japanese aggression. Consequently, he told Roosevelt that he favored the establishment of "strong physical points," or strategically located bases, near Germany and Japan. Since this proposal was compatible with Roosevelt's desire to convert mandated islands and colonies into UN trusteeships, the president warmly endorsed Stalin's suggestion.[76]

As soon as the Tehran Conference ended, Roosevelt and Churchill returned to Cairo, where they continued their conversations from December 2-7. As a concession to Churchill, who in effect had been reduced to Roosevelt's junior partner at Tehran, the president agreed to cancel the invasion of Burma. Stalin's pledge at Tehran to enter the war against Japan after Germany was defeated, Churchill had argued, precluded the need for the Burma operation. In addition, the prime minister pointed out, there would be insufficient numbers of landing craft to support the operation as well as meet the demands of OVERLORD and ANVIL. The other major decision reached at the second Cairo Conference was Roosevelt's appointment, and Churchill's acceptance, of Dwight Eisenhower as the commander of OVERLORD.[77]

## Aftermath of the Tehran and Cairo Conferences

The SEXTANT-EUREKA talks, in the opinion of historian Warren Kimball, "were the most significant in the war." The outlines of postwar Europe and East Asia were drawn, the idea of the United Nations as a peacekeeping body was agreed upon, and the Big Three accepted plans for invasions of northern and southern France. By accepting Soviet control of the Baltic states, altered boundaries for Poland, the need for permanent restraints on German and Japanese power, and a predominant role for the Big Four in maintaining world peace, Roosevelt believed that he had established the foundation of stable Soviet-American relations after the war. The Teheran Conference truly marked the high point of Allied political unity during the war.[78]

Others were not as optimistic as Roosevelt. Churchill, for one, did not think that Stalin would be as cooperative after the war as he was while he needed Anglo-American help. "There might be a more bloody war," he confided to Eden only two days after Tehran. One member of the State Department, Charles Bohlen, wrote that, as a result of the Tehran agreements, "the Soviet Union would be the only important military and political force on the continent of Europe. The rest of Europe would be reduced to military and political impotence."

Indeed, with the Allies at last in agreement on a military strategy against Hitler, the political issues raised at Tehran would now be able to move to the forefront. Ultimately, they would tear apart the Grand Alliance.[79]

# 6

# The Road To Victory, 1944-1945

## The Allied Offensives in Europe, 1944

On June 6, 1944--D-Day--the invasion of France finally began in Normandy. On D-Day and D-Day +1 over 185,000 men and 19,000 vehicles were transported across the English Channel. At the end of eleven days, 641,170 British, Canadian, and American soldiers were fighting in France. OVERLORD was, by far, the greatest amphibious operation in history.

From the first, however, the Germans fought stubbornly and, as a result, the progress of the Allied armies inland was much slower than had been anticipated. But on July 31 General George Patton's Third U.S. Army broke through the German lines near Avranches and quickly fanned out into the rear of the German forces. Fearing complete envelopment, the Germans were forced to pull back rapidly toward the Seine River. On August 25 Paris was liberated. By mid-September the Allies had captured Brussels and advanced to the Dutch and German frontiers.

In the meantime, the Allies continued their slow advance up the Italian peninsula. In January an amphibious force landed at Anzio, almost 100 miles north of the German battle line. Yet it was not until May that Allied forces were able to break out of the Anzio beachhead, forcing the Germans to retreat to a position north of Rome. On June 4 the Italian capital was liberated.

While the Allied armies advanced in France and Italy, the Soviet juggernaut continued its inexorable march from the east. In January 1944 the Red Army reached the eastern prewar Polish boundary. By February they had broken the German encirclement of Leningrad. The following month the Soviets began a great offensive in the south that reached the Pruth River, the 1940 boundary of Rumania, by summer. In compliance with the promise Stalin had made at Tehran, a Soviet offensive on the central Russian front was launched shortly after the Normandy landings began. By August 1 the Red Army had advanced 450 miles and reached the suburbs of Warsaw. In the north, the Soviet army broke through the Finnish lines in June, and forced the Finns to sue for peace in September.

The Soviet advance into the Balkans was equally spectacular. On August 25 Rumania deserted Hitler and joined the Russian side. Two weeks later, on September 9, Bulgaria declared war on Germany. By October 1 the Red Army had overrun Rumania and crossed into Yugoslavia, where it made contact with communist partisans under Josip Broz Tito. Two weeks later, on October 15, Belgrade was liberated. Meanwhile, Soviet and Rumanian troops crossed the Carpathian Mountains and by November 11 reached the outskirts of Budapest, Hungary. By the end of the month, the Hungarian capital was under Soviet control.

## The Soviet Problem

As a result of the Allied progress on all fronts during the summer of 1944, many expected the war in Europe to be over by Christmas. However, as military victory over Germany appeared increasingly inevitable and imminent, political problems that had been glossed over at Tehran, in order to preserve Allied unity, became more and more important. And the rift over strategy and policy that had developed between Roosevelt and Churchill in 1943 only widened during the subsequent year.

The most important point of difference between the Americans and the British concerned Western policy toward the Soviet Union. While Churchill and his colleagues were elated by the collapse of the German eastern front, they were dismayed by the prospect of Soviet domination of Eastern Europe. Before the great Soviet summer offensive of 1944, Churchill had hoped that by conceding Bessarabia, eastern Poland, and the Baltic states to the Soviet Union, it would be possible to create governments in the rest of Eastern Europe that would be fully independent but not hostile to Russia. Eduard Benes, the president of the Czech government-in-exile, seemed to be well on the way to achieving this outcome for his country. Although an anticommunist, Benes believed that cooperation with the Soviet Union would guarantee Czechoslovakia's independence after the war. Accordingly, in December 1943 the Czechs concluded a twenty-year treaty of friendship with the Soviet Union that was modeled after the Anglo-Soviet Treaty of 1942. However, the inability of the London Poles to come to an agreement with Stalin, and the Soviet-dictated armistice terms that were signed by Rumania and Bulgaria in September, led Churchill to believe that the creation of independent states in Eastern Europe was no longer possible. He now feared that the region would be communized.[1]

Motivated partly by intense anticommunism as well as by Britain's traditional concern for the maintenance of the European balance of power, Churchill sought to duplicate the feat performed by British statesmen after the defeat of Napoleon in 1815--preventing Russian domination of the Continent. Yet Britain alone lacked the power to counter the Soviet menace. By the end of 1944 the Soviets were attacking the Germans with some 13,000 tanks, 16,000 frontline aircraft, and 525 divisions totaling 5 million soldiers. By comparison, Britain had only 12 divisions, about 820,000 men, on the western front.[2]

The key to Britain's postwar policy, obviously, was to persuade the United States to maintain a military presence in Europe after the war. A Foreign Office memorandum of March 1944 stated: "It must be our purpose to make use of American power. If we go about our business in the right way, we can steer this great unwieldy barge, the USA, into the right harbor. . . . If we don't, it is likely to continue to wallow in the ocean, an isolated menace to navigation."[3]

In 1943 Churchill had begun to speak, much as he did immediately after World War I, of a more permanent, postwar Anglo-American alliance. At the TRIDENT Conference, in May of that year, he urged the Americans to join Britain in creating a "fraternal association" of their two countries, with common passports and citizenship, joint use of their military bases, and continuation after the war of the Combined Chiefs of Staff. On September 6, 1943, Churchill repeated these themes in an address at Harvard University. The speech was a preview of his famous "Iron Curtain" address at Fulton, Missouri in 1946--without, of course, the provocative references to a Soviet threat for which the Fulton speech would be remembered. In November, while en route to the Tehran Conference, Churchill said to his aide (and future prime minister) Harold Macmillan: "Germany is finished, though it may take some time to clean up the mess. The real problem now is Russia. I can't get the Americans to see it."[4]

The major flaw in Churchill's strategy was that in early 1944 Franklin Roosevelt had no intention of forming a joint front with Britain against Russia. The president did not want a quarrel with the Soviets before the Germans were defeated, and he feared that that would be the likely result of a confrontational policy in Eastern Europe. Moreover, the American people were beginning to look to the United Nations, not the balance of power, nor an alliance with Britain, nor even a U.S. military presence in Europe after the war, as the best approach to preserve the postwar peace. And, again, Roosevelt was not inclined to repeat the mistakes Woodrow Wilson had made at the end of World War I. He was determined not to get too far ahead of American public opinion, which definitely was not oriented toward deep U.S. involvement in postwar European affairs.[5]

Indeed, in 1944 American opinion appeared to be more concerned about the postwar ambitions of Britain than those of the Soviet Union. Americans were repelled by Britain's determination to retain control of India and other imperial possessions after the war. And tempers flared when American and British negotiators quarreled over Middle Eastern oil rights, trade, postwar U.S. economic assistance to Britain, and other economic issues. The British, for their part, feared that the Americans were trying to dominate the postwar international economy at Britain's expense.[6]

# ANVIL

Churchill did not, however, abandon his effort to check Soviet expansion into Central Europe. In early August, after the beachheads in Normandy had been secured, he launched a campaign designed to persuade the Americans to abandon ANVIL, the invasion of southern France. ANVIL, Churchill argued, was an unnecessary operation, since the Allies were now advancing rapidly in northern France without it. The prime minister wanted to use the forces in Italy that were assigned to ANVIL for an amphibious operation designed to cross the Adriatic Sea, land in Yugoslavia, and drive through the Ljubljana Gap into Austria and southern Hungary. He defended the proposed operation on military grounds as likely to be more productive than the advance up the Rhone Valley that was called for in ANVIL. But the political advantages of the operation were no less obvious to him. If successful, Churchill believed, a Balkan invasion would put the Allies in a  position to prevent Soviet domination of Eastern Europe.[7]

Roosevelt, however, refused to accept Churchill's Balkan strategy. He reminded the prime minister that the shortest path to victory--and the agreed strategy at Tehran--was to drive into the heart of Germany from France while the Soviets invaded from the east. As Eisenhower put it in a letter to Marshall on June 20, "achievement of a successful beachhead in France does not--repeat not--of itself imply success in Operation OVERLORD as a whole." Concentration of military forces was the key to success, Eisenhower insisted, and he argued that "wandering off overland via Trieste to Ljubljana is to indulge in conjecture to an unwarranted degree." Besides, Roosevelt wrote Churchill, the difficulties of an advance through the Ljubljana Gap "would seem to far exceed those pictured by you in the Rhone Valley." ANVIL, he added, would give the Allies the port of Marseilles, without which it would be difficult to bring additional U.S. divisions into France. Roosevelt also believed that the abandonment of ANVIL in favor of an eastern strategy would arouse Stalin's suspicions about Anglo-American ambitions in Eastern Europe and thereby jeopardize the understanding he believed he had achieved with the Soviet dictator at Tehran.[8]

Faced with Roosevelt's opposition, Churchill backed down, and ANVIL began as scheduled on August 15. Within a month, the seven French and three American divisions engaged in the operation captured Marseilles and Toulon, drove northward up the Rhone Valley, and linked up with the OVERLORD forces advancing across northern France. However, in spite of the overwhelming success of ANVIL, Churchill still considered it an unwise operation. After the war, he observed that, because of ANVIL, the Allied forces in Italy lost the opportunity to beat the Russians to Vienna, "with all that might have followed therefrom."[9]

## Spheres of Influence

Unable to obtain active American assistance in blocking Soviet domination of Eastern Europe, Churchill developed a two-part alternative strategy. First, he tried to establish--or reestablish--and aid pro-Western governments wherever he could in Eastern Europe. Second, he tried to gain an agreement with Stalin that would define their respective spheres of influence in the region. To Churchill, the only way to deal with the Soviets was on a quid pro quo basis. He feared that Roosevelt's policy of giving something to the Soviets and asking for nothing in return would only encourage Stalin to ask for more and convince him that the West was powerless to deny his requests.

Churchill's effort to conclude a spheres of influence agreement with the Soviet Union began in the spring of 1944. On May 5 Eden proposed to the Soviets that Rumania should be in their sphere while Greece should be in the British sphere. On May 18 the Soviets tentatively accepted the British proposal but asked how the United States would view the arrangement. The Soviet query prompted Churchill to approach the Americans. On May 30 Lord Halifax, the British ambassador in Washington, explained the arrangement to Cordell Hull, but Halifax described it as only a temporary arrangement that would apply only to military operations, not civilian government, in the affected countries. Despite this limitation, Hull objected vigorously to the establishment of any sphere of influence as a throwback to the power politics of the past, which the United States was now trying to replace with the United Nations.[10]

Rejected by Hull, Churchill approached Roosevelt directly on May 31, and again on June 10, asking the president to approve the Anglo-Soviet Balkan arrangement for a trial period of three months. Far more the realist than Hull, Roosevelt was not surprised by Stalin's effort to establish friendly governments in Eastern Europe. Yet, while he was inclined to give the Soviets a relatively free hand in that region, he could not say so openly because of the idealism of Hull, the Congress, and the American people, all of whom, more or less, expected the Soviets to abide by the principles of the Atlantic Charter. Any compromise with the Soviet Union that violated the charter, Roosevelt feared, could generate sufficient opposition within the Senate to block American membership in the United Nations. Moreover, Roosevelt was preparing for another presidential election in November. Consequently, he was acutely sensitive to the opinions of ethnic Americans with ties to Eastern Europe. As a result, as at Tehran, he was reluctant to take a public position that would offend these groups. At the same time, however, he was determined to avoid any action that would risk alienating the Soviet Union, whose military support both he and his advisers believed was essential, not only for the speedy defeat of Germany, but Japan as well. Not surprisingly, Roosevelt's policy in 1944, at least before the presidential election in November, was one of minimizing difficulties with the Soviets while making no public agreements that would lose votes for the Democratic ticket.[11]

Prompted by purely domestic considerations, Roosevelt at first, on June 10, responded negatively to Churchill's sphere of influence proposal. Yet his desire to maintain good relations with the Soviet Union led him to take advantage of Hull's absence from Washington on June 13 and cable Churchill stating that he supported the Anglo-Russian agreement for a trial three-month period. However, the president insisted that "we must be careful to make it clear that we are not establishing any postwar spheres of influence." But fearing opposition from Hull, he did not inform the secretary of state about this reversal. Consequently, when Hull returned to Washington, he drafted and sent another note rejecting the British proposal, only to learn that Roosevelt had already accepted it. No doubt embarrassed by being caught in this subterfuge, the president approved a message to Churchill drafted by Hull on June 22 that complained that the British had not informed the United States about the Balkan arrangement before it was concluded with the Soviets. Still, when the Soviets on July 1 requested to know the American reaction to the Balkan arrangement, the State Department responded that it was acceptable to the United States, but only for a three-month trial period. The State Department also stated that America's interests in the Balkans would be in no way affected by the Anglo-Soviet agreement, a reservation that did much to impair its value to the Soviet Union.[12]

# The Warsaw Uprising

Despite Roosevelt's efforts to remain on good terms with the Russians, Soviet policy toward Poland made it increasingly difficult to do so. In response to the president's and Churchill's urgings, Stalin agreed to see the Polish premier, Stanislaw Mikolajczyk, in early August. The Soviet leader demanded that Mikolajczyk recognize the so-called Curzon Line (which had been proposed by a British statesman, Lord Curzon of Keddleston, in 1920) as an equitable Polish Soviet border, and dismiss certain members of the London government which Stalin considered anti-Soviet. He also insisted that Mikolajczyk come to an agreement with the Lublin Committee. While Mikolajczyk considered the Lublin Poles servile puppets of the Soviets, he agreed to meet with them and to create a coalition government in which he would remain as prime minister. In addition, he agreed to dismiss the most avid anti-Soviet ministers in the London government. But a major obstacle to an agreement between the Polish factions arose over the division of seats in the proposed coalition government. The Lublin Poles wanted fourteen seats for themselves and were willing to allot the London Poles only four.[13]

There was, however, a more important reason for the failure of the talks between the two Polish factions. On August 1, while Mikolajczyk was still in Moscow, an uprising led by the Polish underground, the so-called Home Army, erupted in Warsaw. The Home Army intended to liberate the Polish capital before the arrival of the Red Army, the lead units of which were only six miles from the city. Although Stalin promised to aid the uprising in his final talk with Mikolajczyk on August 9, it was soon obvious that the Soviet leader was more than willing to allow the Germans to destroy his principal rival for control of Poland. After a German counterthrust halted the Soviet advance on Warsaw, Churchill asked Stalin to airlift supplies to the hard-pressed Polish fighters. Stalin replied by denouncing the uprising as "a reckless and fearful gamble," which had been launched without Soviet knowledge. Consequently, he said, the Soviet Union would not assume responsibility for its outcome.[14]

Even Roosevelt, who with Churchill sent a joint message to Stalin on August 20, could not persuade the Soviet dictator to save the Home Army. Stalin rejected his allies' request to order Soviet planes to fly supplies into Warsaw or to allow British and American planes to land on Soviet airfields at the end of their missions to the beleaguered city. When Churchill urged the president to make another joint appeal to Stalin, Roosevelt replied on August 26 that, in view of Stalin's refusal to permit the use of Russian bases to aid the Poles, and the American desire to obtain military bases on Soviet territory for use against Japan, he did not consider another message "advantageous to the long-range general war prospect." The president, quite obviously, was unwilling to confront Stalin over the Warsaw Uprising, believing that ultimately there was little he could do for the beleaguered Poles without Soviet approval and, not wanting to allow Poland to damage the prospects of victory and a postwar Soviet-American understanding, he was unwilling to create a rift in the Grand Alliance over the issue.[15]

Finally, in mid-September, the Soviets began flying in some supplies to Warsaw and then resumed their attack on the city. But the assistance was too little and too late. After the Soviet offensive failed to penetrate the German defenses and the insurgents' supplies were exhausted, the insurrection came to an end on October 4. By then over 250,000 of Warsaw's people, one-fourth of the city's population, were killed in the uprising.[16]

## The Dumbarton Oaks Conference, August-September 1944

The Soviet response to the Warsaw Uprising was only one indication of the growing trouble between the Western Allies and the Soviets on postwar issues. Others arose during the Dunbarton Oaks Conference, which was held in Washington between August 21 and September 28. The conference had been convened in order to establish a new international peacekeeping organization, the United Nations. Before the conference, the Big Three had agreed on the basic framework of the new body. It would consist of four major elements. One was a General Assembly, in which all member nations would have one vote. Another was a Security Council, in which the Big Three plus China and--in a major concession to de Gaulle--France would be permanently seated, with a number of smaller nations elected by the assembly to annual seats. A third element was the Secretariat, which would conduct the day-to-day operations of the organization. The fourth major part of the new world body was an International Court of Justice, modeled after the Permanent Court of International Justice at The Hague. The new court would attempt to mediate international disputes before they led to war.[17]

While agreement on the overall structure of the UN was achieved quickly, the conference was soon faced with two seemingly unresolvable issues. The first concerned representation in the General Assembly. The Soviets, fearing that they would be outnumbered by the votes of the British Commonwealth states and those of the Latin American nations under U.S. influence, proposed that each of the sixteen Soviet republics be seated in the General Assembly. "My God!" Roosevelt exclaimed to Assistant Secretary of State Edward Stettinius, "we could never accept this proposal." Fearing the "explosive" effects the Soviet proposal would have on American opinion, Roosevelt persuaded Andrei Gromyko, the head of the Soviet Dumbarton Oaks delegation, to make no further reference to it during the conference. He also cabled Stalin warning him that the Soviet proposal could wreck the formation of the United Nations. However, Roosevelt added, that he would have no objection to discussing the matter of representation after the new world body was formed.[18]

The second UN issue that caused trouble for Roosevelt concerned the veto power of the Security Council. While the Big Three agreed that each of the permanent members should have the right to veto a decision of the council, the British and the Americans insisted that an exception should be made in cases where one of the permanent members was a party to a dispute. The Soviets, however, emphatically refused to agree to any limitation of the veto power. The unanimity of the great powers, they argued, must be the basis of any action by the Security Council.[19]

The impasse on these UN issues plus Soviet policy toward Eastern Europe raised serious doubts in the minds of Roosevelt and his advisers about the long-range prospects of Soviet-American relations. Yet neither the Americans nor the Soviets were willing to allow the UN issues to disrupt the Grand Alliance. As a result, Stalin agreed to Roosevelt's suggestion that further consideration of the unresolved issues should be postponed until the next summit conference. To preserve the appearance of Allied harmony in the meantime, the announcement at the close of the conference stated that, while some issues remained to be settled, progress had been made toward resolving them.[20]

## The Second Quebec Conference, September 1944

While the Dunbarton Oaks Conference was in session, Roosevelt and Churchill met for a second time in Quebec from September 11 to 16 (the conference was code named OCTAGON) and then traveled to the president's home in Hyde Park, New York, where they continued their discussions on September 18-19.

Churchill was anxious to discuss ways of checking growing Soviet influence in Eastern Europe. The armistice negotiations conducted by the Soviets with Rumania and Bulgaria earlier that month gave the prime minister reason to believe that those countries would be Soviet satellites after the war. He also feared that communist regimes would be established in Yugoslavia and Greece if the West did not act quickly. Consequently, Churchill asked Roosevelt to allow American planes to transport British paratroops into Athens when the Germans withdrew, and he again pushed for an Allied operation across the Adriatic into Yugoslavia. In addition, he asked Roosevelt to join him in writing a cable to Stalin stating that the differences that were arising over Allied policy in Eastern Europe were undermining the Grand Alliance.[21]

With the Polish problem and UN differences fresh in his mind, Roosevelt was more receptive to Churchill's anxieties about the Soviet Union than he had been before. "Our main concern," the president told Archduke Otto of Austria during the Quebec Conference, "is how to keep the communists out of Hungary and Austria." Like Churchill, he was increasingly concerned that the Soviet military presence in the Balkans would become permanent. Accordingly, Roosevelt approved Churchill's request for American assistance in putting British forces into Greece. As a result, when the Germans withdrew their forces from that country in early October, British troops quickly moved in. The president also supported, and the Joint Chiefs of Staff endorsed, British plans for amphibious operations against the Istrian Peninsula in Yugoslavia and for an operation that would put four divisions into Austria following a sudden German collapse. (Neither plan, however, was ever implemented.) The president also "provisionally" accepted Churchill's suggestion for a joint cable to Stalin, warning him of the political dangers of divergent Allied policies toward Eastern Europe.[22]

The troubled relations with the Soviets also affected Anglo-American policy toward the atomic energy issue, which was discussed by Roosevelt and Churchill at Hyde Park. On September 19 the two leaders signed an *aide-mémoire* in which they agreed to cooperate fully after the war in the development of atomic energy for military and commercial purposes. In so doing, they tacitly rejected a proposal by the renowned physicist, Niels Bohr, to share some atomic information with the Soviets as an incentive to winning their support for postwar international control of atomic energy. The *aide-mémoire* not only rejected Bohr's proposal, it also stated that the scientist should be placed under surveillance.[23]

However, the most controversial issue at the Quebec Conference concerned the postwar treatment of Germany. Secretary of the Treasury Henry Morgenthau presented Roosevelt with a plan calling for the dismantling of Germany's industry and the "pastoralization" of her economy in order to make her incapable of waging war. The president liked Morgenthau's plan. "We have got to be tough with Germany," he said, "and I mean the German people not just the Nazis. We either have to castrate the German people or you have got to treat them in such manner so they can't just go on reproducing people who want to continue the way they have in the past."[24]

Churchill, for his part, vehemently rejected the Morgenthau plan when it was presented to him at Quebec on September 13. His accepting it, he explained to Roosevelt, would be tantamount to "chaining himself to a dead German." As early as October 1943, the prime minister had told his cabinet that Britain "must not weaken Germany too much--we may need her against Russia." The destruction of the German arms industry alone, he told the president, would be sufficient to prevent reconstruction of the German war machine. But by the end of the conference, Churchill had reversed himself and accepted the Morgenthau plan. He did so primarily because Roosevelt strongly supported it and because Britain badly needed additional Lend-Lease assistance. In fact, the same day that Churchill gave his support to the Morgenthau plan, he and Roosevelt signed an agreement designed to provide Britain with $3.5 billion worth of continued Lend-Lease assistance after the defeat of Germany as well as a loan of $3 billion for nonmilitary purposes. The agreement would enable the British to use some of their industrial production for domestic consumption and to revive their export trade while still receiving Lend-Lease assistance. Roosevelt attempted to justify this concession to Britain by arguing that it would help keep her strong after the war.[25]

In return for British support for the Morgenthau plan, Roosevelt also agreed to give northwestern Germany to Britain as an occupation zone. He had wanted that part of Germany for the American zone primarily because it offered easy access to the sea, and because he did not want the United States to be in a position where it would have to police France and central Europe after the war. But after the British agreed to place under American control the ports of Bremen and Bremerhaven,

Roosevelt accepted the southwestern part of Germany as the U.S. zone of occupation.[26]

Although the agreement on occupation zones survived intact after the conference closed, the Morgenthau plan and Lend-Lease agreement did not. The Morgenthau plan drew widespread criticism in America when its highlights were leaked to the press. Critics charged that it would stiffen German resistance on the battlefield and thereby prolong the war. Faced with hostile reaction to the plan, Roosevelt dropped it on September 29 and announced that postwar economic policy toward Germany had not been determined. The new Lend-Lease agreement, which was concluded in its final form in November, provided the British with only $5.5 billion, about 20 percent less than had been originally promised. Despite this agreement, after Roosevelt's death, Lend-Lease came to a halt after Japan surrendered.[27]

## Churchill's Trip to Moscow, October 1944

The political future of Eastern Europe was not discussed at length at Quebec or Hyde Park. With the presidential election fast approaching, Roosevelt was unwilling to meet with Stalin to resolve East European problems. But Churchill realized that the rapid advance of the Red Army made it necessary to deal with these problems as soon as possible. Consequently, in October the prime minister decided to see the Soviet leader in Moscow without the president. However, he promised to keep Roosevelt fully informed about the proceedings, and he requested that the president send either Marshall or Stettinius to Moscow to represent the United States.[28]

Roosevelt had ambivalent feelings about Churchill's trip to Moscow. While he viewed with sympathy any effort to improve relations with Stalin, he regarded with trepidation the possibility that the prime minister would make unacceptable commitments to the Soviet leader. His reaction to Churchill's conference proposal reflected his mixed feelings. While he refused to send Stettinius or Marshall, so as not to involve the United States too deeply in the proceedings, he informed Churchill that Averell Harriman, the U.S. ambassador to Moscow, would participate as his observer.[29]

Churchill and Eden arrived in the Soviet capital on October 9. The first topic of their discussions with Stalin was Poland. Churchill quickly revealed that he was quite willing to pressure the London Poles to reach an accommodation with the Soviets in order to get Soviet recognition of British interests elsewhere. "Under dire threats," he recalled, he had "persuaded" Mikolajczyk to come immediately to Moscow. He browbeat the Polish leader into accepting the Curzon Line as the new Soviet-Polish border and insisted that he work out an arrangement with the Lublin Poles for a government of national unity. Mikolajczyk said he would not participate in any government in which the Lublin Poles were in the majority, but Stalin refused to settle for less. Consequently, the talks between the Polish factions made little progress. And while Mikolajczyk accepted the Curzon Line as

Poland's eastern border, he was unable to persuade his London colleagues to do so as well. Accordingly, on November 24, Mikolajczyk resigned the premiership.[30]

In spite of Churchill's unsuccessful effort to force the London Poles to accept Soviet aims in Poland, he was successful in reaching an agreement of sorts with Stalin on the Balkans. The agreement unofficially defined the spheres of influence of the two nations in that region. It recognized a 90 percent British interest in Greece, and set the Soviet interest in that country at 10 percent. For Rumania the same ratio was reversed in favor of the Russians. In Bulgaria the division of interests was set at 75:25, again in favor of the Soviet Union. Yugoslavia and Hungary were divided 50:50. Churchill wrote these percentages on a half-sheet of paper and pushed it across the table to Stalin. The Soviet leader made a large tick with a blue pencil on the paper and passed it back to the prime minister. "Might it not be thought rather cynical," Churchill asked, "if it seemed we had disposed of these issues, so fateful to millions of people, in such an offhand manner? Let us burn the paper." Stalin replied: "No, you keep it."[31]

In addition to the Balkan arrangement, both Stalin and Churchill reached an understanding on their respective interests in the Mediterranean Sea. Stalin accepted Churchill's demand that Britain must be the leading Mediterranean power. In return, Churchill promised the Soviet leader that he would guarantee unrestricted Soviet access between the Black Sea and the Mediterranean by supporting the cancellation of the Montreaux Convention, which allowed Turkey to close the straits connecting the two seas.[32]

Although Harriman was not present when the Balkan and Mediterranean arrangements were made, after he had learned about their details, he warned Churchill and Stalin that Roosevelt would not accept the establishment of spheres of influence. Yet even before the president was informed about the details of the agreement, he cabled Harriman expressing his "active interest that such steps as are practicable should be taken to insure against the Balkans getting us into a future international war." Furthermore, after subsequent messages from Churchill and Harriman confirmed that the Anglo-Soviet deal had divided the Balkans into spheres of interest, Roosevelt did not object.[33]

Roosevelt was also pleased by other news from Churchill. Stalin, the prime minister reported, indicated that Soviet forces would attack the Japanese in Manchuria following the defeat of Hitler, a move that would preclude what appeared to be the necessity of sending American forces to invade China. At the same time, however, Roosevelt asked Churchill to delay any announcement on Poland until after the election, only two weeks away. The Montreaux Convention, the future of Germany, and other matters discussed at Moscow, the president advised the prime minister, would have to be discussed at their next meeting with Stalin.[34]

As result of the Moscow Conference, the Big Three were again led to believe that they might be able to work out their differences over Eastern Europe. The Moscow meeting, Churchill wrote Stalin after the conference, "has shown that there are no matters that cannot be adjusted between us when we meet together in frank and intimate discussion." The Soviet leader echoed these sentiments in a message to Roosevelt: "The talks made it plain that we can without undue difficulty coordinate our policies on all important issues and that even if we cannot ensure immediate solution of this or that problem, such as the Polish question, we have nevertheless more favorable prospects in this respect as well." In response, Roosevelt cabled Stalin that he was "delighted" with the outcome of the conference. In the president's opinion, it would help to build a "satisfactory and a durable peace."[35]

Stalin had every reason to be pleased with the results of his meeting with Churchill. It appeared to him that the British prime minister and the American president were prepared to recognize Soviet domination of Eastern Europe. In return, Stalin was prepared to allow the British a free hand in Greece and, quite possibly, much of Western Europe as well. As a result, while Churchill was busy consolidating British influence in Greece, Stalin strengthened Soviet control over Bulgaria, Rumania, and Poland. The status of Yugoslavia ultimately would depend on the direction taken by Tito, who concluded an agreement on November 1 with the royal government-in-exile making him prime minister, minister of defense, and commander in chief of the Yugoslav armed forces.[36]

While Roosevelt gave tacit recognition to the Anglo-Soviet Balkan arrangement, other American officials reacted to it negatively and with bitterness. It only confirmed their suspicions that Churchill was determined to restore the old diplomacy--with its secret deals, balances of power, and spheres of influence--to the detriment of America's apparent policy of creating a Wilsonian system of international relations, based on a community of power, open diplomacy, and the principle of self-determination. More than a few Americans began to believe that their soldiers were fighting in Europe so that Britain and Russia could divide the spoils. Even Churchill quickly appreciated the negative impact his Balkan arrangement would have on American opinion. As a result, on October 11, one day after the deal with Stalin, he wrote to the Soviet leader that the percentages it contained were no more than a guide for the conduct of their affairs, and that the figures should not be publicized since they would be considered "crude and even callous."[37]

## Anglo-American Tensions over Italy and Greece

Churchill, however, was unable to avert the deterioration of Anglo-American relations that followed in the wake of the British agreement with Russia. British policy in Greece and Italy were largely responsible.

In Italy Churchill objected strongly to the replacement of Prime Minister Badoglio by Ivanoe Bonomi on June 9. Churchill feared Italian conservatives would be denied a role in the new government. But Roosevelt rejected Churchill's arguments against Bonomi, and the British were compelled to recognize the new Italian leader. In November, however, Churchill tried to block the appointment of Count Carlo Sforza as the new Italian foreign minister. He considered Sforza anti-British and far too willing to work with the Italian communists. But Americans considered Sforza an ardent antifascist, and Churchill's opposition to him raised an outcry in the American press. As a result, Stettinius, who had succeeded Hull as secretary of state on December 1 (Hull had resigned for reasons of health), took strong exception to Churchill's opposition. A State Department press release on December 5 described Sforza's appointment as "purely an internal affair," which should not be influenced from the outside.[38]

To the British, however, Italy was a defeated enemy in whose internal affairs the victorious Western Allies had every right to meddle. In a message to Roosevelt on December 6, Churchill wrote that he was much hurt and "astonished at the acerbity" of the State Department's press release. He could not, he said, remember anything the State Department had ever said about the Russians that was so poignant. The Anglo-American tiff over Italy ended when Stettinius apologized for releasing the statement without first consulting the British. Moreover, the Americans did not object when Bonomi formed a cabinet without Sforza on December 9.[39]

In Greece the withdrawal of German troops caused by the Soviet advance into the Balkans made it possible for British troops to enter the country on October 4. Two weeks later the Greek government-in-exile, headed by King George II and led by a cabinet dominated by the Greek oligarchy, returned to Athens. However, the government's control of the country was challenged by antimonarchial partisans who were led by the National Liberation Front (EAM) and its military arm, the National People's Liberation Army (ELAS), both of which were comprised of a coalition of socialists, liberals, and communists. In mid-December, when forces of ELAS tried to seize Athens in order to topple the monarchy, Churchill ordered the British army to fire upon them, arguing that military action was necessary to prevent a communist takeover of the country.[40]

As the situation in Greece deteriorated, Churchill requested American mediation of the conflict. But American opinion reacted hostilely to what they perceived as a British effort to foist an unpopular monarchy on the Greek people. As a result, even though Roosevelt supported Churchill's effort to prevent a communist takeover of Greece, he felt restricted in what he could do to help the British. Nevertheless, on December 13 he did suggest to Churchill that a regency might be the way to avoid civil war in Greece. The British accepted the president's suggestion and proposed to King George that he name Archbishop Damaskinos of Athens to head the regency. At Churchill's request, Roosevelt cabled the king on December 29 supporting the archbishop. On January 1, 1945, a regency was established under Damaskinos. Ten days later, a truce was arranged that produced an uneasy peace between the two hostile Greek factions.[41]

## Toward West European Union

Disillusioned by America's Eastern European policy, some British statesmen, particularly Churchill and Eden, entertained thoughts of creating a Western European military and economic bloc to balance the growing power of the Soviet Union. As a step in this direction, Churchill traveled to Paris on November 11 and informed de Gaulle that he would support an occupation zone for France in Germany and would ask the Americans to equip a French occupation army. Yet Churchill's enthusiasm for a West European defense bloc was not as great as

Eden's. Like earlier British statesmen, the prime minister was reluctant to commit Britain to the defense of weak European countries. Only a permanent security relationship with the United States, Churchill insisted, could maintain the postwar balance of power on the Continent. It was a sentiment fully shared by the British Chiefs of Staff, who saw an American alliance as the essential element of postwar British defense policy.[42]

But Roosevelt was not inclined to support either an alliance with Britain or the creation of a West European bloc. On November 18 he informed Churchill that, after the defeat of Germany, it would be necessary to bring home American troops as quickly as possible. On November 26 he also told the prime minister that he had no objection to a French occupation force in Germany, but when the war was over, it was unlikely that Congress would equip it with American weapons. Roosevelt also vetoed any French presence, and particularly de Gaulle's, at the next summit with Stalin. De Gaulle's participation in the conference, he wrote Churchill on December 6, would "introduce a complicating and undesirable factor."[43]

Stalin, on the other hand, was not as reluctant as Roosevelt to befriend the French leader. On December 2 he informed the president that he was considering a mutual assistance pact with de Gaulle's government. Roosevelt responded that he had no objection to such an agreement, and on December 10 the pact was signed.[44]

## Soviet Recognition of the Lublin Poles

Roosevelt's major European concern, other than victory over Germany, was to prevent the Polish problem from destroying the Grand Alliance. In November he told Harriman that "he wanted to have a lot to say about the settlement in the Pacific, but that he considered the European questions so impossible that he wanted to stay out of them as far as practicable, except for the problems involving Germany." On November 20, in response to former ambassador to Poland Arthur Bliss Lane's urging that he demand Soviet recognition of Polish independence, the president sarcastically asked: "Do you want me to go to war with Russia?"[45]

However, after his reelection to a fourth term, Roosevelt was more willing to deal with the Polish crisis. On December 16 he cabled Stalin asking him to avoid recognizing the Lublin Committee as the provisional government of Poland until they had a chance to meet. But Stalin would not oblige. In a message to the president on December 27 he denounced the London Poles for being anti-Soviet and stated that, because the Lublin Committee represented a majority of Poles, he could not delay its recognition. Roosevelt responded on December 30 by informing Stalin that there was no possibility that the United States would transfer its recognition from the London Poles to the Lublin Committee. Nevertheless, the next day the Soviet government announced that it had recognized the Lublin Committee as the provisional government of Poland. In a conversation with Stimson that day, Roosevelt said that Stalin had every intention of establishing a *cordon sanitaire* of friendly nations in Eastern Europe.[46]

## The Conferences at Malta and Yalta, January-February 1945

Roosevelt had been trying since July 1944 to arrange another summit meeting with Stalin either in Scotland or somewhere in the Mediterranean. But the Soviet leader insisted that the rapid advance of the Red Army as well as poor health made it impossible for him to leave the Soviet Union.[47]

By the beginning of 1945 Roosevelt's own health was not good. His doctor diagnosed his condition as cardiac failure. But when Lord Moran, Churchill's physician, saw him in February 1945, he thought the president was suffering from hardening of the arteries in the brain. Moran, quite prophetically, gave him only a few months to live. The president apparently was never informed about the seriousness of his condition, but considering the decline in energy and physical appearance that he experienced in the last year of his life, it is quite possible that he realized he did not have long to live. Against the advice of all of his advisers, who could not understand why the president of the United States had to travel halfway around the world to see Stalin, Roosevelt agreed to go to Yalta, in the Soviet Crimea. It is entirely possible that he believed it might be his last chance to come to terms with the Soviet leader.[48]

Although Churchill agreed to accompany the president to Yalta, he could not get Roosevelt to accept the need for a preliminary conference prior to their meeting with Stalin. The president again wanted to avoid creating the impression that he and the prime minister were conspiring against the Soviet leader. The most that Churchill could get Roosevelt to do was to meet with him briefly on Malta before each made their own separate way to Yalta. Nevertheless, in their brief encounter, which took place on February 2, no political decisions were made.[49]

The Combined Chiefs of Staff, on the other hand, held substantive military talks on Malta before accompanying Roosevelt and Churchill to Yalta. After the Anglo-American armies had repulsed a major German offensive on the western front in December, the so-called Battle of the Bulge, Eisenhower proposed a plan for a broad frontal advance to the Rhine. General Montgomery, on the other hand, favored a concentrated attack on the lower Rhine, where his Twenty-first British Army Group was positioned. This, of course, meant that Montgomery would lead the Allied advance into Germany. But the Combined Chiefs supported Eisenhower's broad-front strategy. As a result, Patton's Third Army, and not Montgomery's forces, would be the first to cross the last major barrier into the German homeland.[50]

The Combined Chiefs also accepted General Alan Brooke's estimate that the advance of the left wing of the Soviet army through Yugoslavia and Hungary made unnecessary an Anglo-American advance through the Ljubljana Gap. As a result, the Combined Chiefs recommended the transfer of a number of Allied divisions from Italy to the western front. This decision did not please Churchill, who told Roosevelt in their brief Malta meeting, "We should occupy as much of Austria as possible, as it was undesirable that more of Western Europe than necessary should be occupied by the Russians." This was the first time that the prime minister had explicitly suggested to Roosevelt that their military forces be positioned to limit Soviet expansion. The president, however, refused to be drawn into a discussion of the matter.[51]

At long last, on February 4 the Yalta Conference (code named ARGONAUT) began. Unlike the first meeting of the Big Three, at Tehran, the Yalta Conference dealt primarily with political issues. Military matters were emphasized on only the first day of the conference. Here, the Soviets were at a distinct advantage. Since January 12, when Soviet armies had launched an offensive designed to relieve German pressure on the Anglo-American front, the Red Army had advanced 250 miles to the Oder River, only 40 miles from Berlin. With the Anglo-American forces still on the west side of the Rhine, it appeared as though the Soviets themselves would end the war. However, not aware that the Soviets had reached the limit of their lines of communication and supply, some American diplomats urged the president to ratify quickly the German occupation zones recommended by the European Advisory Commission, which gave the Soviets a zone in eastern Germany, before the Red Army could advance into western Germany.[52]

# The German Problem

Most of the second day of the Yalta Conference was spent discussing the postwar treatment of Germany. After Roosevelt again informed Stalin and Churchill that American troops were unlikely to stay in Europe for more than two years after the war, the prime minister insisted that France must help share the burden of occupying Germany. Both Stalin and the president agreed to give the French an occupation zone (in the Rhineland), but they only reluctantly accepted Churchill's suggestion that France must also be given a seat on the Allied Control Council for Germany. Roosevelt did not want France restored to the ranks of the great powers too quickly. The remainder of Germany was to be divided into three occupation zones, one for the British in the northwest of Germany, one for the Americans in the south, and one for the Soviets in the east.[53]

The Allies were not able, however, to agree on the long-term partitioning of the German state. The Soviets wanted Germany divided into several small states. But Churchill opposed a draconian partition, no doubt fearing that a dismembered Germany would become easy prey for Soviet subversion. Roosevelt, who by this time had moderated his hostility toward the Germans, suggested that the issue of partition be tabled for further study. But Stalin refused to do so. As a result, the conference agreed to include a reference to the dismemberment of Germany in the final surrender terms, which were to remain secret until the war was over.[54]

The issue of reparations was also discussed at Yalta. The Soviets wanted to exact $20 billion in reparations from Germany, half of which they wanted for themselves. To avoid the problem of financing German reparations, the Soviets recommended that half of the amount should consist of movable capital, including machinery and rolling stock, which would be seized within two years of war's end. The balance would be taken from current German production over a period of ten years. Although the Soviet plan was calculated to reduce the German heavy-industrial capital plant by 80 percent, unlike the Morgenthau plan, the Soviets did not intend to reduce Germany to a pastoral state.[55]

To the displeasure of Churchill, who blamed reparations for the collapse of the peace after World War I, and who thought the Soviet reparations proposal excessively severe, Roosevelt supported it "as a basis for discussion." But the president refused to consider the idea of a massive American loan to the Soviet Union, which Molotov had proposed shortly before the conference and which might have reduced the amount of reparations the Soviets were seeking. The president apparently accepted the advice of the State Department that the loan should not be offered until the Soviets had made concessions on other issues. In the end, neither Roosevelt nor Stalin was able to win Churchill's support for stringent German reparations and, therefore, no final agreement on the issue was possible at Yalta. Instead, the Big Three agreed to establish a Reparation Commission in Moscow which would study the matter further.[56]

As historian Warren F. Kimball has pointed out, at Yalta Roosevelt refused to propose a security treaty between the United States and the European powers. Even though this idea had been suggested by the former isolationist senator, Arthur Vandenberg, and had received a favorable reaction in the American press, Roosevelt, who had a copy of Vandenberg's proposal with him at Yalta, never raised the subject at the conference. He may have thought, Kimball believes, that a security treaty would interfere with the operation of the United Nations or, more likely, that neither the Senate nor the American people were ready for such a drastic departure from the nation's isolationist tradition. Roosevelt clearly had no desire to repeat Woodrow Wilson's mistake at Versailles. Furthermore, the president had more than enough problems at Yalta without stoking up the embers of American isolationism.[57]

## The Polish Imbroglio

However, the most time-consuming and controversial issue at the Yalta Conference was not Germany. That dubious honor went to Poland. Stalin came to the conference seeking Anglo-American recognition of the Warsaw (Lublin) government, which the Soviet government had recognized on December 30, insisting that it not only enjoyed the support of the Polish people but was also the only government capable of maintaining order in the rear of the Soviet armies as they advanced into Germany. In addition to the Curzon Line, the Soviet leader wanted the Oder and West Neisse rivers to be the new boundary of the Polish state. Churchill, faced with a parliamentary election at war's end, was increasingly sensitive to his public's reaction to Soviet expansion in Eastern Europe. He accepted the Curzon Line but not the Oder-Neisse Line, and he refused to recognize the Warsaw government as representing the will of the Polish people.

The London Poles, on the other hand, accepted the Oder-Neisse Line but not the Curzon Line. Nor did they recognize the legitimacy of the Warsaw government.[58]

Roosevelt, for his part, feared that the controversy over Poland would wreck the conference. He was not prepared to allow the Polish problem to cripple his effort to establish postwar Soviet-American relations on a sound footing at Yalta. As a way out of the stalemate, the president suggested that Stalin alter the Curzon Line by giving Poland the city of Lwow and by creating a new Polish provisional government that would include the London Poles. This, he believed, would assure American opinion that the Polish government really "represented the people."[59]

Stalin responded with an impassioned speech in defense of the Soviet position on Poland. A friendly Poland, he insisted, was vital to the security of the Soviet Union. Poland, he reminded Churchill and Roosevelt, had been more than once the pathway of invaders into Russia. Comparing Poland to Western-supported France, he asked why more was demanded of the Poles than of the French. De Gaulle, he pointed out, had not been elected, yet the French provisional government had been recognized by the Soviet Union. He could not understand why Churchill and Roosevelt could not emulate his action toward France in their policies toward Poland.[60]

Nevertheless, Stalin offered a few concessions that he thought would give his allies a face-saving way out of the Polish problem. To create an illusion of democracy in Poland without weakening Soviet domination of the country, Stalin promised that "all democratic and anti-Nazi parties" would have a right to take part in "free and unfettered elections" in Poland. But he refused to permit Western observations of the Polish elections to ensure that they were really free. Instead, he suggested the establishment of a tripartite commission, composed of Molotov and the American and British ambassadors in Moscow, which would enlarge the Polish government and keep their respective governments informed about developments in Poland. But Stalin also insisted that the communist-dominated Lublin group must be the foundation of the Warsaw government's reorganization and that the Oder-Neisse Line must be the western boundary of Poland.[61]

Roosevelt, like Churchill, was prepared to recognize the Curzon Line as the eastern boundary of Poland but not the Oder-Neisse Line as her western frontier. With the Big Three unable to agree on Poland's western border, it was decided that resolution of the issue must await the final peace conference. Roosevelt and Churchill, however, did accept, albeit reluctantly, the Soviet proposal for reorganizing the Polish provisional government. In effect, this meant that the future of Polish democracy would be largely dependent on Soviet assurances that free elections would be held in Poland. Roosevelt realized this. "Mr. President," his chief of staff, Admiral William Leahy, reacted to the Polish agreement, "this is so elastic that the Russians can stretch it all the way from Yalta to Washington without ever technically breaking it." "I know Bill," Roosevelt replied. "I know it. But it's the best I can do for Poland at this time."[62]

As a means of applying additional restrictions on Soviet behavior in Poland and the other nations of Eastern Europe occupied by the Red Army, Roosevelt proposed a Declaration on Liberated Europe. Drafted by the State Department, the document was designed as an alternative to the spheres of influence agreement reached by Churchill and Stalin the previous October. The declaration committed the Allies to assist liberated peoples in solving their political and economic problems by democratic means, including free elections. "I want this election in Poland to be the first one beyond question," Roosevelt stated. "It should be like Caesar's wife. I did not know her but they said she was pure." Replied Stalin, in a preview of what was to come in Poland, "They said that about her, but in fact she had her sins." Still, both Stalin and Churchill approved the declaration, although the prime minister did so with the understanding that the reference to the Atlantic Charter in the declaration would not apply to the British Empire. Churchill had no intention of permitting the declaration or the president to deprive Britain of her far-flung colonial holdings.[63]

## The United Nations

Roosevelt's policy of avoiding a confrontation with the Soviets over Eastern Europe was partly motivated by his desire to see the United Nations successfully established. Without the UN, he feared, the American people would again see only the old diplomacy at work in Europe and would once again turn their backs on the Old World, as they did after World War I. For Roosevelt, then, creation of the UN was vital to ensure continued American participation in world affairs. And he was prepared to pay a price in his negotiations with Stalin to ensure Soviet cooperation in establishing the new world body.[64]

With respect to the UN, Roosevelt offered Stalin a compromise position on the voting problem. It would establish two kinds of issues that would fall under the jurisdiction of the Security Council. One category would include issues relating to the admission and suspension of member nations, peacekeeping or restoring actions, and arms regulations. This kind of issue would require a unanimous vote of the permanent members of the Security Council. In the second category were quasi-judicial issues, like the question of whether a dispute between member states should be referred to the International Court of Justice. In cases like this, the permanent members of the council would not be permitted to vote if they were a party to the dispute.[65]

Both Stalin and Churchill accepted the American compromise. But Stalin demanded a concession in return: seats in the General Assembly for two or three of the Soviet republics. Churchill supported Stalin's request on the ground that the British Commonwealth had already been allotted multiple seats. Roosevelt reluctantly supported the idea of seating the Soviet republics of the Ukraine and Byelorussia, but he did so only after Churchill and Stalin promised to raise no objections to giving two additional seats to the United States. Roosevelt also required them to keep the multiple seating arrangement secret until the first session of the UN, which the Big Three agreed would be held in San Francisco beginning on April 25, 1945.[66]

While Roosevelt was uneasy about his concession on additional Soviet representation in the General Assembly, Churchill was agitated by Stettinius' proposal to establish UN trusteeships over colonial and dependent nations. The prime minister considered it an American attempt to dismantle the British

Empire. Churchill vehemently exclaimed that he would never permit the UN to thrust "interfering fingers into the life's existence of the British Empire," thereby seeming to confirm Stalin's view that imperialists would rather fight than relinquish their colonies. Later, Eden recalled Stalin's reaction to the prime minister's outburst: "He got up from his chair, walked up and down, beamed, and, at intervals, broke into applause." An embarrassed Stettinius was compelled to assure Churchill that the trusteeship proposal did not apply to the British Empire. The prime minister was not fully mollified until a protocol of the conference specifically stated that only existing mandates of the League of Nations and former enemy territories would be established as UN trusteeships.[67]

# The Far East

There was, in fact, a real basis for Churchill's fear that Roosevelt was trying to dismember the British Empire. In a private meeting with Stalin on February 8, the president questioned the right of Britain and France to have any influence in Asia after the war. Although he had made it clear that Japan would be occupied by the United States, Roosevelt expected that the Soviets would have an interest in Manchuria and Korea. In fact, the president proposed to Stalin that Korea should be established as a trusteeship under American, Soviet, and Chinese supervision. He did not want to offer Britain a share of the Korean trusteeship, but Stalin said that, if the British were denied a role in Korea, Churchill might "kill us." As for the French, Roosevelt told Stalin that they were unfit to govern Indochina, which, the president asserted, suffered grievously under their rule. Indochina, he felt, should become a UN trusteeship.[68]

In this meeting between the Big Two, Stalin also restated the political conditions under which the Soviet Union would enter the war against Japan. He had discussed them with Harriman during a conversation with the ambassador in December, and Harriman in turn had relayed them to the president. Stalin wanted the southern part of Sakhalin Island as well as the Kuril Islands, both of which were Japanese but which once had belonged to czarist Russia. He also desired access to two Chinese ports in Manchuria--Darien and Port Arthur--and joint ownership with China of the Chinese Eastern and Southern Manchurian railroads. Stalin also demanded that China make no attempt to end Soviet hegemony over Outer Mongolia. Roosevelt raised no objection to Stalin's territorial demands on Japan, but he said he would support the concessions from China only if Chiang Kai-shek agreed to give them. Only after Roosevelt responded favorably to Stalin's conditions did the Soviet leader promise to enter the war against Japan, two or three months after the defeat of Germany. The Far Eastern agreement was made a top secret; even Stettinius was not informed about it. And although Eden protested that the agreement should not be concluded without China's signature, Churchill signed it anyhow, arguing that it was the only way to preserve Britain's waning influence in East Asia.[69]

Although, from hindsight, Roosevelt's concessions to Stalin in the Far East appear excessive, the territory demanded by the Soviets was theirs for the taking.

And while the atomic bomb would make Soviet participation in the war against Japan unnecessary, in February 1945 Roosevelt was not sure the bomb would work. Even if it did, it was not expected to be produced in any significant numbers until well into 1946. For this reason, General Marshall argued that Soviet participation would be far more important than the bomb in shortening the war and saving Americans lives; he pressed the president to do everything possible to obtain it. Nor was Roosevelt bothered by the concessions he had made at China's expense. In return for them, Stalin had promised to sign a treaty of friendship with Nationalist China, a factor that could not be weighed lightly in the face of the growing Chinese communist menace to Chiang's government.[70]

## Other Issues at Yalta

Stalin was less successful in getting American and British acquiescence to other Soviet ambitions. While both Roosevelt and Churchill accepted, in principle, a revision of the Montreaux Convention, which gave Turkey the right to close the Dardenelles and Bosporus to foreign warships, nothing was finalized on this matter at Yalta. It was, however, agreed that the issue would be considered later at a conference of the foreign ministers.[71]

An even more potentially explosive issue between the Big Three was Iran. The country had been occupied by the British and the Soviets in 1941 to ensure the safe passage of supplies from the Persian Gulf to the Soviet Union. Both signed a treaty promising to withdraw their troops shortly after the end of the war, and the British promised that they would not seek any advantage in Iran at Russia's expense. In 1942 American troops also were sent to Iran to facilitate Lend-Lease shipments to the Soviet Union. They were soon followed by American companies seeking oil concessions from the Iranian government. Pressed by the Americans, both the Soviets and the British sought similar concessions.[72]

At Yalta both the British and the Americans tried to get the Soviets to sign a document renewing their earlier pledge to withdraw their troops from Iran at war's end. But the Soviets refused to sign the agreement until they received oil concessions from the Iranian government commensurate with those granted to Britain and the United States. While the British and Americans recognized Russia's right to oil concessions in Iran, they refused to make the troop withdrawal contingent on Soviet success in getting them. The Yalta Conference ended with the Iranian issue unresolved. It remained so until it flared into a major Soviet-American crisis a year later.[73]

Indeed, too many problems were raised at the Yalta Conference to be resolved quickly by the Big Three. As a result, Roosevelt and Stalin accepted Churchill's suggestion to arrange periodic meetings of their foreign ministers to deal with them. London was selected as the site of the first foreign ministers' conference. Subsequent meetings would be rotated to each of the three capitals.[74]

## Aftermath of Yalta

After his return to Washington, Roosevelt told the Congress that the Yalta agreements represented a major step toward peace. "It ought to spell the end of the system of unilateral action, the exclusive alliances, the spheres of influence, the balances of power, and all the other expedients that have been tried for centuries-- and have always failed. We propose to substitute for all of these, a universal organization in which all peace-loving nations will finally have a chance to join."[75]

Privately, Roosevelt expressed less confidence in the results of the conference. Upon seeing Adolf Berle, a State Department member and old friend of the president who feared Soviet ambitions, Roosevelt threw his arms up and said: "Adolf, I didn't say the result was good. I said it was the best I could do." The alternative was to risk a war with the Soviet Union, which neither he nor the American people were prepared to consider. In the opinion of historian Robert Dallek, Roosevelt realized that the exaggerated optimism he displayed toward the conference was bound to produce disillusionment later. But he believed that, by the time this occurred, the American commitment to a major role in international affairs would have been placed on a firm foundation.[76]

In the meantime, Roosevelt hoped that Stalin would cooperate by curbing his territorial appetite and by preserving the facade of democracy in Eastern Europe that was created at Yalta. This, however, the Soviet dictator was not inclined to do, at least not to the satisfaction of Western opinion. Stalin violated the Declaration on Liberated Europe within two weeks of signing it by forcing a subservient government on Rumania. In Poland, tedious negotiations to broaden the Warsaw government to include noncommunists got nowhere, and the Soviets proceeded with the liquidation or deportation of Poles who opposed communist rule.[77]

The prestige of the Yalta agreements suffered another serious blow in late March when news of Roosevelt's acquiescence to Stalin's demand for UN seats for the Ukraine and Byelorussia leaked to the press. Neither the president's admission that he supported the arrangement nor his request for triple American representation in the General Assembly sweetened the pill. When the idea of multiple U.S. representation failed to generate any public support, the administration dropped the American claim to more than one seat in the assembly. The manner in which news of multiple Soviet representation in the General Assembly was revealed caused many Americans to wonder what other secret agreements had been concluded at Yalta.[78]

## Churchill Adopts a Hard Line toward the Soviets

In the wake of the dissipation of the high hopes raised at Yalta, Churchill concluded that there was little likelihood that Stalin would cooperate with the West after the war. On March 8 he cabled the president urging a harder line toward Soviet policy in Eastern Europe. The Soviets, he pointed out, had imposed a government on Rumania and were not even going through the motions of conducting elections for a new Polish provisional government. While the prime minister was bothered by Soviet behavior in Poland, he probably was more concerned about its effect on his reelection chances, considering that he had been part of the negotiations that had tacitly recognized Soviet domination of that nation. Even though he understood that the wording of the Declaration on Liberated Europe was imprecise, he still argued that he and the president had been "deceived" at Yalta, and that it would be necessary to press Stalin to create an entirely new government in Poland with free elections supervised by Western observers.[79]

Roosevelt, however, refused to be drawn into a confrontational policy toward the Soviets in Eastern Europe. Rumania, he cabled Churchill on March 12, was not a good test case of Soviet intentions. The country was "in undisputed Soviet control," the president argued, and the Russians could argue that military necessity justified their actions there. As for Poland, Roosevelt said he would not tolerate "a fraud or a mere whitewash of the Lublin Government," but he wanted to avoid any kind of ultimatum to the Soviets, not only because he believed that there was no way to enforce it, but also because he was unwilling to do anything that might jeopardize the approaching San Francisco Conference. Rather than confronting Stalin over Poland, Roosevelt preferred to pressure the Warsaw government to observe the Yalta accord.[80]

The Soviets, however, made it increasingly difficult for Roosevelt to avoid a confrontation over Poland. On March 23 Molotov insisted that the Warsaw government had the right to accept or reject any new members, in effect, meaning that all noncommunists would be excluded from the provisional government. Any request to send observers into Poland, Molotov added, would also have to be approved by the Warsaw government. In response to Molotov's statement, Churchill on March 27 again asked Roosevelt to join him in a protest to Stalin, demanding the creation of an entirely new government in Poland. In a reply two days later, the president recommended that rather than calling for a new government in Poland, they should insist on a strict observation of the Yalta agreement and demand that the tripartite Moscow Commission, not the Warsaw government, should determine which Poles would be included in the provisional government.[81]

## The Last Days of Franklin Roosevelt

By the end of March, some evidence seems to indicate, Roosevelt may have begun to move toward the hard line favored by Churchill. In a message to Stalin on April 1, which was drafted by the State Department but approved by the president, Roosevelt stated that he could not understand why the developments in Rumania "should be regarded as not falling within the terms" of the Declaration on Liberated Europe. Moreover, he added, "a thinly disguised continuation of the present Warsaw regime would be unacceptable and would cause the people of the United States to regard the Yalta agreement as having failed." He concluded: "I wish I could convey to you how important it is for the successful development of our program of international collaboration that this Polish question be settled fairly and speedily." Stalin responded on April 7 by blaming the Polish impasse on the Western Allies who, he charged, were attempting to change the Yalta agreement by refusing to accept the Warsaw government as "the core of a new government of National Unity."[82]

Other points of friction strained Anglo-American relations with the Soviets. In March reports reached Washington that the Soviets were mistreating American prisoners of war whom they had liberated from the Germans. In the same month, Moscow announced that Molotov would be too busy to attend the San Francisco Conference in April. And in late March and early April, Stalin interpreted Anglo-American negotiations (conducted in Bern, Switzerland) to arrange for the surrender of German forces in Italy as an attempt to secure a separate peace with Berlin. In a highly critical cable to Roosevelt on April 3, Stalin implied that the president was deliberately deceiving him about the objectives of the Bern talks.[83]

In fact, Roosevelt was withholding a full explanation of the Bern talks from his Soviet ally. With Anglo-American forces advancing rapidly across Germany after crossing the Rhine in early March, the Combined Chiefs feared that the Soviets would try to delay the surrender negotiations until the Red Army, which was tied down on the Oder River, could launch its offensive against Berlin. Prolongation of the negotiations, the Chiefs believed, would cause a needless loss of American and British lives. Roosevelt angrily denounced Stalin's implied accusation that he was trying to conclude a separate peace, but the president never explained why Soviet representatives were excluded from the Bern talks.[84]

In a message on April 5, Churchill informed Roosevelt that he was "astonished" at the "insulting" tone of Stalin's Bern cable. He wondered if "the brutality of the Russian messages" foreshadowed "some deep change of policy for which they are preparing." With this in mind, Churchill felt it was vital to "join hands with the Russian armies as far to the east as possible and, if circumstances allow, enter Berlin." It was "of the highest importance," he added, "that a firm and blunt stand should be made at this juncture by our two countries in order that the air may be cleared and they realize that there is a point beyond which we will not tolerate insult. If they are ever convinced that we are afraid of them and can be bullied into submission, then indeed I should despair of our future relations with them and much else."[85]

Some of Roosevelt's advisers were also pushing him toward a showdown with the Soviets. On April 3 Harriman cabled from Moscow that "confronted with a definite and firm position on our part, there is a chance that the Soviet Government may yield and allow the Polish negotiations to continue." On April 6 a message to Churchill, drafted by Leahy in the president's name, stated: "We must not permit anybody to entertain a false impression that we are afraid. Our armies will in a very few days be in a position that will permit us to become 'tougher' than has heretofore appeared advantageous to the war effort."[86]

Yet other evidence appears to indicate that Roosevelt intended to continue to avoid, for as long as possible, a confrontation with Stalin. Much to Churchill's chagrin, the president, as well as the U.S. Joint Chiefs of Staff, supported Eisenhower's decision to allow the Red Army to capture Berlin. The decision was prompted primarily by military considerations. Eisenhower put much stock in rumors that the Nazis were preparing a redoubt in the south of Germany, where they would make a last-ditch stand. He also did not want to expend American and British lives to capture territory, lying in the future Soviet occupation zone, from which the Western armies would be compelled to withdraw after the war. Consequently, Eisenhower ordered General Omar Bradley's Twelfth Army Group to move toward Leipzig, to the south of Berlin, and in effect permit the Soviets to take the German capital.[87]

In addition, in a cable to Stalin on April 11, the president regarded the Bern negotiations with the Germans, which ultimately proved unsuccessful, as a misunderstanding that had "faded into the past." "There must not be," he informed Stalin, "mutual distrust" between the Allies that would jeopardize victory over Germany. On the same day, in his next to last message to Churchill, a cable that he personally drafted, the president wrote: "I would minimize the general Soviet problem as much as possible because these problems, in one form or another, seem to arise every day and most of them straighten out, as in the case of the Bern meeting."[88]

The next day, April 12, at 1:15 in the afternoon, while resting at his vacation home in Warms Springs, Georgia, Roosevelt complained of a "terrific headache," before slumping in his chair unconscious. A little over two hours later, the president died, apparently of a cerebral hemorrhage.[89]

## Roosevelt's Wartime Diplomacy: An Assessment

The interpretation of Franklin Roosevelt's wartime diplomacy has been even more controversial than the analysis of his prewar foreign policy.[90]

As early as 1948, William C. Bullitt called the height of naiveté Roosevelt's attempt to accommodate Stalin with almost unlimited wartime aid and territorial concessions, all to win Soviet cooperation in building a stable postwar peace. Equally damaging, Bullitt charged, Roosevelt had ignored the dictum that war is an instrument of policy, and the warnings of the more politically astute Churchill, by making total military victory more important than fashioning a stable political order after the war.[91]

Echoing this criticism, in 1952 Australian journalist and military historian Chester Wilmot charged that Roosevelt, by subordinating all political issues to the goal of winning a total military victory as rapidly as possible, thereby lost the peace. By choosing the cross-Channel strategy instead of Churchill's plan for an invasion of the Balkans, Roosevelt in effect allowed the Soviet Union a free hand in Eastern Europe. He compounded this error at the Yalta Conference, Wilmot asserted, by agreeing to a division of Germany without guaranteeing Western access rights to Berlin, and by vetoing Churchill's pleas for an Anglo-American advance on the German capital as well as on Vienna and Prague. Reflective of the vitriolic criticism that American conservatives would shower on the Yalta accords after Roosevelt's death, Anthony Kubeck charged that the ailing president had been duped by communist sympathizers in the State Department.[92]

Roosevelt's alleged diplomatic naiveté is accentuated in Frederick Marks' recent study. In Marks' opinion, the president's efforts to charm and "appease" the Soviet dictator produced numerous, unnecessary American concessions. Roosevelt did not have to travel halfway around the world twice to meet with Stalin, Marks argues, to concede to the Soviets much more than they were entitled to in Eastern Europe and the Far East. In so doing, the president betrayed not only the East Europeans but America's closest ally in the Far East, Nationalist China. Instead of pursuing the chimera of a cooperative Soviet-American relationship after the war, Marks contends, Roosevelt should have prepared the nation for an inevitable breakdown of the Grand Alliance. Had he been so inclined, Marks writes, the president "might have sided with Churchill on the value of Germany and France as potential makeweights against Soviet power."[93]

Yet other historians have challenged the view that Roosevelt was either a naive Wilsonian idealist, a dupe of Stalin and his agents, or simply a bumbler as a diplomatist. Instead, they view the president as a shrewd statesman who based his wartime strategy and Soviet policy on a realistic assessment of the balance of power that would prevail in postwar Europe. According to this interpretation, Roosevelt was correct in making the defeat of Germany, rather than the prevention of Soviet occupation of Eastern Europe, the major priority of his wartime policy. His approval of the cross-Channel assault rather than Churchill's Balkan strategy, and his decision to postpone territorial decisions as much as possible to the end of the war, preserved the Grand Alliance until ultimate victory over the Axis powers was achieved. Churchill's alternative, this view contends, may have delayed final victory without standing any chance of halting the inexorable march of the Red Army. Indeed, diverting Allied resources to the Balkans, historian Raymond G. O'Connor has argued, may have made it possible for the Soviets to advance even farther into central Europe than they did. Instead, by following the cross-Channel strategy, major Anglo-American armies were able to meet the Soviets deep in Germany, on the Elbe River, rather than farther west.[94]

Reflecting this interpretation, diplomat and historian George Kennan argued that the great mistake of the Western powers was not made during the war but before it began, in the thirties, when the totalitarian dictatorships had been allowed to become so strong militarily that the aid of one of them, the Soviet Union, became essential to defeat the other, Nazi Germany. Postwar Soviet occupation of Eastern Europe, which the American people were not prepared to reverse by military means, was the price the West had to pay to defeat Hitler. Roosevelt could not alter this fact, and never attempted to do so. Instead, the president tried to ameliorate Soviet policy in the eastern part of Europe by trying to assure Stalin that the United States posed no threat to the Soviet Union and by attempting to gain Soviet adherence to the principles of the Atlantic Charter, the Declaration on Liberated Europe, and the United Nations Charter.[95]

To be sure, Roosevelt overestimated his own ability to influence Stalin. Nevertheless, Arthur M. Schlesinger, Jr., has argued that "Roosevelt intuitively understood that Stalin was the *only* lever available to the West against the Leninist ideology and the Soviet system. If Stalin could be reached, then alone was there a chance of getting the Russians to act contrary to the prescriptions of their faith." But the impression that Stalin most probably gained from Roosevelt's efforts to accomodate the Soviet Union's security concerns was that Soviet occupation of Eastern Europe was acceptable to the United States as long as it could be made palatable to American public opinion. In this sense, Roosevelt was Stalin's accomplice in the Soviet occupation of Eastern Europe. And, as Frederick Marks implies, by failing to prepare American opinion for the type of policy the Soviets would follow in Eastern Europe, Roosevelt bears his share of the responsibility for the subsequent Cold War.[96]

However, as Robert Dallek and John Gaddis have pointed out, Roosevelt was not duped into believing that he could completely succeed in gaining Stalin's trust and cooperation, or that the United Nations alone would be capable of restraining the Soviet Union's expansionistic tendencies after the war. This is evident, they argue, in the president's refusal to cooperate with the Soviets in the development of atomic energy, his decision to tie postwar economic assistance to the Soviet Union with political concessions from Stalin, his willingness to station American troops in southern Germany, his determination to acquire American air and naval bases in the Pacific and the Atlantic, and his attempt to use China as a counter to Soviet postwar expansion in Asia. "When Roosevelt did make concessions," Gaddis asserts, "it was generally in areas where Anglo-American power could not feasibly be brought to bear to deny the Russians what they wanted." Roosevelt, Dallek has observed, kept the *Realpolitik* side of his policy hidden from the American people, primarily because he did not believe they were ready to play the role of world's policeman at the end of the war.[97]

To be sure, with hindsight it can be said that Roosevelt did exaggerate the depth of isolationist sentiment that would prevail in postwar America, ironically, perhaps as much as Wilson exaggerated the willingness of the American people to abandon isolationism after World War I. In fact, Roosevelt, in spite of his professions of internationalism, his belief that the United States must play a major role in world affairs, and his understanding of the realities of power politics, was, in a sense, the last isolationist president. Like the isolationists, he refused to the end of his life to become too deeply entangled in Europe's postwar problems, particularly the military security of the Continent. He flatly refused to commit American troops to Europe beyond a one- or two-year occupation period, thereby forcing Churchill to consider the creation of an Anglo-French alliance to fill the military vacuum the withdrawal of U.S. forces would produce.

How long Roosevelt thought he would be able to maintain a militarily aloof attitude toward Europe, and a conciliatory policy toward the Soviet Union, is, of course, impossible to determine, considering his secretiveness and untimely death. However, shortly before he died, rising Soviet-American tensions over Poland, the German surrender negotiations, and other problems produced the first tangible indication that he was prepared to adopt a more confrontational policy toward the Soviet Union once victory over Germany and Japan had been achieved. Yet, because of his death, this transformation in America's approach to the Soviet Union would not. be made by Roosevelt but rather by his successor, Harry S. Truman. Ultimately, it would be Truman's role to complete the transition in American policy from isolationism to more extensive and permanent American military entanglement in the affairs of Europe.

# 7

# The Collapse of the Grand Alliance, 1945-1947

## The New President

Harry S. Truman succeeded Franklin D. Roosevelt in the presidency determined to continue the domestic and foreign policies of his predecessor, including the attempt to create a collaborative relationship with the Soviet Union. Yet within two years after Truman entered the White House, the Grand Alliance had disintegrated, the United States and the Soviet Union had become bitter enemies, and what soon was called the Cold War had begun. Until this day, historians have debated the reasons for this major transformation in American foreign policy.

The new president was at least partly responsible for the breakup of the Grand Alliance. When Truman entered the presidency in April 1945 he knew little about foreign policy, and almost nothing about the complexities of Roosevelt's Soviet diplomacy. His entire experience in government had been in the arena of domestic affairs. After failing in a haberdashery business, he was elected a county official in his native Missouri. In 1934 he ran for and, with the support of "Boss" Tom Pendergast's Kansas City political machine, was elected to the U.S. Senate. Ten years later, he was nominated to be Roosevelt's vice-presidential running mate. Truman, who staunchly supported the New Deal and the president's foreign policy, and who had won acclaim for his work as the head of a Senate committee that had investigated the national defense program during the war, offended neither conservatives nor liberals, and as a result was considered a safe choice for the second spot on the ticket. But as vice president, following Roosevelt's election to a fourth term, Truman was excluded from the president's circle of advisers. In fact, between Roosevelt's return from Yalta and his death, Truman had met with him only twice. Truman was not informed about the Yalta accords, nor even the existence of the atomic bomb project, until after he was sworn in as Roosevelt's successor on April 12, 1945.[1]

# Truman's Initial Approach to the Soviets

To compensate for his lack of diplomatic knowledge, Truman relied heavily on his predecessor's advisers--men whose advice Roosevelt had only selectively accepted. At first, hardliners like Admiral William Leahy, who stayed on as Truman's military chief of staff, Secretary of the Navy James V. Forrestal, and Moscow Ambassador Averell Harriman had the greatest influence on the new president. They urged Truman to resist the Sovietization of Eastern Europe.[2]

Across the Atlantic, Winston Churchill also pressed Truman to take a tougher line against the Soviets. To this end, he pleaded with the president to order American troops to advance as far to the east as possible before the Germans surrendered, thereby increasing the West's bargaining leverage with Stalin. Churchill also pressured Truman to use military force, if necessary, to expel Yugoslavian troops from the Italian city of Trieste, the outskirts of which Tito's forces had occupied in March.[3]

In the face of this pressure, Truman felt compelled to demonstrate that he was not afraid of the Soviets. He assured Harriman that he intended "to be firm with the Russians and make no concessions . . . to win their favor." On April 16 he joined Churchill in sending a message to Stalin insisting that the Soviets abide by the Yalta accord on Poland. On April 23 he personally berated Molotov, who was in Washington on his way to the United Nations organizational conference in San Francisco, for failing to observe that agreement. "I have never been talked to like that in my life," the Soviet foreign minister protested to the president. Truman retorted, "Carry out your agreements and you won't get talked to like that."[4]

A little over two weeks later, on May 11, Truman signed an order abruptly ending Lend-Lease shipments to the Soviet Union, except aid that would be used for the anticipated Soviet war effort against Japan. Although termination of Lend-Lease at the end of the war had been mandated by Congress, some historians now believe that, in spite of Truman's insistence to the contrary, the measure was designed to pressure the Soviets to be more amenable to American desires. The Soviets were indeed shocked by the abruptness of the cutoff. Even ships at sea with cargoes bound for Europe were ordered to return to the United States. The outcry that the move created both in the Soviet Union and among liberals in the United States prompted Truman to modify his cutoff order to permit shipments in transit to proceed to the Soviet Union. However, after the war against Japan was formally ended in September, all Lend-Lease assistance to the Soviet Union was terminated (although goods on order continued to be shipped to the Soviets well into 1947).[5]

The Soviets reacted to Truman's confrontational diplomacy with increased hostility of their own. On April 24 Stalin responded to the joint message of the president and Churchill by accusing the United States and Britain of trying to "dictate" to the Soviet Union their demands concerning Poland. In San Francisco, the UN organization conference was disrupted by acrimonious exchanges between the Soviet and American delegations. In the Balkans, the Soviets intensified their effort to communize the governments of Bulgaria and Rumania. In Poland, the Soviets arrested sixteen leaders of the underground who had been lured out of hiding by a promise of safe passage to Moscow, where they had been invited to discuss the broadening of the Warsaw government. As a result of the rapid deterioration of U.S.-Soviet relations that occurred during Truman's first month in office, the American media began to discuss the possibility of another world war.[6]

## Second Thoughts

In spite of Truman's inclination to confront the Soviets, he also came to appreciate the arguments of less hawkish advisers, like Secretary of War Henry Stimson and Joseph E. Davies, former ambassador to Moscow, that it was essential to avoid a split with the Soviet Union. Davies feared that the breakup of the Grand Alliance would disrupt the American effort to launch the United Nations and would destroy any chance for a postwar settlement in Europe. Stimson told Truman that a break with the Soviets could preclude their participation in the war against Japan, which American military planners considered essential to the ultimate victory.[7]

Stimson also believed that a dispute over Eastern Europe, which, he pointed out, not only was in close geographic proximity to the Soviet Union but also had no tradition of democracy, was not worth the disruption of the Grand Alliance. In fact, Stimson was prepared to recognize tacitly a Soviet sphere of influence in Eastern Europe in exchange for Soviet acquiescence to the establishment of American-administered United Nations trusteeships over Pacific islands that the War Department considered vital to U.S. security. In addition, Stimson hoped that the Soviets would not place any obstacles in the way of the administration's effort to create a U.S. alliance with the nations of Latin America. The legitimacy of such regional pacts within the United Nations framework had yet to be determined.[8]

At the same time, however, neither Stimson, nor America's top military commanders, had any inclination to comply with Churchill's repeated pleas to keep U.S. forces in the Soviet occupation zone after the German surrender. On April 29 Eisenhower informed General Marshall: "I shall *not* attempt any move which I deem militarily unwise merely to gain a political prize unless I receive specific orders from the Combined Chiefs of Staff." Marshall and the Joint Chiefs supported Eisenhower's position. And so, too, did the president. Like the Joint Chiefs of Staff, Truman began to suspect that Churchill was trying to embroil the United States in Eastern Europe and the Mediterranean in order to protect British interests in those regions. He was not about to allow Churchill to impair what he now believed was the paramount objective of securing Soviet participation in the war against Japan. On May 1 he informed the prime minister that he supported Eisenhower's decision to restrict severely the eastward advance of the American armies.[9]

Nor was American public opinion prepared for a confrontation with the Soviets over Eastern Europe. The expectation was widespread that the end of the war in Europe would enable America's soldiers to return home quickly. Few Americans favored keeping large contingents of troops in Europe to preclude what was then considered to be the remote possibility of the continued advance of the Soviet army. In fact, a poll taken in mid-May indicated that almost half (45 percent) of those questioned expected cooperation with the Soviets to continue after the war (38 percent believed it would not). At the same time, Truman was not prepared to allow a dispute over Eastern Europe to jeopardize the future prospects of the new United Nations organization, upon which, the American people had been led to believe, the postwar peace would come to depend.[10]

Stimson had another reason for urging Truman to follow a more cautious policy toward the Soviets--the atomic bomb. The secretary of war wanted to avoid any showdown with the Soviets until after the bomb had been tested, sometime during the approaching summer. "The time now and the method now to deal with Russia," Stimson told Assistant Secretary of War John J. McCloy on May 14, "was to keep our mouths shut and let our actions speak for words. I told him this was a place where we really held all the cards. I called it a royal straight flush and we must not be a fool about the way we play it. They [the Soviets] can't get along without our help and industries and we have coming into action a weapon which will be unique."[11]

Historians have debated the extent to which Truman appreciated the diplomatic implications of the atomic bomb. In his memoirs, the president recalled that he understood that Stimson was at least as much concerned with the role of the atomic bomb in the shaping of history as in its capacity to shorten the war. However, in the spring of 1945, the atomic bomb was still only a hypothetical weapon. As a result, Truman saw no reason why he should not do everything he possibly could to ensure Soviet military assistance against Japan.[12]

## A Return to Accommodation

With these considerations in mind, during May Truman decided to patch up his frayed relationship with Stalin. On May 9 he turned down a request by Churchill for a meeting of the Big Three the British prime minister wanted to convene as soon as possible, while substantial Anglo-American military forces were still deep in the Soviet zone. Truman argued that the pressure of domestic affairs made it impossible for him to leave the country at that time. Later, however, he confided to Davies that the real reason for delaying the summit meeting was to provide additional time to test the atomic bomb.[13]

While Truman on May 20 did approve a recommendation of the Joint Chiefs of Staff to make a show of force against Yugoslavia over Trieste, he also gave Tito a diplomatic way out of the crisis. After a number of American divisions were sent to the Brenner Pass and a naval flotilla sailed into the Adriatic Sea, Tito on May 22 accepted "in principle" Allied proposals which provided for the retention of token Yugoslav civil and military units in the Trieste area while the ultimate fate of the city would be left for the peace conference. While Churchill and American hardliners were pleased by the U.S. show of force against Tito, as historian Lisle Rose has pointed out, Truman in the Trieste affair demonstrated that he would "employ the American military machine solely for the defeat of the Axis powers and the occupation of their homelands--and for nothing else." In June the United States accelerated the withdrawal of its military forces from the

Continent. By the end of the year, there would be less than 300,000 U.S. troops in Europe.[14]

On May 19 Truman persuaded the ailing Harry Hopkins, the personification of Roosevelt's conciliatory policy, to travel to Moscow to try to iron out American differences with Stalin. While Truman told Hopkins that he expected Stalin to keep his Yalta agreements, he did not expect them to be observed literally. In his diary Truman recalled telling Hopkins "that Poland ought to have a 'free election,' at least as free as [Boss] Tom Pendergast . . . would allow." The British, who were not informed about the Hopkins mission until after Stalin had approved it, were not invited to participate.[15]

As a result of the Hopkins mission, which lasted from May 25 to June 6, Soviet-American tensions diminished appreciably during the late spring and early summer of 1945. Stalin responded favorably to the president's request to hold a meeting of the Big Three in or near Berlin during the middle of July. More important, they came to an understanding on the Polish issue. Stalin agreed to allow five non-Lublin Poles and three London Poles, including Stanislaw Mikolajczyk, to participate in the Polish government. While the arrangement in no way threatened Soviet control of Poland, it did give Truman a face-saving way to recognize the Polish government, a step that was taken by the United States on July 5 and, much more reluctantly, by Churchill the same day.[16]

In return for effectively recognizing Soviet domination of Poland, the Soviets did not oppose the U.S. effort to conclude a regional pact with the nations of Latin America, and they made no attempt to obstruct the administration's plan to gain for the United States UN trusteeships in the Pacific. In addition, the Soviets dropped their demand, made at the San Francisco Conference, that the Soviet Union must retain the veto over Security Council discussion as well as action. The Soviets had used the veto demand primarily as leverage to obtain American concessions in Eastern Europe. As a result, the San Francisco Conference was able to complete its work on the UN charter on June 25. The charter, along with a statute permitting American participation in the International Court of Justice, was overwhelmingly approved by the Senate on July 28. On August 8 Truman ratified the charter and signed the statute, which became effective on December 20, 1945. For the first time, the United States joined an international peacekeeping body.[17]

Truman was pleased with the results of Hopkins' mission to Moscow. The United States apparently had resolved the Polish problem, thereby making possible not only Soviet participation in the war against Japan but also American military withdrawal from Europe as well. In addition, Stalin recognized the predominant interests of the United States in Japan and China, and accepted an international trusteeship in Korea. Stimson, for his part, was happy to hear that Truman had set the opening date of the Big Three summit for July 15. The postponement, the secretary of war recorded in his diary, would "give us more time," undoubtedly, to test the atomic bomb.[18]

The British, on the other hand, regarded the Hopkins mission as an unnecessary sellout to Stalin's expansionist ambitions. Churchill was personally shocked to learn that Truman wanted to exclude him from the president's initial meeting with Stalin in order to avoid any suspicion that the Western allies were "ganging up" on the Soviet leader. After the prime minister's heated threat that he would not attend a conference in which he could not participate fully, Truman dropped his plan to meet separately with Stalin. The president, however, refused to stop in London and meet with Churchill before going on to Potsdam. Truman told his aides that he wanted to demonstrate that he was not "in cahoots" with either ally.[19]

## The Potsdam Conference, July-August 1945

The Potsdam Conference (code named TERMINAL), the last of the wartime meetings of the Big Three, convened from July 17 to August 2 in the Cecilienhof, the estate of the last Hohenzollern crown prince, which was located just outside Berlin.

Churchill arrived in Potsdam still determined to resist the growth and consolidation of Soviet influence in Europe. In his first face-to-face conversation with Truman, the prime minister raised once again his design for an Anglo-American partnership, one that he had first proclaimed at Harvard University in 1943. With the aim of protecting Western interests around the globe, he proposed the joint sharing of American and British air and naval bases. The president responded that "all this language was very near his own heart." But, he added, "any plan would have to be fitted in, in some way, as a part of the method of carrying out the policy of the United Nations."[20]

The fact is, Truman and his new secretary of state, former U.S. senator, congressman, supreme court justice, and Roosevelt's "assistant president for domestic affairs," James Byrnes, went to Potsdam determined to clear up the remaining European problems not settled by the Hopkins mission in order to free the United States to concentrate on ending the war with Japan. The details of Soviet participation in the Pacific conflict as well as the organization of German occupation were the primary items on the American agenda at Potsdam. As far as Eastern Europe was concerned, the Americans were not about to take Churchill's advice and "roll back" the Soviet advance. While Truman and Byrnes told Stalin that they expected him to observe the Declaration on Liberated Europe, they were not about to allow a literal interpretation of that document to disrupt Soviet-American relations once again.[21]

Soon after the conference began, the Big Three came to an agreement on the need to establish a council of foreign ministers. In addition to drafting the peace treaties for Germany and her Axis satellites and addressing the "territorial questions outstanding at the termination of the war in Europe," at Byrnes' insistence, the council was also empowered to deal with "other matters" referred to it "from time to time." Byrnes clearly intended to dominate the Council of Foreign Ministers and to use it to create a world hospitable to American interests. The first meeting of the council was scheduled for September in London.[22]

Of much greater importance to Byrnes and the president than the Council of Foreign Ministers, however, was the reaffirmation of Stalin's promise to Hopkins that the Soviet army would be prepared to invade Japanese-held Manchuria by mid-August. Truman, for his part, curtly and nonchalantly informed the Soviet leader that the United States had a weapon of great destructive capability, without specifically mentioning the atomic bomb, which had been tested successfully in the desert of New Mexico on July 16. Stalin tried to downplay the significance of the president's message by telling Truman that he hoped that the United States would make good use of the new weapon against Japan. On July 26 Truman issued a declaration to the Japanese warning them of the terrible consequences of continuing the war but making no specific mention of the atomic bomb.[23]

With respect to Germany, the Big Three at Potsdam agreed that the German nation should be demilitarized, de-Nazified, and democratized. All of this was to occur under the supervision of a four-power Allied Control Commission, comprised of representatives of the Big Three plus France, which, however, was excluded from participation in the Potsdam Conference. In addition, it was decided that the surviving top leaders of the Third Reich would be placed on trial at Nuremberg, Germany, for crimes they had committed during the war.[24]

However, the reparations issue and postwar boundaries of Germany proved more difficult to settle. The Soviets had unilaterally placed German territory east of the Oder-Neisse River line under Polish administration, while they themselves began to loot systematically the area under direct Soviet control. They also insisted upon the observance of an agreement reached at Yalta that called for extracting $20 billion worth of reparations in kind from the Germans, half of which was to be given to the Soviet Union. Truman and Byrnes objected to the Polish administration of German territory and insisted that the Yalta agreement on reparations was only a "basis for discussion."[25]

After days of stalemate on the reparations issue, Byrnes fashioned a three-part compromise that was reluctantly approved by Stalin on the last day of the conference. As one part of the compromise, the Western allies agreed to recognize Polish occupation and administration of the German territory east of the West Neisse line. In return, the Soviets accepted the Western demand that the establishment of Germany's eastern boundary would await a formal peace conference.[26]

In a second part of the compromise, the Big Three agreed that the other defeated Axis powers--Italy, Finland, Hungary, Rumania, and Bulgaria--would be recommended for UN membership contingent upon their acceptance of peace treaties that would be drafted by the Council of Foreign Ministers. However, the Western powers withheld recognition of the governments of Bulgaria, Rumania, and Hungary until they had been suitably "reorganized."[27]

Finally, the Big Three dropped the $20 billion reparations figure formulated at Yalta, and in its place inserted an agreement that each power would extract reparations from within its respective zone, with the Soviets assuming the responsibility for satisfying Polish reparations claims from the German territory under their direct jurisdiction. In addition, the compromise provided for interzonal reparations exchanges, which would enable food from the eastern zone to be exchanged for industrial products from the western zones, a step that would reduce Germany's dependence on Western agricultural exports. It also was agreed that the Ruhr, which was entirely within the British zone, would not be internationalized, as the French had demanded.[28]

In the end, the Soviets received much less at Potsdam than they had first anticipated. They did not get the amount of reparations they had desired, while they were compelled to assume the responsibility for satisfying Poland's reparations claims. Nor were Soviet ambitions in the Mediterranean area fulfilled at Potsdam. Molotov insisted that the Montreaux Convention, which governed international use of the Turkish-controlled Straits of the Bosporus and the Dardanelles, must be revised to give the Soviet Union a share in their administration. During the war, the Soviets complained, the Turks had permitted German warships to enter the Black Sea. In addition, the Soviets wanted the Turks to return territory on the Black Sea that Russia had been forced to cede to Turkey in 1921. Churchill, however, insisted that Britain must receive any and all privileges that would be given to the Soviet Union. Truman, seeking to defuse the issue, proposed that the straits as well as the Rhine and Danube rivers should be internationalized. But Stalin insisted that the Montreaux Convention must be dealt with separately. When the Western Allies refused to do so, the straits issue was referred to the Council of Foreign Ministers for future consideration.[29]

One other issue emerged briefly at Potsdam, one that would grow steadily in importance in the coming months. With the war in Europe over, Churchill demanded that all Allied troops must be withdrawn from Iran, as called for in the Anglo-Soviet Treaty of 1942. Stalin, however, said the Iranian occupation could not be terminated prior to the conclusion of the Pacific war without jeopardizing Lend-Lease shipments to the Soviet Union through that country. As a result, no agreement on Iranian troop withdrawals was reached at Potsdam. Truman, however, did state that American troops would be withdrawn from Iran within sixty days--all U.S. forces were out of the country by January 1, 1946.[30]

While some historians regard the Potsdam Conference as the beginning of the Cold War, Truman and his colleagues were pleased with the agreements it produced. The accords on Germany and Eastern Europe seemed to guarantee that the United States could safely continue to withdraw its military forces from the Continent. While Soviet assistance against Japan was no longer as important as it had appeared it would be before the successful test of the atomic bomb, Truman could take satisfaction from the fact that the Potsdam Conference had preserved the facade of Allied unity, thereby ensuring Soviet participation in the ultimate defeat of the Japanese. Although Admiral Leahy told Truman that "Stalin was a liar and a crook," and could not be trusted, both the president and Byrnes thought that, although the Soviet leader was a hard bargainer, he could be depended upon to keep his Potsdam agreements.[31]

Without a doubt, the individual who suffered most at Potsdam was Winston Churchill. Not only did Truman refuse to take the hardline approach toward the Soviets that the prime minister favored, the Americans gave every indication that they were prepared once again to hand over to Britain the burden of maintaining the balance of power in Europe, now seemingly threatened by the Red Army. Yet Churchill was spared the direct responsibility of leading a greatly weakened Britain in playing this role. On July 28, two days after it was determined that his Conservative Party had been defeated in the general parliamentary election, Churchill's place at the Potsdam Conference was taken by a new prime minister, the leader of the Labour Party, Clement Attlee.[32]

## The London Conference of Foreign Ministers, September-October 1945

Not long after the Pacific war ended, with the Japanese surrender on August 14, the facade of Allied unity that had been preserved at Potsdam began to crumble. In September, at the London Conference of Foreign Ministers, which was called to draft peace treaties for the former German satellites, the first publicized Soviet-American clash took place. Byrnes, who led the American delegation, naively and arrogantly believed that the military and economic superiority that the United States enjoyed at the end of the war would enable the American delegation at London to dictate the terms of the peace treaties. His expectations were quickly shattered. Molotov, who headed the Soviet delegation, ignored the atomic monopoly and vast economic power of the United States and was as difficult as ever. He reiterated an earlier Soviet demand for a share of Italy's African colonies--the Soviets wanted Tripolitania--and insisted that Italy pay $600 million in reparations, one-third of which would go to the Soviet Union. He also made it clear that unless Britain and the United States supported Soviet terms for the peace treaties with Rumania and Bulgaria, he would not accept the Anglo-American draft of the treaty with Italy.[33]

In a series of private meetings with Molotov, Byrnes tried to change the Soviet position. He told Molotov that the Senate would not ratify peace treaties with Bulgaria and Rumania unless they had representative regimes. He even offered Molotov a treaty binding the United States to enforce Germany's demilitarization for twenty-five years in order to remove any excuse for Soviet domination of Eastern Europe. But the Soviet foreign minister remained unmoved. In an attempt to break up the Western bloc that Soviet intransigence had created, Molotov attempted to exclude France and China, whose foreign ministers had been invited to participate in the conference, from a further discussion of the satellite peace treaties. Their participation, he pointed out quite correctly, had not been provided for in the voting instructions agreed upon by the Big Three at Potsdam. Two days later, Molotov demanded the establishment of an Allied Control Council in Japan--composed of representatives from the United States, the Soviet Union, Britain, and China--to supervise the policies of General Douglas MacArthur, the commander-in-chief of American occupation forces. Byrnes rejected both of Molotov's proposals. As a result, the conference broke up early in October with Big Three unity in serious disarray.[34]

Byrnes was disappointed by the collapse of the London Conference. However, the Senate Foreign Relations Committee not only strongly applauded his refusal to compromise with the Soviets, it expressed its hope that he would continue to do so. John Foster Dulles, who had attended the London Conference as a Republican observer, also praised Byrnes' decision to "stand firm for basic principles." It was, Dulles argued, "no longer necessary, nor was it healthy, to hide the fact that fundamental differences now existed between the United States and the Soviet Union."[35]

# The Moscow Conference of Foreign Ministers, December 1945

In the wake of the London Conference, there were disturbing reports that, in addition to pressuring Turkey for a revision of the Montreaux Convention, the Soviets were also using their occupation troops in Iran in an attempt to intimidate the Iranians into granting the Soviet Union oil concessions comparable to those that they were prepared to give Britain and the United States. As a result, by October Truman was beginning to question the wisdom of his accommodationist policy and was starting to believe that a more forceful response to the Soviet Union might again be necessary. Yet Truman was also aware that, with men being discharged from the Army at the rate of 15,200 a day in September, and Congress unreceptive to his proposal for a system of universal military training (a peacetime draft), he had precious little military power to counter the Soviet moves in the Near East. When Budget Director Harold Smith tried to console the president by telling him, "you have an atomic bomb up your sleeve," Truman responded, "but I am not sure it can ever be used." Consequently, Truman, for the time being, suppressed any inclination he may have had to challenge the Soviet maneuvers in the Near East. On October 26 he informed his cabinet that "we were going to find some way to get along with the Russians."[36]

Byrnes was also reluctant to have another face-off with the Soviets. In spite of the congressional and public support he had received after the London Conference, he realized that neither the American atomic monopoly nor economic superiority had had any positive impact on Molotov's attitude. The secretary of state was also increasingly sensitive to the criticism that, while he was denying the Soviets a role in the occupation of Japan, he was demanding a greater American voice in the affairs of Bulgaria and Rumania. He also realized that the Soviet army was unlikely to leave those countries until the peace treaties were signed.[37]

In an attempt to revive the spirit of Yalta, on October 20 and November 2 respectively, the United States recognized the provisional governments of Austria and Hungary. Byrnes also hoped that he could persuade Stalin to be content with an "open" sphere of influence in Eastern Europe. By this arrangement, which the State Department concocted to circumvent the traditional antipathy of the American people to spheres of influence, the nations of Eastern Europe would be required to maintain friendly relations with the Soviet Union; in return, they would be permitted to determine their own governments without Soviet interference. The creation of an "exclusive" sphere of influence in Eastern Europe, one in which the Soviets would determine both the internal and external affairs of these nations, Byrnes and his advisers feared, would threaten the balance of power on the Continent, lead to the creation of an anti-Soviet bloc in Western Europe, and increase the pressure for permanent American military involvement on the Continent. Byrnes simply did not believe that either the American people or the Congress were in any frame of mind to accept a more extensive U.S. commitment to Europe's security in the fall of 1945.[38]

As a result of these considerations, Byrnes believed he had no choice but to try once again to reach an understanding with Moscow. In late November he asked the Soviets to host another meeting of the Council of Foreign Ministers--without French and Chinese participation. In Moscow Byrnes hoped he would be able to bypass the obdurate Molotov and deal directly with Stalin. The Soviets accepted Byrnes' conference proposal, and the Moscow Conference was scheduled to begin in the middle of December. However, the new British foreign secretary, Ernest Bevin, feared an American sellout to the Soviets, and consequently raised strenuous objections to the proposed conference. He agreed to attend only after Byrnes threatened to go to Moscow without him.[39]

Before the secretary of state left for the Soviet capital, he was presented with a report by Mark Ethridge, publisher of the *Louisville Courier Journal*, whom Byrnes had dispatched to Eastern Europe on a fact-finding mission in early October. Ethridge confirmed earlier State Department charges that the Soviets were engaged in extensive interference in the internal affairs of Rumania and Bulgaria. The Ethridge Report concluded that, unless the United States took steps to uphold the Yalta Declaration on Liberated Europe, Rumania and Bulgaria would not regain their independence. But Byrnes was no longer interested in upholding the declaration, at least not literally. He did not want that document to interfere with the completion of the satellite peace treaties, which alone, he believed, would bring about the withdrawal of Soviet troops from Eastern Europe. As a result, Byrnes did not circulate the Ethridge Report until after the Moscow Conference. Truman himself did not see it until January.[40]

At Moscow, Byrnes and the Soviets worked out the kind of compromise the secretary of state wanted. Stalin agreed to token representation for the pro-Western parties (two members each) in the communist-dominated governments of Rumania and Bulgaria. In return, Byrnes stated that the United States was prepared to recognize these governments. The foreign ministers also agreed that a conference to complete the peace treaties would be held in Paris beginning in May 1946. Byrnes also agreed to create an Allied Control Council, which would consult with and advise General MacArthur on occupation measures in Japan. In reality, however, the council would have little control over MacArthur, who was obliged to take its advice only when he decided the "exigencies of the situation" required it. Nevertheless, by completing the agreements on Japan, Bulgaria, and Rumania, Byrnes and the Soviets were able to fashion a face-saving way of recognizing each other's spheres of influence.[41]

Byrnes and the Soviets also reached a compromise agreement on the atomic energy issue. But in doing so, Byrnes ignored Truman's reluctance to share atomic information with the Soviets, as well as an agreement the president had concluded with British Prime Minister Clement Attlee and Canadian Prime Minister William MacKenzie King on November 15. This agreement called for the creation of a UN atomic energy commission which would implement a four-stage process toward nuclear disarmament, including the sharing of atomic information with the Soviets and eventual elimination of nuclear weapons, but only after an international inspection system had been put into operation. However, the plan Byrnes initially offered the Soviets did not require completion of one stage before implementing the next. Only after the British and key congressmen--including Vandenberg and Senator Tom Connally, the Democratic chairman of the Foreign Relations Committee--complained about Byrnes' revision, did the secretary of state reinsert the ordered, stage-by-stage process required by the Truman-Attlee-King agreement. While the Soviets accepted the amendment to the Byrnes plan, they did so only after he agreed to make the activities of the UN atomic energy commission accountable to the Security Council, where Soviet interests could be protected by the veto.[42]

## The Aftermath of the Moscow Conference

Because Byrnes was pleased by the results of the Moscow Conference, he was surprised by the hostile reaction his work provoked in much of the American press and among influential members of the government. Reflecting this view, George Kennan, chargé d'affaires in the Moscow embassy, called Byrnes' Balkan accord "some fig leaves of democratic procedure to hide the nakedness of the Stalinist dictatorship in the respective East European countries." As the Ethridge Report indicated, the Soviets were in the process of creating an exclusive, not an open, sphere of influence in Eastern Europe.[43]

According to Truman's memoirs, he also was unhappy with Byrnes' work in Moscow. The memoirs record that on January 5 Truman had a face-to-face encounter with the secretary of state, in which he called Byrnes' accomplishments at Moscow "unreal." Truman called the Balkan agreement nothing more than "a general promise" from the Soviets; he told Byrnes that he would not recognize the governments of Rumania and Bulgaria as they were then constituted. He also recalled that he criticized the secretary of state for not keeping him fully informed about the proceedings of the conference, much of which he learned about from the press. Truman also remembered telling Byrnes that he would not permit the exchange of information relating to nuclear energy until the Soviets became more cooperative on other issues. Finally, according to Truman's account, he demanded that Byrnes protest the continuing Soviet military pressure on Turkey and Iran "with all the vigor of which we are capable." He concluded: "I'm tired of babying the Soviets."[44]

While considering Truman's memorandum a basis for the president's conversation with Byrnes on January 5, historian Robert Messer argues persuasively that Truman probably did not read it verbatim to the secretary of state, as he claimed to have done, if in fact, he mentioned it at all. Had Truman done so, Byrnes asserted after the memorandum was published in the president's memoirs, he would have resigned on the spot. Messer believes that Truman, in his memoirs, exaggerated the harshness of his discussion with Byrnes primarily to cast on the secretary of state all the responsibility for the administration's unsuccessful effort to reach an understanding with the Soviets. The fact that American policy toward the Soviets did not begin to change until the following month is another reason to believe that there was no "showdown" between Byrnes and Truman in early January. In addition, it was not until April that Byrnes told Truman that he wanted to resign--he said for reasons of health, but more probably because he no longer had the free hand he had previously possessed in conducting the nation's foreign policy. However, Byrnes agreed to stay on until the completion of the peace treaties with Germany's former allies, which would not occur until December 1946.[45]

While Truman probably did not read the January 5 memorandum to Byrnes, it did, nevertheless, indicate that he was increasingly inclined to adopt a less accommodating attitude toward the Soviets. Henceforth, there would be no further attempts to appease the Soviets with territorial concessions or promises of economic assistance. In addition, in 1946 the Truman administration would begin to move--albeit cautiously and slowly--toward a policy of assisting states threatened by Soviet expansion. However, historian Deborah Larson argues that, while adopting a tougher policy toward the Soviets in early 1946, Truman did not abandon his hope that the Soviets would adopt a more cooperative attitude toward the West. The result, according to Larson, was a policy that vacillated between resistance toward Soviet expansion and continued administration attempts to secure the Soviets' cooperation in creating a stable international order.[46]

## The Declaration of the Cold War

Although Truman was still not prepared to break with the Soviets in January 1946, a number of developments in the next several months made it exceedingly difficult for him to build the cooperative relationship with the Soviet Union he still may have wanted. At the London meeting of the United Nations that month, Bevin took the lead in resisting the Soviet effort to intimidate Turkey and Iran. The British foreign secretary clearly hoped to set an example for the United States, one that would prompt the Truman administration to collaborate with Britain in the defense of Western interests. Bevin's stand soon began to have the desired impact on American opinion makers. *Time* invidiously compared Byrnes, whom the magazine called "a habitual compromiser," with the British foreign minister, who "spoke up to the Russians as a great many plain people in pubs and corner drugstores had often wanted to speak." *The Dallas Times Herald* recommended that Truman "swap Jimmy Byrnes to the British for Ernie Bevin and toss in any number of old destroyers it takes to clinch the deal."[47]

Another event that pushed the administration toward a confrontational policy toward the Soviets was a speech delivered by Stalin on February 9. In this address, the Soviet leader downplayed Allied collaboration during the war and stated that future conflicts were inevitable until communism supplanted capitalism on a worldwide basis. He called for a new, five-year economic program to prepare the Soviet Union to defend itself. The speech convinced Harriman that the primary objective of Soviet foreign policy was the global expansion of communism. To U.S. Supreme Court Justice William O. Douglas, Stalin's speech was "the Declaration of World War III."[48]

Although other observers interpreted Stalin's speech as merely an attempt to mobilize the Soviet people for the sacrifices that postwar reconstruction would require, not as a preparation for a war with the West, what aggravated its impact on American opinion was the atmosphere in which it was made. Not only were Soviet troops still in Iran, but they continued to occupy Chinese Manchuria long after the Japanese surrender. And, much to the embarrassment of the administration, the Soviets invoked the Yalta agreements to defend their occupation of Japan's Kuril Islands. As a result, Byrnes was compelled to release the text of the Yalta accords in late January. The congressional and public outcry they produced, particularly against the Far Eastern concessions Roosevelt had made to win Soviet participation in the war against Japan, forced Truman to try to distance himself not only from the Soviets but also from Byrnes, who until this time had prided himself on being at Roosevelt's side at Yalta.[49]

Perhaps of greater impact on American opinion, however, was the revelation by news commentator Drew Pearson on February 3 that a Soviet spy ring, operating in Canada, had been successful in transmitting secret information about the American atomic bomb to the Soviet Union. Truman had been informed about the spy ring the previous September but had said nothing about it publicly. News of the Canadian spy ring, needless to say, did much to dampen public enthusiasm for a nuclear disarmament agreement with the Soviets.[50]

Alarmed by these events, Republican leaders, like Senator Vandenberg, who while in London had discussed American foreign policy at length with Bevin, warned Truman that the Republican Party would no longer support the kind of conciliatory approach toward the Soviet Union that Byrnes had pursued in Moscow. On February 27 Vandenberg told the Senate: "There is a line beyond which compromise cannot go--even if we once crossed that line under the pressures of the exigencies of war." With congressional elections less than seven months away, the administration did not believe it could ignore Vandenberg's words.[51]

## Toward Containment

But even before Vandenberg's warning, the administration was moving in the direction favored by the Republicans. On February 12 the State Department informed the Soviets that the United States was deferring recognition of the Bulgarian government until Bulgaria reached a reparations agreement with Greece. On the same day, for the first time, Byrnes complained to the Austrian government that Soviet policy in that country was undermining the four-power occupation agreement. On February 15, after the administration had recognized the Rumanian government, Byrnes protested the Soviet failure to implement a Potsdam agreement to revise Allied Control Council procedures for Bulgaria, Rumania, and Hungary. He demanded "prompt measures to ensure future compliance." Later in the month, the secretary of state proclaimed that the United States intended "to promote principles of freedom of commerce and navigation in East Central Europe and to support the political independence of peoples of this region."[52]

In a major turn in the American attitude toward Iran, where the administration had heretofore followed a hands-off policy, on February 22 Byrnes instructed George Kennan to inform the Iranian prime minister, Ahmad Qavam, who was then in Moscow negotiating with the Soviets about Iranian oil concessions, that the United States would support Iran's Security Council effort to defend her independence and territorial integrity.[53]

The administration's new Iranian policy, however, was not motivated by purely altruistic motives. More important, as Truman admitted in his memoirs, was the "control of Iran's oil reserves," the removal of which "would be a serious loss for the economy of the Western world." Even more important than Iran's oil, however, were the far vaster oil reserves of nearby Saudi Arabia, where American oil companies were already well established. A study by the Joint Chiefs of Staff in October 1946 argued that the loss of Iran to the Soviet Union would gravely affect American interests in Saudi Arabia and the entire region. An earlier State Department analysis called the oil of Saudi Arabia "a stupendous source of strategic power, and one of the greatest material prizes in world history."[54]

The apparent Soviet threat to the oil of the Middle East also made, for the first time, the defense of Turkey a vital American interest. In late February Byrnes, at Forrestal's prompting, decided to return to Istanbul the body of the Turkish ambassador, who had died in 1944, aboard the *USS Missouri*, the world's most powerful warship. The decision to send the *Missouri* to Turkey was not only a warning to Moscow that the United States would not tolerate Soviet aggression against Turkey, it was also the first step in the creation of a permanent American naval presence in the Mediterranean Sea. Thus, in the space of a few days, Byrnes began the process of aligning the United States with Britain in the defense of the Turkish straits and the oil of the Near East.[55]

The rationale for the new policy of resisting further Soviet expansion was provided on February 22 by an 8,000-word telegram drafted by George Kennan, from his post in the Moscow embassy. Kennan warned the State Department that Soviet hostility toward the capitalist world was inevitable and immutable because it seemed to provide the justification for the oppressive totalitarian system the communists had imposed upon the Soviet people. As a result, for the Soviet Union, Kennan wrote, "there can be no permanent *modus vivendi* with the United States." Consequently, in his opinion, it was not only futile, but dangerous, for the United States to attempt to accommodate Soviet desires. Instead, Kennan recommended that the United States concentrate on containing the expansion of Soviet power and influence until such a time that a more moderate form of government came into being in the Soviet Union.[56]

Kennan later recalled that the official reaction to his "Long Telegram" was "nothing less than sensational." Kennan's "totalitarian-ideological" model of Soviet behavior, historian John Lewis Gaddis has observed, "provided a clear, plausible, and in many ways gratifying explanation of the Russians' failure to cooperate with their former allies in building a lasting peace." In Gaddis' opinion, the Long Telegram also "absolved the United States of responsibility for the breakdown of wartime cooperation; it made any future relaxation of tensions dependent upon changes of heart in Moscow, not Washington." It also offered Truman a middle way between the now unacceptable policy of trying to accommodate Soviet demands and the even more unthinkable alternative of war.[57]

For the first time publicly, Byrnes announced the administration's new approach to the Soviets in an address to the Overseas Press Club in New York on February 28. The United States, the secretary of state declared, intended to act like the great power it was "not only in order to ensure our own security but in order to preserve the peace of the world." In a phrase Truman underlined when he read the speech before it was delivered, Byrnes stated that "we cannot *allow aggression* to be accomplished by *coercion* or *pressure* or *subterfuges* such as *political infiltration*." In delivering this address, Robert Messer observes, "Byrnes announced, with Truman's blessing, his personal declaration of the cold war."[58]

## Churchill's "Iron Curtain" Speech, March 1946

On March 5, less than a week after Byrnes' Overseas Press speech, Winston Churchill, now leader of the opposition party in Parliament, delivered a commencement address in Fulton, Missouri. With Truman present on the speakers' dais, Churchill declared that an "Iron Curtain" had descended from "Stettin in the Baltic to Trieste in the Adriatic." He again called for the creation of a "fraternal association of the English-speaking peoples" to keep the peace. What he had in mind were the things he first suggested in his Harvard speech in 1943: "intimate relationships between our military advisors, leading to a common study of potential dangers, the similarity of weapons and manuals of instruction, the interchange of officers and cadets at technical colleges" and "joint use of all naval and air force bases in the possession of either country all over the world." He concluded: "I am convinced that there is nothing they [the Soviets] admire so much as strength, and there is nothing for which they have less respect than for military weakness." Stalin, responding to Churchill's speech, called it "a dangerous act designed to sow the seeds of discord among the allies and to undermine their collaboration." The former prime minister, Stalin charged, wanted a "war with the USSR."[59]

While some Americans applauded Churchill's tough stand against the Soviets, many criticized his call for an Anglo-American alliance. (One poll indicated that 40 percent of those sampled opposed Churchill's alliance bid, while only 18 percent favored it.) Senator Arthur Capper, an isolationist Republican from Kansas, accused Churchill of trying to "arouse the people of the United States to commit the country to the task of preserving the farflung British Empire." Senators Claude Pepper, Harley M. Kilgore, and Glen Taylor issued a joint statement on March 6 in which they charged that Churchill's "fraternal association" would "cut the throat" of the United Nations. British Ambassador Lord Halifax concluded that as "profound as the uneasiness is about Soviet politics, there is still a strong underlying anxiety [on the part of the American people], if possible, to find a way of cooperation with the Russians."[60]

The president tried to escape the controversy generated by Churchill's speech by claiming that he had not read it in advance. This clearly was false. Both he and Byrnes had read the speech before it was delivered. In fact, Churchill had discussed its contents with Truman at the White House on February 10 and with Byrnes in Florida on February 17. *Time* magazine believed that they had hoped to use the address as a trial balloon designed to gauge the reaction of the American people to a tougher policy toward the Soviet Union. However, in Deborah Larson's opinion, *Time* oversimplified Truman's and Byrnes' intentions. "It is more likely," she has written, "that Truman wished to warn the Russians that there were limits to our patience, and that the United States had other alternatives to cooperation with the Soviets."[61]

## The Iranian Crisis, March-April 1946

While the administration in the next few weeks tried publicly to disassociate itself from the Fulton speech, it did not abandon its policy of "firmness and patience" toward the Soviet Union. On March 5, after Washington learned of ominous Soviet troop movements in Iran, Byrnes made public a note he had sent Moscow demanding Soviet withdrawal from that country. Three days later he demanded an explanation from Moscow for the movement of additional Soviet troops into Iran. The same day, he asked Bevin if Britain would be willing to join the United States in placing the Iranian issue before the Security Council if the Soviets refused to withdraw their troops from the country. On March 16 Byrnes delivered a forceful public address in which he stated: "Should the occasion arise, our military strength will be used to support the purposes and principles of the [UN] Charter."[62]

Responding to the embarrassing exposure of their attempts to intimidate Iran, the Soviets on April 4 concluded an agreement with the Iranians that provided for the withdrawal of Soviet troops from that country by early May. In exchange the Soviets received oil concessions in northern Iran. However, after Soviet troops were safely out of the country, the Iranian parliament, with U.S. support, revoked its oil concession agreement with the Soviet Union.[63]

The Soviet withdrawal from Iran elated the Truman administration. It appeared to confirm the wisdom of the tougher policy toward the Soviets. In the face of a resolute stand by the United States and Britain, the Soviets demonstrated that they would back down. Years later Truman called the administration's response to the Iranian crisis the first of a series of initiatives--including the Truman Doctrine and the Marshall Plan during the subsequent year--that, as he put it, "saved the world."[64]

On the other hand, liberals condemned the administration's new Soviet policy as a betrayal of Franklin Roosevelt's grand design. On March 14 Secretary of Commerce Henry A. Wallace sent a letter to Truman advocating a policy of economic collaboration with the Soviets as a better alternative to, as he described it publicly several days later, "try[ing] to strut around the world and tell people where to get off." However, opinion polls indicated that most Americans no longer supported the kind of conciliatory policy toward the Soviets that Wallace and other Russophiles favored. Sixty percent of those polled in a mid-March sample thought the American approach to the Soviet Union was "too soft"; only 3 percent felt it was "too tough." And Byrnes received widespread acclaim for the strong stand he took against the Soviets in the Iranian crisis. As a result, Truman and his secretary of state believed they could count on solid support as they moved to implement their new policy of "patience with firmness"--or, as it soon came to be called, "containment."[65]

# The Peace Treaties

For the remainder of 1946, Byrnes devoted most his time and energy to the task of drawing up peace treaties for the former satellite states of Germany: Rumania, Bulgaria, Hungary, Italy, and Finland. The Council of Foreign Ministers met in Paris for two sessions (April 25 to May 16 and June 15 to July 12) to draft the treaties. From July 29 to October 15 representatives from twenty-one Allied nations gathered in the French capital to consider the drafts the Big Four had prepared. In November and December the Council of Foreign Ministers met again in New York to put the treaties in their final form.

Byrnes' behavior at the Paris Conference of Foreign Ministers during the spring and early summer of 1946 demonstrated that he was no longer as willing to accommodate Soviet objectives as he had been at the Moscow Conference the previous December. He told George Bidault, the French foreign minister, that he had been subjected to considerable criticism for "appeasing" the Soviets and that, as a result, he "was no longer disposed to make concessions on important questions." To ensure his critics that this was true, Byrnes felt compelled to invite both Senators Vandenberg and Connally to accompany him to Paris. Vandenberg was pleased by Byrnes' performance in the French capital. The secretary of state convinced him that, as the senator put it, "the appeasement days [were] over." As a result, Republican criticism of the administration's foreign policy quickly subsided.[66]

But, in the opinion of historian Patricia Dawson Ward, Vandenberg oversimplified Byrnes' new approach to the Soviets. While avoiding any open concessions that could be regarded as a sign of weakness, out of the public spotlight the secretary of state was still willing to deal with the Soviets. By following a dual strategy of public intransigency and private diplomacy, Byrnes was able to complete all five peace treaties by the end of the year.[67]

The treaties reflected the basic, but tacit, understanding that had prevailed for some time, that is, that the occupying powers would get their way in their respective spheres of influence. Thanks largely to Byrnes' efforts, Italy was dealt with lightly in her treaty. She was required to pay only $300 million in reparations; of that amount, the Soviets received only $100 million. Moreover, Italy's reparations were to be paid, not from current production, as the Soviets desired, but from overseas assets and surplus property whose value was very dubious. In addition, Trieste was not awarded to Yugoslavia but was made an autonomous city under UN supervision, with a border contiguous to Italy. Eventually, in 1954, the city was awarded to the Italians. And, while Italy lost her colonies, they did not go to the Soviet Union. The Dodecanese Islands were awarded to Greece, and Libya was placed under joint Franco-British administration.[68]

In return for getting his way with Italy, Byrnes gave the Soviets just about what they wanted with the other former German allies. While the treaties with these states contained provisions protecting human rights, free trade, and open navigation of the Danube, they soon proved unenforceable. The treaties also ended the operation of the Allied Control Councils in Rumania and Bulgaria, as the Soviets had demanded, thereby removing the last vestiges of Western influence in those two countries. In addition, Moscow was permitted to keep sufficient forces in Hungary and Rumania to secure communication and supply lines to Soviet occupation forces in Austria. The indefinite postponement of an Austrian peace treaty, which Moscow was in no hurry to conclude, ensured that Hungary and Rumania would remain behind the Iron Curtain.[69]

With the peace treaties ratified by the Senate in June and July 1947, nothing stood in the way of the complete communization of Eastern Europe. Only Finland, which was not fully occupied by the Red Army, was allowed to maintain a democratic government. But by the spring of 1947 Washington had lost interest in trying to maintain even the semblance of democracy in the rest of Eastern Europe. After fraudulent elections were held in Rumania and Bulgaria, and noncommunist parties in those countries were crushed, the United States established full diplomatic relations with Bucharest, at the end of July 1947, and recognized the Bulgarian government the following October.[70]

# Germany

Yet as the Truman administration's interest in Eastern Europe waned, its interest in Germany increased. It was not long after the Potsdam Conference that Germany became a major source of friction between the Soviet Union and the West. The Potsdam agreements had called for treating Germany as a single economic unit. The Soviets, however, refused to allow shipments of foodstuffs from their zone, and from the Polish zone, to the largely nonagricultural western zones. As a result, the cost of feeding the inhabitants of western Germany, which had been inundated with refugees from the east, became a major drain on the resources of the Western Allies, and particularly on those of the financially hard pressed British. The economic problems posed by Soviet policy in eastern Germany were only aggravated by the failure of the Allied Control Council to establish a centralized administration for the country. Without it, a common Allied economic policy in Germany proved to be impossible to implement.[71]

According to historian John Gimbel, however, it was the French, and not the Soviets, who were primarily responsible for the inability of the Allies to establish a central administration in Germany. The government of Charles de Gaulle feared that creating a centralized German administration, and treating all of Germany as an economic unit, would be only the first step in the revival of German military power. To prevent this, France advocated the detachment from Germany of the Ruhr, the Rhineland, and the Saar, and the French used their vote on the Allied Control Commission to prevent the establishment of a centralized German administration. Germany's future, de Gaulle told U.S. Ambassador Jefferson Caffery, "is a matter of life and death for us. For you, one interesting question among many others."[72]

But rather than openly blame France for the failure to achieve a common Allied policy toward Germany, Gimbel has argued, the Truman administration attempted to overcome French obstructionism indirectly by publicly putting the onus for Allied disunity entirely on the Soviets, who alone were publicly pressured to change their German policy. On May 3 General Lucius Clay, the U.S. military governor in Germany, halted all reparations shipments out of the American zone until the Soviets, as well as the French, agreed to a common economic policy for all of Germany. Although Clay's order was aimed at both the Soviet Union and France, Under Secretary of State Dean Acheson interpreted it as an attempt to "put Soviet protestations of loyalty to Potsdam to the final test and fix the blame for the breach of Potsdam on the Soviets in case they fail to meet this test." There was, however, no way the Soviets could pass the American test without undermining their own national interests. To the Soviets, treating Germany as an "economic unit" meant implementing a system of state planning and control. To the Americans, however, it meant establishing a system of free trade and enterprise with minimal centralized direction of the economy, all of which would bring Germany into the Western economic bloc.[73]

Four days before Clay ordered the reparations halt, Byrnes had applied another type of diplomatic pressure on the Soviets. On April 29 he again proposed a four-power, twenty-five-year treaty designed to ensure the disarmament of Germany. The treaty, Byrnes promised, would "guarantee that this time the United States was not going to leave Europe after the war." If the Soviets turned it down, Vandenberg believed, it would demonstrate once and for all that what they really wanted was "*expansion* and not security."[74]

Not surprisingly, the Soviets rejected the American requirements for German economic unification and condemned the "unlawful" action of General Clay in halting reparations removals form the American zone. Molotov then revived the original Soviet demand for a fixed reparations sum of $10 billion, which, he pointed out, Roosevelt had accepted at Yalta. In addition, on July 9 the Soviet foreign minister rejected Byrnes proposed security treaty on the grounds that demilitarization of Germany could not be guaranteed until all reparations deliveries had been completed. Viewing Byrnes' proposal as merely a propaganda gesture, Molotov tried to do the Americans one better by calling for a forty-year treaty with more comprehensive military and economic assistance provisions than were featured in the U.S. plan.[75]

According to John Lewis Gaddis, Byrnes now became convinced that a common Allied policy toward Germany would never be possible and that the only way to prevent the communization of the country, while at the same time making the western zones economically viable, was to make the division of Germany permanent. On July 11 he invited all the occupying powers to merge their zones with the American zone in order to form one economic unit. The British accepted immediately, but the French demurred. Later in the year, on December 2, Byrnes and Bevin signed the Bizonal Fusion Agreement, and on January 1, 1947, the two zones became one. John Gimbel, on the other hand, saw Byrnes' move as hastily conceived, and aimed more at averting economic disaster in Germany than it was in alienating the Soviets.[76]

In a speech at Stuttgart on September 6, Byrnes also called for the creation of a German provisional government, one that would pave the way for the eventual reunification of the country. But he also made it clear that the United States would not tolerate a unified Germany under Soviet control. "We do not want Germany to become the satellite of any power," Byrnes told his audience. To ensure that Germany would not fall under Soviet control, he announced a major and historic departure from previous American policy. "As long as there is an occupation army in Germany," he said, "American armed forces will be part of that occupation army." The United States, in effect, was prepared to make Germany a bulwark against the further westward expansion of communism.[77]

Byrnes' Stuttgart speech also had the desired impact on France, the other obstacle to America's ambitions in Germany. Fearful that their German interests would be disregarded by the Americans and British, the French privately assured the United States that they would discuss merging their zone with the Anglo-American bizone after their November 1947 parliamentary election.[78]

Robert Messer believes that Byrnes' Stuttgart speech was directed not only at the French and the Soviets, but also at Americans who balked at the idea of helping the Germans get back on their feet. "The antidote for such fears," Messer has written, "was to raise the specter of 'red fascism' stalking Europe and the world from its lair in the Kremlin." In this sense, the Stuttgart speech anticipated the scare tactics the administration would employ during the following year when it enlarged the American commitment to the defense of Europe.[79]

# The Baruch Plan

Besides Germany, another source of Soviet-American friction during 1946 was the atomic energy issue. On June 14 Bernard Baruch, the U.S. representative to the UN Atomic Energy Commission, presented the American plan for international control of atomic energy. It called for the creation of a UN International Atomic Development Authority, which would manage or own all nuclear resources, plants, and research, all of which would be accessible to every member nation. After the authority had established an effective control system, some time in the indefinite future, all nations would destroy their existing nuclear weapons and refrain from manufacturing any more. The activities of the authority, which included establishing and imposing a system of penalties for violations of its regulations, would not be restricted by a Security Council veto. In addition, Baruch told the General Assembly that "before a country is ready to relinquish any winning weapons, it must have more than words to reassure it." This, he said, required the elimination of all chemical-biological weapons and even "war itself."[80]

Not surprisingly, the Baruch Plan was unacceptable to the Soviet Union. While it would have given the Soviets some information concerning atomic energy--information they probably already possessed--and a vague promise to destroy the U.S. nuclear arsenal in the indefinite future, it would have required the Soviets to assume major risks: loss of the veto on atomic energy matters; international inspection of Soviet scientific, industrial, and military facilities; and the possible curtailment of Soviet atomic energy development.

On June 19 the Soviet delegate to the UN Atomic Energy Commission, Andrei Gromyko, offered a plan that essentially reversed the order of the Baruch Plan. It called for nuclear disarmament and the sharing of atomic secrets before establishing international controls. In effect, the Soviets insisted that the United States must surrender its nuclear advantage in exchange for a vague Soviet promise to participate in a system of international control. Gromyko also stated flatly that the Soviet Union would not accept any curtailment of its Security Council veto power.[81]

Needless to say, the Soviet plan was totally unacceptable to the United States, and on July 5 Baruch formally rejected it. On July 24 Gromyko responded by turning down the American plan. While the Baruch Plan was approved by the UN Atomic Energy Commission on December 30, its rejection by the Soviet Union made this American victory meaningless. As a result, the continuation of the negotiations to halt the inevitable nuclear arms race became another futile exercise in the developing Cold War.[82]

## The Turkish Crisis

Still another source of Soviet-American friction during 1946 was Turkey. Unable to secure Western cooperation in revising the Montreaux Convention, on August 7 the Soviets sent the Turks another note insisting upon the need for a new treaty providing for joint Turkish-Soviet control of the straits and granting the Soviet Union the right to establish naval bases in the Dardanelles.[83]

Until 1946 Washington had attached little importance to Turkey's problems with the Soviets. But with the deterioration in Soviet-American relations that occurred during that year, Turkey assumed an enhanced status in the eyes of the administration. American military planners began to see Turkey as a base of military operations against the Soviet Union in the event that war erupted. "If war occurred," historian Melvyn Leffler has explained, "Turkey could slow down a Soviet advance to Suez and North Africa, attack Soviet oil resources, provide a cover for bombers heading toward Moscow, bottle up Soviet submarines in the Black Sea, destroy Soviet shipping, and launch a possible ground offensive into the Soviet heartland. It was indispensable, then, to encourage Turkey to resist Soviet demands in peacetime and to thwart Soviet advances in wartime." With these considerations in mind, on August 15 the departments of State, War, and the Navy, supported by the Joint Chiefs of Staff, presented Truman with a report that concluded that the Soviets were attempting to gain control of Turkey as a base from which to dominate Greece, the eastern Mediterranean, and the Middle East. To prevent this, the report recommended that the United States "resist with all means any Soviet aggression against Turkey."[84]

Truman accepted this recommendation. "We might as well find out," he said to Acheson, "whether the Russians were bent on world conflict now as in five or ten years." On August 19 Acheson informed the Soviets that the United States firmly believed that Turkey should continue to have the sole responsibility for the defense of the straits. In late August, as a show of force in support of the Turks, a naval task force led by the new aircraft carrier, the *Franklin D. Roosevelt*, was sent to the eastern Mediterranean. The following month, Forrestal announced the creation of the U.S. Sixth Fleet, which would be stationed permanently in the Mediterranean. The United States, in effect, was telling the Soviets that it was no longer following an isolationist policy toward that part of the world.[85]

The strong American show of support for the Turks reinforced their determination to resist the Soviet demands to revise the Montreaux Convention. As a result, the crisis atmosphere over Turkey slowly subsided, thereby adding further strength to the conviction of the Truman administration that the Soviets respected American military power. In addition, historian Jonathan Knight has observed, during the Turkish crisis the United States began to abandon the distinction it had traditionally made between war and peace as polar opposites. No longer capable of taking refuge behind the oceans, Americans began to see international politics as Stalin did--"the continuation of war by other means."[86]

## The British Loan

The Iranian and Turkish crises also had a profound influence on the attitudes of the Congress and American people toward U.S. cooperation with Britain. The British had not only welcomed the new American naval presence in the Mediterranean, they had provided the U.S. fleet with access to British ports. Until the value of British support in these crises became evident, neither the Congress nor the American people favored giving Britain a long-term, low-interest (2 percent per annum) $3.75 billion loan that the administration and the British had negotiated in December 1945. American conservatives did not want to help a socialist government in Britain. Liberals argued that the loan would commit the United States to the defense of British imperialism. And isolationists feared the loan would contribute to the erosion of American financial solvency. An October 1945 Gallup poll showed that American opinion was three to one against the loan. As late as April 1946 the loan bill encountered several hostile amendments in both houses of Congress and a filibuster in the Senate.[87]

However, largely because of the new American appreciation of Britain's strategic value to the United States, which was accentuated by the increasing Soviet-American tension, the British loan was approved by the Senate on May 10, 1946, by a 43-30 margin, and passed in the House in mid-July by a vote of 219-155. Observed Lord Halifax, "the main propulsive force . . . behind the loan" was "Stalin, whose tactics have erected a greater volume in favor of support of Britain than our unaided efforts could probably ever have achieved."[88]

What undoubtedly made the passage of the British loan all the more galling to the Soviets was their own inability to get anything in the way of a credit from the Americans. In January 1945 Molotov had requested a $6 billion loan. After Truman entered the White House, his administration did consider offering the Soviets a $1 billion credit. But, for the Soviets, the conditions the Americans attached to the loan were unacceptable. They included Soviet willingness to create a political and economic "open door" in Eastern Europe, acceptance of American trade principles, and Soviet membership in the World Bank and International Monetary Fund, all of which the Soviets considered a capitalist attempt to undermine their socialist system.[89]

But the deterioration in Soviet-American relations that occurred during the winter of 1946 also contributed to the administration's declining interest in a loan to the Soviet Union. In early March the Department of State made the bizarre and false announcement that the formal Soviet loan request had been "lost." In October Averell Harriman told the National Press Club that the Soviet loan was no longer a "current issue." Yet he also admitted a month later that the Soviet failure to obtain an American loan had "increased [their] tendency to take unilateral action," and "may have contributed to their avaricious policies in the countries occupied or liberated by the Red Army."[90]

## The Wallace Challenge

The increasingly anti-Soviet and pro-British policy the Truman administration adopted during 1946 did not go unchallenged. It was criticized severely by Commerce Secretary Henry Wallace in a 5,000-word letter to Truman on July 23. Unlike George Kennan, Wallace believed the Soviets had legitimate reasons for fearing the United States. These included U.S. arming of the Western Hemispheric nations, the American atomic bomb, the acquisition of military bases outside the United States, and American diplomatic and military support for Britain in the Middle East and eastern Mediterranean. The effort to create an armed peace based on the atomic bomb, Wallace warned Truman, would "inevitably result in a neurotic, fear ridden, itching-trigger psychology" that was bound to affect the security of the United States as other nations developed atomic weapons. To Wallace, the only solution to an otherwise inevitable nuclear arms race was "atomic disarmament" and an effective system of enforcing it. Truman in response simply acknowledged receipt of Wallace's letter.[91]

Undeterred, Wallace continued his criticism of the administration's foreign policy in a speech at Madison Square Garden on September 12. There, he called for the renewal of Roosevelt's conciliatory approach to the Soviet Union. "'Getting tough,'" he said, "never brought anything real and lasting--whether for schoolyard bullies or businessmen or world powers. . . . The tougher we get, the tougher the Russians will get." As an alternative, Wallace called for the mutual recognition of Soviet and American spheres of interest. "Whether we like it or not," he said, "the Russians will try to socialize their sphere of influence just as we try to democratize our sphere of influence."[92]

Wallace's attack on the "firm but patient" policy that Byrnes had been pursuing for more than six months embarrassed the secretary of state, who at that time was facing off with the Soviets in the Paris peace conference. Byrnes cabled Truman and threatened to resign if the president did not disassociate himself from Wallace's views. Byrnes' threat also placed Truman in an embarrassing position. The president had made no objection to Wallace's speech, after quickly thumbing through it two days before it was delivered, because he did not want to lose, so close to the November congressional election, the liberal support Wallace enjoyed. Yet Truman also did not want to undermine the bipartisan foreign policy that he and Byrnes had fashioned since the spring. Renewed Republican charges of administration appeasement, which were sure to follow if Truman sided with Wallace, would be even more damaging to congressional Democrats than a presidential split with Wallace. When a promise by Wallace, that he would not speak out on foreign policy issues until after the election, did not satisfy Byrnes,

Truman felt he had no alternative but to face the wrath of the liberals. On September 20 he fired Wallace.[93]

# The Clifford-Elsey Report

Three days after Wallace left office, Truman received a copy of a report by presidential counselor Clark Clifford and his aide, George Elsey, which called for an even tougher policy toward the Soviets than the administration had been following. In so doing, the Clifford-Elsey Report ignored earlier intelligence estimates that considered the Soviet Union so severely devastated by the Germans in World War II--including 20 million Soviet people killed and 1,700 towns, 31,000 factories, and 100,000 collective farms destroyed--that it was in no condition to wage an aggressive war. Also ignored were American intelligence estimates that concluded that, while the Soviets were capable of mobilizing 6 million troops in thirty days and 12 million in six months--enough force to overrun Europe and much of Asia--the Soviet military lacked a long-range strategic air force, atomic weapons, and an ocean-going navy, all of which the United States possessed, and all of which American analysts believed would be sufficient to check any aggression by the Soviet Union for the foreseeable future. Years later, in explaining why these estimates were ignored, Clifford said that Truman "liked things in black and white."[94]

Accordingly, the Clifford-Elsey Report concluded that the Soviets were increasing their military power and their sphere of influence in preparation for an inevitable conflict with the United States. Restating the main thesis of Kennan's containment doctrine, the report emphasized that the main objective of the United States should be to persuade the Soviet Union that war was not inevitable. This was to be accomplished primarily by maintaining American military strength, particularly the capability to wage atomic and biological warfare. The "mere fact of preparedness," the report stated, "may be the only powerful deterrent to Soviet aggressive action and in this sense the only sure guaranty of peace." The report also stated the United States "should entertain no proposal for disarmament as long as the possibility of Soviet aggression exists."[95]

The Clifford-Elsey Report also recommended that the United States should be prepared to join Britain in supporting "all democratic countries which are in any way menaced or endangered by the U.S.S.R." Yet it also recognized that the American public and congressional opinion were not yet prepared for close military cooperation with Britain or any countries threatened by Soviet aggression. Consequently, it stated that American economic assistance should be the preferred method of assistance to these countries, with military aid to be offered only as a last resort. The report concluded that "only a well-informed public will support the stern policies which Soviet activities make imperative and which the United States government must adopt." To this end, the report recommended making known to the American people the complete record of "Soviet evasion, misrepresentation, and aggression."[96]

Truman read the Clifford-Elsey Report carefully but at once impounded it. "This is so hot," he told Clifford, that "if this should come out now it could have an exceedingly unfortunate impact on our efforts to try to develop some relationship with the Soviet Union." This statement, and other events, in the opinion of historian Deborah Larson, demonstrated that, despite the strains that America's relationship with the Soviet Union experienced during the year, Truman was not yet ready for a complete break with the Soviets. She argues that the president was encouraged by an interview Stalin gave on September 24, in which the Soviet leader stated that neither poor relations, nor war, with the West was inevitable. According to Larson, Truman tried to reciprocate Stalin's gesture a month later by telling the United Nations General Assembly that "we must not permit differences in economic and social systems to stand in the way of peace." The normally stone-faced Molotov told the president that his speech was "great." As a result, Larson believes, Truman ended 1946 "waffling between confrontation and collaboration" toward and with the Soviets, and was unable to perceive any alternatives to this mixed approach except the unacceptable--war.[97]

While Truman may have been sincere in his desire to preserve a nonhostile relationship with the Soviets, it is also quite possible that he was simply trying to retain liberal votes for the Democractic Party by not widening the Soviet-American breach shortly before the approaching congressional election. Historian William O. McCagg, Jr., argues that "Western observers did not take Stalin's peace talk of late 1946 very seriously." Moreover, while Stalin's words may have changed, his actions did not. In late January 1947 rigged elections in Poland cemented the communist hold on that nation's government. A month later, the arrest by Soviet occupation troops of a leading Hungarian noncommunist politician, Bela Kovacs, indicated that Hungary would follow Poland's example. In February 1947, for the first time, an American official publicly labeled the Soviet Union an aggressive power; by then, the brief thaw of late 1946 and early 1947 was clearly over.[98]

## The Truman Doctrine

In the end, a severe winter in Europe, a renewal of civil warfare in Greece, another financial crisis in Britain, and the election of a parsimonious Congress persuaded Truman to abandon, once and for all, Roosevelt's policy of trying to accommodate Soviet security requirements.

On February 21, 1947, the economically hard pressed British government informed the State Department that it was no longer capable of maintaining a military presence in Greece. Hurt by a shortfall in coal production and severe blizzards that paralyzed more than half of their industrial production, the British had nearly exhausted $5 billion in American and Canadian loans and were compelled to reduce their armed forces by over 300,000 men (out of 1.5 million). While still a great power, Britain clearly was no longer a world power.[99]

The renewal of civil warfare in Greece resulted from the election of a conservative government and the restoration of the monarchy the preceding year. Without continued financial assistance, which Britain could no longer provide, the British warned Washington, it was quite likely that the Greek government would succumb to a communist-led guerrilla movement aided and abetted by Albania,

Yugoslavia, and Bulgaria. Besides Greece, the British told the State Department, Turkey would also need economic and military aid, assistance again that could only come from the United States.[100]

Until the fall of 1946 the Truman administration had been reluctant to consider the Greek problem. The corrupt and repressive government of Constantine Tsaldaris repelled even staunch supporters of Greece. Moreover, the Greek government had squandered several hundred million dollars worth of UN and American economic assistance, and the State Department was reluctant to give them any more. But the Turkish crisis during the preceding summer produced a temporary change of heart in Washington. On September 24 Byrnes agreed to lift restrictions on the sale of U.S. military equipment to Greece, Turkey, and Iran. However, official enthusiasm for assisting Greek soon cooled, partly because the administration was still reluctant to provoke the Soviets, and partly because it continued to be dissatisfied with the Tsaldaris government. In October the administration decided to supply Greece with only limited economic aid and to allow the British to carry the burden of providing military aid.[101]

The inability of Britain to carry that burden alone, however, compelled the Truman administration to play a more active part in assisting Greece. On February 26, five days after the British notes were delivered to the State Department, George Marshall, who had succeeded Byrnes as secretary of state on January 21, presented Truman with a memorandum representing the consensus of the departments of State, War, and the Navy that the collapse of Greece would threaten American security. It recommended that the United States "should take immediate steps to extend all possible aid to Greece and, on a lesser scale, to Turkey." Without questioning the recommendation, Truman agreed to submit the necessary legislation to the Congress.[102]

The next day, the president called congressional leaders to the White House to enlist their support. Marshall told the congressmen that, "if Greece should dissolve into civil war, it is altogether probable that it would emerge as a communist state under Soviet control." Using an early form of the domino theory, Marshall warned that the fall of Greece could lead to the overthrow of pro-Western governments in Turkey, Hungary, Austria, Italy, and France. Marshall's argumentation was supplemented by a more forceful presentation from Acheson, who described the crises in Greece and Turkey as a part of a global struggle between the forces of freedom and totalitarianism, which the United States could ignore only to its own ultimate peril.[103]

The congressmen were shaken by Acheson's presentation; they quickly agreed to support the administration's legislation. But Senator Vandenberg warned Truman that the only way he could gain the support of the American people, who were not particularly aroused by the Greek crisis, and of the Congress, which was now controlled by cost-conscious Republicans, was to tell them bluntly that the aid was necessary to prevent Greece and Turkey from falling to communism. Truman fully agreed. Isolationist sentiment was still sufficiently strong in the United States that Americans probably would not support assistance to Greece and Turkey in order to maintain pro-Western governments in these strategically important countries. However, they were likely to do so, Truman reasoned, if the administration emphasized the ideological aspects of the Soviet-American confrontation. Still, the president realized, as he told his cabinet on March 7, that persuading the American people to abandon their traditional policy of nonentanglement in purely European problems would be "the greatest selling job ever facing a president." By assuming the British burden in Greece and Turkey, the United States would be doing just that.[104]

On March 12 Truman made his sales pitch to a joint session of Congress. In requesting $300 million in aid for Greece and $100 million for Turkey, the president portrayed the Greek civil war as a major battle in the global struggle between democracy and communism. To prevent further communist expansion, he asserted "that it must be the policy of the United States to support free peoples who are resisting attempted subjugation by armed minorities or by outside pressures."[105]

Reaction to the president's speech was mixed. While it attracted strong support from the media, a large minority of liberal Americans believed it was excessively militaristic. Conservative isolationists, like Ohio's Republican senator, Robert Taft, criticized the cost of the Greek and Turkish aid programs--as well as other aid programs he believed were sure to follow. But it proved impossible for liberal and conservative critics of the Truman Doctrine to overcome the public's latent fear of communist expansion that the president's speech so effectively stimulated. Moreover, most congressmen and senators were reluctant to impair American prestige by rejecting a foreign policy request by the chief executive. As a result, on April 22 the Senate approved the administration's aid bill by a margin of 67 to 23. On May 8 the bill passed in the House by 287 to 107.[106]

Although the Truman Doctrine is usually considered the first step toward a worldwide American commitment to defend anticommunist regimes, neither the president nor his chief advisers had any intention of policing the world. Acheson assured the Congress that it would have the final say on any requests for assistance to other countries, and that it would not be asked to do so unless vital American interests were jeopardized--as, he argued, was the case in Greece and Turkey. Although Acheson insisted that the administration had not launched an "ideological crusade" against communism, others have not been so sure. In the opinion of historian Robert M. Hathaway, "sweeping globalism" was not only an important result of the Truman Doctrine, it was also "to some extent a response to and a rejection of suspicions that the United States was merely standing in for Great Britain."[107]

In addition, as John Lewis Gaddis has observed:

> By presenting aid to Greece and Turkey in terms of ideological conflict between two ways of life, Washington officials encouraged a simplistic view of the Cold War which was, in time, to imprison American diplomacy in an ideological straitjacket almost as confining as that which restricted Soviet foreign policy. Trapped in their own rhetoric, leaders of the United States found it difficult to respond to the conciliatory gestures which emanated from the Kremlin following Stalin's death and, through their inflexibility, may well have contributed to the perpetuation of the Cold War.[108]

## Why the Grand Alliance Collapsed

Truman's diplomatic inexperience was at least partially responsible for the collapse of the Grand Alliance. It made him susceptible to the views of subordinates whose advice Roosevelt took only selectively. At first, Truman followed the recommendations of hardliners--Forrestal, Leahy, and Harriman--and tried to be "tough" with the Soviets. But he then was persuaded by others-- including Davies, Stimson, and the Joint Chiefs of Staff--that a confrontational policy toward the Soviet Union would jeopardize the administration's effort to bring the Soviets into the war against Japan. Prompted by this consideration primarily, Truman quickly returned to Roosevelt's conciliatory policy. He tacitly recognized a Soviet sphere of influence in Eastern Europe while paying lip service to the Declaration on Liberated Europe. In return, Stalin gave both tacit and formal recognition to American predominance in Latin America, Italy, Japan, China, and the Pacific, as well as British predominance in Greece and Western Europe. Had matters stood here, perhaps the Cold War could have been avoided--or at least postponed.

But, in American eyes, Stalin overreached himself. He made demands upon Iran and later upon Turkey that aroused the opposition of anti-Soviet hardliners within the administration, Republican Party, and the news media. Many of these elements were already agitated by the creation of communist police states in Eastern Europe, Stalin's hostile speech of February 9, 1946, Kennan's Long Telegram, the revelation of a Soviet atomic spy ring, and Churchill's Fulton address. It appeared to an increasing number of Americans that there were no limits to Stalin's territorial ambitions. As a result, the past American effort to accommodate Soviet desires in order to maintain the Grand Alliance after the war became synonymous with the Western effort to appease Hitler before that conflict. After the Truman administration released the documentation of the Yalta Conference in January 1946, Yalta became synonymous with Munich--a sellout. The result was to make the continuation of Roosevelt's conciliatory policy toward the Soviet Union politically impossible for Truman after March 1946.

To be sure, Stalin was encouraged to move against Iran and Turkey by the lack of interest the United States had displayed toward these countries before 1946 and by the rapid decline of British military power after the war. The power vacuum that existed in the Near East and the eastern Mediterranean at the end of the war prompted the Soviet leader to take what action he could to expand Soviet influence in these regions while conditions for doing so appeared favorable. But American officials and military leaders began to see the Soviet moves against Iran and Turkey as a threat to the growing American oil interests in the Near East, and particularly in Saudi Arabia, as well as to the balance of power in Europe, which Britain was no longer capable of maintaining by herself. With the memory of World War II still fresh in American minds, the Truman administration began moving toward a permanent U.S. military presence in these regions.

The growing American antagonism toward the Soviets was also fueled by a number of other events during Truman's first year in office. With regard to Germany, they included Soviet-American differences over reparations, the German-Polish border, and the political and economic nature of a reunified

German state. In addition, the inability of the Soviet Union and the United States to agree upon an international arrangement for the control of atomic energy helped to make a nuclear arms race inevitable--and promoted distrust between the superpowers. The weakness of the United Nations also proved to be a point of friction between the United States and the Soviet Union. Instead of a forum for resolving international differences, the world body quickly became a focus of Cold War confrontation. No doubt, the demise of the common enemy--Germany--made disagreements that were papered over during the war inevitable once that conflict ended.

Much has been made of the economic causes of the Cold War by so-called revisionist historians. They argue that America sought a global "open door" policy of equal trade and investment opportunity, private enterprise, multilateral cooperation in foreign commerce and freedom of the seas--all of which threatened to undermine the Soviet sphere of influence. Revisionists conclude that the American effort to create a world based on capitalistic and democratic principles made the Cold War inevitable.[109]

On the other hand, historian Robert Pollard points out that the United States had invited the Soviet Union to join the Marshall Plan, but the Soviets refused to do so, believing their economy would become vulnerable to capitalistic manipulation. According to Pollard, an American reconstruction loan to the Soviet Union was possible until the Soviet crackdown in Poland.[110]

Nevertheless, it is also true that the United States did attempt to use economic leverage--for example, the suspension of Lend-Lease and the rejection of a loan to the Soviet Union--to modify Soviet behavior. As a consequence, the Soviets were led to believe that the Americans had sinister motives behind their economic aid proposals. Others have argued that it would have been foolhardy for the United States to provide the Soviet Union with the economic wherewithal to threaten American interests in Europe and Asia. The United States, in other words, this view holds, had no good reason to facilitate the economic recovery of the Soviet Union, considering the threat the Soviets posed to Western Europe.[111]

Still others believe that the Soviet threat to Western Europe and to other Western interests in the Near East and the eastern Mediterranean has been exaggerated. The late political scientist Hans Morgenthau, for example, argued that "Stalin sought to expand Soviet control primarily into territories adjacent to Russia, the traditional objectives of Russian expansionism," and had neither the ambition, nor the capability, considering the devastation the Soviet Union had suffered during the war, to dominate the world, or even Western Europe. Morgenthau saw Soviet moves against Turkey and Iran, as well as in the Far East, as marking the "traditional limits of Russian expansionism." As Stalin told Eden during World War II: "The trouble with Hitler is that he doesn't know where to stop. I know where to stop."[112]

Nor, in Morgenthau's opinion, was Stalin really concerned about the spread of communism outside of Russia's traditional zones of opportunity. For Stalin, Morgenthau argued, "Communist orthodoxy was a means to an end, and the end was the power of the Russian state traditionally defined." Stalin, he added, did not at first care about the ideological character of the governments of Eastern Europe as long as they were "friendly" to the Soviet Union. The Soviet leader initially tried working with noncommunists in Germany, Rumania, and Hungary. But they proved unreliable, thus forcing him to turn to indigenous communist parties, whose dependency upon the Red Army for their existence ensured that they would be "friendly" to the Soviet Union. Americans failed to appreciate the limited nature of Stalin's ambitions, Morgenthau argued, while the Soviet leader could not understand the nature of American susceptibilities. As a result, in Morgenthau's opinion, the Cold War was to some extent the product of mutual misunderstanding.[113]

The limit of Stalin's ambitions is, of course, impossible to determine, not only because of the inaccessibility to Western analysts of Soviet archival materials, but also because one cannot replay the historical process to see how far the Soviets would have extended their hegemony had there not been an American containment policy. But Truman, lacking his predecessor's diplomatic skills, agitated by Soviet behavior in Eastern Europe and in the Middle East, pressured by hardliners in the Republican Party and from within his own administration, facing a presidential election campaign in 1948, decided he could not afford to test the limits of Soviet expansionism through a continuation of Roosevelt's strategy of patient conciliation. As a result, a policy of openly resisting Soviet demands replaced one of attempting to satisfy them.

To be sure, the American people, while increasingly suspicious of Soviet actions in Eastern Europe and the Near East, were not at first prepared to favor a more active U.S. role in the affairs of these regions. The American people were not yet willing to become entangled in Europe's problems even after it became evident that Eastern Europe was becoming a part of the Soviet bloc. To arouse public support for the administration's decision to provide economic aid to Greece and Turkey, Truman had to convince the public and the Congress that there was a Soviet plan for world domination. By painting the struggle in ideological terms, Truman, in the short run, was able to obtain congressional and public support for the doctrine that bears his name, and the United States took a major step toward abandoning its traditional policy of isolationism. But in the long run, the consequences were almost a half-century of repeated Soviet-American confrontations in Europe, Asia, and the Middle East--an outcome we now call the Cold War.

# 8

# The Creation of the North Atlantic Alliance, 1947–1950

## The Aftermath of the Truman Doctrine

In spite of the willingness of the Truman administration to extend economic aid to Greece and Turkey, the United States was still not ready to make any major military commitments to the defense of Europe. Even the Joint Chiefs of Staff, who strongly backed military aid to Turkey, considered "political, economic, and psychological factors" more important. As a result, the naval presence established by the United States in the eastern Mediterranean was kept small. And when, in the summer of 1947, the British announced that they would withdraw the last of their troops, some 5,000 men, from Greece, the administration successfully persuaded them to stay longer, eventually until 1954.[1]

Yet in spite ot the reluctance of the American government and people to become militarily involved in the defense of Europe, only two years after the Truman Doctrine was announced, the United States joined a European alliance, the North Atlantic Treaty Organization (NATO), thereby completing the gradual abandonment of the century-and-a-half-old tradition of American isolationism.

## The Marshall Plan

The closing phase of American isolationism began with the failure of the Moscow Conference of Foreign Ministers in early 1947 (March 10-April 24). The conference, which was called primarily to resolve German problems, was unable to reach agreement on any of the German issues, including reparations, the creation of a centralized administration, and ultimately reunification of the country. The Soviets attempted to head off the merger of the Western occupation zones by offering to accept the unification of Germany--after the Western powers had withdrawn their military forces from the country--in return for partial Soviet control of the Ruhr. Marshall countered with a proposal for four-power control of the Ruhr as well as Upper Silesia, an offer that was rejected by Molotov. As a result, the Truman administration concluded that the only way Germany would be reunified was under Soviet control. For the Americans, the continued partition of Germany was far more preferable.[2]

While in Europe, Marshall not only gained a new appreciation of the depth of Soviet irascibility, he also observed at first hand the economic difficulties the Europeans were facing. The unexpectedly good year which Western Europe had experienced in 1946 was followed by a sharp decline in production and trade during the winter and spring of 1947. As a result, there were food riots in the Ruhr, bread shortages in France, another financial crisis in Britain, and communist victories in Italian municipal elections. The large balance-of-payments deficits that West European nations ran up, particularly with the United States (estimated at $4.25 billion in fiscal 1948), meant that, without additional U.S. credits, the continental countries would be unable to buy American goods. Indeed, the administration feared that without massive American financial assistance, the economies of Western Europe would soon collapse, leaving the Soviet Union as the dominant power on the Continent. With these considerations in mind, Marshall not only concluded that the economic recovery of Western Europe was essential to the maintenance of the balance of power, but also that Germany's rehabilitation was the key ingredient in that recovery. "Without a revival of German production," he told Congress, "there can be no revival of Europe's economy."[3]

The French, however, balked at the prospect of reviving Germany's industrial plant, fearing that the resuscitation of German military might would follow soon thereafter. To reassure the French that the United States would not again abandon them to a revived German militarism, the State Department conceived a plan for massive economic aid to all the nations of Europe. In this way, Germany's economy--and military potential--would not be rebuilt faster than the economies of her neighbors. Moreover, by including the Germans as a part of an economic aid program for all of Europe, the administration hoped to preclude France from blocking Germany's recovery. Further, the officials of the State Department reasoned, a Germany integrated in an economically revitalized Europe would be able to resist communist expansion without Germany once again dominating the Continent--and without a major U.S. military commitment to European security.[4]

In an address at Harvard University on June 5, 1947, Marshall announced the State Department's idea of offering American economic assistance to the nations of Europe. But he provided no specifics as to what form this aid program would take, insisting that the initiative for planning it "must come from Europe." In an attempt to avoid the overt anti-Soviet implications of the Truman Doctrine, Marshall stated that American policy was "directed not against any country or doctrine, but against hunger, poverty, deprivation and chaos."[5]

Yet while the European Recovery Program (ERP), which the Marshall Plan was officially entitled, was one of the most generous acts of any nation in history, it was not without manipulative undertones. The offer, a State Department memorandum revealed, was designed in "such a form that the Russian satellite countries would either exclude themselves by their unwillingness to accept the proposed conditions or agree to abandon the exclusive Soviet orientation of their economies." In his Harvard address, Marshall warned that those who "seek to perpetuate human misery in order to profit therefrom . . . will encounter the opposition of the United States."[6]

On June 13 Ernest Bevin, Britain's foreign secretary, accepted Marshall's suggestion that the Europeans take the initiative in determining their economic needs. With French cooperation, the European states, including those in the Soviet bloc, were invited to attend an ERP conference in Paris. On June 26 Molotov arrived in the French capital with eighty-nine economic experts and clerks, a clear indication that the Soviets intended to give the American offer serious consideration. But Soviet participation in the Marshall Plan was precluded by Molotov's insistence that each nation must independently determine its own economic needs and then ask the United States to provide the money to meet them. The Soviets did not want to participate in a joint program that would require them to furnish economic data to the United States and other nations. The French and British, however, wanted to draft a plan for the whole of Europe. In addition, Molotov also demanded that the former Axis states, including Germany, must be excluded from the program so as not to revive their military might before the rest of Europe could be rebuilt. When the Anglo-French formula prevailed, Molotov angrily left the conference on July 2, warning that the Marshall Plan would divide "Europe into two groups of states, creating new difficulties in the relations between them."[7]

The Soviets opposed the Marshall Plan not only because they did not want to save capitalism in Western Europe, but primarily because they feared that the American program would undermine Soviet control of Eastern Europe. To preclude the latter, a Soviet crackdown on the satellite states was instituted in the wake of Molotov's departure from Paris. On July 9, under Soviet pressure, the Poles and Czechs, who had expressed interest in Marshall's proposal, reversed themselves and announced that they could not attend the Paris conference because their presence "might be construed as an action against the Soviet Union." In August rigged elections in Hungary brought that nation firmly into the Soviet camp. In October 1947 the Soviets created the Cominform (Communist Information Bureau) to strengthen their political control over the world communist movement. By the end of the year, the last vestiges of opposition parties had been erased in Poland, Bulgaria, and Rumania. In January 1949 the Soviets established their own alternative to the Marshall Plan, the Council for Mutual Economic Assistance (COMECON), a centralized agency designed to stimulate the economic recovery of Eastern Europe under the aegis of the Soviet Union.[8]

On July 12, in Paris, the representatives of sixteen European countries accepted the American aid program. They also declared: "The German economy must be integrated into the European economy in such a way that it contributes to a general improvement in the standard of living." In response, the Truman administration moved quickly to design a strategy that would win congressional approval of the European Recovery Program. On December 9, 1947 the president requested an initial fifteen-month appropriation of $6.6 billion, and $17 billion over a four-year period. But while Truman argued that the amount requested was only 5 percent of the cost of World War II and 3 percent of national income in 1948, it was still too much for the tight-money, Republican-controlled Congress.

Moreover, the Congress insisted that the Europeans assure the United States that the money would not be wasted. In the end, Senator Vandenberg was able to persuade the administration to reduce the initial fifteen-month appropriation from $6.8 billion to a first-year amount of $5.3 billion, in order to eliminate the requirement for a four-year authorization, and to strengthen a "self-help" provision that empowered the president to terminate American aid to uncooperative aid recipients.[9]

Many of the arguments that were employed by the administration to gain congressional approval of the Truman Doctrine were again used for the Marshall Plan. Administration spokesmen sought to portray ERP as vital to the security of the United States. In January 1948 Marshall told the Senate Foreign Relations Committee that the economic aid program would help to restore the balance of power in Europe, thereby meeting the primary objective of America's involvement in World War II. The alternative, he warned, could be another world war with "tremendous appropriations for national security." In effect, the Economic Recovery Program, Marshall argued, would enable the United States to maintain peace in Europe and halt the expansion of communism without a far more costly war--or a major American military contribution. The cost-effectiveness side of ERP eventually proved to be very useful in persuading economy-minded Republicans and Democrats to approve the program.[10]

## Bevin's Bid for an American Alliance

Although the United States offered a massive program of economic assistance to the nations of Western Europe, Britain's foreign minister, Ernest Bevin, believed that ultimately Europe's security could only be guaranteed by a Western alliance involving the United States. In late 1946 and early 1947 Bevin engineered negotiations leading to the signing in March 1947 of the Treaty of Dunkirk, which created a fifty-year Anglo-French alliance against Germany. However, in spite of the alliance's German orientation, Bevin considered the Soviet Union, not Germany, the primary threat to Western Europe. He feared that, without an Anglo-French alliance, France would be subverted by her powerful communist party, which was aided and abetted by the Soviet Union. Belgium and the Netherlands soon expressed an interest in joining the Anglo-French alliance. However, without an American military commitment to European defense, Bevin at first feared that a wider Western alliance would only dangerously exacerbate relations with the Soviets, who would regard the alliance as directed primarily against them rather than the Germans.[11]

But the failure of still another meeting of the Council of Foreign Ministers (in London, from November 25 to December 15, 1947) to resolve the German problem convinced Bevin that a wider Western alliance was necessary not only to counter Soviet military power, but also to integrate Germany's economic might into the Western bloc. On December 17 Bevin told Marshall that there was an urgent need for some form of Western democratic system comprising America, Britain, France, Italy, and the British Dominions. "This would not be a formal alliance," he assured Marshall, "but an understanding backed by power, money, and resolute action." Not mentioning any specifics, Bevin told the secretary of state that he envisioned "a sort of spiritual federation of the West." He suggested that the effort to create such an association should begin with Anglo-American military talks. Marshall expressed general agreement with Bevin's ideas but informed him that, before American support could be officially given, the United States would need to know more precisely what the foreign secretary had in mind.[12]

Later, John D. Hickerson, director of the State Department's Office of European Affairs, learned from officials in the British Foreign Office that Bevin was thinking in terms of two circles of defense. The inner one would include European states bound tightly by an alliance, while the second, outer circle would encompass a more loosely bound association of states that would include the United States and the British Dominions. After receiving this information, Marshall informed Lord Inverchapel, the British ambassador in Washington, that he "wished to see the United States do everything which it properly can in assisting the European nations in bringing a project along this line to fruition."[13]

With this encouragement, Bevin delivered a fiery speech to Parliament on January 22, 1948, calling for a military association of the West European states. Economic cooperation, he declared, was not enough to resist Soviet aggression and subversion; military cooperation was now necessary. Bevin planned to use the Dunkirk Treaty as the nucleus of the new arrangement he had in mind. The other West European states, including the Benelux countries (Belgium, the Netherlands, and Luxembourg), and even Italy, would be invited to participate in the alliance. The military pact Bevin envisioned would serve a dual purpose: it would offer the French security against the possibility of renewed German aggression, while it would lay the groundwork for a wider Atlantic alliance, ultimately involving the United States, which would be directed implicitly against the Soviet Union.[14]

It soon became clear to the British foreign secretary, however, that the extent of American support for a European alliance was shallower than Marshall's initial encouragement had suggested. Key leaders in the State Department--Under Secretary of State Robert Lovett, Counselor Charles Bohlen, and Policy Planning Director George Kennan--all regarded as premature the idea of an American military alliance with Western Europe. Kennan, for one, believed that the Western Europeans should complete the task of economic recovery and achieve political unification before proceeding to a military pact. There was also a general fear within the department that a formal American alliance with Western Europe and a permanent U.S. military presence on the Continent would not be approved by Congress, where there was still substantial opposition to entangling alliances with European powers.[15]

Nor, in Kennan's opinion, was an alliance necessary. Having fought a costly war to rid the Continent of Nazism, he argued, the United States was not about to permit its domination by the Soviet Union--with or without American participation in a European alliance. Kennan believed, as he wrote some months later, that the appropriate eventual goal of American policy should be the withdrawal of both U.S. and Soviet troops from the "heart of Europe" and "the encouragement of the growth of a third force which can absorb and take over the territories between the two." Yet Kennan admitted that, until this could be arranged, the United States would have to provide military support to the West Europeans. Still, he believed that an American military commitment to Europe should take the form of a presidential pronouncement, modeled on the Monroe Doctrine, rather than a formal treaty of alliance.[16]

Even John Hickerson, who was strongly in favor of a military alliance with Western Europe, did not support Bevin's plan to expand the Dunkirk Treaty to include the Benelux countries. Because the Dunkirk pact was aimed against Germany, Hickerson thought it would be of dubious value because it failed to deal with "the real threat to Western Europe which came from further East." Furthermore, the Congress wanted to strengthen Germany as a barrier against Soviet expansion, Hickerson pointed out, not to maintain her status as an enemy state. What was needed, Hickerson told Inverchapel, was a multilateral defense pact modeled after the Inter-American Treaty of Reciprocal Assistance, which the United States and the Latin American states had signed at Rio de Janiero in September 1947. In the Rio Pact, the military assistance obligation was "open ended," that is, not directed at any particular country. Instead, it was designed to cover aggression from any quarter, even from signatories of the treaty.[17]

However, Hickerson did tell the British ambassador that if the Europeans felt that "no regional organization could be complete without the United States," and if the proposed organization "was closely associated with the Charter of the United Nations," the idea of an American association with such a grouping "might receive a favorable reception." But Hickerson attached an important condition on American association with the West European states: the initiative for such action must come from the Europeans. Hickerson argued that Congress would be more likely to support such an arrangement if the West European states had demonstrated first "that they were resolved and able to stand on their own feet."[18]

The American response placed the British in a vicious circle. The West Europeans were unwilling to form an alliance among themselves until they had obtained security assurances from the United States. But the Americans would not give those assurances until the West Europeans had first demonstrated the principle of self-help. What compounded Bevin's predicament was the unwillingness of his own government to make a security commitment to Western Europe without a prior American security guarantee.[19]

With Britain in another acute economic crisis, and with very limited military resources, the British Chiefs of Staff, along with Prime Minister Attlee--in a replay of the strategic situation that Britain had faced during the interwar era--were anxious to avoid continental commitments. At the end of 1947, the British Chiefs, with cabinet approval, had decided that they would send no land forces to Europe in the event of a war, and that the Royal Air Force would be based exclusively at bases in Great Britain. While they realized that public knowledge of this decision would undermine the resolve of the Western Europeans to resist Soviet pressure, the British Chiefs were not prepared to go further without a complementary American commitment to the defense of the Continent. Indeed, it was not until May 10, 1948, almost two months after Britain had signed the Brussels Treaty (which bound her to an alliance with the Benelux countries as well as to France), that Bevin, with the assistance of Field Marshal Montgomery and Defense Minister A. V. Alexander, was able to persuade Attlee and the British Chiefs that Britain must fight on the Continent alongside her new allies. Yet while the British accepted the American condition that the West European nations must act first, they did not reduce their pressure on the United States to become actively involved in the defense of the Continent.[20]

But the Americans were not the only obstacle to British plans for a wider alliance. The negotiations for the Western Union, as the Brussels alliance was called, reached a stalemate in February when France insisted that the alliance should be based on multilateral treaties modeled on the Dunkirk Treaty, which was specifically directed against Germany. The French feared that any other arrangement would appear to be directed against the Soviets, whom France did not want to risk offending without a written defense arrangement with the United States. In February and March 1948, during the first session of a London conference of Western powers (the United States, Britain, France, Belgium, the Netherlands, and Luxembourg), which was called to discuss the creation of a West German state, the French refused to merge their occupation zone with Bizonia--the combined American and British zones--until they had received a guarantee that the resources of the Ruhr and the Saar would not be used to rearm the Germans. The Benelux countries, on the other hand, believed that Soviet communism posed a greater threat to Western Europe than Germany, the Western portions of which they hoped would one day join the Western Union. The Americans supported this view, and as a result, the British changed their minds and did so also.[21]

## The Czechoslovak Coup, February 1948

The French became more amenable to the Anglo-American position on the Western Union and Germany after Czech communists staged a coup d'état in Prague in late February. Since 1943 the Czechs had managed to coexist with the Soviets while keeping open their frontiers with the West. However, the decision of the Czech government, a coalition of the Communist Party and noncommunist parties, to apply for Marshall Plan assistance alarmed and infuriated the Soviets. Fearful that Czechoslovakia might fall into the Western camp, Stalin ordered the Czech communists to take over the Prague government. Backed by the might of the Soviet army deployed on Czechoslovakia's borders, on February 29 President Eduard Benes capitulated to the Czech communists' demand to give them complete control of the government. Two weeks later, on March 10, the noncommunist foreign minister, Jan Masaryk, was found dead in a courtyard next to his office window. The communists asserted that Masaryk's death was a suicide, but most in the West, including Truman, believed he had been murdered.[22]

The West was shocked by the dramatic events in Czechoslovakia. Recalling how Hitler had subverted the independence of that country only ten years earlier, many saw the Prague coup as an ominous step to another war. Warned Averell Harriman: "There are aggressive forces in the world coming from the Soviet Union which are just as destructive as Hitler was, and I think are a greater menace than Hitler was." Truman reminded the nation that the Soviet Union and its agents had "destroyed the independence and democratic character of a whole series of nations in Eastern and Central Europe." Now it was clear, at least in Truman's mind, that they intended to extend their ruthless course of action "to the remaining free nations of Europe."[23]

In addition to overthrowing the Czech government, the Soviets put pressure on Norway and Finland. The Soviets wanted "mutual assistance" agreements with these two countries that would permit Soviet forces to pass through, and fortify certain portions of, their territory. Norway quickly appealed to London and Washington for assistance against the Soviets. But Finland, which shared a long frontier with the Soviet Union, was in no position to resist. As a result, the Finns signed a mutual defense treaty with the Soviet Union on April 6.[24]

The Soviet moves in central and northern Europe caused a war scare in the West. It was fueled by a telegram the Pentagon received from General Clay on March 5. Clay's telegram stated in part: "Within the last few weeks, I have felt a subtle change in Soviet attitudes which I cannot define but which now gives me a feeling that war may come with a dramatic suddenness." However, eleven days later, on March 16, the U.S. intelligence community informed the White House that, based on its estimates, it did not believe the Soviet Union would initiate military action within the next two months. Nevertheless, it added, "there was an ever present possibility that some miscalculation or incident may result in military movements towards areas at present unoccupied by the U.S.S.R." It was later determined that the primary purpose of Clay's telegram, according to the editor of his papers, was to help the Pentagon win congressional approval for additional military appropriations.[25]

Prompted by the events in Europe, Truman addressed both houses of Congress on March 17. He affirmed his determination to resist the "ruthless" ways and "growing menace" of Soviet expansion. And, in what many thought was a prelude to American rearmament, he urged swift funding of the European Recovery Program, enactment of legislation establishing Universal Military Training, and temporary reinstatement of Selective Service, which he had allowed to lapse a year earlier. Within twelve days the Congress responded to the events in Europe by approving the ERP. The measure passed in the Senate by a 183 to 86 margin and in the House by a vote of 329 to 74. On April 1 Truman signed a foreign assistance act that would commit the United States, over the next four years, to give $12.4 billion, most in the form of grants, to the European participants in the Marshall Plan. While Congress rejected Universal Military Training, it did approve a Selective Service bill. It also approved funds for a seventy-group Air Force, some 25 percent larger than the Pentagon had requested. The war scare of March 1947 was in no small part responsible for the Congress' actions.[26]

## The Brussels Treaty, March 1948

The Soviet Union's aggressive moves in central and northern Europe provided additional impetus for American association with a Western alliance. Taking advantage of the Soviet threat to Norway in particular, on March 11 Bevin suggested to the Americans that what was needed was a security system not only encompassing Western Europe but the North Atlantic and the Mediterranean as well. Bevin's reference to a North Atlantic pact was a stroke of genius, for it touched upon an area even more vital to American security than Western Europe.[27]

Alarmed by the Prague coup and Soviet pressure against Norway and Finland, the administration was finally prompted to move. On March 12 Marshall informed Inverchapel: "We are prepared to proceed at once in the joint discussions on the establishment of an Atlantic security system." To this end, the Truman administration acted to facilitate the conclusion of the Brussels Treaty. To ameliorate French insecurity, the United States promised to maintain its occupation forces in Germany indefinitely. In return, France agreed to allow the West Germans to participate in the European Recovery Program and dropped their demand for a European alliance based on the Dunkirk Treaty in favor of one modeled on the Rio Pact.[28]

As a result, on March 17 Britain, France, and the Benelux countries signed a fifty-year military alliance. It bound its members to meet an "armed attack in Europe" upon any one member, from any quarter, with "all the military and other aid and assistance in their power." The open-ended nature of the treaty made possible the eventual participation of Germany, a prerequisite for eventual American association with the Brussels powers. Six months later, the Brussels powers formed a Western Defense Organization, the Western Union, embodying a Consultative Council of Foreign Ministers and a Defense Committee. The latter body would be assisted by a Joint Chiefs of Staff, which Field Marshal Montgomery was appointed to head.[29]

In his speech to Congress on March 17, Truman responded to the signing of the Brussels Treaty by calling it "a notable step in the direction of unity in Europe for the protection and preservation of civilization." He added, "This development deserves our full support." Yet, in spite of the support that the president gave the Brussels Pact, there was still considerable uncertainty within the administration concerning the wisdom of the United States joining a European alliance. While Truman's advisers wanted to give the Western Union all possible support, including American association in a wider alliance, they were reluctant to have the United States undertake the kind of military commitment that would make such a pact effective, primarily because they believed that such a commitment would be rejected by the Congress.[30]

## The Pentagon Talks, March-April 1948

Nevertheless, shortly after Truman's speech to Congress pledging U.S. support for Western European defense, American, Canadian, and European officials began to search for a formula to implement the president's wishes. As a first step, the United States invited representatives of Britain and Canada to attend a series of "security conversations" at the Pentagon. The talks, which extended from March 22 to April 1, addressed not only the question of how the United States could assist the Brussels powers but how a North Atlantic alliance could be created as well. From the first, the British pressed for an American commitment to provide military assistance to the Western Union in the event of aggression in Europe. However, U.S. Ambassador to Britain Lewis Douglas responded that "full American support should be *assumed,* for the purpose of the current conversations," but "no commitments could be developed without the support of the Congress." This position, which was motivated by the administration's concern for a possible election-year leak, was "somewhat reluctantly" accepted by the British. The American delegation was also aware of Congress' opposition to any automatic-war requirement, the likes of which was contained in Article 6 of the Brussels Treaty. Consequently, they argued in favor of language comparable to that contained in the Rio Pact, which simply obliged signatories to react to external attacks with appropriate measures rather than the kind of more specific commitment contained in the Brussels Treaty.[31]

At the sixth and final meeting of the Pentagon Conference on April 1, John Hickerson introduced a paper which recommended that the parties should attempt to create a formal defensive alliance covering Western Europe, North America, and the islands of the North Atlantic. As a first step toward this end, the Truman administration, Hickerson proposed, should ask the Brussels powers to invite Norway, Sweden, Denmark, Iceland, Italy, Canada, Ireland, Portugal, and the United States to join an expanded alliance which would include them. Hickerson also recommended that, "when circumstances permit," Germany, Austria, and Spain should be invited to participate as well. Pending the conclusion of this wider alliance, Hickerson suggested, the United States would consider an armed attack in the North Atlantic area against any member of the Brussels pact as an attack against the United States. In addition, Hickerson recommended that Britain and the United States should declare that they would not "countenance any attack on the political independence or territorial integrity of Greece, Turkey, or Iran," and that "they would feel bound fully to support these states under Article 51 of the Charter of the United Nations."[32]

The final draft of the Pentagon Conference's summary report adopted Hickerson's recommendations. Still, as Hickerson cautioned, agreement on the report did not imply an American commitment to defend Europe, but rather represented "only a concept of what is desired at the working level." Other American officials feared that even military conversations with the Brussels powers would increase pressure on the United States to change its defense strategy, unless such talks were limited to the coordination of production and supplies.[33]

## The Vandenberg Resolution

In the meantime, a debate took place within the Truman administration concerning the form an American association with Western Europe should take. Kennan and State Department Counselor Charles Bohlen, who did not participate in the Pentagon talks, argued that, rather than joining a formal alliance, the United States should give a unilateral guarantee to Europe that would take the form of a presidential declaration similar to the Monroe Doctrine. This, Kennan argued, would allow the United States the maximum amount of freedom in determining its involvement in European security, thereby avoiding the criticism that the United States was entangling itself in a permanent alliance. Military staff talks, Kennan recommended, would allow the Europeans to know exactly what the United States would do in the event of Soviet aggression.[34]

On the other hand, Robert Lovett and John Hickerson believed that, to be effective, the association with Europe should be defined in a treaty of alliance containing specified reciprocal obligations. A treaty was necessary, they argued, not only because the French were demanding a precise, formal guarantee from the United States, but also because the Congress would insist upon a role in approving any American military commitment to Europe, even one resulting from a presidential declaration.[35]

On April 11, however, Senator Vandenberg told Lovett that an attempt to get a two-thirds affirmative vote in the Congress on a pact involving the type of military guarantees envisaged by the State Department was likely to end in failure. The Senate, he said, would be particularly opposed to any treaty that would automatically obligate the United States to go to war. Rather than the precise and formal obligations specified in the Brussels Treaty, Vandenberg suggested that the Congress would be more likely to approve an association with Europe modeled on the Rio Pact.[36]

The Joint Chiefs of Staff were also bothered by the prospect of an open-ended security commitment to Western Europe. They believed that the United States had neither the troops nor the support material necessary to fight a ground war in Europe. American strategy, they reminded the administration, was based on strategic aerial bombardment, not ground combat. The Congress also disapproved of extensive military aid to rearm Western Europe, let alone a formal alliance with those nations, while Marshall Plan appropriations were still under consideration.[37]

Nevertheless, on April 13 the National Security Council (which was established in 1947 to coordinate the activities of the State Department with those of the newly created Defense Department and Central Intelligence Agency) approved a directive, NSC 9, which recommended that the United States participate in a North Atlantic defense system, as outlined in the Pentagon report, but not participate in the Western Union. Yet, while the Americans refused to join the Brussels pact, the British did take comfort from the American willingness to join a North Atlantic alliance, which, in their estimation, would serve as effectively in tying the United States to the defense of Western Europe.[38]

With the approval of Marshall and John Foster Dulles, Lovett and Vandenberg devised a strategy designed to overcome any congressional or Pentagon opposition to an American military commitment to West European security. Vandenberg would introduce a resolution (S.R. 329) in the Senate stating that the United States should associate, "by constitutional process, with such regional and other collective arrangements as are based on continuous and effective self-help and mutual aid, and as affect its national security." In effect, American participation in any collective security agreement would not automatically commit the United States to go to war, but would require prior congressional approval. The self-help and mutual aid provision was designed to reassure reluctant senators that the entire burden of defending Western Europe would not fall upon the United States. After the Senate passed the resolution, the State Department would arrange to have the Brussels powers ask the United States to consult with them on defense matters. The president then would announce that the United States was prepared to do so on the basis of conditions set forth in the Vandenberg Resolution.[39]

On May 11 Vandenberg introduced his resolution into the Senate Foreign Relations Committee. Eight days later, that committee passed it unanimously. On June 11, 1948, the full Senate passed the resolution by a vote of 64 to 4, thereby authorizing the executive branch to create an American military tie to Europe. What is surprising is the lack of debate that preceded this momentous departure from the century-and-a-half-old tradition of American isolationism. "One who reads the *Congressional Record* of June 11," Vandenberg's son recalled, "may well wonder whether some members of the Senate were fully aware of the far-reaching action they were taking on that occasion. The language of the Vandenberg Resolution was general--perhaps even a bit vague--and it was impossible to know exactly what the framers had in mind." No doubt, the senators were influenced by Vandenberg's assurances that, as the committee report stated, "the resolution has been designed to avoid open-ended or unlimited commitments and to require reciprocity of aid." However, while the Vandenberg Resolution may have been viewed as a "vague" commitment to a military association with Western Europe, it was nevertheless to become a pillar of the emerging North Atlantic alliance.[40]

Not surprisingly, the Brussels powers reacted favorably to the passage of the Vandenberg Resolution. As a result, on June 17 the French Assembly, by the narrow vote of 300 to 286, approved five major agreements reached at a second session of the London Conference on Germany. One called for the convening of a German assembly by September 1 that would draft a constitution for a West German state. Another provided that the new nation would be economically integrated into Western Europe. A third agreement created an international authority designed to oversee the Ruhr industrial basin. A fourth agreement provided that U.S. forces would stay indefinitely in Germany. And, finally, the Americans, British, and French promised to coordinate more closely their economic policies in their respective zones. As a step in this direction, on June 18 the three Western powers began to introduce a common currency into their occupation zones.[41]

## The Berlin Blockade

The Soviets were alarmed by the steps to unify the western zones. They regarded the creation of a West German state tied militarily, politically, and economically to the enormous power of the United States as a new German menace. To forestall this development, the Soviets applied pressure to the most vulnerable Western position in Germany, the divided city of Berlin, 125 miles deep inside the Soviet zone. Taking advantage of the absence of a formal agreement concerning the access rights of the Western powers to the city, the Soviets began to restrict ground travel to West Berlin on March 31, 1948. On June 24 the Soviets responded to the implementation of the new currency arrangement in the western zones by halting all western land traffic into the city.[42]

On June 28 Truman responded with determination to the Soviet blockade of Berlin. "We [are] going to stay, period," Forrestal recalled the president saying. As Marshall saw the situation, "We had the alternative of following a firm policy in Berlin or accepting the consequences of the failure of the rest of our European policy." Accordingly, the United States reacted strongly to the Soviet blockade. A Western counterblockade of the Soviet zone was implemented, denying the Soviets badly needed industrial goods, and a massive airlift of supplies into West Berlin was begun. Further, on July 15 the United States ordered, with British approval, the dispatch of sixty B-29s to airbases in Britain. Although the planes were dubbed "atomic bombers" by the press, they were not equipped to carry nuclear weapons; in all probability, however, this was not known by the Soviets. As a result, the threat of American nuclear retaliation against the Soviet Union, once tacit, was now explicit.[43]

The threat of nuclear destruction, however, was not the primary factor responsible for the Soviet decision to end the blockade the following May. Not only was the Soviet effort unable to dislodge the Western powers from Berlin, the Western counterblockade of the Soviet zone proved to be painful as well. Worse, from the Soviet perspective, the Berlin blockade also hastened rather than forestalled the creation of a West German state, the German Federal Republic in May 1949. (The Soviets retaliated later that year by organizing a puppet government, styled the German Democratic Republic, in the eastern zone, thereby completing the division of Europe into rival spheres of Soviet and American influence.) Equally, if not more, painful for the Soviets, the Berlin blockade proved to be a major impetus for drawing the United States into an alliance with the West Europeans, thereby ultimately creating an American military presence on the Continent, a development Stalin had long sought to prevent.[44]

## The Washington Exploratory Talks

On July 6, 1948, shortly after the Berlin blockade began, representatives of the United States, Britain, France, Canada, Belgium, the Netherlands, and Luxembourg began a series of meetings in Washington to determine the nature of America's military association with the Brussels powers. Simultaneously, in accordance with a revised version of NSC 9--NSC 9/2--which was approved in early June, the United States began discussions in London with the Western Union to devise a common strategy to resist Soviet aggression and to draw up a coordinated military supply plan.[45]

The American position for the Washington talks was governed by another version of NSC 9--NSC 9/3--which President Truman had approved on July 2. While NSC 9/3 recommended full compliance with the Vandenberg Resolution, it expressed the hope that the development of a common military strategy, and an assistance program based on the concept of reciprocal aid, would suffice to meet the expanded American commitment to Western Europe. However, NSC 9/3 also stated that if "some further political commitment was necessary at this time to bolster public confidence in Western Europe, the U.S. Government should discuss with the parties to the Brussels Treaty some form of association by the U.S., and if possible Canada, along the lines recommended in the Senate [Vandenberg] resolution." It concluded by adding that "nothing should be done requiring congressional action prior to next January," that is, after the inauguration, to avoid making an alliance treaty a bone of contention in the approaching presidential election.[46]

Needless to say, for the very same reason--fear of isolationist sentiment--the Truman administration was opposed even to discussions concerning the sending of American combat troops to Europe. Moreover, American policymakers did not yet believe that a major U.S. military presence on the Continent was necessary, for few thought that the Soviets were preparing an attack on Western Europe. Charles Bohlen considered the value of a North Atlantic alliance to be primarily "psychological" in nature. It would revive the morale of the West and particularly of the French, who continued to view an American alliance as insurance at least as much against German aggression as against an attack from the Soviet Union.[47]

On August 6, however, the French flatly stated that they were dissatisfied with the type of alliance envisioned by the Americans. Modeled as it was on the Rio Pact, the French viewed it as nothing more than a consultative agreement that, because it shunned "precise engagements of a military character," was "insufficient" to deal with the Soviet menace. The French insisted that the treaty of alliance must be based upon a "more precise and definite mutual obligation" than was contained in the Rio Pact. They also demanded the creation of a unified Western military command structure as well as the immediate dispatch of American military supplies and combat troops to France. The French attitude so enraged Marshall that he threatened to end the Washington talks forthwith. Their demands were "fantastic," Ambassador Caffery informed the French government, since it was the United States, and not France, that was "doing the favors." Nevertheless, Marshall also realized that French support was necessary to implement the American conception of the Atlantic pact as well as to win their acceptance of Germany's economic revitalization. Consequently, in August the administration agreed to reequip the three French divisions stationed in Germany.[48]

As a result of this American concession, the French dropped their overt opposition to the U.S. plan for the Atlantic alliance, and the Washington talks ended on September 9 with the Truman administration securing essentially what it had wanted. In the Washington Paper, as the summary of the talks was called, it was agreed that a North Atlantic security system would be the product of a formal treaty based upon the Vandenberg Resolution and modeled primarily on the Rio Pact and only secondarily on the Brussels Treaty. As such, the Vandenberg Resolution's provisions calling for "self help and mutual aid" meant that American military assistance would supplement, not replace, European defense efforts. The Rio Pact pattern, eventually embodied in Article 5 of the North Atlantic Treaty, would ensure that, rather than the automatic military assistance the Europeans desired, the U.S. response to aggression in the area covered by the alliance would be governed by "constitutional processes," thereby requiring congressional approval. In addition, it was decided that Denmark, Norway, Iceland, Portugal, Sweden, Ireland, and eventually Italy would be considered for membership in the alliance. Although Truman initially opposed including Italy in the alliance, because she was not an Atlantic power, Acheson was able to persuade him to change his mind. Not only was France likely to block completion of the alliance until Italy was included, Acheson pointed out to the president, Italy would play a vital role in the defense of the Mediterranean. The ultimate membership of western Germany and Franco's Spain was also envisioned but put off until public opinion could be prepared to accept the idea.[49]

By October 29, 1948, Canada and all the Brussels powers had informed the United States that they were ready to begin negotiations on a North Atlantic treaty. They asked Washington to suggest a starting date for the talks. But again the Truman administration decided to wait until after the November presidential election before beginning the negotiations. Truman recalled in his memoirs that he had "always kept in mind the lesson of Wilson's failure in 1920." He added that he "meant to have legislative cooperation."[50]

## Military Planning

While the United States and Western Europe were taking the initial steps toward a North Atlantic alliance, they also moved steadily toward a unified military strategy. The defense ministers of the Western Union had already stated, in the spring of 1948, that "in the event of an attack by Russia, the five [Brussels] powers are determined to fight as far east as possible in Germany." This, they believed, would assure "sufficient time for American military power to intervene decisively." However, in the wake of America's rapid military withdrawal from Europe after World War II, the thought that a Soviet attack could be checked in Germany by the Western powers did not have much support from military planners in the United States. In Germany, a mere 200,000 soldiers (including two British, three French, and two American divisions) faced over half a million Soviet troops organized in nearly thirty fully equipped divisions, and many more divisions in the Soviet Union and Eastern Europe. "All the Russians need to get to the Channel," remarked Robert Lovett, "is shoes."[51]

Historian Matthew A. Evangelista, on the other hand, argues that Allied military planners exaggerated the capabilty of the Soviets to launch a successful invasion of Western Europe. Not only did the Soviets lack the economic power to wage a major war with the Western powers, they did not have the military superiority Westerners believed they had during the immediate postwar years. Although the Soviets possessed far more combat divisions than those of the West, probably as many as 175, most of those divisions were not at full combat strength, and most of their troops were engaged in occupation duties in Eastern Europe and reconstruction work in the Soviet Union. For this reason, in Evangelista's estimation, only thirty-one Soviet divisions could have been used in a surprise attack on Western Europe, rather than the sixty-seven the Joint Chiefs of Staff originally estimated in 1947. Moreover, even though the Western powers had fewer divisions than the Soviets, Western divisions had more men per division (16,000-18,000) than those of the Soviet Union (9,000-12,000). When total available manpower of the Western powers in Germany and Austria (about 400,000 troops) is added to that of the home armies of France (270,000), the Netherlands (108,000), Belgium (50,000), and Denmark (22,000), Evangelista argues, the Western powers would have had more than adequate manpower to check a Soviet attack. He also asserts that both the Soviets and Western military planners came to realize that the balance of military power in Europe was roughly equal, but that the Joint Chiefs of Staff continued to use their initial, and inaccurate, higher estimate of Soviet military power. "It is difficult to avoid the impression," Evangelista concludes, "that many in the West intentionally exaggerated the Soviet conventional threat to Europe in order to gain U.S. congressional and popular support for the NATO alliance."[52]

The best that could be done with the forces on hand, American military planners stated, in a war plan (code named HALFMOON) that was approved by the Joint Chiefs of Staff in March 1948, would be to conduct an orderly retreat of the British and U.S. occupation forces in Germany to the Channel ports, where they could be transported to Britain, as they were during the battle of Dunkirk in World War II. Once American and British forces had been reinforced in Britain, another invasion of the Continent would take place to liberate the areas occupied by the Red Army. In the meantime, Soviet military installations and industrial centers would be subjected to Anglo-American strategic bombardment, including atomic bombs.[53]

However, America's military planners did not know that, at least until 1950, the United States had neither the bombs nor the bombers to implement a successful strategic attack upon the Soviet Union. In the spring of 1947 the United States had no more than a dozen atomic bombs--none of them ready for immediate use-- and probably no more than 100 nuclear weapons by the end of 1948. At the start of 1948, the Air Force had only thirty-three bombers capable of carrying atomic bombs. Furthermore, a number of the twenty targeted cities were beyond the maximum range of the B-29s based in Western Europe. In effect, at least until 1950, the Western powers would have been hard pressed to halt a Soviet offensive beyond the Rhine, let alone on it.[54]

Still, in 1948, and particularly after the Berlin blockade had begun, the Anglo-American occupation forces in Germany, despite their small size, began to acquire a symbolic role as a barrier to the further westward expansion of Soviet influence. The decision to make a stand on the Continent, rather than to withdraw from it, first appeared in a National Security Study, NSC 20/4, which was approved by the president on November 24, 1948. The continental strategy, however, was motivated not only by political factors, but by economic and strategic considerations as well. American planners realized that they could not expect France to incur the risks of alienating the Soviet Union by participating in the Economic Recovery Program, fusing the French occupation zone in Germany with Bizonia, and joining a North Atlantic alliance, if the United States and Britain planned to withdraw as rapidly as possible from the Continent in the event of war. Moreover, having decided to invest $12 billion in the economic rehabilitation of Western Europe under the Marshall Plan, it made no sense to hand over those resources to the Soviets without a fight.[55]

The decision to stand in Europe proved to be a revolutionary change in the traditional strategic doctrine of the United States, which had always rejected a permanent American military presence on the Continent. The decision had far-reaching consequences. It meant that any Soviet attack against Western Europe--in spite of the constitutional-process requirement that eventually would be contained in Article 5 of the North Atlantic Treaty--would automatically involve the United States in military action against the Soviet Union. In effect, the United States became a de facto member of a European alliance even before the negotiations for the North Atlantic Treaty were concluded.

Now that it was accepted that U.S. forces would fight on the Continent, questions of command, weapons, equipment, supply, and reinforcement had to be considered. In the wake of the Berlin crisis, France wanted to coordinate an emergency war plan with the Americans and British and to name a commander-in-chief for the Western forces in Germany. In response, the Joint Chiefs of Staff authorized General Clay to coordinate his plans with the French and British. And, pending the conclusion of the North Atlantic alliance, Truman accepted Marshall's recommendation to place American occupation troops in Germany under the command of Field Marshal Montgomery, who was appointed the commander of Western Union forces in October. But the president added "that we must be very careful not to allow a foreign commander to use up our own men before he goes into action *in toto*." As much as any other factor, the decision to place U.S. forces in Germany under a foreign commander dictated full American participation in the emerging alliance.[56]

## The Negotiation of the North Atlantic Treaty

Shortly after Truman's stunning upset victory over his Republican rival, Governor Thomas E. Dewey of New York, the United States and the European powers began negotiations for a North Atlantic alliance. By December 24, 1948, the draft of a treaty was completed. Article 3 of the draft treaty would require all signatories to provide "continuous and effective self help and mutual aid." Article 4 would oblige them to consult with each other regarding any threat to the territorial integrity, political independence, or security of any member state. Article 5, the so-called heart of the treaty, provided that an attack against any one of the signatories would be regarded as an attack against all, requiring the parties to respond to any such aggression by taking appropriate individual and collective action. It was also provided in Article 5 to limit membership, as far as possible, to the countries of the immediate North Atlantic area. Later, however, it was decided to include in the area of the alliance both Italy, because of its vital position in the Mediterranean, and Algeria, because it still was a part of metropolitan France. Article 8 called for the establishment of a council and a defense committee to deal with matters concerning implementation of the treaty. At first, agreement on the duration of the treaty was not possible. But eventually it was agreed that the treaty would extend twenty years (unless it was renewed), that it would be reviewed after ten years, and that any member was free to withdraw from the alliance after giving one-year notice of its intention to do so.[57]

The initial draft of the treaty, however, was not acceptable to key members of the Senate. In particular, Senators Vandenberg, Connally, and Henry Cabot Lodge, Jr. (the grandson of Woodrow Wilson's arch-rival), were not happy with the original version of Article 5, which stated in part that each member would take "forthwith such military or other action, individually and in concert with the other Parties, as may be necessary to restore and assure the security of the North Atlantic area." To these senators, Article 5 looked like an automatic obligation to declare war. In February 1949 they told Dean Acheson, who succeeded Marshall as secretary of state the preceding month, that they hoped it would be possible "to find more neutral language than that contained in the present draft." But the French complained that other alliances were far more binding and that "a bad impression" would result "if the wording of the Atlantic Pact were weaker than the Rio Pact."[58]

Under senatorial pressure, however, Acheson provided the Senate Foreign Relations Committee with a revised version of the treaty. In it, Article 5 was changed to read that each member would "assist the party or parties so attacked by taking forthwith, individually and in concert with the other parties, such action, including the use of armed forces, as it deems necessary to restore and maintain the security of the North Atlantic area." Another article, Article 11, stated that all the provisions of the treaty were to be "carried out by the Parties in accordance with their respective constitutional processes." In effect, the revised treaty did not bind the United States to the military defense of Western Europe. In fact, as historian Timothy P. Ireland points out, a strict military commitment would not exist until sufficient U.S. troops were sent to Europe to make an organized defense of the Continent possible. And this would not occur until 1951.[59]

## Ratification of the North Atlantic Treaty

On April 4, 1949, the North Atlantic Treaty was signed in an elaborate ceremony in Washington. But it still had to gain the approval of the U.S. Senate before it went into effect. Two major hurdles stood in the path of ratification. One involved the nature of the guarantee provided by Article 5, and the other, its implementation under Article 3. The State Department had the unenviable responsibility of trying to convince the West Europeans that the American commitment to their defense would be strong while, at the same time, assuring the Congress that the treaty did not constitute an "entangling" military alliance.[60]

The administration's difficulties were complicated by the fact that a number of powerful senators were prepared to fight the treaty "every step of the way." Among the opponents of the treaty were hard-core isolationists, like Forrest Donnell (Rep.-Mo.), William Jenner (Rep.-Ind.) and Kenneth Wherry (Rep.-Neb.). Although ardent anticommunists, these senators were also strongly opposed to "automatic" commitments to use force. Consequently, they concentrated their attack on what was for them the treaty's challenge, contained in

Article 5, to Congress' exclusive right to declare war. Donnell in particular was indignant when a newspaper reported that Acheson had told Norwegian Foreign Minister Oskar Lange that "in joining the Alliance, the American Government would subscribe to the principle that an attack on one member nation was an attack on all, and this would be interpreted as a moral commitment to fight." Donnell vigorously protested "the inclusion in the pact of any such provision."[61]

Reflecting the concern of these senators, still another isolationist, Senator Robert A. Taft, argued that the treaty was in fact a military alliance that would automatically drag the United States into a European war. Like George Kennan, Taft wanted the North Atlantic Treaty to provide nothing more than a political guarantee, analogous to the Monroe Doctrine, with no provisions for military assistance, which, he believed, would preserve the ability of the United States to decide which European wars it would enter. But while Taft was unhappy with Article 5 of the treaty, he was even more dissatisfied with Article 3, which, he insisted, required the United States to provide the West Europeans with massive amounts of military assistance--Taft estimated that as much as $24 billion, enough to equip sixty divisions, might be necessary.[62]

In fact, there was some substance to Taft's charge. To compensate for the weakening of Article 5, the French had turned to the "mutual aid" clause of Article 3 as a way to involve the United States more deeply in Europe's security. To the French, the definition of "mutual aid" required American military assistance to help Western Europe rearm. Many senators, on the other hand, were of the opinion that nothing in the proposed treaty, including Article 3, required the United States to supply military equipment to the Europeans. Said Vandenberg, "I think a man can vote for this treaty and not vote for a nickel to implement it." In other words, to many senators like Vandenberg, the treaty itself was sufficient to deter Soviet aggression; a massive and expensive program to rearm the West European countries, on the other hand, was not needed.[63]

At first, Acheson, in testimony before the Senate Foreign Relations Committee, tried to persuade the senators that they were free to reject the administration's Military Assistance Program (MAP), most of whose $1.5 billion initial appropriation would go to the West European nations, and still approve the North Atlantic Treaty. But under questioning, he was forced to admit that Article 3 of the treaty did in fact commit the United States to adhere to the principle of "mutual aid," and, as a consequence, the treaty and MAP were quite inseparable. In the end, Article 3 and MAP survived the hearings largely because consideration of the military aid program was postponed until after the treaty had been approved. As a result, most senators were led to believe that they could vote for the treaty without necessarily being obliged to support a costly military assistance program.[64]

Interestingly, all of the old--that is, pre-World War II--isolationists did not oppose the treaty. In fact, some, like Senators Vandenberg and Alexander Wiley (Rep.-Wis), were among the treaty's staunchest defenders. Vandenberg argued that neither of the two world wars would have occurred had the North Atlantic Treaty existed before them. Senator Wiley suggested that the treaty would not only prevent Western Europe from falling "into Russia's lap," but the economic cooperation called for in Article 2 could help to relieve unemployment in the United States.[65]

On the other hand, more than a few critics of the treaty feared that it would lead the United States into war. Said Mrs. Clifford A. Bender, a Methodist Church spokeswoman: "History indicates that the most that can be achieved by military alliances is a temporary balance of power, while they eventually give rise to increasing insecurity and a menacing arms race, ending in war." Perhaps the most vicious attack on the treaty came from Henry Wallace, who had challenged Truman for the presidency in the 1948 election. Wallace argued that the treaty would harden differences between the United States and the Soviet Union, and could lead to war. He added that it also would drain American resources, create a dependent Europe, and undermine the credibility of the United Nations.[66]

To overcome opposition to the treaty itself, the administration followed a strategy designed to convince the Senate that, rather than being a drastic departure from America's traditional isolationist policy, the treaty was in line with the most sacred "isolationist" pronouncements of the past. In this sense, the administration argued that the treaty was, like the Monroe Doctrine, a warning to potential aggressors. The treaty was also held to be in accord with Washington's Farewell Address, which had recommended temporary alliances to deal with extraordinary emergencies. Some argued that the North Atlantic alliance was unlike traditional European alliances because it was purely defensive in nature.[67]

In the end, the administration's strategy succeeded in persuading the overwhelming majority of senators that the treaty was only an extension of, rather than a major departure from, America's traditional policy toward Europe. On July 21, 1949, the Senate approved the treaty by an 82 to 13 margin. Only three of the nine remaining isolationists who had opposed American involvement in the last European war--Taft, William Langer, and Edwin C. Johnson--voted against the treaty.[68]

## The Creation of NATO

On the day Truman signed the North Atlantic Treaty, July 25, 1949, he also sent to the Congress a one-year, $1.5 billion Mutual Defense Assistance bill, thereby confirming the intimate linkage between the two policies. Opponents of the bill repeated many of the same arguments that were used against the treaty. It would, they argued, represent the final abandonment of the United Nations and serve as the prelude to the deployment in Europe of U.S. combat forces. War, in their opinion, could be the only result. The administration, in response, assured the Senate that it had no intention of either sending additional U.S. troops across the Atlantic or of rearming Germany in order to shore up Europe's defenses. "We are not arming ourselves and our friends to start a fight with anybody," Truman argued. "We are building defenses so that we won't have to fight." He asked, "Which is better, to make expenditures to save the peace, or to risk all our resources and assets in another war?" Nevertheless, it was not until October 6, two weeks after Truman had announced the explosion of a Soviet atomic bomb in late August, that the Congress passed the Mutual Defense Assistance bill. The vote in the House was 224 to 109 in favor, while the margin in the Senate was 55 to 24.[69]

However, before the funds for the Mutual Defense Assistance bill could be released, Congress had deferred the bulk of the aid until an organizational structure for the alliance had been created that included Germany. The move was initiated by Vandenberg and John Foster Dulles (who was appointed to fill a vacancy in one of New York's Senate seats) because they feared that, if France received extensive military equipment and Germany was excluded from the alliance, the Germans might join the Soviet bloc.[70]

The result was the creation of the North Atlantic Treaty Organization (NATO). The new organization included a North Atlantic Council (composed of the alliance's foreign ministers), a Defense Committee (made up of defense ministers), a Defense Financial and Economic Committee (in which finance ministers would be represented), a Military Committee (made up of the alliance's chiefs of staff), a Military Production and Supply Board, and five Regional Planning Groups. The organization of the regional groupings expressed the strategic concerns of the alliance's member states. The Northern European Group included Denmark, Norway, and Britain. The Western European Group comprised Belgium, France, Luxembourg, the Netherlands, and Britain. The Southern European-Western Mediterranean Group included France, Italy, and Britain. A fourth group consisted of only Canada and the United States. The fifth grouping, the North Atlantic Group, included all of the members of the alliance except Italy and Luxembourg. Reflecting the vestiges of American isolationist sentiment, the United States accepted full membership in only the latter two groups. It became only a "consulting member" on the planning committees of the first three groupings. With NATO established, Truman was able to approve the release to the Europeans of Mutual Defense Assistance payments.[71]

On January 27, 1950, the president also approved a "Strategic Concept" for the new alliance. Again indicative of the American desire to play a limited role in Europe's defense, the strategic guidance required each member of the alliance to undertake tasks for which, considering its location and capabilities, it was "best suited." The primary U.S. responsibility would be strategic bombing ("with all types of weapons") and cooperation with Britain in securing sea and air lanes. The guidance stipulated that, "Initially, the hard core of ground forces will come from European nations. Other nations will give aid with the least possible delay and in accordance with over-all plans."[72]

Despite the Truman administration's arguments to the contrary, by ratifying the North Atlantic Treaty and then participating in the creation of NATO, the United States had abandoned two of its most time-honored traditions: avoiding entanglement in permanent alliances, a policy first annunciated in George Washington's Farewell Address, and maintaining the separation between Europe's affairs and those of the Western Hemisphere, a policy first promulgated in the Monroe Doctrine. The Truman administration, in effect, had persuaded the American people to abandon, perhaps once and for all, an isolationist posture toward Europe that was over three centuries old.

# Conclusion:
# The Entangling Alliance

Why did the United States pursue an isolationist policy toward Europe for most of its history? Why did Americans abandon isolationism in the twentieth century?

The roots of American isolationism lie deep in the nation's colonial past. The first settlers, separated from Europe by distance and time, were compelled by necessity to develop their own patterns of behavior and thought, and ultimately their own nation. The relative peace, freedom, and economic opportunity that the New World offered contrasted quite glaringly with the constant warfare, social and economic inequity, religious intolerance, and political oppression that characterized the Old World. Reinforced by the Declaration of Independence and the Constitution, Americans quite easily came to regard themselves as morally and politically superior to Europeans. This sense of superiority provided additional justification for the desire most Americans possessed to separate themselves as much as possible from Europe's problems.

American isolationism was also encouraged by George Washington's 1796 Farewell Address. In it, the first president urged his fellow citizens to avoid permanent alliances in order to concentrate their energy on developing the young nation. James Monroe, in his declaration of 1823, reinforced the advice of the Farewell Address by stating that the United States had no intention to interfere in Europe's affairs and, in turn, would tolerate no further European colonization in the New World.

Yet while the first presidents regarded American nonentanglement in Europe's political problems as essential to the welfare of the young nation, they also realized that its peace, prosperity, and independence were to a great extent dependent on the existence of a balance of power in Europe. For this reason, they did not exclude the possibility of American participation in temporary alliances or military action designed to maintain the European balance of power. Indeed, the effectiveness of the Monroe Doctrine throughout most of the nineteenth century was based on the support the British navy gave it, for until late in the century America's navy could not enforce it. Nor did the first presidents think that America's isolation from Europe's political affairs need be permanent. One day, they foresaw, America would be sufficiently strong to play a major role in the affairs of the world as well as in Europe.

Throughout the last three-quarters of the nineteenth century, however, Americans concentrated on domestic affairs, including the Civil War, Reconstruction, settlement of the West, and industrialization. The energy Americans gave to these affairs, and the strength the nation acquired by successfully doing so, only augmented the American proclivity to remain secure behind the oceans and avoid European entanglements. However, as the United States industrialized, and its trade and foreign investments grew, Americans found themselves increasingly involved in the affairs of the world as well as the European continent. In addition, technological developments, including steel battleships and submarines, began to reduce the security offered the nation by the Atlantic and Pacific oceans.

Reacting to these developments at the dawn of the twentieth century, Theodore Roosevelt was the first president to insist that the United States could no longer maintain an isolationist attitude toward Europe. Roosevelt believed that the security of the United States was intimately tied to a strong U.S. navy patrolling the Atlantic and the Pacific Oceans and a close American friendship with Great Britain. He further argued that the United States must play a major role in maintaining a balance of power in Europe, one that he believed was increasingly threatened by the expansion of German military power.

However, neither the American people nor either of Roosevelt's two immediate successors, William Howard Taft and Woodrow Wilson, supported the idea of an American role in maintaining the European balance of power. Most Americans still believed that the oceans would continue to protect the United States from aggression. Even after World War I began and Germany threatened to overrun the Continent, Americans did not favor U.S. military intervention in the conflict. Eventually the United States did enter the war. But it did so primarily to uphold U.S. neutral rights disregarded by Germany's decision to launch unrestricted submarine attacks on American shipping. Only a few Americans saw intervention as a necessary way to restore the European balance of power now jeopardized by German military power.

Indeed, after victory was achieved, rather than reestablishing the balance of power in Europe, perhaps by engaging the United States in an alliance with Britain and France, Woodrow Wilson sought to establish a community of power based on American membership in the League of Nations and U.S. participation in a program of advancing free trade, disarmament, and the mediation of international disputes.

For a variety reasons, however, the United States Senate rejected the Treaty of Versailles and with it American participation in the League of Nations. More than a few Americans feared that the League of Nations would unduly restrict U.S. sovereignty and violate the Monroe Doctrine. Some believed the treaty was excessively harsh toward Germany and would eventually involve the United States in another war with that country. Ultimately, Wilson's refusal to accept reservations favored by Senator Henry Cabot Lodge doomed the treaty to extinction in the Senate.

Still, after the treaty was rejected, the United States only partly reverted to isolationism. While rejecting a military commitment to Europe's security, the administrations of Warren Harding, Calvin Coolidge, and Herbert Hoover expanded America's involvement in the economic and political affairs of the Continent. These administrations sent American observers to the League of Nations, participated in disarmament conferences with European nations, and facilitated American private loans to Germany. But they also refused to give the Europeans, and particularly the French, the kind of security guarantees that may have averted the increase in international tensions that followed in the wake of the Great Depression and the rise to power in Germany of Adolf Hitler.

While Americans were dismayed by Hitler's program to destroy the Versailles system, they were much more upset with America's former allies, Britain and France, and other European nations that had defaulted on war debts owed to the United States. In 1934 Congress passed the Johnson Debt Default Act, which prohibited American loans to nations in default. The following year witnessed the high-water mark of interwar isolationist sentiment when Congress passed the first Neutrality Act, which was designed to prevent American involvement in foreign wars by prohibiting loans to belligerent nations.

President Franklin D. Roosevelt, like his predecessor and distant cousin Theodore, believed the United States had to play a major role in maintaining not only a European, but also a world, balance of power, which was increasingly menaced in the thirties by the rise of militarists in Germany, Italy, and Japan. But being an astute politician, Roosevelt followed an oblique, and often duplicitous, strategy in countering the prevailing isolationist sentiment in the United States. After proclaiming his determination to maintain American neutrality, he undertook a program of public education designed to alert the American people to the growing menace of the Axis nations. He also worked to revise the Neutrality Act, and succeeded in doing so, to the point where it became incapable of fulfilling its initial objective--keeping America out of war.

Roosevelt also encouraged, perhaps belatedly and inadequately, in the opinion of some historians, the British to take the lead in resisting Axis aggression in Europe and Asia. Only after war erupted in Europe, and Winston Churchill became prime minister in May 1940, was it possible for Roosevelt to form an effective collaborative relationship with Britain. The Destroyer Deal, the Lend-Lease Act, and U.S. naval patrol of the Atlantic were the major steps in America's growing involvement in the defense of Great Britain.

Roosevelt also took the first steps toward bringing the Soviet Union into a "Grand Alliance" that would eventually defeat the Axis nations. Soon after the Soviet Union was invaded by the Germans in June 1941, Roosevelt initiated an all-out effort to supply the Soviet war effort, culminating in the extension of Lend-Lease to the Soviet Union four months later.

But events in the Far East, rather than in Europe, were ultimately responsible for bringing the United States into the war. Not willing to see China succumb to Japanese aggression, Roosevelt gradually increased the economic pressure on Japan to the point where the Japanese had to choose between two excruciating alternatives: either the abandonment of their program to conquer much of the Far East or war with the United States. In launching a surprise attack on Pearl Harbor and other U.S. possessions in the Pacific, they opted for the latter alternative.

Roosevelt hoped that the Grand Alliance, in addition to bringing about the defeat of the Axis nations, his primary objective during the war, would serve as the foundation for a stable postwar international system. At the Tehran Conference in November and December 1943, the outlines of such a postwar world were drawn. There Roosevelt, Churchill, and Stalin agreed on the creation of the United Nations, the postwar Soviet annexation of the Baltic states, altered boundaries for Poland, the need for permanent restraints on German and Japanese power, and a predominant role for the Big Three plus China in maintaining world peace.

However, even before the Axis nations were defeated, problems emerged that would eventually tear apart the Grand Alliance. They included the postwar role of the United Nations and atomic energy, Soviet occupation policy in Eastern Europe, and the future of Germany. Roosevelt tried to ameliorate the harshness of Soviet occupation policy in Eastern Europe by attempting to assure Stalin that the United States posed no threat to the Soviet Union and by trying to gain Soviet adherence to the principles of the Atlantic Charter, the Declaration on Liberated Europe, and the United Nations Charter. But while he overestimated his ability to influence the Soviet dictator, he never completely counted on gaining Stalin's trust. He demonstrated this, among other ways, by refusing to share American atomic know-how and technology with the Soviets. Apparently, the atomic bomb was the insurance Roosevelt felt he needed in case friendly postwar relations with the Soviets proved to be impossible.

Yet, in spite of any personal doubts Roosevelt may have had about the future of Soviet-American relations, he never publicized them. Fearing the revival of isolationist sentiment after the war, Roosevelt refused to consider concluding a postwar alliance with Britain and France in the event that East-West relations soured. And, for the same reason, he also rejected an American military presence on the Continent beyond a one- or two-year occupation of Germany. His refusal to commit the United States to the postwar security of Europe, beyond support for the United Nations Charter, meant that the transition from isolationism to more extensive and permanent American involvement in Europe's defense would occur during the administration of his successor, Harry S. Truman.

The development of an American commitment to European security during Truman's administration was a gradual and unven process. Indeed, at the end of the war in Europe, as Roosevelt had planned, the United States engaged in a rapid withdrawal of its forces from the Continent, leaving small occupation forces in Germany as the legacy of its once powerful military presence in Europe. At the end of the war, the Truman administration considered Germany the greatest potential threat to European peace, and clearly expected the Soviets and the British to bear the burden of keeping her in check for the foreseeable future.

But by 1947 the United States came to see the Soviet Union, not Germany, as the major obstacle to lasting peace on the Continent. The Soviets not only had established communist regimes in the areas of Europe they had liberated from the Nazis, but they also appeared to threaten the states of Western Europe that had been liberated by the Anglo-American armies.

The nature of the Soviet threat to Western Europe has been a matter of controversy to historians. To be sure, in the late 1940s, few of America's military or political leaders believed that the Soviet Union was contemplating a military invasion of Western Europe. Although the Soviets had substantial forces in Eastern Europe, the extensive damage the Soviet Union had suffered during the war, as well as the even more ruinous destruction which the Soviet Union could expect to suffer from American atom bombs if another war erupted, made another conflict unthinkable both for the Soviets and for the West, at least for the foreseeable future.

But Truman, lacking his predecessor's diplomatic skills, agitated by Soviet occupation policy in Eastern Europe and aggressive moves in the eastern Mediterranean and Iran, pressured by hardliners in the Republican Party and from within his own administration, and facing a presidential election campaign in 1948, believed he no longer could afford to follow Roosevelt's conciliatory approach toward the Soviet Union. As a result, by 1947 containment replaced conciliation.

The communist coup in Czechoslovakia, the Soviet Union's pressure on Finland and Norway, and the Soviet blockade of Berlin--all of which were directly related to the end of the conciliatory American policy toward the Soviet Union-- only reinforced an emerging Cold War consensus in the West that held that, if the United States once again withdrew into isolation, Western Europe would again fall under the domination of an aggressive power, and American military forces again would have to fight on the Continent.

After the death and destruction caused by the world wars, both of which began in Europe, and both of which eventually involved the United States, the American people, prompted in part by the Truman administration, came to the realization that it would be far less expensive in lives and wealth to attempt to prevent another such conflict than to engage in it after it had begun. Moreover, the security once provided by the oceans continued to diminish. The development of long-range aircraft made the United States increasingly vulnerable to attack, as the Japanese demonstrated so dramatically at Pearl Harbor. As a result, Americans gradually came to believe that their nation's defensive frontiers should be established not only in the western Pacific but on the European continent as well.

But even after the Soviet Union's aggressive tendencies had been confirmed in the eyes of Americans, the Truman administration sought to limit America's new commitment to European security to primarily economic assistance, believing that Britain could and would bear the major military responsibility for defending the Continent against the Soviets. As a result, in the Truman Doctrine and, far more extensively, in the Marshall Plan, the United States made a major economic commitment to the security of noncommunist Europe.

Yet the British government was able to convince the administration that American economic assistance would not be enough, and that a U.S. military commitment to Europe was needed to check Soviet aggression. British Foreign Secretary Ernest Bevin, in particular, was able to overcome U.S. opposition to joining an alliance with Europe by proposing a North Atlantic security pact, which in the end proved acceptable to the Americans. The first step in the conclusion of a North Atlantic alliance was the 1947 Anglo-French Treaty of Dunkirk. Although directed at Germany, the Dunkirk Treaty served as the nucleus of the Brussels Pact of 1948, which bound Britain and France to the defense of the Benelux countries as well as themselves. The Brussels Pact, in turn, served as the nucleus of the much wider North Atlantic pact, which bound the United States and Canada to the defense of fourteen European countries.

France and, more passively, Germany also played important roles in the creation of NATO. The Truman administration came to see a Germany rehabilitated both politically and economically not only as a powerful barrier to Soviet domination of Western Europe, but also as a vital ingredient in the economic recovery of Europe. In the wake of the inability of the Western powers to reach an agreement with the Soviet Union on common Allied policy toward Germany, the United States took the lead in uniting into one political and economic entity the Western occupation zones. The West Germans were given Marshall Plan aid and eventually were organized into an independent state.

To restore West Germany, however, the United States had to satisfy the security concerns of the French, who feared the revival of German militarism perhaps even more than the military power of the Soviet Union. Cognizant that the United States had ignored French security concerns before both world wars, the Truman administration took steps to assure France that America would not abandon her again. In September 1946 Secretary of State James Byrnes promised that U.S. occupation troops would remain in Germany indefinitely. In ratifying the North Atlantic Treaty, the United States assured France that America would defend her against aggression from whatever source, Germany or the Soviet Union.

Key Truman administration officials also played major roles in the creation of NATO, not only by helping to draft the North Atlantic Treaty, but also by gaining support for the treaty's ratification. Truman, whose own support was obviously vital to the creation of NATO, singled out the contribution of Secretary of State Dean Acheson. According to the president, Acheson drove home "the point that NATO would have no meaning at all unless a really joint effort was made at common defense and mutual aid." But the roles of other critical administration players--including George Marshall, Robert Lovett, and John Hickerson--cannot be ignored. On the congressional side, the role of Senator Vandenberg was important. With considerable help from the State Department, Vandenberg drafted the resolution that, when approved by the Senate, placed that body in line with the administration's effort to conclude an alliance with the West European states.[1]

However, even after the United States had decided to join a North Atlantic alliance, the Truman administration and the Congress opposed an open-ended American commitment to European security. The Europeans favored a North Atlantic alliance based upon the Dunkirk and Brussels treaties, which required an "automatic" commitment to help defend against an armed attack on another signatory by using "all the military and other means" available. The Americans, on the other hand, favored a more limited commitment, one modeled on the Rio Pact, which allowed each signatory to decide on the nature of its response to an aggressor. The nature of the guarantee that finally emerged in the treaty that was signed and ratified in 1949 conformed closely to this American objective.

The Europeans, and particularly the French, sought compensation for the weaker American commitment contained in Article 5 by placing greater emphasis on Article 3, which called for mutual assistance on the part of the treaty's parties. Eventually, in 1951, it was this article, more than Article 5, which would bind the United States to the military defense of the Continent. Once American combat troops returned to the Continent in that year, it would become axiomatic that any

Soviet attack on Western Europe, in spite of Article 5, would automatically bring the United States into another European war. By then, the process of involving the United States in an entangling alliance with European nations would be completed.

# Notes

## PREFACE

1. John Milton Cooper, Jr., *The Vanity of Power: American Isolationism and the First World War, 1914-1917* (Westport, Conn.: 1969), 1-2, 5. For a brief summary of the major interpretations of isolationism, see Cooper, 250-57. Alexander DeConde, "On Twentieth Century Isolationism," in Alexander DeConde, ed., *Isolation and Security: Ideas and Interests in Twentieth Century American Foreign Policy* (Durham, N.C.: 1957), 3-32. See also Manfred Jonas, "Isolationism," in Alexander DeConde, ed., *Encyclopedia of American Foreign Policy* (New York: 1978), 496-506.

2. Albert K. Weinberg, "The Historical Meaning of the Doctrine of Isolationism," *American Political Science Review* 34 (September 1940), 539-47.

## INTRODUCTION

## AMERICAN ISOLATIONISM UNTIL 1901

1. Thomas A. Bailey, *A Diplomatic History of the American People*, 6th ed. (New York: 1958), 22-23. Cushing Strout, *The American Image of the Old World* (New York: 1963), 6.

2. Max Savelle, "Colonial Origins of American Diplomatic Principles," *Pacific Historical Review* 3 (1934), 335.

3. Gerald Stourzh, *Benjamin Franklin and American Foreign Policy*, 2nd. ed. (Chicago: 1969), 120.

4. Moncure Daniel Conway, ed., *Writings of Thomas Paine* (New York: 1894), I, 86, 88; Paine's emphases.

5. Ibid., I, 79; Paine's emphases.

6. Francis Wharton, *The Revolutionary Diplomatic Correspondence of the United States* (Washington, D.C.: 1889), VI, 136.

7. Gaillard Hunt, ed., *Journals of the Continental Congress, 1774-1789* (Washington, D.C.: 1922), XXIV, 394.

8. James D. Richardson, ed., *A Compilation of the Messages and Papers of the Presidents, 1789-1902* (Washington, D.C.: 1904), I, 222-23.

9. Ibid.

10. Ibid. Robert Ellis Jones, "Washington's Farewell Address and Its Applications," in Burton Ira Kaufman, *Washington's Farewell Address: The View from the Twentieth Century* (New York: 1969), 43.

11. Richardson, I, 223. John C. Fitzpatrick, ed., *Writings of George Washington* (Washington, D.C.: 1931-1944), XXXV, 29-31.

12. William Appleman Williams, "The Age of Mercantalism: An Interpretation of the American Political Economy, 1763 1828," *William and Mary Quarterly*, 3rd ser., 15 (October 1958), 419-37, Williams' emphasis.

13. Richardson, I, 323.

14. Adrienne Koch and William Peden, eds., *The Life and Selected Writings of Thomas Jefferson* (New York: 1944), 383, 395, 382.

15. Strout, 28.

16. Worthington C. Ford, ed., *The Writings of John Quincy Adams* (New York: 1917), VII, 49.

17. Edward Howland Tatum, Jr., *The United States and Europe, 1815-1823: A Study in the Background of the Monroe Doctrine* (Berkeley, Calif.: 1936), 244.

18. Andrew A. Lipscomb, ed., *The Writings of Thomas Jefferson* (Washington, D.C.: 1903), XV, 477. Richardson, II, 209, 218. Charles F. Adams, ed., *Memoirs of John Quincy Adams* (Philadelphia: 1874-1877), VI, 179.

19. Koch and Peden, 708.

20. John Bassett Moore, *American Diplomacy* (New York: 1905), 139.

21. Norman A. Graebner, ed., *Ideas and Diplomacy: Readings in the Intellectual Tradition of American Foreign Policy* (New York: 1964), 141.

22. Strout, 35.

23. Foster Rhea Dulles, *America's Rise to World Power, 1898-1954* (New York: 1963), 10-11.

24. Charles A. Beard and G.H.E. Smith, *The Idea of National Interest* (New York: 1934), 361-62.

25. Richardson, VI, 366.

26. Mark Twain, *The Innocents Abroad: Or The New Pilgrims Progress,* in Charles Neider, ed., *The Complete Travel Books of Mark Twain* (Garden City, N.Y.: 1966) I, 170.

27. Richardson, VIII, 301.

28. Carl Schurz, "Manifest Destiny," *Harper's New Monthly Magazine* 87 (October 1893), 743.

# CHAPTER ONE

# THE EMERGENCE OF AMERICAN INTERNATIONALISM, 1901-1921

1. Richard Hofstadter, *The American Political Tradition: And the Men Who Made It* (New York: 1974), 272.

2. Robert Dallek, *The American Style of Foreign Policy: Cultural Politics and Foreign Affairs* (New York: 1983), 34-35.

3. Alfred Thayer Mahan, *The Interest of America in Sea Power: Past and Present* (Boston: 1897). George E. Mowry, *The Era of Theodore Roosevelt, 1900-1912* (New York: 1958), 149. For examples of Roosevelt's application of idealism in the use of U.S. military power, see Frederick W. Marks III, "Morality as a Drive Wheel in the Diplomacy of Theodore Roosevelt," *Diplomatic History* 2 (Winter 1978), 43-62.

4. Manfred Jonas, *The United States and Germany* (Ithaca, N.Y.: 1984), 59-60. Daniel M. Smith, *The Great Departure: The United States and World War I, 1914-1920* (New York: 1965), 10. Thomas A. Bailey, "Dewey and the Germans at Manila Bay," *American Historical Review* 35 (October 1939), 59-81.

5. Roosevelt to Lodge, June 19, 1901, in Henry Cabot Lodge, *Selections from the Correspondence of Theodore Roosevelt and Henry Cabot Lodge* (New York: 1925), I, 493-94. Richard H. Collin, *Theodore Roosevelt, Culture, Diplomacy, and Expansion: A New View of American Imperialism* (Baton Rouge: 1985), 154-86.

6. Spring-Rice to Roosevelt, September 14, 1896, in Stephen Gwynn, ed., *The Letters and Friendships of Sir Cecil Spring-Rice: A Record* (London: 1929), I, 210-11.

7. Roosevelt to Spring-Rice, August 5, 1896, in Elting Morrison, ed., *The Letters of Theodore Roosevelt* (Cambridge, Mass.: 1951), I, 555.

8. Mowry, 148.

9. André Tardieu, "Three Visits to Mr. Roosevelt," *The Independent* 64 (April 16, 1908), 862-63. Raymond A. Esthus, "Isolationism and World Power," *Diplomatic History* 2 (Spring 1978), 117-29.

10. William Henry Harbaugh, *Power and Responsibility: The Life and Times of Theodore Roosevelt* (New York: 1961), 274. Raymond A. Esthus, "The Taft-Katsura Agreement: Reality or Myth?" *Journal of Modern History* 31 (March 1959), 46-51.

11. Mowry, 195. Raymond A. Esthus, *Theodore Roosevelt and the International Rivalries* (Waltham, Mass.: 1970), 66-111.

12. Calvin DeArmond Davis, *The United States and the First Hague Peace Conference* (Ithaca, N.Y.: 1962), 37, 202. Alexander DeConde, *A History of American Foreign Policy*, 2nd. ed. (New York: 1971), 396.

13. Calvin DeArmond Davis, *The United States and the Second Hague Conference: American Diplomacy and International Organization, 1899-1914* (Durham, N.C.: 1976), 140-61. DeConde, *A History of American Foreign Policy*, 396-97.

14. Davis, *The United States and the Second Hague Conference*, 323-26.

15. Ray Stannard Baker and William E. Dodd, eds. *The Public Papers of Woodrow Wilson* (New York: 1925-1927), III, 147.

16. Ibid., II, 294.

17. Robert E. Osgood, *Ideals and Self-Interest in America's Foreign Relations* (Chicago: 1953), 144-45. John Milton Cooper, *The Warrior and the Priest: Woodrow Wilson and Theodore Roosevelt* (Cambridge, Mass.: 1983), 266-87.

18. Alexander L. and Juliette L. George, *Woodrow Wilson and Colonel House: A Personality Study* (New York: 1964), 114, 272, 6, 8. 160.

19. Edwin A. Weinstein, James William Anderson, and Arthur S. Link, "Woodrow Wilson's Personality: A Reappraisal," *Political Science Quarterly* 93 (Winter 1978), 585-98. For the response of the Georges, see Alexander L. and Juliette L. George, "Woodrow Wilson and Colonel House, A Reply to Weinstein, Anderson, and Link," *Political Science Quarterly* 96 (Winter 1981), 641-65, and their "Comments on 'Woodrow Wilson Re-examined: The Mind-Body Controversy Redux and Other Disputations,'" *Political Psychology* 4 (1983), 307-12. For the titles of works dealing with Wilson's health, see Arthur Link, ed., *The Papers of Woodrow Wilson* (Princeton, N.J.: 1966- ), LIV, ix-xi (hereafter cited as *PWW*), and Lloyd E. Ambrosius, *Woodrow Wilson and the American Diplomatic Tradition: The Treaty Fight in Perspective* (New York: 1987), 222, n. 23.

20. Baker and Dodd, III, 226.

21. Ibid., III, 302-7; IV, 407-14.

22. Norman Gordon Levin, Jr., *Woodrow Wilson and World Politics: America's Response to War and Revolution* (New York: 1968), 126.

23. Smith, *The Great Departure*, 25-26. Osgood, 174-75.

24. Kurt Wimer, "Woodrow Wilson and World Order," in Arthur S. Link, ed., *Woodrow Wilson and a Revolutionary World, 1913-1921* (Chapel Hill, N.C.: 1982), 152.

25. Ambrosius, *Woodrow Wilson and the American Diplomatic Tradition*, 17. Arthur S. Link, *Woodrow Wilson and the Progressive Era, 1900-1917* (New York: 1954), 179-80.

26. Link, *Woodrow Wilson and the Progressive Era, 1900-1917*, 185. Osgood, 206-7.

27. Link, *Woodrow Wilson and the Progressive Era*, 180-182. John Milton Cooper, Jr., *The Vanity of Power: American Isolationism and the First World War, 1914-1917* (Westport, Conn: 1969), 87-98.

28. Link, *Woodrow Wilson and the Progressive Era*, 188.

29. Ibid., 190.

30. Arthur S. Link, ed., *Woodrow Wilson: Revolution, War, and Peace* (Arlington Heights, Ill.: 1979), 21-63. U.S. Department of State, *Foreign Relations of the United States: 1915*, Supplement: *The World War* (Washington, D.C.: 1928), 98-100.

31. *Official German Documents Relating to the World War* (New York: 1923), II, 1317-19. See also I, 128-50.

32. Smith, *The Great Departure*, 6.

33. Baker and Dodd, IV, 428-32. Link, *Woodrow Wilson: Revolution, War, and Peace*, 67-68.

34. *Official German Documents*, II, 1337. Baker and Dodd, V, 6-16. Link, *Woodrow Wilson: Revolution, War, and Peace*, 68-71.

35. Baker and Dodd, V, 6-16.

36. Osgood, 143, 273.

37. *Congressional Record*, 65th Cong., special session, April 4, 1917, vol. 54, 223-36, 212-14; 65th Cong., 2nd sess., July 10, 1917, vol. 55, 4893.

38. Robert H. Ferrell, *Woodrow Wilson and World War I, 1917-1921* (New York: 1985), 84, 87. Klaus Schwabe, *Woodrow Wilson, Revolutionary Germany, and Peacemaking, 1918-1919: Missionary Diplomacy and the Realities of Power* (Chapel Hill, N.C.: 1985), 30-39.

39. U.S. Department of State, *Foreign Relations of the United States: 1917, Supplement: The World War* (Washington, D.C.: 1932), I, 24-29. Baker and Dodd, V, 155-62.

40. Baker and Dodd, IV, 414; V, 352-56. Ambrosius, *Woodrow Wilson and the America Diplomatic Tradition*, 53.

41. Albert Shaw, ed., *The Messages and Papers of Woodrow Wilson* (New York: 1924), II, 852.

42. Smith, *The Great Departure*, 108. U.S. Department of State, *Papers Relating to the Foreign Relations of the United States: 1918,* Supplement: *The World War* (Washington, D.C.: 1933), I, 381-83. *PWW*, LI, 416-19.

43. The text of the Treaty of Versailles appears in U.S. Department of State, *Papers Relating to the Foreign Relations of the United States: The Paris Peace Conference, 1919* (Washington, D.C.: 1947), XIII, 57-756 (hereafter cited as *FRUS: PPC*).

44. Link, *Woodrow Wilson: Revolution, War, and Peace*, 97. David Stevenson, "French War Aims and the American Challenge, 1914-1918," *Historical Journal* 22 (1979), 877-94.

45. Ray Stannard Baker, *Woodrow Wilson and World Settlement* (New York, 1922), II, 253-57.

46. Levin, 159-60. *FRUS: PPC*, III, 1002, 972-74; V, 700, 527-28. Baker, *Woodrow Wilson and World Settlement*, III, 494.

47. Link, *Woodrow Wilson: Revolution, War, and Peace*, 102.

48. Ibid., 101.

49. Norman A. Graebner, *America as a World Power: A Realist Appraisal from Wilson to Reagan* (Wilmington, Del.: 1984), xviii-xix. Richard N. Current, "The United States and 'Collective Security,'" in Alexander DeConde, ed., *Isolation and Security: Ideas and Interests in Twentieth Century American Foreign Policy* (Durham, N.C.: 1957), 33-37.

50. Graebner, *America as a World Power*, xix. George M. Trevelyan, *Grey of Fallodon* (Boston: 1937), 356-59. George W. Egerton, *Great Britain and the Creation of the League of Nations* (Chapel Hill, N.C.: 1978), 24-31. Baker and Dodd, III, 184-88.

51. The text of the League of Nations Covenant appears in *FRUS: PPC*, XIII, 69-106. Baker and Dodd, VI, 227. *PWW*, LIV, 188.

52. David Hunter Miller, *The Drafting of the Covenant* (New York: 1928), I, 243-60. Baker, *Woodrow Wilson and World Settlement,* III, 236-37. Baker and Dodd, V, 343.

53. *FRUS: PPC,* V, 117-18. Louis A. R. Yates, *The United States and French Security, 1917-1921* (New York: 1957), 61-62, 64-68. Levin, 172. Smith, *The Great Departure,* 157. Lloyd E. Ambrosius, "Wilson, the Republicans, and French Security after World War I," *Journal of Modern History* 59 (September 1972), 341-52.

54. Smith, *The Great Departure,* 139.

55. Robert Lansing, *War Memoirs* (New York: 1935), 340.

56. *FRUS: PPC,* III, 648, 584.

57. Lansing Diary, October 28, 1919, quoted in Frederick S. Calhoun, *Power and Principle: Armed Intervention in Wilsonian Foreign Policy* (Kent, Ohio: 1986), 240.

58. Herbert Hoover, *The Ordeal of Woodrow Wilson* (New York: 1958), 135-36. *PWW,* LVI, 182, 230-43, 331-34. Frank Costigliola, *Awkward Dominion: American Political, Economic, and Cultural Relations with Europe, 1919-1933* (Ithaca, N.Y.: 1984), 39-55.

59. U.S. Department of State, *Papers Relating to the Foreign Relations of the United States, 1918: Russia* (Washington, D.C.: 1931-1932), II, 484-85 (hereafter cited as *FRUS, 1918: Russia*). Link, *Woodrow Wilson: Revolution, War, and Peace,* 96. *PWW,* XLVII, 620-22; XLVIII, 285-88.

60. A. Whitney Griswold, *The Far Eastern Policy of the United States* (New York: 1958), 223-28. Betty Miller Unterberger, *America's Siberian Expedition, 1918-1920* (Durham, N.C.: 1956), 88. *FRUS, 1918: Russia,* II, 287-90. *PWW,* XLVI, 527-55, 590-91, 598.

61. *FRUS, 1918: Russia,* II, 287-90. U.S. Department of State, *Papers Relating to the Foreign Relations of the United States, 1919: Russia* (Washington, D.C.: 1937), 391 (hereafter cited as *FRUS, 1919: Russia*). Calhoun, 189-218. Betty Miller Unterberger, "Woodrow Wilson and the Russian Revolution," in Link, *Woodrow Wilson and a Revolutionary World,* 49-104. *PWW,* LIV, 183.

62. *FRUS: PPC,* III, 581-84, 663-64, 648-49, 676-77, 686. Levin, 211.

63. *FRUS, 1919: Russia,* 74, 77-80. John M. Thompson, *Russia, Bolshevism, and the Versailles Peace* (Princeton, N.J.: 1966), 152-72.

64. *FRUS: PPC,* III, 1042-43. Levin, 216-17. Thompson, 149-77. Unterberger, "Woodrow Wilson and the Russian Revolution," 84-85. *FRUS, 1919: Russia,* 85-89. Beatrice Farnsworth, *William C. Bullitt and the Soviet Union* (Bloomington, Ind.: 1967), 32-70. *PWW,* LVII, 459-60.

65. Levin, 223-25. *FRUS, 1919: Russia,* 352-53, 367-70, 374-79.

66. Thompson, 299, 302, 304-8. Levin, 230-31.

67. Winston S. Churchill, *The Aftermath* (New York: 1929), 285.

68. *FRUS, 1919: Russia,* 620-23.

69. Baker and Dodd, VI, 18-19.

70. Shaw, II, 773, 821.

71. Henry Cabot Lodge, *The Senate and the League of Nations* (New York: 1925), 146-47, 201-2.

72. Foster Rhea Dulles, *America's Rise to World Power, 1898-1954* (New York: 1955), 119-20. Cooper, *Vanity of Power*, 134-42.

73. Link, *Woodrow Wilson: Revolution, War, and Peace*, 110-11.

74. Smith, *The Great Departure*, 182.

75. William C. Widenor, *Henry Cabot Lodge and the Search for an American Foreign Policy* (Berkeley, Calif.: 1980), 325-26, 331-32.

76. Thomas A. Bailey, *Woodrow Wilson and the Great Betrayal* (New York: 1945), 70. Widenor, 326.

77. *Congressional Record*, 65th Cong., 3rd sess., December 21, 1918, vol. 57, 727. Widenor, 295.

78. Ambrosius, "Wilson, the Republicans, and French Security After World War I," 341-52.

79. For a text of the reservations, see *Congressional Record*, 66th Cong., 1st sess., November 19, 1919, vol. 58, 8773 and 66th Cong., 2nd sess., March 19, 1920, 4599. David Mervin, "Henry Cabot Lodge and the League of Nations," *Journal of American Studies* 4 (February 1971), 201-14.

80. Baker and Dodd, V, 451. Smith, *The Great Departure*, 135. Seth P. Tillman, *Anglo-American Relations at the Paris Peace Conference of 1919* (Princeton, N.J.: 1961), 281-97. Miller, I, 322-23, 442-50. *PWW*, LVI, 82-83. Melvyn P. Leffler, *The Elusive Quest: America's Pursuit of European Stability and French Security, 1919-1933* (Chapel Hill, N.C.: 1979), 9.

81. Lodge, *The Senate and the League of Nations*, 172-77.

82. Link, *Woodrow Wilson: Revolution, War, and Peace*, 115, 120.

83. Bailey, *Woodrow Wilson and the Great Betrayal*, 259.

84. Ralph Stone, *The Irreconcilables: The Fight Against the League of Nations* (Lexington, Ky.: 1970), 87. Link, *Woodrow Wilson: Revolution, War, and Peace*, 122-23. See also Kurt Wimer, "Woodrow Wilson Tries Conciliation: An Effort that Failed," *The Historian* 25 (August 1963), 419-38.

85. John Maynard Keynes, *The Economic Consequences of the Peace* (New York: 1920), 225. Dulles, 118.

86. Edwin A. Weinstein, *Woodrow Wilson: A Medical and Psychological Biography* (Princeton, N.J.: 1981), 363.

87. James E. Watson, *As I Knew Them* (Indianapolis: 1936), 201-2.

88. Smith, *The Great Departure*, 197, 122.

89. Stone, 152-58.

90. Graebner, *America as a World Power*, xxiv-xxviii, 1-2.

91. Link, *Woodrow Wilson: Revolution, War, and Peace*, 128. Arthur S. Link, *The Higher Realism of Woodrow Wilson and Other Essays* (Nashville: 1971), 125-54.

92. Ambrosius, *Woodrow Wilson and the American Diplomatic Tradition*, xii, 8-9.

93. Levin, 260.

# CHAPTER TWO

# REPUBLICAN ISOLATIONISM, 1921-1933

1. Thomas N. Guinsberg, *The Pursuit of Isolationism in the United States Senate from Versailles to Pearl Harbor* (New York: 1982), 52. John D. Hicks, *Republican Ascendancy, 1921-1933* (New York: 1960), 25.

2. Hicks, 31. U.S. Department of State, *Papers Relating to the Foreign Relations of the United States: 1921* (Washington, D.C.: 1936), II, 29-33 (hereafter cited as *FRUS* followed by the title of its volume). Betty Glad, *Charles Evans Hughes and the Illusions of Innocence: A Study in American Diplomacy* (Urbana, Ill.: 1966), 212.

3. *FRUS*: 1921, II, 29-33. Kurt and Sarah Wimer, "The Harding Administration, the League of Nations, and the Separate Peace Treaty," *Review of Politics* 29 (January 1967), 24.

4. Glad, 213, 235.

5. Ibid., 214. William Appleman Williams, "The Legend of Isolationism in the 1920s," *Science and Society* 48 (Winter 1954), 1-20, and his *The Tragedy of American Foreign Policy* (Cleveland: 1959), 128-31. For two convincing rebuttals to Appleman's "Open Door" thesis, see Robert James Maddox, "Another Look at the Legend of Isolationism in the 1920s," *Mid-America* 53 (January 1971), 35-43, and John Braeman, "The New Left and American Foreign Policy during the Age of Normalcy: A Re-examination," *Business History Review* 57 (Spring 1983), 73-104. Frank Costigliola, *Awkward Dominion: American Political, Economic, and Cultural Relations with Europe, 1919-1933* (Ithaca, N.Y.: 1984), 58-60.

6. Selig Adler, *The Isolationist Impulse: Its Twentieth-Century Reaction* (London: 1957), 137-61. Historian Charles A. Beard described the chief characteristics of interwar isolationism as "rejection of membership in the League of Nations; non-entanglement in the political controversies of Europe and Asia; non-intervention in the wars of these continents; neutrality, peace, and defense for the United States through measures appropriate to those purposes; and the pursuit of a foreign policy friendly to all nations disposed to reciprocate." Charles A. Beard, *American Foreign Policy in the Making, 1932-1940* (New Haven, Conn.: 1946), 17.

7. *FRUS: 1921*, I, xvii-xviii.

8. Eugene P. Trani and David L. Wilson, *The Presidency of Warren G. Harding* (Lawrence, Kan.: 1977), 146.

9. Robert H. Ferrell, *American Diplomacy in the Great Depression: Hoover-Stimson Foreign Policy, 1929-1933* (New Haven, Conn: 1957), 31.

10. *FRUS: 1923* (Washington, D.C.: 1938) I, 10-24.

11. Glad, 187. Trani and Wilson, 147-48.

12. *Congressional Record*, 69th Cong., 1st sess., February 2, 1927, vol. 67, 2824-25.

13. Glad, 193.

14. Trani and Wilson, 148-49.

15. Norman A. Graebner, *America as a World Power: A Realist Appraisal from Wilson to Reagan* (Wilmington, Del.: 1984), 10-11.

16. Robert H. Ferrell, "The Peace Movement," in Alexander DeConde, ed., *Isolation and Security: Ideas and Interests in Twentieth-Century American Foreign Policy* (Durham, N.C.: 1957), 99, 103. Charles DeBenedetti, *Origins of the Modern Peace Movement, 1915-1929* (Millwood, N.Y.: 1978), 47.

17. DeBenedetti, 47, 49.

18. Ibid., 59, 74, 83.

19. Ferrell, "The Peace Movement," 101.

20. De Benedetti, 83. Ferrell, "The Peace Movement," 102.

21. DeBenedetti, 59, 61, 64-65.

22. John Chalmers Vinson, *The Parchment Peace: The United States Senate and the Washington Conference, 1921-1922* (Athens, Ga.: 1955), 45.

23. Trani and Wilson, 151.

24. William R. Braested, *The United States Navy in the Pacific, 1909-1922* (Austin, Tex.: 1971), 493. DeBenedetti, 70.

25. Braested, 498.

26. Ibid., 552, 562, 559. Costigliola, 82.

27. Braested, 558, 560.

28. Ibid., 563-64. *FRUS: 1921*, I, 18, 28-29.

29. Hicks, 134-35. Gaddis, 97-98.

30. U.S. Department of State, *Conference on the Limitation of Armament, Washington, November 12, 1921-February 6, 1922* (Washington, D.C.: 1922), 60, 62. Harold and Margaret Sprout, *Toward a New Order of Sea Power: American Naval Policy and the World Scene, 1918-1922* (Princeton, N.J.: 1940), 155.

31. *Conference on the Limitation of Armament*, 64. *FRUS: 1922* (Washington, D.C.: 1937), I, 247-67.

32. Sprout and Sprout, 221. *FRUS: 1922*, I, 250.

33. Sprout and Sprout, 195. Glad, 276. For the Billy Mitchell controversy, see Russell Weigley, *The American Way of War: A History of United States Military Strategy and Policy* (New York: 1973), 223-41.

34. *FRUS: 1922*, I, 90-99, 265-66.

35. Ibid., I, 33-37.

36. Ibid., I, 276-87.

37. Thomas H. Buckley, *The United States and the Washington Conference, 1921-1922* (Knoxville, Tenn.: 1970), 165.

38. Braested, 625. Vinson 207, 202, 198. Buckley, 178, 183-184.

39. Glad, 299.

40. Ibid., 301.

41. Hicks, 49.

42. Braested, 632.

43. *FRUS: 1922*, I, 392-94. Costigliola, 108.

44. Carole Fink, *The Genoa Conference: European Diplomacy, 1921-1922* (Chapel Hill, N.C.: 1984), 29. J. Néré, *The Foreign Policy of France from 1914 to 1945* (London: 1975), 11, 19. Walter A. McDougall, *France's Rhineland*

*Diplomacy, 1914-1924: The Last Bid for a Balance of Power in Europe* (Princeton, N.J.: 1978), 7.

45.  Néré, 12.

46.  Arnold Wolfers, *Britain and France between Two Wars: Conflicting Strategies of Peace Since Versailles* (New York: 1940), 37, 14, 17.

47.  Wolfers, 13. Carole Fink, "European Politics and Security at the Geneva Conference of 1922," in Carole Fink, Isabel V. Hull, and MacGregor Knox, eds., *German Nationalism and the European Response, 1890-1945* (Norman, Okla.: 1985), 141.

48.  Sprout and Sprout, 182. Melvyn P. Leffler, *The Elusive Quest: America's Pursuit of European Stability and French Security, 1919-1933* (Chapel Hill, N.C.: 1979), 36. Fink, *The Genoa Conference*, 35, 80.

49.  Hicks, 136. Glad, 219.

50.  Hicks, 136.

51.  Melvyn P. Leffler, "American Policy Making and European Stability, 1921-1933," *Pacific Historical Review* 46 (May 1977), 212-14.

52.  Michael J. Hogan, *Informal Entente: The Private Structure of Cooperation in Anglo-American Economic Diplomacy, 1918-1928* (Columbia, Mo.: 1977), 51-52. Melvyn Leffler, "The Origins of Republican War Debt Policy, 1921-1923: A Case Study in the Application of the Open Door Interpretation," *Journal of Modern History* 59 (December 1972), 592-94.

53.  Alexander DeConde, *A History of American Foreign Policy*, 2nd. ed. (New York: 1971), 557. Hicks, 138. Henry Blumenthal, *Illusion and Reality in Franco-American Diplomacy, 1914-1945* (Baton Rouge: 1986), 153-54.

54.  Fink, *The Genoa Conference*, 26. *FRUS: 1922*, II, 199-202.

55.  Stephen A. Schuker, *The End of French Predominance in Europe: The Financial Crisis of 1924 and the Adoption of the Dawes Plan* (Chapel Hill, N.C.: 1976), 6, 16. Sally Marks, "The Myths of Reparations," *Central European History* 11 (1978), 254-55.

56.  Schuker, 22, 25. Wolfers, 56-58. Leffler, *The Elusive Quest*, 82.

57.  *FRUS: 1923* (Washington, D.C.: 1938), II, 70-73. Schuker, 183. Glad, 231. Costigliola, 111-27.

58.  Hogan, 68-69. Glad, 228.

59.  Wolfers, 37. Leffler, *The Elusive Quest*, 113-14.

60.  Walter C. Langsam, *Documents and Readings in the History of Europe since 1919*, rev. ed. (Chicago: 1951), 205-15.

61.  Wolfers, 346, 348, 351.

62.  Ibid., 351-52, 354

63.  David D. Burks, "The United States and the Geneva Protocol of 1924: 'A New Holy Alliance?'" *American Historical Review* 64 (July 1959), 897.

64.  Ibid., 896-97, 901-2, 905.

65.  William J. Newman, *The Balance of Power in the Interwar Years, 1919-1939* (New York: 1968), 205-27.

66.  Jon Jacobson, *Locarno Diplomacy: Germany and the West, 1925-1929* (Princeton, N.J.: 1972), 64-65, 40, 366. Manfred F. Enssle, "Stresemann's Diplomacy Fifty Years after Locarno: Some Recent Perspectives," *The Historical Journal* 20 (1977), 942-43.

67. Jacobson, 15-16, 37.

68. *FRUS: 1925* (Washington, D.C.: 1940), I, xii-xiii.

69. Jacobson, 30. See also Jean-Baptiste Duroselle, "The Spirit of Locarno: Illusions of Pactomania," *Foreign Affairs* 50 (July 1972), 752-64.

70. Jacobsen, 30, 105, 239.

71. *FRUS: 1926* (Washington, D.C.: 1941), I, 42-44. 51-56, 80-100. *FRUS: 1927* (Washington, D.C.: 1942), I, 163-66. Leffler, *The Elusive Quest,* 159.

72. *FRUS: 1926,* I, 109-11, 80-84. Leffler, *The Elusive Quest,* 160.

73. Leffler, *The Elusive Quest,* 160.

74. *FRUS: 1927,* I, 1-9.

75. Ibid., I, 10-12, 14. Hicks, 148. Raymond G. O'Connor, *Perilous Equilibrium: The United States and the London Naval Conference of 1930* (Lawrence, Kan.: 1962), 16.

76. David Carlton, "Great Britain and the Coolidge Naval Disarmament Conference of 1927," *Political Science Quarterly* 83 (December 1968), 573. Gerald E. Wheeler, *Prelude to Pearl Harbor: The United States Navy and the Far East, 1921-1931* (Columbia, Mo.: 1963), 131-57. *FRUS: 1927,* I, 124-27, 142-59. B.J.C. McKercher, *The Second Baldwin Government and the United States, 1924-1929* (Cambridge, Eng.: 1984), 55-76.

77. Jacobson, 187-88. *FRUS: 1928* (Washington, D.C.: 1942), I, 268-70, 282-86.

78. Jacobson, 207. O'Connor, 22.

79. DeBenedetti, 73. Robert James Maddox, *William E. Borah and American Foreign Policy* (Baton Rouge: 1969), 135-43.

80. DeBenedetti, 186. *FRUS: 1927,* II, 611-13.

81. DeBenedetti, 194-95. Jean-Baptiste Duroselle, *From Wilson to Roosevelt: Foreign Policy of the United States, 1913-1945* (Cambridge, Mass.: 1963), 180.

82. Francis P. Walters, *A History of the League of Nations* (New York: 1952), I, 386.

83. DeBenedetti, 198-99, 203-4. Maddox, *William E. Borah and American Foreign Policy,* 150-82.

84. Leffler, *The Elusive Quest,* 162-63. *FRUS: 1928,* I, 1-2.

85. DeBenedetti, 205. *FRUS: 1928,* I, 3-5.

86. *FRUS: 1928,* I, 107-8.

87. Ibid., I, 153-57. Robert H. Ferrell, *Peace in Their Time: The Origins of the Kellogg-Briand Pact* (New Haven, Conn.: 1952), 201.

88. John C. Vinson, *William E. Borah and the Outlawry of War* (Athens, Ga.: 1957), 171. William S. Myers, ed., *The State Papers and Other Public Writings of Herbert Hoover* (Garden City, N.Y.: 1934), I, 79-80.

89. Norman Graebner, ed., *Ideas and Diplomacy: Readings in the Intellectual Tradition of American Foreign Policy* (New York: 1964), 519.

90. Ibid., 520.

91. Roland N. Stromberg, *Collective Security and American Foreign Policy* (New York: 1963), 60.

92. Ferrell, *American Diplomacy,* 40. For a discussion of the historiography of Hoover's foreign policy, see Selig Adler, "Hoover's Foreign Policy and the New Left," in Martin L. Fausold, ed., *The Hoover Presidency: A Reappraisal*

(Albany, N.Y.: 1974), 153-63 and Joan Hoff Wilson, "A Reevaluation of Herbert Hoover's Foreign Policy," in Fausold, 164-86.

93. Ferrell, *American Diplomacy*, 41.

94. Ibid., 20.

95. Hogan, 221-22.

96. Jacobson, 272. Costigliola, 210-17.

97. Ferrell, *American Diplomacy*, 111. Duroselle, *From Wilson to Roosevelt*, 194.

98. Ferrell, *American Diplomacy*, 116-17. *FRUS: 1931* (Washington, D.C.: 1946), I, 33-35.

99. Leffler, *The Elusive Quest*, 241-43. *FRUS: 1931*, I, 47-48, 62-65, 161-63.

100. *FRUS: 1932* (Washington, D.C.: 1947), I, 687-91, 817-18. Ferrell, *American Diplomacy*, 110-119. Leffler, *The Elusive Quest*, 290-99.

101. Duroselle, *From Wilson to Roosevelt*, 203.

102. Leffler, *The Elusive Quest*, 219.

103. *FRUS: 1929* (Washington, D.C.: 1944), III, 1-37.

104. *FRUS: 1930* (Washington, D.C.: 1945), I, 2, 24-25.

105. Ibid., I, 36-39, 45-46, 55-56, 63-65, 75-79, 92-95. O'Connor, 88-90. Leffler, *The Elusive Quest*, 222-23.

106. *FRUS: 1930*, I, 79-82, 89, 92-95. Leffler, *The Elusive Quest*, 224-28.

107. *FRUS: 1930*, I, 107-25.

108. Leffler, *The Elusive Quest*, 226.

109. DeConde, *A History of American Foreign Policy*, 514.

110. *FRUS: 1930*, I, 101. Leffler, *The Elusive Quest*, 227-28.

111. *FRUS: 1932* (Washington, D.C.: 1948), I, 34-39. Néré, 119.

112. *FRUS: 1932*, I, 180-82, 211-14. Herbert Hoover, *The Memoirs of Herbert Hoover* (New York: 1952), II, 352-57.

113. *FRUS: 1932*, I, 121-26, 108-12, 356-58, 360-61, 380-86, 473-80, 489-508. Leffler, *The Elusive Quest*, 287-88.

114. Christopher Thorne, *The Limits of Foreign Policy: The West, the League, and the Far Eastern Crisis of 1931-1933* (New York: 1972), 3-4.

115. Ibid., 283-84, 288-99, 331-45.

116. Hoover, II, 366, 372-73. Thorne, 299-301. *FRUS: Japan, 1931-1941* (Washington, D.C.: 1943), I, 76.

117. Leffler, "American Policy Making and European Stability, 1921-1933," 209.

118. Ibid. For a more sympathetic view of the Republican foreign policy, see John Braeman, "Power and Diplomacy: The 1920s Reappraised," *Review of Politics* 44 (July 1982), 342-69.

# CHAPTER THREE

# FRANKLIN D. ROOSEVELT, THE ISOLATIONISTS, AND THE AGGRESSORS, 1933-1939

1. Robert Dallek, *Franklin D. Roosevelt and American Foreign Policy, 1932-1945* (New York: 1979), 7-9. Franklin D. Roosevelt, "On Your Own Heads," *Scribner's Magazine,* January-June 1917, 414.

2. Frank Freidel, *Franklin D. Roosevelt: The Apprenticeship* (Boston: 1952), 241.

3. William E. Kinsella, Jr., *Leadership in Isolation: Franklin D. Roosevelt and the Origins of the Second World War* (Cambridge, Mass: 1978), 11-13.

4. Elliott Roosevelt, ed., *F.D.R.: His Personal Letters, 1928-1945* (New York: 1950), I, 466-67. Dallek, 11-12. Kinsella, 19. Frank Freidel, *Franklin D. Roosevelt: The Ordeal* (Boston: 1954), 18.

5. Frank Freidel, *Franklin D. Roosevelt: The Triumph* (Boston: 1956), 250-54. Louis Wehle, *Hidden Threads of History: Wilson through Roosevelt* (New York: 1953), 110. Edgar B. Nixon, ed., *Franklin D. Roosevelt and Foreign Affairs: January 1933-January 1937* (Cambridge, Mass.: 1969), I, 23-24.

6. Robert E. Osgood, *Ideals and Self-Interest in America's Foreign Relations* (Chicago: 1953), 411.

7. Gerhard L. Weinberg, *The Foreign Policy of Hitler's Germany: Diplomatic Revolution in Europe, 1937-1939* (Chicago: 1980), 2-3. Eberhard Jackel, *Hitler's World View: A Blueprint for Power,* Herbert Arnold, trans. (Cambridge, Mass.: 1972), 27-46.

8. David L. Porter, *The Seventy-sixth Congress and World War II: 1939-1940* (Columbia, Mo.: 1979), 28. Samuel I. Rosenman, ed., *The Public Papers and Addresses of Franklin Delano Roosevelt* (New York: 1938), I, 14.

9. U.S. Department of State, *Papers Relating to the Foreign Relations of the United States: 1933* (Washington, D.C.: 1950), I, 673-74. Dallek, 38.

10. Dallek, 40. Melvyn P. Leffler, *The Elusive Quest: America's Pursuit of European Stability and French Security, 1919-1933* (Chapel Hill, N.C.: 1979), 356-57.

11. Wayne S. Cole, *Roosevelt and the Isolationists, 1932-1945* (Lincoln, Neb.: 1983), 92. Frederick W. Marks III, *Winds over Sand: The Diplomacy of Franklin Roosevelt* (Athens, Ga.: 1988), 28-29.

12. Willard Range, *Franklin D. Roosevelt's World Order* (Athens, Ga.: 1959), 7. *FRUS: 1933,* I, 210. Gerhard L. Weinberg, *The Foreign Policy of Hitler's Germany: Diplomatic Revolution in Europe, 1933-1939* (Chicago: 1970), 143. Dallek, 68.

13. *FRUS: 1933,* I, 43-54, 144.

14. Ibid., I, 156. U.S. Department of State, *Peace and War: United States Foreign Policy, 1931-1941* (Washington, D.C.: 1943), 188-89. Robert A. Divine, *The Illusion of Neutrality* (Chicago: 1962), 51.

15. *FRUS: 1933,* I, 364-67, 369-78. Cordell Hull, *The Memoirs of Cordell Hull* (New York: 1948), I, 229-30. Dallek, 47, 72.

16. Weinberg, *The Foreign Policy of Hitler's Germany: 1933-1936*, 161, 163-66. Edward W. Bennett, *German Rearmament and the West, 1932-1933* (Princeton, N.J.: 1979), 450, 475, 479, 508. *FRUS: 1933*, I, 238-41, 243-47, 265.

17. Bennett, *German Rearmament*, 480-84. *FRUS, 1933*, I, 273. Keith Feiling, *The Life of Neville Chamberlain* (London: 1946), 226.

18. John Wheeler-Bennett and Stephen Heald, eds., *Documents on International Relations: 1935* (London: 1936), I, 58-64.

19. Anthony Adamthwaite, *France and the Coming of the Second World War, 1936-1939* (London: 1977), 24-29, 354-58. Robert J. Young, *In Command of France: French Foreign Policy and Military Planning, 1933-1940* (Cambridge, Mass.: 1978), 162. James Thomas Emmerson, *The Rhineland Crisis, 7 March 1936: A Study in Multilateral Diplomacy* (London: 1977), 48-53, 62-71, 130-49. Weinberg, *The Foreign Policy of Hitler's Germany: 1933-1936*, 251. Arnold A. Offner, *American Appeasement: United States Foreign Policy and Germany, 1933-1938* (Cambridge, Mass.: 1969), 144-45. P.M.H. Bell, *The Origins of the Second World War in Europe* (London: 1986), 210-11.

20. Offner, 132.

21. Elliott Roosevelt, I, 475. Kinsella, 43. Dallek, 103.

22. Dallek, 95.

23. Ibid., 95-97.

24. Gilbert N. Kahn, "Presidential Passivity on a Nonsalient Issue: President Franklin D. Roosevelt and the 1935 World Court Fight," *Diplomatic History* 4 (Spring 1980), 137-60. Robert D. Accinelli, "The Roosevelt Administration and the World Court Defeat, 1935," *The Historian* 40 (May 1978), 463-78.

25. Dallek, 75. *FRUS: 1933*, I, 380-84, 386-95.

26. *FRUS: 1935* (Washington, D.C.: 1953), I, 68-70. Cole, 77. *FRUS: 1933*, I, 303-4.

27. Nixon, II, 263, 291, 315-19. Stephen E. Pelz, *Race to Pearl Harbor: The Failure of the Second London Naval Conference and the Onset of World War II* (Cambridge, Mass.: 1974), 143. Dorothy Borg, *The United States and the Far Eastern Crisis of 1933-1938* (Cambridge, Mass: 1964), 104-11.

28. *FRUS: 1934* (Washington, D.C.: 1951), 415-19. Dallek, 90. Pelz, 197-98, 200-8.

29. U.S. Congress, Special Senate Committee Investigating the Munitions Industry, *Hearings: Munitions Industry*, 73rd and 74th Cong., 1934-1936, pts. 1-39. U.S. Congress, Special Senate Committee on Investigation of the Munitions Industry, *Munitions Industry: Report on Existing Legislation*, 74th Cong., 1st sess., 1936, Senate Report 944, pt. 5, 1-9, 58.

30. Cole, 160.

31. David Reynolds, *The Creation of the Anglo-American Alliance, 1937-41: A Study in Competitive Co-operation* (Chapel Hill, N.C.: 1982), 29. Cole, 149, 154. *FRUS: 1935*, I, 363-64.

32. Robert A. Divine, *The Reluctant Belligerent: American Entry into World War II*, 2nd. ed. (New York: 1979), 22. *Peace and War*, 272.

33. Brice Harris, Jr., *The United States and the Italo-Ethiopian Crisis* (Stanford, Calif.: 1964), 2-20, 62-72.

34. *FRUS: 1935*, I, 797-804. *Peace and War*, 283-84.

35. Hull, I, 432-33. *FRUS: 1935*, I, 803-4. Divine, *Illusion of Neutrality*, 130.

36. Bell, 171. Wheeler-Bennett and Heald, *Documents on International Relations: 1935*, II, 360-62. Harris, 97-111.

37. Harris, 138-39. Dallek, 117.

38. David F. Schmitz, *The United States and Fascist Italy, 1922-1940* (Chapel Hill, N.C.: 1988), 170-71.

39. Harris, 141. Divine, *The Illusion of Neutrality*, 130-34, 139-61.

40. F. Jay Taylor, *The United States and the Spanish Civil War* (New York: 1956), 21-38. Richard P. Traina, *American Diplomacy and the Spanish Civil War* (Bloomington, Ind.: 1968), 3-10.

41. Raymond Sontag, *A Broken World, 1919-1939*, 304-5. Bell, 216-17. Traina, 27-45.

42. Divine, *Reluctant Belligerent*, 33. Traina, 204-7.

43. Douglas Little, *Malevolent Neutrality: The United States, Great Britain, and the Origins of the Spanish Civil War* (Ithaca, N.Y.: 1985), 238. Leo V. Kanawada, Jr., *Franklin D. Roosevelt and American Catholics, Italians, and Jews* (Ann Arbor, Mich.: 1982), 54-55. Traina, 46-54. *Peace and War*, 32-33, 323-29.

44. *FRUS: 1938* (Washington, D.C.: 1955), 188-92. Divine, *Illusion of Neutrality*, 170. Dallek, 136, 143. Taylor, 199, 207. Traina, 84-98.

45. Weinberg, *The Foreign Policy of Hitler's Germany: 1933-1936*, 331-37, 345-46. Offner, 165.

46. Howard Jablon, "Franklin Roosevelt and the Spanish Civil War," *Social Studies* 56 (February 1965), 59-69.

47. *Congressional Record*, 76th Cong., 1st sess., March 1, 1937, vol. 84, 1677. Bernard Baruch, "Neutrality," *Current History* 44 (June 1936), 43.

48. Divine, *Illusion of Neutrality*, 181, 174.

49. Divine, *Reluctant Belligerent*, 37. *Congressional Record*, 76th Cong., 1st sess., March 3, 1937, vol. 84, 1778.

50. *Peace and War*, 355-65.

51. Divine, *Illusion of Neutrality*, 198-99, 166.

52. Borg, 276-83, 300.

53. Ibid., 334-54. *Congressional Record*, 75th Cong., 1st sess., August 19, 1937, vol. 81, 2187. Divine, *Illusion of Neutrality*, 203-4, 209-10. *Peace and War*, 380

54. *Peace and War*, 383-87. Borg, 369-86.

55. Marks, 69, 74.

56. Cole, 243. Borg, 387-98. Elliott Roosevelt, II, 719.

57. *FRUS: 1937* (Washington, D.C.: 1954), I, 665-70. *FRUS: 1938*, I, 115-32.

58. *FRUS: Japan, 1931-1941* (Washington, D.C.: 1943), I, 517-20, 551-52. John Morton Blum, *From the Morgenthau Diaries*, vol. I: *Years of Crisis, 1928-1938* (Boston: 1959), 490-91. Harold I. Ickes, *The Secret Diary*, vol. II: *The Inside Struggle, 1936-1939* (New York: 1954), 274-75, 279. Pelz, 199. James R. Leutze, *Bargaining for Supremacy: Anglo-American Naval Collaboration: 1937-1941* (Chapel Hill, N.C.: 1977), 18-19, 21-28. Borg, 497-98. John McVickar

Haight, "Franklin D. Roosevelt and a Naval Quarantine of Japan," *Pacific Historical Review* 40 (1971), 219, 221. Lawrence R. Pratt, "The Anglo-American Naval Conversations on the Far East of January 1938," *International Affairs* 47 (October 1971), 745-63. William R. Rock, *Chamberlain and Roosevelt: British Foreign Policy and the United States, 1937-1940* (Columbus, Ohio: 1988), 49, 52.

59. Cole, 271. Ernest C. Bolt, Jr., *Ballots before Bullets: The War Referendum Approach to Peace in America, 1914-1941* (Charlottesville, Va.: 1977), 152. Divine, *Illusion of Neutrality*, 219-20.

60. *Peace and War*, 400-1. Cole, 253.

61. Rosenman, VII, 68-71. *Peace and War*, 403-5.

62. Cole, 266-70, 273. *Fortune* 18 (July 1938), 37. Divine, *Illusion of Neutrality*, 221.

63. Callum A. MacDonald, *The United States, Britain, and Appeasement* (London: 1981), 42. Haight, "Franklin D. Roosevelt and a Naval Quarantine of Japan," 221. Michael Howard, *The Continental Commitment: The Dilemma of British Defense Policy in the Era of Two World Wars* (London: 1972), 120-21. Rock, 55-58.

64. *FRUS: 1937*, IV, 85. Borg, 406-7. Elliott Roosevelt, II, 718-19. Offner, 194-97. Rock, 42-45.

65. MacDonald, *The United States, Britain, and Appeasement*, 43. *FRUS: 1938* (Washington, D.C.: 1955), I, 119.

66. MacDonald, *The United States, Britain, and Appeasement*, 21. Callum A. MacDonald, "The United States, Appeasement and the Open Door," in Wolfgang J. Mommsen and Lothar Kettenacker, eds., *The Fascist Challenge and the Policy of Appeasement* (London: 1983), 400-1. Hull, II, 1069-82. *FRUS: 1941*, IV, 600-85.

67. MacDonald, *The United States, Britain, and Appeasement*, 24-25.

68. Sumner Welles, *The Time for Decision* (New York: 1944), 66. *FRUS: 1938*, I, 120-22.

69. MacDonald, *The United States, Britain, and Appeasement*, 18. Anthony Eden, *Facing the Dictators* (Boston: 1962), 634-45, 699-700.

70. Rock, 58-68, 71-72.

71. Weinberg, *The Foreign Policy of Hitler's Germany: 1937-1939*, 38-51. MacDonald, *The United States, Britain, and Appeasement*, 71-72. Jay Pierrepont Moffat, *The Moffat Papers*, Nancy Harvison Hooker, ed. (Cambridge, Mass: 1956), 190-91. Rock, 67-68, 80-86.

72. Samuel Viscount Templewood, *Nine Troubled Years* (London: 1954), 273. Offner, 234. *FRUS: 1938*, I, 473. Rock, 92-96.

73. Count Galeazzo Ciano, *Ciano's Diary, 1937-1938* (London: 1954), 94-95.

74. Hull, I, 582. *FRUS: 1938*, I, 147-48. Dallek, 158. Rock, 94.

75. Juri Hochman, *The Soviet Union and the Failure of Collective Security, 1934-1938* (Ithaca, N.Y.: 1984), 52. See also Marcia Lynn Toepfer, "The Soviet Role in the Munich Crisis: An Historiographical Debate," *Diplomatic History* 1 (Fall 1977), 341-57.

76. MacDonald, *The United States, Britain, and Appeasement*, 79, 94.

77.  *FRUS: 1938*, I, 649-50. E. L. Woodward and Rohan Butler, eds., *Documents on British Foreign Policy*, 3rd ser. (London: 1954), VII, 627.

78.  Woodward and Butler, 3rd ser., VII, 627-30.

79.  *FRUS: 1938*, I, 660-61, 72-73. Kinsella, 123. Dallek, 164-65. *Peace and War*, 425-26, 428-29. MacDonald, *The United States, Britain, and Appeasement*, 103-4. Marks, 142-47.

80.  William L. Langer and S. Everett Gleason, *The Challenge to Isolation, 1937-1940* (New York: 1964), 35. Divine, *Reluctant Belligerent*, 59.

81.  *FRUS: 1938*, III, 316; V, 419-20.

82.  Dallek, 171. John Blum, *From the Morgenthau Diaries*, vol. II: *Years of Crisis, 1938-1941* (Boston: 1965), 48-49.

83.  John McVickar Haight, Jr., *American Aid to France, 1938-1940* (New York: 1970), 60-63. MacDonald, *The United States, Britain, and Appeasement*, 121.

84.  MacDonald, *The United States, Britain, and Appeasement*, 121-22, 112-13. Ickes, II, 474.

85.  Porter, 21. *Peace and War*, 447-49.

86.  Divine, *Reluctant Belligerent*, 60.

87.  Cole, 297, 305. Dallek, 181.

88.  Cole 306-7. Dallek, 181-82. Divine, *Illusion of Neutrality*, 238-39. Haight, *American Aid to France*, 130-31.

89.  Divine, *Reluctant Belligerent*, 60-61. *Congressional Record*, 76th Cong., 1st. sess, February 2, 1939, vol. 84, pt. 1, 1347.

90.  *The New York Times*, March 12, 1939. Tom Connally, *My Name is Tom Connally* (New York.: 1954), 226. Divine, *Illusion of Neutrality*, 242-43. *Congressional Record*, 76th Cong., 1st. sess., March 20, 1939, vol. 84, 2923-26.

91.  Divine, *Illusion of Neutrality*, 244.

92.  Elliott Roosevelt, II, 873. Divine, *Reluctant Belligerent*, 62.

93.  Divine, *Reluctant Belligerent*, 63. Hull, I, 643.

94.  Divine, *Reluctant Belligerent*, 63-64. Divine, *Illusion of Neutrality*, 275.

95.  Divine, *Illusion of Neutrality*, 276-79.

96.  Divine, *Reluctant Belligerent*, 67. James V. Compton, *The Swastika and the Eagle: Hitler, the United States, and the Origins of the Second World War* (London: 1968), 33.

97.  Norman A. Graebner, *America as a World Power: A Realist Appraisal from Wilson to Reagan* (Wilmington, Del.: 1984), 55.

98.  Rock, 170-71. Sir Arthur Willert, *Washington and Other Memories* (Boston: 1972), 214-19.

99.  *Peace and War*, 455-58. *FRUS: 1939* (Washington, D.C.: 1956), I, 130-33, 88. Reynolds, 61. Rock, 178-80.

100.  Teddy J. Ulrichs, "A.J.P. Taylor and the Russians," in Gordon Martel, ed., *The Origins of the Second World War Reconsidered: The A.J.P. Taylor Debate after Twenty-five Years* (Boston: 1986), 164-65.

101.  Kinsella, 97. Edward M. Bennett, *Franklin D. Roosevelt and the Search for Security: American-Soviet Relations, 1933-39* (Wilmington, Del.: 1985), 136.

102. Thomas R. Maddux, *Years of Estrangement: American Relations with the Soviet Union, 1933-1941* (Tallahassee, Fla.: 1980), 99. Reynolds, 39. Larry William Fuchser, *Neville Chamberlain and Appeasement: A Study in the Politics of History* (New York: 1982), 182-83.

103. Graebner, 59-60.

104. Weinberg, *The Foreign Policy of Hitler's Germany: 1937-1939*, 573-76. Jonathan Haslam, *The Soviet Union and the Struggle for Collective Security in Europe, 1933-39* (New York 1984), 231.

105. Maddux, 53. Joseph E. Davies, *Mission to Moscow* (New York: 1941), 450.

106. *FRUS: 1939*, I, 360-62, 368. *Peace and War*, 479-80. Weinberg, *The Foreign Policy of Hitler's Germany: 1937-1939*, 638-39.

107. J. Garry Clifford, "Both Ends of the Telescope: New Perspectives on FDR and American Entry into World War II," *Diplomatic History* 13 (Spring 1989), 218.

108. Ibid., 229.

109. Bennett, 192.

110. Clifford, 216. Marks, 61, 287, 280.


# CHAPTER FOUR

# THE ROAD TO WAR, 1939-1941

1. *Peace and War: United States Foreign Policy, 1931-1941* (Washington, D.C.: 1943), 483-86.

2. Robert Dallek, *Franklin D. Roosevelt and American Foreign Policy, 1932-1945* (New York: 1979), 199. Cordell Hull, *The Memoirs of Cordell Hull* (New York: 1948), I, 684. William L. Langer and S. Everett Gleason, *The Challenge to Isolation, 1937-1940* (New York: 1964), 286-88. *Peace and War*, 488-94. Joseph P. Lash, *Roosevelt and Churchill, 1939-1941: The Partnership that Saved the West* (New York: 1976), 64-66.

3. Langer and Gleason, *The Challenge to Isolation*, 471, 207. Richard M. Leighton, "The American Arsenal Policy in World War II: A Retrospective View," in Daniel R. Beaver, ed., *Some Pathways in Twentieth-Century History: Essays in Honor of Reginald Charles McGran* (Detroit: 1969), 225. Dallek, 203. For the development of American strategy, see Mark M. Lowenthal, "Roosevelt and the Coming of the War: The Search for United States Policy, 1937-42," *History* 16 (July 1981), 413-40.

4. David L. Porter, *The Seventy-sixth Congress and World War II: 1939-1940* (Columbia, Mo.: 1979), 55. *Peace and War*, 486-88. Thomas N. Guinsberg, *The Pursuit of Isolationism in the United States Senate from Versailles to Pearl Harbor* (New York: 1982), 223. Robert A. Divine, *The Reluctant Belligerent: American Entry into World War II*, 2nd. ed. (New York: 1979), 74.

5. Porter, 65.

6. Divine, *Reluctant Belligerent*, 77.

7. Guinsberg, 240. Roosevelt to White, December 14, 1939, Elliott Roosevelt, ed., *F.D.R.: His Personal Letters: 1928-1945* (New York: 1950), II, 968.

8. *Peace and War*, 514-15.

9. Ibid., 76, 545-49.

10. Dallek, 228. *Peace and War*, 551-52.

11. *Peace and War*, 552. Langer and Gleason, *The Challenge of Isolation*, 496.

12. *Peace and War*, 553-54.

13. Langer and Gleason, *The Challenge of Isolation*, 474-75. *Peace and War*, 527-32. Samuel Eliot Morison, *History of United States Naval Operations in World War II*, vol. I: *The Battle of the Atlantic, September 1939-May 1943* (Boston: 1962), 27-28. Divine, *Reluctant Belligerent*, 90.

14. Robert E. Osgood, *Ideals and Self-Interest in America's Foreign Relations* (Chicago: 1953), 409.

15. Divine, *Reluctant Belligerent*, 93. Warren F. Kimball, *Churchill and Roosevelt: The Complete Correspondence* (Princeton, N.J.: 1984), I, 37-38, 50. Winston Churchill, *The Second World War*, vol. II: *Their Finest Hour* (Boston: 1949), 24.

16. Divine, *Reluctant Belligerent*, 93.

17. *Peace and War*, 83-84, 564-68. Divine, *Reluctant Belligerent*, 96.

18. Robert E. Sherwood, *Roosevelt and Hopkins: An Intimate History*, rev. ed. (New York: 1948, 1950), 191. Dallek, 248-51.

19. Churchill, II, 559-67. *Peace and War*, 599-608.

20. *Peace and War*, 100-2, 628. Samuel I. Rosenman, ed., *The Public Papers and Addresses of Franklin D. Roosevelt* (New York: 1941), IX, 607. Patrick J. Hearden, *Roosevelt Confronts Hitler: America's Entry Into World War II* (DeKalb, Ill.: 1986), 39.

21. *The New York Times*, January 13, 1941. Arthur Vandenberg, Jr., and J. A. Morris, eds., *The Private Papers of Senator Vandenberg* (Boston: 1952), 10.

22. U.S. Congress, Joint Committee on the Investigation of the Pearl Harbor Attack, *Hearings: Pearl Harbor Attack*, "Report of the United States-British Staff Conversations," March 27, 1941, 79th Cong., 1st sess., (1946), XV, 1485-1550.

23. Ibid. Osgood, 421.

24. Hearden, 194-96. *Pearl Harbor Attack*, V, 2292. John Blum, *From the Morgenthau Diaries*, vol. II: *Years of Crisis, 1938-1941* (Boston: 1965), 253-54. Waldo Heinrichs, *Threshold of War: Franklin D. Roosevelt and American Entry into World War II* (New York: 1988), 47-48, 56, 66-67.

25. *Peace and War*, 662-72. Dallek, 266-67. Kimball, I, 209.

26. Vojtech Mastny, *Russia's Road to the Cold War: Diplomacy, Warfare, and the Politics of Communism, 1941-1945* (New York: 1979), 32.

27. Raymond James Sontag and James Stuart Beddie, eds., *Nazi-Soviet Relations, 1939-1941: Documents from the Archives of the German Foreign Office* (Washington, D.C.: 1948), 217-54, 260-64.

28. Winston S. Churchill, *The Second World War,* vol. III: *The Grand Alliance* (Boston: 1950), 371-72, 382.

29. Ibid., 369. *FRUS: 1941* (Washington: 1958), I, 766. Sherwood, 303-4.

30. Joseph Davies, *Mission to Moscow* (New York: 1941), 475-76, 492-93.

31. Dallek, 212. Raymond H. Dawson, *The Decision to Aid Russia, 1941: Foreign Policy and Domestic Politics* (Westport, Conn.: 1959), 290.

32. Elliott Roosevelt, II, 1177. Sherwood, 417.

33. Dallek, 208-9. Porter, 94, 123. Divine, *Roosevelt and World War II,* (Baltimore: 1969), 78. Dawson, 16.

34. *FRUS: 1941,* I, 768. Dawson, 121.

35. *FRUS: 1941,* I, 802-14. Sherwood, 328-33. Divine, *Roosevelt and World War II,* 83.

36. William L. Langer and S. Everrett Gleason, *The Undeclared War: 1940-1941* (New York: 1953), 543-46. *FRUS: 1941,* I, 789.

37. Dallek, 279. Elliott Roosevelt, II, 1202. Dawson, 213.

38. Dawson, 99-100, 108.

39. *FRUS: 1941,* I, 784. Churchill, III, 392. Lynn Etheridge Davis, *The Cold War Begins: Soviet-American Conflict over Eastern Europe* (Princeton, N.J.: 1974), 12.

40. Kimball, I, 221-22. *FRUS: 1941,* I, 342. Dawson, 136. Churchill, III, 392.

41. Churchill, III, 433.

42. *FRUS: 1941,* 367-69.

43. Leland M. Goodrich, ed., *Documents on American Foreign Relations* (Boston: 1942), IV, 214-16.

44. Davis, 15-17. Dallek, 284-85.

45. Sherwood, 361. *FRUS: 1941,* I, 832, 1002-3. Langer and Gleason, *Undeclared War,* 796-97.

46. *Congressional Record,* 77th Cong., 1st sess., October 8, 1941, vol. 87, 7734. Dawson, 281-83. *Department of State Bulletin* 5 (1941), 365-66.

47. Henry L. Stimson Diary (Unpublished MS, Sterling Memorial Library, Yale University, New Haven, Conn.), August 28, 1941. Lash, 422.

48. Divine, *Reluctant Belligerent,* 134-36.

49. Ibid., 134. Langer and Gleason, *Undeclared War,* 570-74.

50. *Peace and War,* 103-4, 640-48. Langer and Gleason, *Undeclared War,* 579. Divine, *Reluctant Belligerent,* 132-33.

51. Kimball, I, 229. Lash, 401-2. Stimson Diary, July 21, 1941.

52. Patrick Abbazia, *Mr. Roosevelt's Navy: The Private War of the U.S. Atlantic Fleet, 1939-1942* (Annapolis, Md.: 1975), 223-31. Hearden, 203. H. L. Trefousse, *Germany and American Neutrality, 1939-1941* (New York: 1969), 41, 86.

53. Langer and Gleason, *Undeclared War,* 743-47, 753-55. Lash, 417-21. Sidney Lens, *The Forging of the American Empire* (New York: 1971), 321.

54. Abbazia, 265-80, 293-308. Goodrich, IV, 127. Langer and Gleason, *Undeclared War,* 756-57. Divine, *Reluctant Belligerent,* 152.

55. Dallek, 288. Divine, *Roosevelt and World War II,* 45.

56. *FRUS: Japan, 1931-1941* (Washington, D.C.: 1943), II, 189, 201-2, 216-18, 222-23, 165-66. Dallek, 240-41.

57. Dallek, 270, 273.

58. Wayne S. Cole, *Roosevelt and the Isolationists, 1932-1945* (Lincoln, Neb.: 1983), 493. Alfred L. Castle, "William R. Castle and Opposition to U.S. Involvement in an Asian War, 1939-1941," *Pacific Historical Review* 54 (August 1985), 337-51.

59. Norman A. Graebner, *America as a World Power: A Realist Appraisal from Wilson to Reagan* (Wilmington, Del.: 1984), 79. Elliott Roosevelt, II, 1174. *FRUS: Japan, 1931-1941*, II, 266-67. Dallek, 274.

60. Divine, *Reluctant Belligerent*, 127. Jonathan G. Utley, *Going to War With Japan: 1937-1941* (Knoxville, Tenn.: 1985), 153-56. Michael A. Barnhart, *Japan Prepares for Total War: The Search for Economic Security, 1919-1941* (Ithaca, N.Y.: 1987), 237-41. Heinrichs, 134-35, 177-79.

61. Dallek, 299-300. Hearden, 213. *FRUS: Japan, 1931-1941*, II, 554-55. Langer and Gleason, *Undeclared War*, 694-97.

62. *FRUS: Japan, 1931-1941*, II, 549-50. Hearden, 216. Langer and Gleason, *Undeclared War*, 849-56.

63. Utley, 167-71.

64. *FRUS: Japan, 1931-1941*, II, 755-56. Paul W. Schroeder, *The Axis Alliance and Japanese-American Relations, 1941* (Ithaca, N.Y.: 1958), 76-81.

65. Kimball, I, 215, 275-78. *FRUS: 1941* (Washington, D.C.: 1956), 661-65. Dallek, 306-7. Elliott Roosevelt, II, 1245-46. *FRUS: Japan, 1931-1941*, II, 768-70.

66. Utley, 174-75. Stimson Diary, November 25-26, 1941. Hearden, 218-21. Raymond A. Esthus, "President Roosevelt's Commitment to Britain to Intervene in a Pacific War," *Mississippi Valley Historical Review* (June 1963), 34-35.

67. Gordon W. Prange, *Pearl Harbor: The Verdict of History* (New York: 1986), 36-44, 136-37. Hans L. Trefousse, *Pearl Harbor: The Continuing Controversy* (Malabar, Fla.: 1982), 41. Sherwood, 431. Churchill, III, 606-7.

68. Vandenberg, 1.

69. Utley, 181.

70. Frederick W. Marks III, *Winds over Sand: The Diplomacy of Franklin Roosevelt* (Athens, Ga.: 1988), 40-119. Heinrichs, 178-79.

71. Dallek, 289.

72. Divine, *Roosevelt and World War II*, 47.

73. Dallek, 289.

# CHAPTER FIVE

# THE GRAND ALLIANCE, 1941-1943

1. *FRUS: The Conferences at Washington, 1941-1942, and Casablanca, 1943* (Washington, D.C.: 1968), 7 (hereafter cited as *FRUS: Washington and*

*Casablanca Conferences).* Winston S. Churchill, *The Second World War*, vol. III: *The Grand Alliance* (Boston: 1950), 608. Robert E. Sherwood, *Roosevelt and Hopkins: An Intimate History*, rev. ed. (New York: 1948, 1950), 445.

2. *FRUS: Washington and Casablanca Conferences*, 21-26. Warren F. Kimball, *Churchill and Roosevelt: The Complete Correspondence* (Princeton, N.J.: 1984), I, 292-313.

3. John Lewis Gaddis, *The United States and the Origins of the Cold War, 1941-1947* (New York: 1972), 67. Winston S. Churchill, *The Second World War*, vol. IV: *The Hinge of Fate* (Boston: 1950). Kimball, I, 292. Maurice Matloff and Edwin M. Snell, *Strategic Planning for Coalition Warfare, 1941-1942* (Washington, D.C.: 1953), 104-5.

4. Sherwood, 11, 296-98. William Hardy McNeil, *America, Britain, and Russia: Their Cooperation and Conflict, 1941-1946* (New York: 1970), 104-5. Matloff and Snell, *Strategic Planning for Coalition Warfare, 1941-1942*, 105.

5. *FRUS: Washington and Casablanca Conferences*, 161-68, 208, 262-65. Churchill, IV, 24-35. *FRUS: 1942* (Washington, D.C.: 1962), II, 124-25.

6. *FRUS: Washington and Casablanca Conferences*, 256-62.

7. Ibid., 376-77.

8. McNeil, 109.

9. Richard W. Steele, *The First Offensive 1942: Roosevelt, Marshall, and the Making of American Strategy* (Bloomington, Ind.: 1973), 76, 80. Churchill, IV, 190, 314. Kimball, I, 436-37.

10. Kimball, I, 458.

11. McNeil, 174. Churchill, IV, 314-20, 322-25.

12. Forrest C. Pogue, *George C. Marshall: Ordeal and Hope, 1939-1942* (New York: 1966), 319-20. Kimball, I, 458.

13. Anthony Eden, *The Reckoning* (Boston: 1945), 334-38. Churchill, III, 630, 696.

14. Joseph Stalin, *The Great Patriotic War of the Soviet Union* (New York: 1945), 44. Churchill, IV, 327.

15. Churchill, IV, 327. *FRUS: 1942*, III, 538. Robert Dallek, *Franklin D. Roosevelt and American Foreign Policy, 1932-1945* (New York: 1979), 296.

16. *FRUS: 1942*, III, 505-12. Cordell Hull, *The Memoirs of Cordell Hull* (New York: 1948), II, 1172.

17. Llewellyn Woodward, *British Foreign Policy in the Second World War* (London: 1971), II, 251-52.

18. Sherwood, 563-64. *FRUS: 1942*, III, 582-83.

19. Sherwood, 574-75, 577. *FRUS: 1942*, III, 583.

20. Churchill IV, 342; Churchill's emphasis. *FRUS: 1942*, III, 598.

21. Churchill, IV, 382-84, 432-35. *FRUS: Washington and Casablanca Conferences*, 433-38.

22. Robert C. Wedemeyer, *Wedemeyer Reports!* (New York: 1958), 160. Sherwood, 602.

23. Martin Gilbert, *Winston S. Churchill*, vol. VII: *Road to Victory, 1941-1945* (Boston: 1986). Ministry of Foreign Affairs of the U.S.S.R., *Stalin's Correspondence with Churchill, Attlee, Roosevelt and Truman, 1941-1945* (Moscow: 1957), II, 44; I, 52-56, 60-61. Churchill, IV, 270-71.

24. Steel, 174. Sherwood, 611-12. Churchill, IV, 447-48.

25. Maxwell Philip Schoenfeld, *The War Ministry of Winston Churchill* (Ames, Iowa: 1972), 176-77.

26. Julian G. Hurstfield, *America and the French Nation, 1939-1945* (Chapel Hill, N.C.: 1986), 162-63. *FRUS: 1942*, II, 453-57.

27. Kimball, II, 3. *FRUS: 1942*, II, 431. Milton Viorst, *Hostile Allies: FDR and Charles de Gaulle* (New York: 1965), 126.

28. *FRUS: 1942*, II, 437. Churchill, IV, 632. Viorst, 131. Hurstfield, 166-67.

29. Charles de Gaulle, *The War Memoirs of Charles de Gaulle*, vol. II: *Unity: 1942-1944*, Richard Howard, trans. (New York: 1959), 270.

30. Kimball, II, 255, 257.

31. De Gaulle, II, 88. Viorst, 91, 105-8.

32. McNeil, 46. Viorst, 178-9. *Stalin's Correspondence*, I, 139.

33. Schoenfeld, 182. *FRUS: 1942*, III, 478-79. *Stalin's Correspondence*, I, 75, 77, 80, 82.

34. Winston Churchill, *The Second World War*, vol. V: *Closing the Ring* (Boston: 1951), 3-16. Gilbert, 261.

35. Churchill, IV, 649-65. *FRUS: The Washington and Casablanca Conferences*, 488, 559, 738-52. Mark A. Stoler, *The Politics of the Second Front: American Military Planning and Diplomacy in Coalition Warfare, 1941-1943* (Westport, Conn.: 1977), 67-68.

36. *FRUS: The Washington and Casablanca Conferences*, 560, 631, 716-18, 785-89, 509-12, 595-97. Stoler, 70, 67. Dallek, 371.

37. Churchill, IV, 683, 692-93. Forrest C. Pogue, *George C. Marshall: Organizer of Victory, 1943-1945* (New York: 1973), 21-23, 26-31.

38. *FRUS: The Washington and Casablanca Conferences*, 727.

39. Churchill, IV, 688-91. Gabriel Kolko, *The Politics of War: The World and United States Foreign Policy, 1943-1945* (New York: 1968), 24.

40. Churchill, IV, 742-43. *Stalin's Correspondence*, I, 87, 95, 106, 110-12, II, 53. Kimball, II, 131-35, 139-40.

41. Kimball, II, 389-402, 192-93, 203-5. *FRUS: 1942*, III, 381-82, 390. *Stalin's Correspondence*, II, 60-61. NcNeil, 276.

42. Orville H. Bullitt, ed., *For the President: Personal and Secret: Correspondence Between Franklin D. Roosevelt and William C. Bullitt* (Boston: 1972), 575-79.

43. William C. Bullitt, "How We Won the War and Lost the Peace," *Life*, August 30, 1948, 94.

44. Gaddis, 64-65. Wedemeyer, 228-30.

45. *FRUS: The Washington and Casablanca Conferences*, 942.

46. Kimball, II, 153-54. *Stalin's Correspondence*, II, 63-64.

47. *FRUS: The Conferences at Washington and Quebec, 1943* (Washington, D.C.: 1970), 26-27.

48. Ibid., 348, 367-68, 193-95, Stoler 93, 95.

49. Kimball, II, 217-18, 244, 285-90. *Stalin's Correspondence*, II, 70, 136-41. *FRUS: 1943* (Washington, D.C.: 1963), III, 553.

50. *FRUS: 1943*, III, 557-62, 682-87, 690, 695-96, 708-9. Vojtech Mastny, "Stalin and the Prospects of a Separate Peace in World War II," *American Historical Review* 77 (December 1972), 1365-88.

51. Kimball, II, 214.

52. Churchill, V, 64. Kimball, II, 360-67, 380-81.

53. *FRUS: The Conferences at Washington and Quebec*, 1024-26, 1037-39. Kimball, II, 430.

54. McNeil, 308.

55. Ibid., 307-10. *FRUS: 1943*, III, 382-83.

56. Churchill, V, 128-29, 135-36.

57. *FRUS: The Conferences at Washington and Quebec*, 1222-24, 1290-92. Stoler, 125-28. Maurice Matloff and Edwin M. Snell, *Strategic Planning for Coalition Warfare, 1943-1944* (Washington, D.C.: 1959), 249-59. Gilbert, 520-28.

58. *Stalin's Correspondence*, II, 83, 90.

59. *FRUS, 1943*, I, 577-70, 771-81.

60. Leland M. Goodrich and Marie J. Carroll, eds., *Documents on American Foreign Relations*, vol. VI: *July 1943-June 1944* (Boston: 1945), 229-30, 315, 318. Hull, II, 1314-15. Robert A. Divine, *Second Chance: The Triumph of Internationalism in America During World War II* (New York: 1967), 153.

61. Hull, II, 1284-87.

62. Ibid., 1283-84, 1297-99, 1305-6.

63. Kimball, II, 606.

64. Churchill, V, 290-93. Gilbert, 537, 543-44. Matloff and Snell, *Strategic Planning for Coalition Warfare, 1943-1944*, 303-4. Stimson Diary, October 29, 1943. Stoler, 133-34.

65. *FRUS: The Conferences at Cairo and Tehran, 1943* (Washington, D.C.: 1961), 3-80. Kimball, II, 544. *Stalin's Correspondence*, II, 105.

66. Kimball, II, 597, 578-79.

67. Ibid., 608-9.

68. *FRUS: The Conferences at Cairo and Tehran, 1943*, 494-97, 505-8, 538-39, 545-48. Kimball, II, 610. Stimson Diary, December 5, 1943.

69. *FRUS: The Conferences at Cairo and Tehran, 1943*, 600.

70. Ibid., 594, 598-601.

71. Dallek, 436-37.

72. *FRUS: The Conferences at Cairo and Tehran, 1943*, 595. Kimball, II, 611.

73. *FRUS: The Conferences at Cairo and Tehran, 1943*, 255-56. Matloff and Snell, *Strategic Planning for Coalition Warfare, 1943-1944*, 342.

74. *FRUS: The Conferences at Cairo and Tehran, 1943*, 531.

75. Ibid., 530.

76. Ibid., 530-32.

77. *FRUS: The Conferences at Cairo and Tehran, 1943*, 725-26.

78. Kimball, II, 616-17, 612-13.

79. Dallek, 439.

# CHAPTER SIX

# THE ROAD TO VICTORY, 1944-1945

1. William Hardy McNeil, *America, Britain, and Russia: Their Cooperation and Conflict, 1941-1946* (New York: 1970), 410. Gabriel Kolko, *The Politics of War: The World and United States Foreign Policy, 1943-1945* (New York, 1968), 123-28. Vojtech Mastny, *Russia's Road to the Cold War: Diplomacy, Warfare, and the Politics of Communism, 1941-1945* (New York: 1979), 133-44.

2. Terry H. Anderson, *The United States, Great Britain, and the Cold War, 1944-1947* (Columbia, Mo.: 1981), 11-12.

3. Ibid., 12-13. Winston S. Churchill, *The Second World War*, vol. V: *Closing the Ring* (Boston: 1951), 129-30.

4. Fraser J. Harbutt, *The Iron Curtain: Churchill, America, and the Origins of the Cold War* (New York: 1986), 48. John W. Wheeler-Bennett and Anthony Nichols, *The Semblance of Peace: The Political Settlement after the Second World War* (New York: 1972), 290.

5. McNeil, 404. Robert E. Sherwood, *Roosevelt and Hopkins: An Intimate History*, rev. ed. (New York: 1948, 1950), 786, 827. Cordell Hull, *The Memoirs of Cordell Hull* (New York: 1948), II, 1656-57.

6. Harbutt, 61-62.

7. Winston S. Churchill, *The Second World War*, vol. VI: *Triumph and Tragedy* (Boston: 1953), 62-64. Warren F. Kimball, *Churchill and Roosevelt: The Complete Correspondence* (Princeton, N.J.: 1984), III, 197-98. Robert Dallek, *Franklin D. Roosevelt and American Foreign Policy, 1932-1945* (New York: 1979), 456-57.

8. Francis L. Loewenheim, Harold D. Langley, and Manfred Jonas, eds., *Roosevelt and Churchill: Their Secret Wartime Correspondence* (New York: 1975), 548-49. Churchill, VI, 64-66. Alfred D. Chandler, Jr., et. al., eds., *The Papers of Dwight D. Eisenhower: The War Years* (Baltimore: 1970), III, 1938.

9. Churchill, VI, 100.

10. Kimball, *Roosevelt and Churchill*, III, 153, 177. See also Warren F. Kimball, "Naked Reverse Right: Roosevelt, Churchill, and Eastern Europe, from TOLSTOY to Yalta--and a Little Beyond," *Diplomatic History* 9 (Winter 1985), 1-24.

11. Kimball, *Roosevelt and Churchill*, III, 153-54. *FRUS: 1944*, (Washington, D.C.: 1965-1966), V, 114-15. Churchill, VI, 75-77. McNeil, 404.

12. Kimball, *Roosevelt and Churchill*, III, 177, 182, 201-3. Hull, II, 1454-58.

13. Llewellyn Woodward, *British Foreign Policy in the Second World War* (London: 1971), III, 197-200. Kimball, *Roosevelt and Churchill*, III, 260.

14. Ministry of Foreign Affairs of the U.S.S.R., *Stalin's Correspondence with Churchill, Attlee, Roosevelt and Truman, 1941-1945* (Moscow: 1957), I, 254. Churchill, VI, 134. Woodward, III, 202-12.

15. Kimball, *Roosevelt and Churchill*, III, 281-83, 295-96. Churchill, VI, 135, 140. *Stalin's Correspondence*, I, 254-55.

16. Dallek, 465. Woodward, III, 218-21.
17. *FRUS: 1944*, I, 653-98.
18. Ibid., 737-38, 744, 758-59. *Stalin's Correspondence*, II, 158-59.
19. *FRUS: 1944*, I, 743, 788, 806-7. *Stalin's Correspondence*, II, 160.
20. Dallek, 467.
21. Ibid., 468-69.
22. *FRUS: The Conference at Quebec, 1944* (Washington, D.C.: 1972), 367, 490.
23. *FRUS: The Conference at Quebec, 1944*, 492-93.
24. Ibid., 86-91. Dallek, 472.
25. *FRUS: The Conference at Quebec, 1944*, 325-26, 344-46, 360-63, 169-73, 177-81. Anderson, 11. John Morton Blum, *From the Morgenthau Diaries*, vol. III: *Years of War, 1941-1945* (Boston: 1967), 310. Churchill VI, 134. Warren F. Kimball, *Swords or Ploughshares? The Morgenthau Plan for Defeated Nazi Germany, 1943-1946* (Philadelphia: 1976), 37-41.
26. *FRUS: The Conference at Quebec, 1944*, 381, 392, 476.
27. Kimball, *Swords or Ploughshares?*, 41-44. Blum, III, 375-83, 314-22.
28. Churchill, VI, 216.
29. Churchill, VI, 217. Kimball, *Roosevelt and Churchill*, 342, 344. Dallek, 478-79.
30. Loewenheim, 514.
31. Churchill, VI, 227-28.
32. Kimball, *Roosevelt and Churchill*, 351.
33. *FRUS: 1944*, IV, 1005-10. *Stalin's Correspondence*, II, 164. Churchill, VI, 231.
34. Churchill, VI, 237. Kimball, *Roosevelt and Churchill*, 365-66.
35. Churchill, VI, 243. *Stalin's Correspondence*, II, 165. Kimball, *Roosevelt and Churchill*, 371.
36. Harbutt, 78. Woodward, III, 351-52. *FRUS: The Conferences at Malta and Yalta, 1945* (Washigton, D.C.: 1955), 250-54.
37. Churchill, VI, 231-35.
38. Loewenheim, 510. Dallek, 504. Woodward, III, 458. *FRUS, 1944*, III, 1162.
39. Kimball, *Roosevelt and Churchill*, III, 437-39. 266-71.
40. Churchill, VI, 289. Woodward, III, 383-88, 410-14. Kolko, 173-74.
41. Churchill, VI, 299-301, 322-24. Kimball, *Roosevelt and Churchill*, 455-56. Woodward, III, 419, 435.
42. Kimball, *Roosevelt and Churchill*, III, 390-92.
43. *FRUS: The Conferences at Malta and Yalta*, 286-87, 291.
44. Ibid., 288-92.
45. W. Averell Harriman and Ellie Abel, *Special Envoy to Churchill and Stalin: 1941-1946* (New York: 1975), 369. Arthur Bliss Lane, *I Saw Poland Betrayed* (Indianapolis: 1948), 66.
46. *FRUS: The Conferences at Malta and Yalta*, 217-19, 221-25. *Stalin's Correspondence*, I, 289-92. Stimson Diary, December 31, 1944.
47. *FRUS: The Conferences at Malta and Yalta*, 12-27.

48. Lord Moran, *Churchill: Taken from the Diaries of Lord Moran* (Boston: 1966), 242-43. Sherwood, 845.

49. *FRUS: The Conferences at Malta and Yalta*, xi.

50. Ibid., 464-67, 470-74, 481-82.

51. Ibid., 486, 543. Kimball, *Roosevelt and Churchill*, III, 523.

52. Kimball, *Roosevelt and Churchill*, III, 524.

53. Dallek, 509-10. *FRUS: The Conferences at Malta and Yalta*, 616-19, 628-30.

54. *FRUS: The Conferences at Malta and Yalta*, 113-18. Kimball, *Roosevelt and Churchill*, III, 527-28.

55. *FRUS: The Conferences at Malta and Yalta*, 620-22, 630-31.

56. Blum, III, 305. Kimball, *Roosevelt and Churchill*, 528. *FRUS: The Conferences at Malta and Yalta*, 621, 971.

57. Kimball, *Roosevelt and Churchill*, III, 528.

58. *Stalin's Correspondence*, II, 181. Diane Shaver Clemens, *Yalta* (New York: 1970), 173.

59. Kimball, *Roosevelt and Churchill*, III, 526. *FRUS: The Conferences at Malta and Yalta*, 667, 677-78. Dallek, 513.

60. *FRUS: The Conferences at Malta and Yalta*, 679-81.

61. Ibid., 973. Kimball, *Roosevelt and Churchill*, III, 527.

62. *FRUS: The Conferences at Malta and Yalta*, 974. William D. Leahy, *I Was There* (New York: 1950), 315-16.

63. *FRUS: The Conferences at Malta and Yalta*, 860-63, 918-19, 854.

64. Dallek, 508. William C. Widenor, "American Planning for the United Nations: Have We Been Asking the Right Questions?" *Diplomatic History* 6 (Summer 1982), 264-65.

65. *FRUS: The Conferences at Malta and Yalta*, 660-67, 682-86.

66. Ibid., 660-67. Kimball, *Roosevelt and Churchill*, III, 527.

67. *FRUS: The Conferences at Malta and Yalta*, 844, 771-72. Anthony Eden, *The Reckoning* (Boston: 1945), 595. Clemens, 242. Kimball, *Roosevelt and Churchill*, III, 530-33.

68. Clemens, 247-49. *FRUS: The Conferences at Malta and Yalta*, 770.

69. *FRUS: The Conferences at Malta and Yalta*, 378-79, 768-71.

70. Ibid., 396-99. Kimball, *Roosevelt and Churchill*, III, 527. Dallek, 519.

71. *FRUS: The Conferences at Malta and Yalta*, 982.

72. Ibid., 748-49. Clemens, 246.

73. *FRUS: The Conferences at Malta and Yalta*, 738-40, 877, 982.

74. Ibid., 974-75.

75. Leland M. Goodrich and Marie J. Carroll, eds., *Documents on American Foreign Relations*, vol. VII: *July 1944-June 1945* (Boston: 1947), 28.

76. Beatrice B. Berle and Travis B. Jacobs, eds., *Navigating the Rapids, 1918-1971: From the Papers of Adolf A. Berle* (New York: 1973), 477. Dallek, 521.

77. Kimball, *Roosevelt and Churchill*, III, 625. *FRUS: 1945* (Washington, D.C.: 1967), V, 142-44, 530.

78. McNeil, 578.

79. Kimball, *Roosevelt and Churchill*, III, 545-51.

80.  Ibid., 560-64.
81.  *FRUS: 1945*, V, 180-82. Kimball, *Roosevelt and Churchill*, III, 585-89, 593-94.
82.  *FRUS: 1945*, V, 194-96. *Stalin's Correspondence*, II, 211-18.
83.  *Stalin's Correspondence*, II, 197, 200-201, 205-6. *FRUS: 1945*, III, 737.
84.  Dallek, 526. Kimball, *Roosevelt and Churchill*, III, 586-87, 609-12. *Stalin's Correspondence*, II, 207-8.
85.  Kimball, *Roosevelt and Churchill*, III, 613.
86.  *FRUS: 1945*, V, 197. Kimball, *Roosevelt and Churchill*, III, 617.
87.  Kimball, *Roosevelt and Churchill*, III, 607-9, 616, 602-3. Chandler, IV, 2551, 2560-62.
88.  Kimball, *Roosevelt and Churchill*, III, 629-30.
89.  Ibid., 631.
90.  For a review of the historiography of Roosevelt's wartime diplomacy, see Mark A. Stoler, "World War II Diplomacy in Historical Writing: Prelude to Cold War," in Gerald K. Haines and J. Samuel Walker, eds., *American Foreign Relations: A Historiographical Review* (Westport, Conn.: 1981), 187-206.
91.  William C. Bullitt, "How We Won the War and Lost the Peace," *Life*, August 30, 1948, 82-97.
92.  Chester Wilmot, *The Struggle for Europe* (New York: 1952), 707-17. Anthony Kubeck, *How the Far East Was Lost: American Policy and the Creation of Communist China, 1941-1949* (Chicago: 1963), 94-101.
93.  Frederick W. Marks III, *Winds over Sand: The Diplomacy of Franklin Roosevelt* (Athens, Ga.: 1988), 177, 173.
94.  Raymond G. O'Connor, *Diplomacy for Victory: F.D.R. and Unconditional Surrender* (New York: 1971), 103-4.
95.  George F. Kennan, *American Diplomacy, 1900-1950* (Chicago: 1951), 74-90.
96.  Arthur M. Schlesinger, Jr., "Origins of the Cold War," *Foreign Affairs* 46 (October 1967), 47.
97.  John Lewis Gaddis, *Russia, the Soviet Union, and the United States: An Interpretive History* (New York: 1978), 167-68. Dallek, 534.

# CHAPTER SEVEN

# THE COLLAPSE OF THE GRAND ALLIANCE, 1945-1947

1.  Margaret Truman, *Harry S. Truman* (New York: 1973), 203. Alonzo L. Hamby, "The Mind and Character of Harry S. Truman," in Michael J. Lacey, ed., *The Truman Presidency* (New York: 1949), 19-53.
2.  Walter Millis, ed., *The Forrestal Diaries* (New York: 1951), 48-51.

*FRUS: 1945* (Washington, D.C.: 1967), V, 231-34, 252-55.

3. Winston S. Churchill, *The Second World War*, vol. VI: *Triumph and Tragedy* (Boston: 1953), 551-52. Harry S. Truman, *Memoirs*, vol. I: *Year of Decisions* (Garden City, N.Y.: 1955), 239, 243.

4. *FRUS: 1945*, V, 232, 211-12, 219-21, 256-58. Harry S. Truman, I, 82.

5. *FRUS: 1945*, V, 999-1000. Harry S. Truman, I, 228, 254-59. George C. Herring, Jr., "Lend-Lease and the Origins of the Cold War, 1944-1945," *Journal of American History* 56 (June 1969), 105-7. Geir Lundestad, *The American Non-Policy Towards Eastern Europe, 1943-1947* (Tromso, Norway: 1978), 379-84.

6. *FRUS: 1945*, IV, 263-64; V, 540-41, 281-84. Deborah Welch Larson, *Origins of Containment: A Psychological Explanation* (Princeton, N.J.: 1985), 174.

7. Larson, 174-75. *FRUS: 1945*, V, 252-54.

8. *FRUS: 1945*, I, 25-27, 312-21, 350-51, 614, 731, 734-39. *FRUS: 1945*, V, 252-55. Lisle A. Rose, *Dubious Victory: The United States and the End of World War II* (Kent, Ohio: 1973), 171-76.

9. Alfred D. Chandler, Jr., et. al., eds., *The Papers of Dwight D. Eisenhower: The War Years* (Baltimore: 1970), IV, 2662; Eisenhower's emphasis. Harry S. Truman, I, 245.

10. Hadley Cantril and Mildred Strunk, *Public Opinion: 1935-1946* (Princeton, N.J.: 1951), 371. Rose, 101. *FRUS: 1945*, V, 233.

11. Henry L. Stimson Diary, May 14, 1945.

12. Harry S. Truman, I, 87.

13. Daniel Yergin, *Shattered Peace: The Origins of the Cold War and the National Security State* (Boston: 1977), 101. *FRUS: The Conference of Berlin (The Potsdam Conference)* (Washington, D.C.: 1960), I, 4, 8.

14. Rose, 124-26. Roberto Rabel, "Prologue to Containment: The Truman Administration's Response to the Trietse Crisis of May 1945," *Diplomatic History* 10 (Spring 1986), 155-56. Richard A. Best, Jr., *"Co-operation with Like-Minded Peoples": British Influences on American Security Policy* (Westport, Conn.: 1986), 86.

15. Harry S. Truman Diary, May 23, 1945, quoted in Larson, 177-78.

16. *FRUS: Potsdam Conference*, I, 735, 737-38. *FRUS: 1945*, V, 300-6. Eduard Mark, "American Policy Towards Eastern Europe and the Origins of the Cold War, 1941-1946: An Alternative Interpretation," *Journal of American History* 68 (September 1981), 327.

17. Fraser J. Harbutt, *The Iron Curtain: Churchill, America, and the Origins of the Cold War* (New York: 1986), 106. *FRUS: 1945*, I, 1, 706-7, 819, 825-26.

18. Stimson Diary, June 6, 1945.

19. *FRUS: Potsdam Conference*, I, 92-93. John Morton Blum, ed., *The Price of Vision: The Diary of Henry A. Wallace, 1942-1946* (Boston: 1973), 454-55. Terry H. Anderson, *The United States, Great Britain, and the Cold War, 1944-1947* (Columbia, Mo.: 1981), 68-72. Rose, 192-93.

20. Harbutt, 112.

21. *FRUS: Potsdam Conference*, II, 357-65, 370-72. Rose, 281-82.

22. *FRUS: Potsdam Conference*, II, 1479. Robert L. Messer, *The End of an Alliance: James F. Byrnes, Roosevelt, Truman, and the Origins of the Cold War* (Chapel Hill, N.C.: 1982), 110.

23. *FRUS: Potsdam Conference*, II, 1474-76.

24. Ibid., 1501-5.

25. James F. Byrnes, *Speaking Frankly* (New York: 1947), 81-82.

26. *FRUS: Potsdam Conference*, II, 533-34, 1509. Rose, 297.

27. *FRUS: Potsdam Conference*, II, 1509-10.

28. Ibid., 1505-6. Byrnes, *Speaking Frankly*, 85.

29. *FRUS: Potsdam Conference*, II, 512-18, 533-34, 1509, 256-59, 1427-28, 304, 258, 365-67, 538.

30. Ibid., 237, 309, 1389.

31. Rose, 298-99. Harry S. Truman, I, 380. Anderson, 79.

32. Anderson, 70 80.

33. Byrnes, *Speaking Frankly*, 97. *FRUS: 1945*, II, 163-66. John Lewis Gaddis, *The United States and the Origins of the Cold War, 1941-1947* (New York: 1972), 264-65.

34. *FRUS: 1945*, II, 194-97, 243-44, 246-47, 292-93, 313-15, 336-39, 357-58, 487-88. Gaddis, *Origins*, 265-66.

35. James L. Byrnes, *All in One Lifetime* (New York: 1958), 357-60. Gaddis, *Origins*, 267.

36. Gary R. Hess, "The Iranian Crisis of 1945-46 and the Cold War," *Political Science Quarterly* 89 (March 1974), 125-26. Harold Smith Diary, October 5, 1945, quoted in Larson, 223-24. Blum, 501-2.

37. Gaddis, *Origins*, 276.

38. Byrnes, *Speaking Frankly*, 107. Eduard Mark, "Charles E. Bohlen and the Acceptable Limits of Soviet Hegemony in Eastern Europe: A Memorandum of 18 October 1945," *Diplomatic History* 3 (Spring 1979), 207-13.

39. Byrnes, *All in One Lifetime*, 318-19. *FRUS: 1945*, II, 582-83, 588-91, 593-95, 597.

40. *FRUS: 1945*, IV, 405-6, 409-10. *FRUS: 1945*, V, 633-37.

41. *FRUS: 1945*, II, 752-56, 821-22, 770-71, 819. Byrnes, *Speaking Frankly*, 115-17. Gaddis, *Origins*, 280-81.

42. *FRUS: 1945*, II, 69-73, 92-96. Messer, 143-44.

43. George F. Kennan, *Memoirs, 1925-1950* (Boston: 1967), 284.

44. Harry S. Truman, I, 551-52.

45. Byrnes, *All in One Lifetime*, 346-47, 353-55, 400-3. Messer, 156-66.

46. Larson, 252.

47. Anderson, 108, 116-17. *Time*, February 18, 1946, 25-26. *The Dallas Times Herald* is quoted in Anderson, 109.

48. Stalin's speech appears in *Vital Speeches* 12 (March 1, 1946), 300-304. Gaddis, *Origins*, 299-301.

49. Larson, 252-55. Messer, 169-78. Athan Theoharis, "Roosevelt and Truman on Yalta: The Origins of the Cold War," *Political Science Review* 87 (June 1972), 239-41.

50. Harbutt, 159. Gaddis, *Origins*, 252-53, 301-2. Messer, 185-86.

51.  Arthur H. Vandenberg, Jr., and J. A. Morris, eds., *The Private Papers of Senator Vandenberg* (Boston: 1952), 248. The text of Vandenberg's speech appears in *Vital Speeches* 12 (March 15, 1946), 322-26.

52.  *FRUS: 1946* (Washington, D.C.: 1969), V, 307, 229; VI, 74-75. Harbutt, 166-67.

53.  *FRUS: 1946*, VII, 334-35.

54.  Harry S. Truman, *Memoirs*, Vol. II: *Years of Trial and Hope* (Garden City, N. J.: 1956), 95. *FRUS: 1946*, VII, 524, 529-32. *FRUS: 1945*, VIII, 45. Joyce and Gabriel Kolko, *The Limits of Power: The World and United States Foreign Policy, 1945-1954* (New York: 1972), 242, 236.

55.  Byrnes, *All in One Lifetime*, 351. Millis, 141. Bruce Robellet Kuniholm, *The Origins of the Cold War in the Near East: Great Power Conflict and Diplomacy in Iran, Turkey, and Greece* (Princeton, N.J.: 1980), 335-37.

56.  The text of the Long Telegram appears in Thomas H. Etzold and John Lewis Gaddis, eds., *Containment: Documents on American Policy and Strategy, 1945-1950* (New York: 1978), 30-63.

57.  Kennan, 294. John Lewis Gaddis, *The Long Peace: Inquiries into the History of the Cold War* (New York: 1987), 40. Messer, 183.

58.  Messer, 188, 190; Truman's emphases. The text of Brynes' speech appears in *Vital Speeches* 12 (March 15, 1946), 326-29.

59.  The text of Churchill's speech appears in *Vital Speeches* 12 (March 15, 1946), 329-32. William Taubman, *Stalin's American Policy: From Entente to Détente to Cold War* (New York: 1982), 140.

60.  *Public Opinion Quarterly* 10 (Winter 1946-1947), 264. Gaddis, *Origins*, 309. Larson, 266.

61.  Harbutt, 161, 168. Gaddis, *Origins*, 307. Byrnes, *All in One Lifetime*, 349. Byrnes, *Speaking Frankly*, 119-20. Larson, 265.

62.  *FRUS: 1946*, VII, 340-42, 345-48. Hess, 137.

63.  Messer, 267. Kolko, 241. Harbutt, 251-52.

64.  Messer, 185.

65.  Harry S. Truman, I, 555-56. Gaddis, *Origins*, 315, 284.

66.  Harbutt, 269. Vandenberg, 2.

67.  Patricia Dawson Ward, *The Threat of Peace: James F. Byrnes and the Council of Foreign Ministers, 1945-1946* (Kent, Ohio: 1979), 175.

68.  Redvers Opie, Joseph W. Ballantine, Paul Birdsall, et. al., *The Search for Peace Settlements* (Washington: D.C.: 1951), 95-103.

69.  Ibid., 144-72.

70.  Lundestad, 345, 103.

71.  Ward, 119.

72.  John Gimbel, "Cold War Historians and the Occupation of Germany," in Hans A. Schmitt, *U.S. Occupation in Europe After World War II* (Lawrence, Kans.: 1978), 89-91. *FRUS: 1945*, III, 890.

73.  *FRUS: 1946*, V, 541-42, 545-47, 549. Robert A. Pollard, *Economic Security and the Origins of the Cold War, 1945-1950* (New York: 1985), 94-99.

74.  The text of the treaty proposed by Byrnes appears in *FRUS: 1946*, II, 190-93. Ward, 94. Vandenberg and Morris, 268; Vandenberg's emphasis.

75. Byrnes, *Speaking Frankly*, 171-76. *FRUS: 1946*, II, 146-47, 166-73, 431-32; V, 561-62.

76. Gaddis, *Origins*, 328, 330-31. Pollard, 101-3. Gimbel, "Cold War Historians and the Occupation of Germany," 91-92.

77. The text of Byrnes' speech appears in *Vital Speeches* 12 (September 15, 1946), 706-9.

78. *FRUS: 1946*, V, 605.

79. Messer, 205. Ward, 140.

80. U.S. Department of State, *Documents on Disarmament, 1945-1959* (Washington, D.C.: 1960), I, 13.

81. Ibid., I, 17-24.

82. Gregg Herken, *The Winning Weapon: The Atomic Bomb and the Cold War, 1945-1950* (New York: 1980), 174-78.

83. *FRUS: 1946*, VII, 827-29.

84. Melvyn P. Leffler, "Strategy, Diplomacy, and the Cold War: The United States, Turkey, and NATO, 1945-1952," *Journal of American History* 71 (March 1985), 815, *FRUS: 1946*, VII, 821-22, 840-42.

85. Harry S. Truman, II, 96-98. *FRUS: 1946*, VII, 847-48. Jonathan Knight, "American Statecraft and the 1946 Black Sea Straits Controversy," *Political Science Quarterly* 90 (Fall 1975), 467, 454.

86. Knight, 466.

87. Pollard, 70, 71. Justus D. Doenecke, *Not to the Swift: The Old Isolationists in the Cold War Era* (Lewisburg, Pa.: 1979), 62, 65. Peter G. Boyle, "The British Foreign Office View of Soviet-American Relations, 1945-1946." *Diplomatic History* 3 (Summer 1979), 318.

88. Boyle, 318.

89. *FRUS: 1945*, V, 945-47. Thomas G. Paterson, "The Abortive American Loan to Russia and the Origins of the Cold War, 1943-1946," *Journal of American History* 56 (June 1969), 70, 75, 81, 84.

90. Paterson, 86-90.

91. Messer, 207. Blum, 589-601. Yergin, 251.

92. The text of Wallace's speech appears in *Vital Speeches* 12 (October 1, 1946), 738-41.

93. Byrnes, *Speaking Frankly*, 240-41. Byrnes, *All In One Lifetime*, 370-76. Harry S. Truman, I, 557-60. Millis, 206-10.

94. The text of the Clifford-Elsey Report appears in Etzold and Gaddis, 64-71. Melvyn P. Leffler, "The American Conception of National Security and the Beginnings of the Cold War, 1945-48," *American Historical Review* 89 (April 1984), 381, 360-62, 369.

95. Etzold and Gaddis, 64-71.

96. Ibid.

97. Margaret Truman, 297. Larson, 301.

98. William O. McCagg, Jr., *Stalin Embattled: 1943-1948* (Detroit: 1978), 259, 257-58.

99. *FRUS: 1947* (Washington, D.C.: 1971), V, 32-37. Pollard, 118.

100. Lawrence S. Wittner, *American Intervention in Greece, 1943-1949* (New York: 1982), 57-59.

101.  *FRUS: 1946*, VII, 209-13, 223, 257, 262-63, 285-86.

102.  *FRUS: 1947*, V, 58-59.

103.  Dean Acheson, *Present at the Creation: My Years in the State Department* (New York: 1969), 219.

104.  Larson, 307. Pollard, 123.

105.  *Public Papers of the Presidents of the United States: Harry S. Truman, 1947* (Washington, D.C.: 1963), 178-79.

106.  Doenecke, 76-86. Pollard, 124-25.

107.  Larson, 314. Robert M. Hathaway, *Ambiguous Partnership: Britain and America, 1944-1947* (New York: 1981), 303.

108.  Gaddis, *Origins*, 352.

109.  Geoffrey S. Smith, "'Harry, We Hardly Know You': Revisionism, Politics and Diplomacy, 1945-1954," *American Political Science Review* 70 (June 1976), 560-82.

110.  Pollard, 247-48.

111.  Taubman, 126-33.

112.  Lloyd C. Gardner, Arthur Schlesinger, Jr., and Hans J. Morgenthau, *The Origins of the Cold War* (Waltham, Mass.: 1970), 94-95.

113.  Ibid., 96, 102.

## CHAPTER EIGHT

## THE CREATION OF THE NORTH ATLANTIC ALLIANCE, 1947-1950

1.  *FRUS: 1947* (Washington, D.C.: 1972), V, 114. Robert A. Pollard, *Economic Security and the Origins of the Cold War, 1945-1950* (New York: 1985), 128.

2.  Timothy P. Ireland, *Creating the Entangling Alliance: The Origins of the North Atlantic Treaty Organization* (Westport, Conn.: 1981), 22. *FRUS: 1947*, II, 767, 789-90. Norman A. Graebner, *Cold War Diplomacy*, 2nd. ed. (New York: 1977), 45. John Lewis Gaddis, *The Long Peace: Inquiries into the History of the Cold War* (New York: 1987), 55.

3.  Melvyn P. Leffler, "The United States and the Strategic Dimensions of the Marshall Plan," *Diplomatic History* 12 (Summer 1988), 279. Pollard, 134. *FRUS: 1947*, III, 204-19, 230-32. Ireland, 134. Walter LaFeber, *America, Russia, and the Cold War, 1945-1975*, 3rd. ed. (New York: 1976), 59, 61-62.

4.  Pollard, 144. *FRUS: 1947*, III, 197-201, 220-30. *FRUS: 1948* (Washington, D.C.: 1974), III, 7; II, 515-18.

5.  The text of Marshall's address appears in *FRUS: 1947*, III, 237-39.

6.  *FRUS: 1947*, III, 228, 237-39.

7.  Ibid., 299-303. LaFeber, 60.

8.  LaFeber, 60. *FRUS: 1947*, III, 318-22. Pollard, 136-40.

9. Alfred Grosser, *The Western Alliance: European-American Relations,* Michael Shaw, trans. (New York: 1982), 63. Pollard, 146. Arthur H. Vandenberg, Jr., and J. A. Morris eds., *The Private Papers of Senator Vandenberg* (Boston: 1952), 88.

10. U.S. Congress, Senate Committee on Foreign Relations, *Hearings: European Recovery Program,* 80th Cong., 2nd sess. (Washington, D.C.: 1948), pt. 1, 36. Pollard, 151.

11. Richard A. Best, Jr., *"Co-operation with Like-minded Peoples": British Influences on American Security Policy, 1945-1949* (Westport, Conn.: 1986), 149-51. Alan K. Henrikson, "The Creation of the North Atlantic Alliance, 1948-1952," *Naval War College Review* 33 (May/June 1980), 7-8. Sean Greenwood, "Return to Dunkirk: The Origins of the Anglo-French Treaty of March 1947," *The Journal of Strategic Studies* 6 (December 1983), 49-65.

12. *FRUS. 1947,* II, 815-17.

13. Martin H. Folly, "Breaking the Vicious Circle: Britain, the United States, and the Genesis of the North Atlantic Treaty," *Diplomatic History* 12 (Winter 1988), 61. *FRUS: 1948,* III, 9.

14. Great Britain, *Parliamentary Debates* (Commons), 5th series, vol. 446 (1947-1948), 383-410.

15. *FRUS: 1948,* III, 7-8. Folly, 62-63.

16. *FRUS: 1948,* III, 287. Best, 160-61. Folly, 70-71.

17. John Baylis, "Britain, the Brussels Pact and the Continental Commitment," *International Affairs* 60 (Autumn 1984), 622. *FRUS: 1948,* III, 9-12. Ireland, 223.

18. *FRUS: 1948,* III, 9-12. Baylis, 622.

19. Folly, 63. Baylis, 623. *FRUS: 1948,* III, 19.

20. Folly, 65. Baylis, 623.

21. *FRUS: 1948,* II, 63-65; III, 26-29, 14-16, 33-34. Folly, 66.

22. *FRUS: 1948,* III, 34-35; IV, 747-54.

23. Graebner, 44.

24. *FRUS: 1948,* III, 46-48. Alfred Goldberg, gen. ed., *History of the Office of the Secretary of Defense,* vol. I: Steven L. Rearden, *The Formative Years: 1947-1950* (Washington, D.C.: 1984), 279.

25. Rearden, 218. Lucius D. Clay, *Decision in Germany* (Garden City, N.Y.: 1950), 354. Jean Edward Smith, ed., *The Papers of General Lucius D. Clay: Germany, 1945-1949* (Bloomington, Ind.: 1974), II, 568-69. Rearden, 283. Jean Edward Smith, "The View from USFET: General Clay's and Washington's Interpretation of Soviet Intentions in Germany," in Hans A. Schmitt, ed., *U.S. Occupation Policy in Europe after World War II* (Lawrence, Kan.: 1978), 176.

26. *Public Papers of the Presidents of the United States: Harry S. Truman, 1948* (Washington, D.C.: 1964), 182-86 (hereafter cited as *PPT: 1948*). Pollard, 152. LaFeber, 73.

27. *FRUS: 1948,* III, 46-48. Folly, 68.

28. *FRUS: 1948,* III, 48. Ireland, 75.

29. The text of the Brussels Treaty appears in Raymond Dennett and Robert K. Turner, eds., *Documents on American Foreign Relations* (Princeton, N.J.:1950), X, 584-88.

30. *PPT: 1948*, 184. Best, 158-59.
31. *FRUS: 1948*, III, 60; Douglas' emphasis. Best, 164.
32. *FRUS:1948*, III, 71-75.
33. Ibid., 72, 78.
34. George F. Kennan, *Memoirs, 1925-1950* (Boston: 1967), I, 407. Daryl J. Hudson, "Vandenberg Reconsidered: Senate Resolution 239 and American Foreign Policy," *Diplomatic History* 1 (Winter 1977), 49-50. *FRUS: 1948*, III, 61-67, 108-9.
35. Ireland, 80. Leffler, 291.
36. *FRUS: 1948*, III, 82-84.
37. Ibid., I, pt. 1, 563.
38. Ibid., III, 85-88. Folly, 70.
39. *FRUS: 1948*, III, 92-96, 104-8, 116-19.
40. The text of the Vandenberg Resolution appears in *FRUS: 1948*, III, 135-36. Vandenberg and Morris, 411. Ireland, 100.
41. *FRUS: 1948*, II, 285-94, 305-17.
42. Avi Shlaim, *The United States and the Berlin Blockade, 1948-1949: A Study in Crisis Decision-Making* (Berkeley, Calif.: 1983), 110-68.
43. Walter Millis, ed., *The Forrestal Diaries* (New York: 1951), 454. LaFeber, 77. Daniel Yergin, *Shattered Peace: The Origins of the Cold War and the National Security State* (Boston: 1977), 377-79.
44. Yergin, 385, 395-96. Frank A. Nikovich, *Germany and the United States: The Transformation of the German Question Since 1945* (Boston: 1988), 68-73. Clay, 393-440. Herbert Feis, *From Trust to Terror: The Onset of the Cold War, 1945-1950* (New York: 1970), 366-74.
45. *FRUS: 1948*, III, 139, 148.
46. Ibid., III, 140-41.
47. Pollard, 226.
48. Ireland, 107. Leffler, 292-93. *FRUS: 1948*, III, 206-8, 142-43.
49. Ireland, 104-5. The text of the Washington Paper appears in *FRUS: 1948*, III, 237-48. Nikolaj Petersen, "Bargaining Power Among Potential Allies: Negotiating the North Atlantic Treaty, 1948-49," *Review of International Studies* 12 (1986), 198.
50. *FRUS: 1948*, III, 270. Harry S. Truman, *Memoirs*, vol. II: *Years of Trial and Hope, 1946-1952* (Garden City, N.Y.: 1956), 243.
51. *FRUS: 1948*, III, 125-26. Henrikson, 11.
52. Matthew A. Evangelista, "Stalin's Postwar Army Reappraised," *International Security* 7 (Winter 1982/1983), 110-38.
53. Best, 177-78.
54. Gregg Herken, *The Winning Weapon: The Atomic Bomb in the Cold War, 1945-1950* (New York: 1980), 197, 241, 220.
55. Ibid., 266. Leffler, 293. *FRUS: 1948*, III, 125; I, pt. 2, 662-69.
56. Best, 186-87. *FRUS: 1948*, III, 221-22, 276, 660.
57. The draft of the North Atlantic Treaty appears in *FRUS: 1948*, III, 333-43.
58. Ireland, 110-11. *FRUS: 1948*, III, 335. *FRUS: 1949* (Washington, D.C.: 1975), IV, 74, 76.

59. *FRUS: 1949*, IV, 108-10, 113-17. U.S. Congress, Senate, Committee on Foreign Relations, *Hearings: The Vandenberg Resolution and the North Atlantic Treaty*, 80th Cong., 2nd sess. and 81st Cong., 1st sess., Historical Series (Washington, D.C.: 1973), 106, 131-32. Ireland, 6-7.

60. Ireland, 119.

61. Ibid. Gaddis Smith, *Dean Acheson*, 70-71, vol. XVI of Robert H. Ferrell, ed., *The American Secretaries of State and Their Diplomacy* (New York: 1966). *Congressional Record*, 81st Cong., 1st sess., February 14, 1949, vol. 95, 1163-69.

62. *Congressional Record*, 81st Cong., 1st sess., July 11, 1949, vol. 95, 9205-9.

63. Henrikson, 23, 221.

64. U.S. Congress, Senate, Committee on Foreign Relations, *Hearings: North Atlantic Treaty*, 81st Cong., 1st sess. (Washington. D.C.. 1949), 12. Ireland, 119. David S. McLellan, *Dean Acheson, The State Department Years* (New York: 1976), 164-67.

65. *Congressional Record*, 81st Cong., 1st sess., March 30, 1949, vol. 95, 3443.

66. *Hearings: North Atlantic Treaty*, 1007, 417-21, 431-32. Robert A. Divine, "The Cold War and the Election of 1948," *Journal of American History* 59 (June 1972), 90-110.

67. LaFeber, 84. Justus D. Doenecke, *Not to the Swift: The Old Isolationists in the Cold War Era* (Lewisburg, Pa.: 1979), 155.

68. Doenecke, 155.

69. Doenecke, 156-59. Truman, II, 251-52. LaFeber, 84.

70. Henrikson, 27. U.S. Congress, Senate, Joint Session on Foreign Relations and Committee on Armed Services, *Hearings: Military Assistance*, 81st Cong., 1st sess. (Washington, D.C.: 1974), 123-24.

71. Henrikson, 27. *FRUS: 1949*, IV, 330-37.

72. *FRUS: 1949*, IV, 353-56.


# CONCLUSION

## THE ENTANGLING ALLIANCE

1. Harry S. Truman, *Memoirs*, vol. II: *Years of Trial and Hope, 1946-1952* (Garden City, N.Y.: 1956), 253. Alan K. Henrikson, "The Creation of the North Atlantic Alliance, 1948-1952," *Naval War College Review* 33 (May/June 1980), 32.

# Suggested Readings

## GENERAL HISTORIES

For the historiography of American diplomacy, see Gerald K. Haines and J. Samuel Walker, eds., *American Foreign Relations: A Historiographical Review* (Westport, Conn.: 1981) and Jerald A. Combs, *American Diplomatic History: Two Centuries of Changing Interpretations* (Berkeley, Calif.: 1983).

Among the best of the realist interpretations of American diplomatic history are the volumes by Norman A. Graebner, *Foundations of American Foreign Policy: A Realist Appraisal from Franklin to McKinley* (Wilmington, Del.: 1985), *America as a World Power: A Realist Appraisal from Wilson to Reagan* (Wilmington, Del.: 1984), and *Ideas and Diplomacy: Readings in the Intellectual Tradition of American Foreign Policy* (New York: 1964). Another is Robert E. Osgood's *Ideals and Self-Interest in America's Foreign Relations* (Chicago: 1953).

For an important revisionist interpretation, see William Appleman Williams, *The Shaping of American Diplomacy* (Chicago: 1956) and *The Tragedy of American Foreign Policy* (Cleveland: 1959).

Bibliographical material dealing with American isolationism can be found in Justus D. Doenecke, *The Literature of Isolationism: A Guide to Non-Interventionist Scholarship, 1930-1972* (Colorado Springs, Colo.: 1972) and his "The Literature of Isolationism, 1972-1983: A Bibliographical Guide," *The Journal of Libertarian Studies* 7 (Spring 1983), 157-84.

For general histories of Anglo-American diplomacy, see H. C. Allen, *Great Britain and the United States: A History of Anglo-American Relations, 1783-1952* (New York: 1953); Charles S. Campbell, Jr., *From Revolution to Rapprochement: The United States and Great Britain, 1783-1900* (New York: 1974); and Donald Cameron Watt, *Succeeding John Bull: America in Britain's Place, 1900-1975* (Cambridge, Eng.: 1984).

German-American relations are examined in Manfred Jones, *The United States and Germany: A Diplomatic History* (Ithaca, N.Y.: 1984).

# CHAPTER 1: 1901-1921

For the historiography of Roosevelt's diplomacy, see Paolo E. Coletta, "The Diplomacy of Theodore Roosevelt and William Howard Taft," in Gerald K. Haines and J. Samuel Walker, eds., *American Foreign Relations: A Historiographical Review* (Westport, Conn: 1981), 91-114.

For surveys of Roosevelt's foreign policies, see the classic, Howard K. Beale, *Theodore Roosevelt and the Rise of America to World Power* (Baltimore: 1956); Raymond A. Esthus, *Theodore Roosevelt and the International Rivalries* (Waltham, Mass.: 1970); Richard H. Collin, *Theodore Roosevelt: Culture, Diplomacy, and Expansion* (Baton Rouge: 1985); and Frederick W. Marks III, *Velvet on Iron: The Diplomacy of Theodore Roosevelt* (Lincoln, Neb.: 1979). For an interesting comparison of Roosevelt and Woodrow Wilson, see John Milton Cooper, Jr., *The Warrior and the Priest, Woodrow Wilson and Theodore Roosevelt* (Cambridge, Mass.: 1983).

Anglo-American relations during the era of Theodore Roosevelt are examined in Charles S. Campbell, *Anglo-American Understanding, 1898-1903* (Baltimore: 1957); Lionel Morris Gelber, *The Rise of Anglo-American Friendship: A Study in World Politics, 1898-1906* (Hamden, Conn.: 1966); and Bradford Perkins, *The Great Rapprochement: England and the United States, 1895-1914* (New York: 1968).

Japanese-American relations are discussed in Raymond A. Esthus, *Theodore Roosevelt and Japan* (Seattle: 1966); Charles E. Neu, *An Uncertain Friendship: Theodore Roosevelt and Japan, 1906-1909* (Cambridge, Mass.: 1967); Eugene P. Trani, *The Treaty of Portsmouth: An Adventure in American Diplomacy* (Lexington, Ky.: 1969); and John A. White, *The Diplomacy of the Russo-Japanese War* (Princeton, N.J.: 1964).

The origin and development of the concept of international organization are examined in Warren F. Kuehl, *Seeking World Order: The United States and International Organization to 1920* (Nashville: 1969). For The Hague conferences, see Calvin DeArmond David, *The United States and the First Hague Peace Conference* (Ithaca, N.Y.: 1962) and *The United States and the Second Hague Peace Conference: American Diplomacy and International Organization, 1899-1914* (Durham, N.C.: 1978).

For the historiography of Wilson's diplomacy, see Edith James, "Wilsonian Wartime Diplomacy: The Sense of the Seventies," in Gerald K. Haines and J. Samuel Walker, eds., *American Foreign Relations: A Historiographical Review,* 115-32. For the historiography of America's entrance into the war, see Daniel M. Smith, "National Interest and American Intervention, 1917: An Historiographical Approach," *Journal of American History* 52 (June, 1965), 5-24; Victor John Porto, "Woodrow Wilson, the War, and the Interpretations: 1917-1970," *Social Studies* 63 (1972), 22-31; and Jerald A. Combs, *American Diplomatic History: Two Centuries of Changing Interpretations* (Berkeley, Calif.: 1983), 132-52. For a summary of the major interpretations of Wilson's European diplomacy, see Lloyd E. Ambrosius, "The Orthodoxy of Revisionism: Woodrow Wilson and the New Left," *Diplomatic History* 1 (Summer 1977), 199-214, and Combs, 113-31.

Several books by the preeminent Wilson scholar, Arthur S. Link, are essential to an understanding of the president. They are *Wilson* (Princeton, N.J.: 1947), *Woodrow Wilson: Revolution, War, and Peace* (Arlington Heights, Ill: 1979), and *Woodrow Wilson and a Revolutionary World: 1913-1921* (Chapel Hill, N.C.: 1982). Link is also the editor of the monumental *The Papers of Woodrow Wilson*, of which sixty-two volumes have been published to date (1966-1990).

For psychobiographies of Wilson, see Alexander L. and Juliette L. George, *Woodrow Wilson and Colonel House: A Personality Study* (New York, 1964) and, the more vindictive, Sigmund Freud and William C. Bullitt, *Thomas Woodrow Wilson, Twenty-eighth President of the United States: A Psychological Study* (Boston: 1967).

For surveys of Woodrow Wilson's diplomacy, see Frederick S. Calhoun, *Power and Principle: Armed Intervention in Wilsonian Foreign Policy* (Kent, Ohio: 1986); and Daniel M. Smith, *The Great Departure: The United States and World War I, 1914-1920* (New York: 1965). John Milton Cooper, Jr.'s *The Vanity of Power: American Isolationism and the First World War, 1914-1917* (Westport, Conn.: 1969) describes the varieties of isolationist and internationalist sentiments on the eve of America's entry into the war.

Wilson's philosophy of international relations is discussed in the heavily documented work by Norman Gordon Levin, Jr., *Woodrow Wilson and World Politics: America's Response to War and Revolution* (New York: 1968).

For Wilson's policies during the war years, see Robert H. Ferrell, *Woodrow Wilson and World War I, 1917-1921* (New York: 1985) and Patrick Devlin, *Too Proud to Fight: Woodrow Wilson's Neutrality* (New York: 1975).

For Wilson's relations with the French, see Louis A. R. Yates, *United States and French Security, 1917-1921* (New York: 1957).

Anglo-American relations are covered in Kathleen Burk, *Britain, America and the Sinews of War, 1914-1918* (Boston: 1985); George W. Egerton, *Great Britain and the Creation of the League of Nations: Strategy, Politics, and International Organization, 1914-1919* (Chapel Hill, N.C.: 1978); Joyce Grigsby Williams, *Colonel House and Sir Edward Grey: A Study in Anglo-American Diplomacy* (Lanham, Md.: 1984); and Laurence W. Martin, *Peace without Victory: Woodrow Wilson and the British Liberals* (New Haven, Conn.: 1958).

Wilson's policy toward Germany is discussed in Klaus Schwabe, *Woodrow Wilson, Revolutionary Germany, and Peacemaking, 1918-1919: Missionary Diplomacy and the Realities of Power*, Rita and Robert Kimber, trans. (Chapel Hill, N.C.: 1985).

For Wilson and the Bolshevik Revolution, see Betty Miller Unterberger, *America's Siberian Expedition, 1918-1920: A Study of National Policy* (Durham, N.C.: 1956); Gerhard Schulz, *Revolutions and Peace Treaties, 1917-1920* (London: 1967); Lloyd C. Gardner, *Safe for Democracy: The Anglo-American Response to Revolution, 1913-1923* (New York: 1984); John A. Sweetenham, *Allied Intervention in Russia, 1918-1919* (London: 1967); and John M. Thompson, *Russia, Bolshevism, and the Versailles Peace* (Princeton, N.J.: 1966).

Important secondary accounts of the Versailles negotiations are provided by Thomas A. Bailey, *Woodrow Wilson and the Lost Peace* (New York: 1944);

Arthur Walworth, *America's Moment: 1918: American Diplomacy at the End of World War I* (New York: 1977); his *Wilson and His Peacemakers: American Diplomacy at the Paris Peace Conference, 1919* (New York: 1986); and Lloyd E. Ambrosius, *Woodrow Wilson and the American Diplomatic Tradition: The Treaty Fight in Perspective* (New York: 1987).

For the ratification battle, see Thomas A. Bailey, *Woodrow Wilson and the Great Betrayal* (New York: 1945); Henry Cabot Lodge, *The Senate and the League of Nations* (New York: 1925); William C. Widenor, *Henry Cabot Lodge and the Search for an American Foreign Policy* (Berkeley, Calif.: 1980); and Ralph Stone, *The Irreconcilables: The Fight Against the League of Nations* (Lexington, Ky.: 1970). For a compilation of excerpts from some of the major interpretations dealing with the defeat of the League, see Ralph A. Stone, ed., *Wilson and the League of Nations* (New York: 1967).

# CHAPTER 2: 1921-1933

Among the surveys of American diplomacy during the twenties and early thirties are Lewis Ethan Ellis, *Republican Foreign Policy 1921-1933* (New Brunswick, N.J.: 1968); John D. Hicks, *Republican Ascendancy, 1921-1933* (New York: 1960); Jean-Baptiste Duroselle, *From Wilson to Roosevelt: Foreign Policy of the United States, 1913-1945* (Cambridge, Mass.: 1963); Thomas N. Guinsberg, *The Pursuit of Isolationism in the United States Senate from Versailles to Pearl Harbor* (New York: 1982); and Frank Costigliola, *Awkward Dominion: American Political, Economic, and Cultural Relations with Europe, 1919-1933* (Ithaca, N.Y.: 1984).

The historiography of the diplomacy of the twenties is examined in Ernest C. Bolt, Jr., "Isolation, Expansion, and Peace: American Policy Between the Wars," in Gerald K. Haines and J. Samuel Walker, eds., *American Foreign Relations: A Historiographical Review,* 133-57; Jon Jacobson, "Is There a New International History of the 1920s?" *American Historical Review* 88 (July 1983), 617-45; and Robert James Maddox, "Another Look at the Legend of Isolationism in the 1920s," *Mid-America* 53 (January 1971), 35-43.

For the diplomacy of Harding and Hughes, see Eugene P. Trani and David L. Wilson, *The Presidency of Warren G. Harding* (Lawrence, Kan.: 1977); Betty Glad, *Charles Evans Hughes and the Illusions of Innocence: A Study in American Diplomacy* (Urbana, Ill.: 1966); Dexter Perkins, *Charles Evans Hughes and American Democratic Statesmanship* (Boston: 1956); and Merlo John Pusey, *Charles Evans Hughes* (New York: 1951).

Coolidge's and Kellogg's diplomacy is covered in Lewis Ethan Ellis, *Frank B. Kellogg and American Foreign Relations, 1925-1929* (New Brunswick, N.J.: 1961) and Robert H. Ferrell, *Peace in Their Time: The Origins of the Kellogg-Briand Pact* (New Haven, Conn.: 1952). For Borah's influence on American foreign policy, see Robert James Maddox, *William E. Borah and American Foreign Policy* (Baton Rouge: 1969).

The Hoover-Stimson policies are examined in Robert H. Ferrell, *American Diplomacy in the Great Depression: Hoover-Stimson Foreign Policy, 1929-1933* (New Haven, Conn.: 1957).

American economic diplomacy is discussed in Herbert Feis, *The Diplomacy of the Dollar: First Era, 1919-1932* (Baltimore: 1950); Carl P. Parrini, *Heir to Empire: United States Economic Diplomacy, 1916-1923* (Pittsburgh: 1969); Joan Hoff Wilson, *American Business and Foreign Policy, 1920-1933* (Lexington, Ky.: 1971); and Joseph Brandes, *Herbert Hoover and Economic Diplomacy: Department of Commerce Policy: 1921-1928* (Pittsburgh: 1962).

For naval disarmament, see Stephen Roskill, *Naval Policy between the Wars: The Period of Anglo-American Antagonism, 1919-1929* (London: 1968); Harold Sprout and Margaret Sprout, *Toward a New Order of Sea Power: American Naval Policy and the World Scene, 1918-1922* (Princeton, N.J.: 1940); William R. Braested, *The United States Navy in the Pacific, 1909-1922* (Austin: 1971); Gerald E. Wheeler, *Prelude to Pearl Harbor: The United States Navy and the Far East, 1921-1931* (Columbia, Mo.: 1963); Thomas H. Buckley, *The United States and the Washington Conference, 1921-1922* (Knoxville, Tenn.: 1970); Roger Dingman, *Power in the Pacific: The Origins of Naval Arms Limitation, 1914-1922* (Chicago: 1976); John Chalmers Vinson, *The Parchment Peace: The United States Senate and the Washington Conference, 1921-1922* (Athens, Ga.: 1955); and Raymond G. O'Connor, *Perilous Equilibrium: The United States and the London Naval Conference of 1930* (Lawrence, Kan.: 1962).

America's relations with the League of Nations and the World Court are discussed in Denna Frank Fleming, *The United States and World Organization, 1920-1933* (New York: 1938); his *The United States and the World Court* (Garden City, N.Y.: 1945); Roland N. Stromberg, *Collective Security and American Foreign Policy: From the League of Nations to NATO* (New York: 1963); and Francis P. Walters, *A History of the League of Nations* (New York: 1952).

For the American peace movement, see Robert H. Ferrell, "The Peace Movement," in Alexander DeConde, ed., *Isolation and Security: Ideas and Interests in Twentieth-Century American Foreign Policy* (Durham, N.C.: 1957), 82-106; Charles DeBenedetti, *Origins of the Modern Peace Movement, 1915-1929* (Millwood, N.Y.: 1978); and Charles Chatfield, *For Peace and Justice: Pacifism in America, 1914-1941* (Knoxville, Tenn.: 1971).

For Anglo-American relations, see Michael J. Hogan, *Informal Entente: The Private Structure of Cooperation in Anglo-American Economic Diplomacy, 1918-1928* (Columbia, Mo.: 1977) and Carole Fink, *The Genoa Conference: European Diplomacy, 1921-1922* (Chapel Hill, N.C.: 1984).

Franco-American relations are covered in J. Néré, *The Foreign Policy of France from 1914 to 1945* (London: 1975); Henry Blumenthal, *Illusion and Reality in Franco-American Diplomacy,1914-1945* (Baton Rouge: 1986); Melvyn P. Leffler, *The Elusive Quest: America's Pursuit of European Stability and French Security, 1919-1933* (Chapel Hill, N.C.: 1979); Walter A. McDougall, *France's Rhineland Diplomacy, 1914-1924: The Last Bid for a Balance of Power in Europe* (Princeton, N.J.: 1978); Stephen A. Schuker, *The End of French Predominance: The Financial Crisis of 1924 and the Adoption of the Dawes Plan* (Chapel Hill,

N.C.: 1976); Marc Trachtenberg, *Reparations in World Politics: France and European Economic Diplomacy* (New York: 1980); and David Strauss, *Menace in the West: The Rise of French Anti-Americanism in Modern Times* (Westport, Conn.: 1978).

An old but excellent interpretative study of Anglo-French relations during the interwar years is provided by Arnold Wolfers, *Britain and France between Two Wars: Conflicting Strategies of Peace Since Versailles* (New York: 1940).

For German-American relations, see Jon Jacobson, *Locarno Diplomacy: Germany and the West, 1925-1929* (Princeton, N.J.: 1972) and Edward W. Bennett, *German Rearmament and the West, 1932-1933* (Princeton, N.J.: 1979).

American policy during the Manchurian crisis is discussed in Christopher Thorne, *The Limits of Foreign Policy: The West, the League, and the Far Eastern Crisis, 1931-1933* (New York: 1972).

# CHAPTERS 3-4: 1933-1941

Important collections of Roosevelt's papers are Elliott Roosevelt, ed., *F.D.R.: His Personal Letters, 1928-1945*, 2 vols. (New York: 1950) and Samuel I. Rosenman, ed., *The Public Papers and Addresses of Franklin Delano Roosevelt*, 13 vols. (New York: 1938-1950). Presidential papers dealing with foreign policy are contained in Edgar Nixon, ed., *Franklin D. Roosevelt and Foreign Affairs First Series, 1933-1937*, 3 vols. (Cambridge, Mass: 1969) and Donald B. Schewe, ed., *Second Series, 1937-1939*, 14 vols. (Clearwater, Fla.: 1972).

For overviews of Roosevelt's foreign policy, see Willard Range, *Franklin D. Roosevelt's World Order* (Athens, Ga.: 1959) and Robert Dallek, *Franklin D. Roosevelt and American Foreign Policy, 1932-1945* (New York: 1979).

For the historiography of American diplomacy in the thirties, see Gerald K. Haines, "Roads to War: United States Foreign Policy, 1931-1941," in Gerald K. Haines and J. Samuel Walker, eds., *American Foreign Relations: A Historiographical Review* (Westport, Conn.: 1981), 159-86.

An excellent account of the development of revisionism during the twenties and thirties is provided by Warren I. Cohen, *The American Revisionists: The Lessons of Intervention in World War I* (Chicago: 1967).

Roosevelt's battle with the isolationists is discussed in three works by Wayne S. Cole: *America First: The Battle Against Intervention, 1940-1941* (Madison, Wis.: 1953); *Roosevelt and the Isolationists, 1932-1941* (Lincoln, Neb.: 1983); and *Charles A. Lindbergh and the Battle against American Intervention in World War II* (New York: 1974). See also Manfred Jones, *Isolationism in America, 1935-1941* (Ithaca, N.Y.: 1966); David L. Porter, *The Seventy-sixth Congress and World War II: 1939-1940* (Columbia, Mo.: 1979); Robert A. Divine, *The Illusion of Neutrality* (Chicago: 1962); and Justus D. Doenecke, "Isolationism of the 1930s and 1940s: An Historiographical Essay," in R. W. Sellen and T. W. Bryon, eds., *American Diplomatic History: Issues and Methods* (Carrolton, Ga.: 1974), 5-39; and Doenecke's "Power, Markets, and Ideology: The Isolationist Response to Roosevelt Policy, 1940-1941," in Leonard P. Liggio and James J.

Martin, eds., *Watershed of Empire: Essays on New Deal Foreign Policy* (Colorado Springs, Colo.: 1976), 132-61.

For sympathetic accounts of the isolationists, see Michele F. Stenehjem, *An American First: John T. Flynn and the America First Committee* (New Rochelle, N.Y.: 1976); Ronald Radosh, *Prophets on the Right: Profiles of Conservative Critics of American Globalism* (New York: 1975); and James T. Patterson, *Mr. Republican: A Biography of Robert A. Taft* (Boston: 1972).

Richard W. Steele, *Propaganda in an Open Society: The Roosevelt Administration and the Media, 1933-1941* (Westport, Conn.: 1985), discusses Roosevelt's efforts to mold public opinion to support his foreign policies. For a study of public opinion in the Chicago area, see James C. Schneider, *Should America Go to War? The Debate over Foreign Policy in Chicago, 1939-1941* (Chapel Hill, N.C.: 1989). For the background of the Selective Service Act, see J. Garry Clifford and Samuel R. Spencer, Jr., *The First Peacetime Draft* (Lawrence, Kan.: 1986).

Among the best general histories of the origins of the Second World War are Maurice Baumont, *The Origins of the Second World War*, Simone de Couvreur Ferguson, trans. (New Haven, Con.: 1978); William Carr, *Poland to Pearl Harbor: The Making of the Second World War* (Baltimore: 1985); P.M.H. Bell, *The Origins of the Second World War in Europe* (London: 1986); and Donald Cameron Watt, *How War Came: The Immediate Origins of the Second World War, 1938-1939* (New York: 1989).

For the historiography of the origins of the Second World War, see Gordon Martel, ed., *The Origins of the Second World War Reconsidered: The A.J.P. Taylor Debate after Twenty-five Years* (Boston: 1986), E. M. Robertson, *The Origins of the Second World War: Historical Interpretations* (New York: 1971); and J. Garry Clifford, "Both Ends of the Telescope: New Perspectives on FDR and American Entry into World War II," *Diplomatic History* 13 (Spring 1989), 213-30.

America's entry into World War II is examined in William S. Langer and S. Everett Gleason, *The Challenge to Isolation, 1937-1940* (New York: 1964); their *The Undeclared War: 1940-1941* (New York: 1953); Patrick Abbazia, *Mr. Roosevelt's Navy: The Private War of the U.S. Atlantic Fleet, 1939-1942* (Annapolis, Md.: 1975); Waldo Heinrichs, *Threshold of War: Franklin D. Roosevelt and American Entry into World War II* (New York: 1988); William E. Kinsella, Jr., *Leadership in Isolation: Franklin D. Roosevelt and the Origins of the Second World War* (Cambridge, Mass.: 1978); Robert A. Divine, *The Reluctant Belligerent: American Entry into World War II*, 2nd ed. (New York: 1979); and a highly critical collection of essays by Frederick W. Marks III, *Winds over Sand: The Diplomacy of Franklin Roosevelt* (Athens, Ga.: 1988).

For the historiography of America's entry into World War II, see Wayne S. Cole, "American Entry into World War II: A Historiographical Appraisal," *Mississippi Valley Historical Review* (March 1957), 595-617, and Justus D. Doenecke, "Beyond Polemics: An Historiographical Re-Appraisal of American Entry into World War II," *History Teacher* 12 (February 1979), 217-51.

Anglo-American relations are covered in William R. Rock, *Chamberlain and Roosevelt: British Foreign Policy and the United States, 1937-1940* (Columbus,

Ohio: 1988); Callum A. MacDonald, *The United States, Britain, and Appeasement, 1936-1939* (New York: 1981); David Reynolds, *The Creation of the Anglo-American Alliance, 1937-41: A Study in Competitive Co-operation* (Chapel Hill, N.C.: 1982); and James R. Leutze, *Bargaining for Supremacy: Anglo-American Naval Collaboration: 1937-1941* (Chapel Hill, N.C.: 1977). See also John Baylis, *Anglo-American Defence Relations, 1939-1980* (New York: 1981).

For U.S. policy toward Germany, see H. L. Trefousse, *Germany and American Neutrality, 1939-1941* (New York: 1969); Arnold A. Offner, *American Appeasement: United States Foreign Policy and Germany, 1933-1938* (Cambridge, Mass.: 1969); and James V. Compton, *The Swastika and the Eagle: Hitler, the United States, and the Origins of the Second World War* (Boston: 1967). Robert Edwin Herzstein, *Roosevelt and Hitler: Prelude to War* (New York: 1989), deals primarily with the efforts of the German-American Bund to turn America into a Nazi state.

Franco-American relations are examined in Henry Blumenthal, *Illusion and Reality in Franco-American Diplomacy, 1914-1945* (Baton Rouge: 1986) and John McVickar Haight, Jr., *American Aid to France, 1938-1940* (New York: 1970).

For Soviet-American relations, see Hugh DeSantis, *The Diplomacy of Silence: The American Foreign Service, the Soviet Union, and the Cold War, 1933-1947* (Chicago: 1983); Thomas R. Maddux, *Years of Estrangement: American Relations with the Soviet Union, 1933-1941* (Tallahassee: 1980); Edward M. Bennett, *Franklin D. Roosevelt and the Search for Security: American-Soviet Relations, 1933-1939* (Wilmington, Del.: 1985); and Warren F. Kimball, *"The Most Unsordid Act": Lend-Lease, 1939-1941* (Baltimore: 1969).

For American-Italian relations, see Brice Harris, Jr., *The United States and the Italo-Ethiopian Crisis* (Stanford, Calif.: 1964) and David F. Schmitz, *The United States and Fascist Italy, 1922-1940* (Chapel Hill, N.C.: 1988).

U.S. policy during the Spanish Civil War is examined in F. Jay Taylor, *The United States and the Spanish Civil War* (New York: 1956); Richard P. Traina, *American Diplomacy and the Spanish Civil War* (Bloomington, Ind.: 1968); and Douglas Little, *Malevolent Neutrality: The United States, Great Britain, and the Origins of the Spanish Civil War* (Ithaca, N.Y.: 1985).

For Japanese-American relations, see Dorothy Borg, *The United States and the Far Eastern Crisis of 1933-1938* (Cambridge, Mass.: 1964); Dorothy Borg and Shumpei Okamoto, eds., *Pearl Harbor as History: Japanese-American Relations, 1933-1941* (New York: 1973); Michael A. Barnhart, *Japan Prepares for Total War: The Search for Economic Security, 1919-1941* (Ithaca, N.Y.: 1987); Jonathan G. Utley, *Going to War with Japan: 1937-1941* (Knoxville, Tenn.: 1985); and Stephen E. Pelz, *Race to Pearl Harbor: The Failure of the Second London Naval Conference and the Onset of World War II* (Cambridge, Mass.: 1974).

The Pearl Harbor attack is examined in Roberta Wohlstetter, *Pearl Harbor: Warning and Decision* (Stanford: 1962); Gordon W. Prange, *At Dawn We Slept: The Untold Story of Pearl Harbor* (New York: 1981); and his *Pearl Harbor: The*

*Verdict of History* (New York: 1986). See also Hans L. Trefousse, *Pearl Harbor: The Continuing Controversy* (Malabar, Fla.: 1982).

# CHAPTERS 5-6: 1941-1945

For Roosevelt's wartime diplomacy, see Robert Dallek, *Franklin D. Roosevelt and American Foreign Policy, 1932-1945* (New York: 1979); Robert A. Divine, *Roosevelt and World War II* (Baltimore: 1969); his *Second Chance: The Triumph of Internationalism in America during World War II* (New York: 1967); Gaddis Smith, *American Diplomacy During the Second World War, 1941-1945;* 2nd ed. (New York: 1965); and Raymond G. O'Connor, *Diplomacy for Victory: FDR and Unconditional Surrender* (New York: 1971). See also Cordell Hull, *The Memoirs of Cordell Hull,* 2 vols. (New York: 1948) and Robert E. Sherwood, *Roosevelt and Hopkins: An Intimate History,* rev. ed. (New York: 1948, 1950).

The historiography of the American diplomacy during the war is examined in Mark A. Stoler, "World War II Diplomacy in Historical Writing: Prelude to Cold War," in Gerald K. Haines and J. Samuel Walker, eds., *American Foreign Relations: A Historiographical Review* (Westport, Conn.: 1981), 187-206. A prominent revisionist interpretation is provided by Gabriel Kolko, *The Politics of War: The World and United States Foreign Policy, 1943-1945* (New York, 1968).

Roosevelt's military strategy is examined in Eric Larrabee, *Commander in Chief: Franklin Delano Roosevelt, His Lieutenants, and Their War* (New York: 1987); Mark S. Watson, *United States Army in World War II: Chief of Staff: Prewar Plans and Preparations* (Washington, D.C: 1950); Samuel E. Morison, *The Battle for the Atlantic, September 1939-May 1943* (Boston: 1947); Maurice Matloff and Edwin M. Snell, *Strategic Planning for Coalition Warfare, 1941-1942* (Washington, D.C.: 1953); by the same authors, *Strategic Planning for Coalition Warfare, 1943-1944* (Washington, D.C.: 1959); Richard W. Steele, *The First Offensive, 1942: Roosevelt, Marshall, and the Making of American Strategy* (Bloomington, Ind.: 1973); Mark A. Stoler, *The Politics of the Second Front: American Military Planning and Diplomacy in Coalition Warfare, 1941-1943* (Westport, Conn.: 1977); and Arthur L. Funk, *The Politics of Torch: The Allied Landings and the Algiers Putsch, 1942* (Lawrence, Kan: 1974). Postwar military strategy is discussed in Michael S. Sherry, *Preparing for the Next War: American Plans for Postwar Defense, 1941-45* (New Haven, Conn.: 1977).

General Marshall's wartime role is described in Forrest C. Pogue, *George C. Marshall: Ordeal and Hope, 1939-1942* (New York: 1966) and his *George C. Marshall: Organizer of Victory, 1943-1945* (New York: 1973).

Anglo-American diplomacy affecting the Pacific war is examined in Christopher Thorne, *Allies of a Kind: The United States, Britain, and the War Against Japan, 1941-1945* (New York: 1978).

For Roosevelt's and Churchill's wartime correspondence, see Francis L. Loewenheim, Harold D. Langley, and Manfred Jonas, eds., *Roosevelt and Churchill: Their Secret Wartime Correspondence* (New York: 1975) and the more extensive collection by Warren F. Kimball, *Churchill and Roosevelt: The*

*Complete Correspondence, 1939-1945*, 3 vols. (Princeton, N.J.: 1984). Also important, although obviously biased, are Churchill's wartime memoirs, *The Second World War*, 6 vols. (Boston: 1948-1953).

Britain's wartime diplomacy is examined in Sir Llewellyn Woodward, *British Foreign Policy in the Second World War*, 5 vols. (London: 1970-1976).

Important works dealing with Churchill's wartime role are Lord Moran, *Churchill: Taken from the Diaries of Lord Moran: The Struggle for Survival, 1940-1964* (Boston: 1966); Martin Gilbert, *Winston S. Churchill*, vol. VII: *Road to Victory, 1941-1945* (Boston: 1986); and Maxwell Philip Schoenfeld, *The War Ministry of Winston Churchill* (Ames, Iowa: 1972).

Various aspects of Roosevelt's wartime Soviet diplomacy are examined in George C. Herring, *Aid to Russia, 1941-1946: Strategy, Diplomacy, and the Origins of the Cold War* (New York: 1973); John Lewis Gaddis, *The United States and the Origins of the Cold War, 1941-1947* (New York: 1972); Paul D. Mayle, *Eureka Summit: Agreement in Principle and the Big Three at Tehran, 1943* (Newark, N.J.: 1987); Lynn Ethridge Davis, *The Cold War Begins: Soviet-America Conflict over Eastern Europe* (Princeton, N.J.: 1974); Diane Shaver Clemens, *Yalta* (New York: 1970); John L. Snell, ed., *The Meaning of Yalta: Big Three Diplomacy and the New Balance of Power* (Baton Rouge: 1956); and Russell D. Buhite, *Decisions at Yalta: An Appraisal of Summit Diplomacy* (Wilmington, Del.: 1986).

Anglo-American relations with the Soviet Union are dealt with in William Hardy McNeil, *America, Britain, and Russia: Their Cooperation and Conflict, 1941-1946* (New York: 1970); Terry H. Anderson, *The United States, Great Britain, and the Cold War, 1944-1947* (Columbia, Mo.: 1981); and Fraser J. Harbutt, *The Iron Curtain: Churchill, America, and the Origins of the Cold War* (New York: 1986). See also W. Averell Harriman and Ellie Abel, *Special Envoy to Churchill and Stalin: 1941-1946* (New York: 1975).

Stalin's wartime diplomacy is examined in Vojtech Mastny, *Russia's Road to the Cold War: Diplomacy, Warfare, and the Politics of Communism, 1941-1945* (New York: 1979). Stalin's correspondence with his allies is contained in Union of Soviet Socialist Republics, Ministry of Foreign Affairs, *Stalin's Correspondence with Churchill, Attlee, Roosevelt and Truman, 1941-1945*, 2 vols. (Moscow: 1957). See also Joseph Stalin, *The Great Patriotic War of the Soviet Union* (New York: 1945).

For Roosevelt's difficult relationship with the French, see Julian G. Hurstfield, *America and the French Nation, 1939-1945* (Chapel Hill, N.C.: 1986) and Milton Viorst, *Hostile Allies: FDR and Charles de Gaulle* (New York: 1965).

Roosevelt's policy toward Germany is described in Warren F. Kimball, *Swords or Ploughshares?: The Morgenthau Plan for Defeated Nazi Germany, 1943-1946* (Philadelphia: 1976).

For the creation of the United Nations, see Robert A. Divine, *Second Chance: The Triumph of Internationalism in the United States during World War II* (New York: 1967).

# CHAPTERS 7-8: 1945-1950

For an overview of the Truman presidency, see Robert J. Donovan, *Conflict and Crisis: The Presidency of Harry S. Truman, 1945-1948* (New York: 1977); his *Tumultuous Years: The Presidency of Harry S. Truman, 1949-1953* (New York: 1982); and Michael J. Lacey, ed., *The Truman Presidency* (New York: 1989). One of the best biographies of President Truman is Margaret Truman's *Harry S. Truman* (New York: 1973).

For personal accounts of the Truman administration's diplomacy, see Harry S. Truman, *Memoirs,* 2 vols. (New York: 1955-56); James F. Byrnes, *Speaking Frankly* (New York: 1947); his *All in One Lifetime* (New York: 1958); and Dean Acheson, *Present at the Creation: My Years in the State Department* (New York: 1969).

Secondary accounts dealing with the diplomacy of James F. Byrnes are Robert Messer, *The End of an Alliance: James F. Byrnes, Roosevelt, Truman, and the Origins of the Cold War* (Chapel Hill, N.C.: 1982) and Patricia Dawson Ward, *The Threat of Peace: James F. Byrnes and the Council of Foreign Ministers, 1945-1946* (Kent, Ohio: 1979).

For George C. Marshall's diplomacy, see Forrest C. Pogue, *George C. Marshall: Statesman* (New York: 1987) and Mark A. Stoler, *George C. Marshall: Soldier-Statesman of the American Century* (Boston: 1989). For Dean Acheson's diplomacy, see David S. McLellan, *Dean Acheson: The State Department Years* (New York: 1976).

Among the numerous works dealing with the origins of the Cold War are Daniel Yergin, *Shattered Peace: The Origins of the Cold War and the National Security State* (Boston: 1977); John Lewis Gaddis, *The United States and the Origins of the Cold War, 1941-1947* (New York: 1972); Bruce Robellet Kuniholm, *The Origins of the Cold War in the Near East: Great Power Conflict and Diplomacy in Iran, Greece, and Turkey* (Princeton, N.J.: 1980); Deborah Welch Larson, *Origins of Containment: A Psychological Explanation* (Princeton, N.J.: 1985); Lisle A. Rose, *Dubious Victory: The United States and the End of World War II* (Kent, Ohio: 1973); her *After Yalta: America and the Origins of the Cold War* (New York: 1973); Gabriel Kolko and Joyce Kolko, *The Limits of Power: The World and United States Foreign Policy, 1945-1954* (New York: 1972); Barton J. Bernstein, ed., *Politics and Policies of the Truman Administration* (New York: 1970); Thomas G. Paterson, *On Every Front: The Making of the Cold War* (New York: 1979); and his *Soviet-American Confrontation: Postwar Reconstruction and the Origins of the Cold War* (New York: 1973).

For an introduction to the historiography of the Cold War, see J. Samuel Walker, "Historians and Cold War Origins: The New Consensus," in Gerald K. Haines and J. Samuel Walker, eds., *American Foreign Relations: A Historiographical Review* (Westport, Conn.: 1981), 207-36. See also Richard S. Kirkendall, *The Truman Period as a Research Field* (Columbia, Mo.. 1974) and Geoffrey S. Smith, "'Harry, We Hardly Know You': Revisionism, Politics and Diplomacy, 1945-1954," *American Political Science Review* 70 (June 1976), 560-82.

American policy toward Eastern Europe is discussed in Geir Lundestad, *The American Non-Policy Toward Eastern Europe, 1943-1947* (Tromso, Norway: 1978) and Lynn Ethridge Davis, *The Cold War Begins: Soviet-American Conflict over Eastern Europe* (Princeton, N.J.: 1974).

The impact of the atomic bomb on the Cold War is discussed in Martin J. Sherwin, *A World Destroyed* (New York: 1975); Barton J. Bernstein, ed., *The Atomic Bomb: The Critical Issues* (Boston: 1976); Gar Alperovitz, *Atomic Diplomacy: Hiroshima and Potsdam*, rev. ed. (New York: 1987); and Greg Herken, *The Winning Weapon: The Atomic Bomb and the Cold War, 1945-1950* (New York: 1980).

The economic aspects of Truman's foreign policy are discussed in Robert A. Pollard, *Economic Security and the Origins of the Cold War, 1945-1950* (New York: 1985); Michael J. Hogan, *The Marshall Plan: America, Britain, and the Reconstruction of Western Europe, 1947-1952* (Cambridge, Eng.: 1987); and John Gimbel, *The Origins of the Marshall Plan* (New York: 1976).

For U.S. policy toward Germany, see Frank Ninkovich, *Germany and the United States: The Transformation of the German Question Since 1945* (Boston: 1988); Avi Shlaim, *The United States and the Berlin Blockade, 1948-1949: A Study in Crisis Decision-Making* (Berkeley, Calif.:1983); John Gimbel, *The American Occupation of Germany: Politics and the Military, 1945-1949* (Stanford, Calif.: 1968); and Bruce Kuklick, *American Policy and the Division of Germany* (Ithaca, N.Y.: 1972).

Anglo-American relations are discussed in Richard A. Best, Jr., *"Co-operation with Like-Minded Peoples": British Influences on American Security Policy* (Westport, Conn.: 1986); Fraser J. Harbutt, *The Iron Curtain: Churchill, America, and the Origins of the Cold War* (New York: 1986); Terry H. Anderson, *The United States, Great Britain, and the Cold War, 1944-1947* (Columbia, Mo.: 1981); Robert M. Hathaway, *Ambiguous Partnership: Britain and America, 1944-1947* (New York: 1981); and Ritchie Ovendale, *The English-Speaking Alliance: Britain, the United States, the Dominions and the Cold War, 1945-1951* (London: 1985).

For Soviet policy, see Vojtech Mastny, *Russia's Road to the Cold War: Diplomacy, Warfare, and the Politics of Communism, 1941-1945* (New York: 1979); William O. McCagg, Jr., *Stalin Embattled: 1943-1948* (Detroit: 1978); and William Taubman, *Stalin's American Policy: From Entente to Détente to Cold War* (New York: 1982).

For the creation of NATO, see Colin Gordon, *The Atlantic Alliance: A Bibliography* (London: 1978); Timothy P. Ireland, *Creating the Entangling Alliance: The Origins of the North Atlantic Treaty Organization* (New York: 1981); Don Cook, *Forging the Alliance: NATO, 1945-1950* (New York: 1989); Lawrence S. Kaplan, *The United States and NATO: The Formative Years* (Lexington, Ky.: 1984); and his *A Community of Interests: NATO and the Military Assistance Program, 1948-1951* (Washington, D.C.: 1980). See also Lawrence S. Kaplan, Robert W. Clawson, and Raimondo Luraghi, eds., *NATO and the Mediterranean* (Wilmington, Del.: 1985); Alfred Goldberg, gen. ed., *History of the Office of the Secretary of Defense*, vol. I: *The Formative Years: 1947-1950*, by Steven L. Rearden,(Washington, D.C.: 1984); and Olav Riste,

*Western Security: The Formative Years: European and Atlantic Defence, 1947-1953* (New York: 1985). The resistance of the isolationists to NATO is described in Justus D. Doenecke, *Not to the Swift: The Old Isolationists in the Cold War Era* (New York: 1979).

# Index

# J

**About the Author**

**RONALD E. POWASKI** teaches advanced placement American history at Euclid Senior High School in Euclid, Ohio. He also teaches American history, part-time, at John Carrol University and Cleveland State University. Mr. Powaski has authored *March to Armageddon: The United States and the Nuclear Arms Race, 1939 to the Present* and *Thomas Merton on Nuclear Weapons.*